Belfast's Unholy War

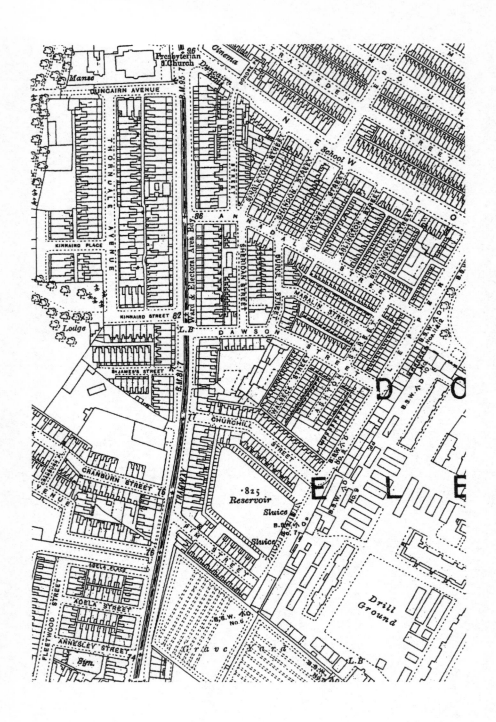

BELFAST'S UNHOLY WAR

The Troubles of the 1920s

ALAN F. PARKINSON

FOUR COURTS PRESS

This book was set in 11 on 14pt Adobe Garamond
by Mark Heslington, Northallerton, North Yorkshire for
FOUR COURTS PRESS LTD
7 Malpas Street, Dublin 8, Ireland
Email: info@four-courts-press.ie
and in the United States for
FOUR COURTS PRESS
c/o ISBS, 920 N.E. 58th Avenue, Suite 300, Portland, OR 97213.

A catalogue record for this title is available from the British Library.

ISBN 1–85182–792–7 hbk

Printed in Great Britain by
MPG Books Ltd, Bodmin, Cornwall

Contents

Illustrations

All photographs appear courtesy of the *Belfast Telegraph*.

Acknowledgments

I would like to express my gratitude to a host of people who helped me out in a variety of ways in completing what turned out to be a five-year project. Many of these, including Doreen Corcoran, Keith Haines, Fred Heatley, John Quinn and Denis Smyth, were involved in local history groups. Others expressed interest in my work, frequently suggesting further lines of enquiry. This group included Joe Graham, Davy Matthews, Bernadette and Pauline O'Hare and Brian Reilly. Several office-bearers in the Catholic Church endeavoured to help me in my research. They included Bishop Tony Farquhar, Father Patrick O'Donnell of Clonard Monastery and archivists, the Revd John Gates (Ara Coeli, Armagh), the Revd George O'Hanlon (Down and Connor) and Sister Dominic Savio of the Cross and Passion Order.

My research took me to many libraries in the United Kingdom and Ireland. I am indebted to the staff at the Public Record Office in Kew and the British Newspaper Library at Colindale in London, the UCD Archive Office and the State Paper Office in Dublin, and to librarians at the Public Record Office of Northern Ireland, Linenhall and Central Libraries in Belfast. Particular thanks are extended to the ever-helpful staff in the Newspaper Library section of Belfast Central Library. Staff at the Ulster Museum and the Folk and Transport Museums advised me about available photographic evidence and Walter McAuley at the *Belfast Telegraph* was especially helpful with such requests. Permission to reproduce photographs was granted by the *Belfast Telegraph*, and PRONI approved reproduction of a boycott poster. John Hewitt's poem, 'The Troubles, 1922' appears on p. 191 by permission of the Blackstaff Press on behalf of the estate of John Hewitt.

Other individuals and institutions proved to be helpful in different ways. Louis Edmondson and his colleagues at the BBC (Northern Ireland) forwarded scripts of radio programmes on the Twenties' Troubles and Allison Murphy was most thoughtful in facilitating interviews with two 'veterans' of the conflict. I would also like to express my gratitude to Terence Blakely for planting the seed of the idea for this project in my mind some six years ago and for his subsequent interest in its progress. Professional advice was given by experts in this field. My thanks go to Professor George Boyce, of the University of Wales (Swansea) and Dr Eamon Phoenix, of Stranmillis University College in Belfast. I benefited considerably from a lecturing visit to America early in 2001, when I presented papers on this subject at the University of North Florida and the University of Illinois. I am indebted to my employer, London South Bank University, for financing this trip and for allocating additional leave during the final phase of my research and also to academic colleagues on the Jacksonville and Springfield campuses. The staff at Four Courts Press have again proved to be helpful and understanding towards a writer who was constantly behind on his proposed schedule. Thanks especially to Michael and Ronan, for their professional interest and friendship.

My family have again been tolerant and helpful in different ways. My wife Janet, daughter Katherine and son Nicholas have been ready, despite their own onerous schedules, to help with proof-reading, whilst my younger son, Thomas, who shares an interest in Irish history with his father, has been of immeasurable help, tracking documents in various records offices and especially during the final phase of editing. Finally, I am indebted to the many conflict 'veterans', including my father John, who responded to my requests for interviews. Their fascinating accounts of what life was like for young people growing up in Belfast at a difficult time were particularly illuminating and a whole chapter is devoted to their memories. Sadly several of them passed on before my work reached its publication phase. This book is dedicated to these respondents and also to the many innocent victims of the Twenties' Troubles.

Introduction

Belfast's war of the early 1920s is conspicuous in that it remains the only major event in the city's twentieth century history which has not yet warranted its own study.[1] To an extent, the circumstances behind the events of these years are shrouded in mystery, whilst the events themselves have been interpreted in a one-dimensional manner. Described as the 'forgotten conflict', the 1920s Belfast discord has, as a consequence of this lack of investigative research, been dismissed as a 'pogrom' or a 'siege' and thus regarded as Belfast's own distinctive version of the wider Irish war of the period.[2] The accuracy of such terms will be considered later, but it is important to state at this juncture that perceptions of this conflict tend to be restricted to images of rampant sectarianism, state-sanctioned butchery, mindless urban shooting and bombing and even allegations of ethnic cleansing. Other related aspects which are less likely to have been considered in depth include the role of the IRA in fermenting discord, the influence of events south of the newly-created border (not least the imposition of economic sanctions), an explanation of the authorities' inability to cope adequately with a deteriorating security situation and, most fundamentally, what it was like to live during those turbulent times. In this book, therefore, a wide range of issues pertaining to events in Belfast between 1920 and 1922 will be examined in an honest endeavour to tell the story of the period.

Apart from two contemporary partisan accounts of selected incidents, a chapter in a book on the theme of religious conflict in the city, and references to specific events within general and local historical accounts, there has been comparatively little coverage of this subject.[3] Indeed, this is the first work devoted to the 1920s' Belfast conflict. However, certain writers have focussed on specific aspects of strife in Belfast during the post Great War period. These include critical accounts of the activities of the Ulster Special Constabulary and more recently, sympathetic studies of the role of the IRA in the city and life on board the internment ship SS *Argenta*.[4] In general, observers have drawn their readers' attention to the unparalleled scale of the violence, the familiarity of its patterns with previous disturbances and the inter-relationship between the city's communal violence and an unprecedented flurry of political activity.[5]

What then have been the conclusions of historians writing about this subject? The inevitability of civil unrest and the tinderbox nature of Ulster society at that time – 'a sectarian timebomb ready to be detonated by agitators' – was central to Andrew Boyd's explanation of events.[6] Although some observed clear linkage between the cyclical nature of the street disturbances and that on similar urban streets during the previous century, others have pointed out that their intermittent, extended nature helped distinguish them from nineteenth-century riots.[7] Historians have divided over whether there was a commonality of experience, in terms of shared suffering and grief, during these two blood-stained years in Belfast. Many have emphasised the greater discomfort of the Catholic community though others have regarded such interpretations as simplistic.[8] Whilst some viewed events in the North as being detached from those elsewhere in Ireland on account of their sharply internecine nature, other writers have been more circumspect, suggesting that, although events in Belfast developed their own momentum, they were clearly conditioned by events occurring elsewhere on the island.[9] Finally, historians have frequently turned their attention to assessing the culpability of the state for what occurred on Belfast's streets over this two year period. Some have limited their criticism to the perceived inefficiency of the agencies of law and order, whilst others suggest governmental orchestration of the campaign of violence in the city.[10] Even historians from a unionist background have been critical of governmental inactivity.[11]

What makes the oversight of this 'forgotten war' even more surprising is that the events of these years proved to be of considerable importance in determining long term attitudes and responses of both the authorities and Catholic community. The blood-letting, and especially the IRA's accountability for much of that, exaggerated as it may have been, appeared to Craig and subsequent Unionist leaders to justify a reactionary response which inevitably resulted in a diminution of basic human liberties. These drastic measures, it was argued, were necessary in order to maintain border security and thus protect the new state's very existence.[12] With the exception of smaller scale street riots in 1935, Belfast was, largely on account of grim memories of the early 1920s and especially the reactions of those in authority to the disturbances, not to experience communal rioting on a sustained basis until 1968. The effects of the Twenties' disturbances on the psyche of both sections of the community were also profound. Unionists' cognisance of the vulnerability of their territory had been heightened by the conflict and they keenly endorsed the 'safety first' measures of consecutive administrations, with their joint emphasis on sustaining high levels of security and maintaining the political status quo. Belfast's nationalists were also conditioned by their experiences during the 1920s. For Catholics, their initial mistrust of a seemingly lethargic Unionist administration and its inability to protect them against marauding mobs and gunmen, meant they were unwilling to alter such views once the violence desisted. In other words, the communal suffering engendered during those dismal times created a lasting atmosphere of mistrust and subsequent non co-operation which endured for nearly half a century and proved to be the catalyst for the next bout of prolonged sectarian rioting in the city.

Despite the scale of the Twenties' violence, its acknowledged significance and compactness as a research topic, there remains a dearth in the number and quality of books and articles on the subject. Why is this so? There are a number of possible explanations. A plethora of literature about this period of wider Irish history, if not the actual topic, does exist. Historians and journalists alike have chosen to write in copious detail about the Anglo-Irish War, the Treaty and the Civil War and to focus on glamorous personalities such as Michael Collins, which might well have had the effect of deterring other writers from concentrating on a similar chronological period. Also, northern readers have been bombarded by works on every conceivable subject related to the modern conflict, including many on security issues which might well appear to be more immediate and enticing. Indeed, by choosing a field of enquiry which appears to closely mirror the present, there is an increased tendency for writers to select specific aspects of the 1920s' conflict which have a closer resonance with contemporary Belfast, rather than focus on the broader canvas of life in the city during the early 1920s. Not surprisingly therefore, despite the passage of some eighty years, the Twenties' Troubles have been regarded as being too 'close' and potentially controversial for honest analysis. Others have been deterred by discrepancies between press accounts of the disturbances, the bland, incomplete and far from illuminating nature of police reports and the withdrawal, or partial closure, of other government records.[13] These drawbacks can lead to uncertainty in proclaiming culpability for specific crimes. Another reason for the low creative output in this subject area is the despairing nature of its story – a bloody, gloomy and nihilistic episode in modern Irish history, which commentators have avoided at all costs.[14] Perhaps the most important requirement for such a study is that its subject matter should be addressed in an investigative and dispassionate manner. I shall endeavour to pursue this approach in my account of these troublesome years.

DISTINCTIVE FEATURES

The impact of the 1920s' violence in Belfast, both in terms of its dominance of the provincial and national security picture as well as its influence on the lives of ordinary people, was unparalleled. Considering the volume of attention paid to events elsewhere in Ireland during this crucial period, it would be easy to forget that Belfast was at 'the centre of Irish violence during the national revolution'.[15] With at least 90% of the fatalities in Northern Irish security incidents between 1920 and 1922 occurring in the city, which also witnessed a majority of violent deaths in Ireland as a whole, Belfast appeared to carry 'the burden of the Anglo-Irish struggle'.[16] Although the number of casualties far outweighs those of previous conflicts in the city, a word of warning needs to be directed towards this question of 'casualty counting'.[17] As with subsequent disturbances, attempts to record the victims of violence – based as they are on incidents noted by the authorities or in the press – failed to take into consideration those casualties who were treated by sympathetic doctors or even buried in secret. Nor should those victims of accidental shootings or of criminal, rather than sectarian attacks, be confused with those deliberately targeted by gunmen and bombers. Additionally, the records need to be used with caution, as they do not always indicate precisely the circumstances of such incidents. Thus, the selective nature of press coverage of specific attacks, motivated as it was by political or sectarian consideration, resulted in a far from complete account of the security situation, whilst police records are only reliable from November 1921 when the new northern administration assumed responsibility for security matters.

It is also important, especially for the purposes of this study, to distinguish between fatalities of the conflict in Belfast from those in Northern Ireland as a whole.[18] An additional complication in providing statistical analysis of the 1920s' Troubles is that many existing records restrict the period of conflict to that beginning with the shipyard expulsions in July 1920 and ending with the start of the Civil War in June 1922, rather than extending it to include the final Troubles-related killings a few months later.[19] Consequently, estimates of fatalities in the city range from 416 to 455, with my own revised figure of 498.[20] The other conflict statistics are also interesting. Over 2,000 people were seriously injured and over £3 million damage was done to the city's economy.[21] It is also difficult to accurately assess the number of people evicted from both their jobs and homes.[22] However, Boyd's estimation that around 10,000 were expelled from the workplace and 23,000 were made homeless is a reasonably accurate one.[23]

Hostilities between the various factions in the city also corresponded with a period of intense political activity and change across the whole of Ireland, and this activity was meaningful because it proved to be instrumental in determining the atmosphere on Belfast's streets. Thus, during the two years of conflict, Belfast's citizens experienced the political debate surrounding the Government of Ireland Bill, elections for a new regional parliament, tense political negotiations in London preceding the Treaty, ongoing political dialogue involving Lloyd George, Churchill, Craig, Collins and de Valera which culminated in two abortive pacts between north and south, and the transfer of security responsibility to the new administration in Belfast, which was fully operational by the time civil war started in the rest of the island. It was these influences largely outside the city's boundaries – high profile and potentially historic meetings between leading political figures in London and Dublin, political claims over the jurisdiction of northern territory by Sinn Féin, concerns over the violence in the south, initially during the Anglo-Irish War and towards the end of the northern conflict, and anxiety over civil war in the south and west (especially the plight of Protestants in these areas) – which helped to fuel tension at local level. Although it is difficult to gauge the extent to which this 'external' activity actually precipitated specific security incidents in the north, its impact on Belfast's loyalist community, in particular, was considerable. The high profile political focus on the north inflamed the situation, providing local activists with excuses and opportunities to break the law.

Apart from the unparalleled scale of the conflagration and the impact of outside events on community interaction within Belfast, there were other elements which determined the nature of events on the city's streets, often distinguishing them from previous disturbances. These had generally been confined to fist-fighting, stone throwing and occasional exchange of gunfire, frequently leading to police or military intervention. The disturbances were also inclined to be short-term in their duration and restricted to a comparatively limited number of areas. Whilst some of these characteristics are discernible in the 1920s' disturbances, there was a substantial increase in the scope of the violence, its range of militant actions and the number of people likely to be affected by its consequences. One big difference between the Twenties' Troubles and the last sustained rioting over 30 years previously was the enhanced civilian access to more sophisticated and potent firearms. By 1920, the increased range and firing frequency afforded by more sophisticated weaponry meant that a considerably greater number of potential victims was inevitable. There were also other forms of weaponry available to paramilitaries at this time. Therefore, the Mills bomb, which could easily be lobbed into a terraced house or crowded tramcar, was a real threat to those relaxing at home or proceeding to work. Fatal attacks could now be executed from the safety of the miscreant's own area or from the periphery of opposing hinterland, whilst the ready availability of high velocity rifles and sometimes machine-guns, meant that more people could be targeted by snipers operating from considerable distances. Thus, improvements in military technology meant that a wider number and range of people than in the past were liable to be at risk. In a post-war, battle-hardened world, women, children, the elderly and handicapped were considered by both sides to constitute appropriate targets, despite the habitual outpourings of disgust which ritualistically followed each atrocity.

Yet again a disproportionate amount of suffering was experienced by the city's working-class population, but in 1920 the conflict was also to make a considerable impact upon the lives of all Belfast's citizens, who were subject to regular curfew restrictions on their movements, road-blocks, security checks on the city streets, gunfire in central thoroughfares and incendiary attacks on business premises. However, with a few notable exceptions, it was the city's large industrial population, both Catholic and Protestant, which were most vulnerable, both in terms of life protection and in the diminution of their basic liberties (especially those pertaining to their right to work and live where they wanted).

Though these differences in the nature and extent of the Twenties' Troubles are real and marked, it would be disingenuous to deny they conform to a distinctive, cyclical pattern of disturbances in the city.[24] There were also a number of similar trends between the 1920s' feud and the modern Troubles. Firstly, similar locations were chosen for sectarian attack throughout 150 years of street disturbances, especially the interface areas in the west, north and east of the city.[25] Also, commercial premises were constant targets in an orchestrated IRA campaign in 1922 just as they would be half a century later. Additionally, allegations of police brutality against Catholics were rife in both conflicts (if anything, the animosity between sections of the police and nationalists were stronger in the early 1920s). Finally, in both 'wars', the majority of victims were innocent people endeavouring to proceed with the business of everyday life when they were cruelly and mercilessly cut down by bullet or bomb. In both periods raw feelings of hatred, anger, fear, panic and occasionally outright terror mingled together. For those with little direct experience of trouble in their own area, visits to the city centre could be exciting, though on occasions they produced tragic repercussions. There were also some contrasting features between the respective conflicts. With the exception of one year in the more recent Troubles, the 1920s' 'war' was distinctive on account of its relative intensity and comparative brevity which contrasted sharply with the protracted, spasmodic nature of the modern conflict.[26] Other marked differences include the demographic balance, which saw the relatively small Catholic population of 1920 in a more perilous position than their 1969 counterparts.[27] There was also a marginal difference in the character of Belfast's theatres of war, with its central streets being more likely to experience gunfire than in the modern conflict.

YET MORE TROUBLES ...

The immediate sectarian and political backdrop to the disturbances in Belfast during the summer of 1920 is described in detail in the next section. However, a brief outline of communal violence in the nineteenth century and a summary of events both in the north and south of Ireland during the early part of the twentieth century is necessary to set the context. Changing demographic patterns, bans and restrictions on Orange processions for much of the century and tension created by imminent political change precipitated street disturbances in Belfast on at least six occasions in the nineteenth century. It was another cruel irony in the city's development that the commercial progress which had led to the influx of Catholic workers from the south and west to Belfast during the mid nineteenth century following the industrialisation of the Lagan Valley, also resulted in the creation of an environment of political stalemate and growing sectarian tension.[28] The growth in the city's Catholic population resulted in the revitalisation of the Orange Order and the targeting of gangs of Catholic workers, especially those employed in the docks.[29] Disturbances tended to occur in similar areas, particularly in the west of the city, frequently during the summer period, though not necessarily as a direct consequence of the Orange marches.[30] The Shankill Road and Millfield districts provided the battlegrounds for the 1829 disturbances, whilst Sandy Row was the focal point for agitation following a visit to the city in 1841 by Daniel O'Connell.[31] Riots could also be intense and enduring, with the disturbances of 1857 lasting up to six weeks.[32] Trouble also erupted in the west of the city, around the Brickfields, some 15 years later when many features of subsequent disturbances were recorded, including military intervention after police handling of a situation had failed, the burning-out of families of a different religious persuasion and exodus to other, 'friendly' districts. There is a timeless quality about a press report of the Battle of the Brickfields in 1872.

> The police tried in vain to separate them [the two factions] and the military were sent for: sixty men of the 4th Royal Dragoons, and a detachment of the 78th Highlanders, forced the combatant mobs apart ... The houses on the Shankill Road and adjoining streets have been gutted by mobs who took the furniture out and burnt it in the street ... It was pitiable to see the families leaving their houses as though going into captivity or exile, and hear the lamentations of the women and children, Protestants living in Catholic districts and Catholics living in Protestant districts have found it necessary to change their quarters and go to their respective friends for protection.[33]

The most costly disturbances in Belfast during the nineteenth century – both in terms of human life and commercial damage – occurred in 1886, as a direct consequence of tension caused by the introduction of Gladstone's first Home Rule Bill at Westminster. Whilst violence erupted in the familiar interface areas of west Belfast, there were also reports of disturbances in the city centre and, to its north, in York Street, which were to experience substantial trouble in the 1920s. These riots, also like subsequent disturbances, witnessed the targeting of Catholics in the shipyards and attacks on public houses. Over 50 people were believed to have died in the three-month bout of violence, 371 injuries were officially recorded and 442 arrests made.[34] Commercial losses were also high. Apart from 190 Catholics expelled from the shipyards, 31 pubs were looted and over £90,000 damage was caused.[35] Although the 1886 disturbances were nowhere near the duration or scale of those in the early 1920s, the increased severity of the city's final disturbances of the nineteenth century and specific quarrying of Catholic workmen and business premises, provided miscreants of the next generation with a model for action.

The sheer idiosyncrasy of the northern situation and its unique communal divisions might tempt one to distinguish between events there in the early part of the twentieth century and those occurring elsewhere in Ireland. However, despite the unusual circumstances and parochial nature of the Ulster conflict, it is essential that one relates events in the north to the wider Irish war, as each conflict impacted immeasurably upon the other. Nationalists and unionists had been desperately close to experiencing civil war during the summer of 1914. Asquith's third Home Rule Bill, although refraining from bestowing republican status on Ireland, proposed the establishment of an all-Ireland legislature based in Dublin, and had been on the verge of becoming law when war broke out in Europe. Not for the first time Ulster proved to be the major stumbling-block as the British attempted to solve the Irish problem. A private army, the Ulster Volunteer Force (UVF), over 100,000 strong, had been founded early in 1913, and under the command of ex-British Army generals, was, especially after gun-smuggling along the Antrim and Down coasts early in 1914, fully prepared for action, if their leader, Sir Edward Carson, so decreed.[36] Ulster's Unionist community, in a display of unprecedented solidarity, conducted its campaign both on the streets and at Westminster, with Carson, Sir James Craig and their numerous supporters on the British mainland (including Conservative Party leader Bonar Law) organising petition-signings and 'monster' rallies both in Ireland and Great Britain, to promote support for the Ulster cause.[37] In stark contrast with the early 1920s, the tight discipline imposed by the unionist political and military leadership during this Edwardian period ensured that sectarian disturbances were averted.[38]

In a unique display of agreement, both Irish paramilitary groups, the UVF and John Redmond's Irish Volunteers, answered the call of the British Empire and thousands volunteered to serve in France. The Ulster Volunteers formed the 36th Ulster Division, which was to serve with distinction at the Somme.[39] As so many of its workforce was serving in France, the Harland and Wolff shipyard and other industrial concerns recruited replacement labourers, many of them Catholic migrants from outside Ulster. When the Great War ended and the soldiers demobilised, they found themselves out of work when they returned home. This was interpreted by many loyalists as 'Sinn Féiners getting the boys' jobs' and although it was blatantly unjust to classify all Catholic workers like this, those who had started work at the shipyards during the war were inevitably going to be in a vulnerable position when the troops returned home. Like the majority of the Irish population, 'loyal Ulster' was shocked and disturbed by events in Dublin during the Easter Rising in 1916. Unlike the rest of Ireland Ulster Unionists retained this condemnatory attitude towards Sinn Féin, once the war in Europe reached its successful conclusion. This disdain for republicanism grew after the war, as Sinn Féin consolidated its political position, notably at the General Election the following year and peaked in its intensity as war was waged against the military agents of British rule in Ireland. Crucially many of the victims of the Anglo-Irish War were Ulster-born policemen and Protestant farmers living in remote areas of the south and west. Although high profile attacks tended to involve undercover British intelligence officers such as those killed in Dublin on Bloody Sunday in November 1920, northern loyalists were convinced that a campaign of ethnic cleansing was being conducted against their co-religionists in the south.

When the conflict commenced in Belfast during the summer of 1920, the war against the British was at its peak. As will be noted later, the columns of the unionist press and the speeches of their politicians were brimming with references to the latest atrocity against a Protestant farmer or a northern policeman in the south and west. Claims of their opponents' atrocities were exaggerated but the propaganda value of such stories was immense. Northerners were also concerned by political developments. Sinn Féin's predominant position elsewhere in Ireland and their apparently successful combination of physical force methods and popular politics worried unionists, who were increasingly perturbed by the effects of their campaign on British public opinion and politicians. Newspapers which had in pre-war days sided with unionists, now began to criticise them, especially for appearing to block an Irish settlement. More critically, they had initially been wary of the British Government's proposed political settlement, the Better Government of Ireland Bill, which was introduced in the House of Commons in March 1920, believing that the proposed devolved administration which was on offer, formed the antithesis of what they had campaigned for less than a decade before.[40]

THE BOOK'S STRUCTURE

A few brief comments need to be made about the structure of this book. Its title clearly illustrates its focus on the conflict within the city of Belfast and not the whole of the north. I did not extend my range to cover the entire area of Ulster, or the newly-created state of Northern Ireland for a number of reasons. Firstly, the nature of the northern 'war' was epitomised by the mix of urban guerrilla warfare and the murky escapades of men in uniform experienced in Belfast, which suffered the vast majority of the region's fatalities. Whereas many of the attacks in the border areas, such as IRA 'lightning' raids and 'reprisal' attacks by the Special Constabulary, reflected what was going on elsewhere in Ireland, the sectarian tit-for-tat shootings, tram bombings and sniper fire directed at civilians in busy thoroughfares personified the peculiar nature of the northern conflict. Also, some of the more significant attacks which occurred elsewhere in Ulster and their impact on the pattern of events in Belfast, are discussed here. Nor should the book be regarded as the mere exposition of a lengthy sectarian casualty list. Whilst an honest, rigorous attempt is made to revise previous estimations of conflict victims this work is concerned more with describing the nature of the violence and analysing its implications, than merely providing raw statistical information designed for fuelling sectarian point-scoring. Nor is the book restricted to a simple exposure of the terror created by policemen, the IRA or loyalists between 1920 and 1922. It contextualises security incidents by providing analysis of political developments and encourages the reader to empathise with the precarious lot of Belfast citizenry during these dangerous years.

Although the structure of the book is generally determined by chronological considerations reflected in the three main sections each of which is devoted to a year of the conflict, I have also adopted, where appropriate, a thematic approach. Therefore, whilst there is a systematic attempt to outline events during this period, specific issues are discussed in separate chapters within each of the three main sections. Whole chapters are devoted to an analysis of political developments, including the Craig-Collins pacts, the election of the new Belfast Parliament and the royal visit to open this institution. Similar detail is afforded to other important influences on the conflict, including the economic boycott of northern goods orchestrated by the Dublin administration, the formation of the Special Constabulary and the childhood memories of conflict 'veterans'. The story behind what was arguably the most vicious of all the crimes of this period, the McMahon murders, is also given a chapter of its own, whilst analysis of other key themes is provided within appropriate chapters. To inform the reader, extensive endnotes are provided and the appendices include a chronological summary of events and a glossary containing short biographies of the conflict's leading personalities.

Several questions will be asked in this book. Like any honest historian, I will

not pretend to have all the answers, but the issues will be revisited and analysed. The following is a list of questions which will be asked and should serve the purpose of acting as 'markers' for the reader. What sparked off the Troubles and to what degree might it be argued that the violence might have been averted, or at least, contained? What were the fears of the two communities? Did the events of 1920–2 constitute a 'pogrom'? What was the role of the IRA in Belfast at this time? To what extent was the British administration culpable for not intervening in a more proactive manner, especially in the area of security? How did press comment and political propaganda fuel the street disturbances? In what ways did the high profile political negotiations, legislation, elections and opening of the new administration heighten the tension on the streets? What truth is there in nationalist claims that there was at least substantial collusion between the police and loyalist murder gangs and possibly the direct involve-ment of some individual officers? Was any police liability for such crimes intentional or was it simply due to negligence? What was the rationale behind loyalist violence and to what extent was it organised? What policies did the administration adopt in order to cope with the terror on the streets and how effective did these prove to be? How did political, economic and military influ-ences elsewhere in Ireland impact upon events in Belfast? How did the authorities and voluntary agencies deal with problems of social deprivation accentuated by the street violence? What was the conflict's legacy for the new northern state? What was it like to live in the city, especially for children, during this difficult time?

It is my intention to provide both a detailed narrative of events and an analysis of their repercussions. In doing so, I will endeavour to describe events as accurately as possible and where the truth is unclear, I will make informed inferences. Above all, I hope to tell the story of these years, warts and all, and aim to paint a picture of what it was like to have lived in Belfast during those eventful years. The first section explores the ways in which a variety of factors combined to precipitate the start of disturbances in the city during July 1920.

1920

Start of the Storm

'We tell you this – that if, having offered you help, you are your-selves unable to protect us from the machinations of Sinn Féin, and you won't take our help, well then, we will tell you that we will take the matter into our own hands.'

Sir Edward Carson,
speaking to Belfast Orangemen, 12th July 1920

Chapter 1

Bonfire sparks

'WE WILL TAKE THE MATTER INTO OUR OWN HANDS'

Ulster was far from insulated against the repercussions of the war proceeding unabated in the rest of Ireland. Although the onslaught against British military forces, or as it became known, the Anglo-Irish War, can be traced back to the beginning of 1919, it escalated during the early summer of 1920, both in terms of its intensity and the area affected. The loyalist press, as well as spiritual and political leaders, gave vent to their feelings about the 'flying columns' of IRA volunteers who ambushed sorely-pressed RIC personnel in their barracks and on patrol. The view that the rest of Ireland was rapidly descending into anarchy which was in danger of spreading to Ulster, grew stronger in 1920 as 'incendiarism' outrages against Protestant-owned properties in several Irish counties proliferated.[1] Concern grew for co-religionists in the south and west of Ireland and in June 1920 the General Assembly of the Presbyterian Church passed a resolution expressing 'sympathy with all loyal citizens who reside in those parts of Ireland where they are exposed to terror and outrage'.[2] The substantial press coverage of the terror campaign in the rest of Ireland resulted in feelings of 'intense indignation' in Belfast, where it was believed Catholics were 'approving the outrages being committed in the south and the west'.[3] Indeed, the evictions from shipyards and factories, which had initially been understated in the loyalist press and by their political representatives, were to be regarded by them as a predictable regional outcome of a wider national conflict, exacerbated by inappropriate governmental response to atrocities elsewhere in Ireland.

However, the city was more influenced by events occurring in other parts of Ulster, especially in what was soon to become the border zone between the new states. Following substantial losses in local elections and the appointment of the city's first nationalist mayor, tension increased in Derry. Street riots occurred as republican prisoners were being moved into the city's Bishop Street jail, towards the end of April and further mayhem erupted on 15 May when there was evidence of both IRA and UVF involvement. Ill feeling within particular

districts of Derry led to Catholic homes being destroyed in the Waterside area
and reprisal attacks against Protestants in the Bogside. 1500 soldiers were drafted
in to the city on 23 June and the army were obliged to utilise curfew restraints
to restore order. The sheer volatility of the situation – nearly 40 people were
killed in Derry inside two months – provided further grim warning about what
might happen in Belfast, especially when a plethora of factors – economic,
political and cultural – coincided at one particular time.[4]

An obvious spark to light an enormous conflagration was the annual Twelfth
of July celebration in the city. Although the staging of traditional parades had
not sparked street disturbances for many years, the fears which many expressed
about imminent marches were real and understandable. However, the sheer
force of external influences in the summer of 1920 – the spread of death and
destruction throughout the south and west of Ireland, including many attacks
on Protestants, the ongoing passage of the Better Government of Ireland Bill
and the increasing proximity of violence to Belfast, as witnessed by events in
Derry – combined to create a most threatening situation in Belfast. Fears of
potential civil war in Ulster were voiced by no less an influential organ than the
Times. A leading article shortly before the parade pointed to the 'immediacy' of
the danger in Ulster, and noted the concern caused by events in Derry.
Explaining how Ulster was 'different' to the rest of Ireland, and hinting that
loyalists were 'preparing for hostilities', the *Times* made a plea for the parade to
be suspended:

> The [Orange] celebrations, in the country's present temper, are a chal-
> lenge, and they ought not to be held. In Derry, where a lesson has been
> learnt, there is agreement not to hold them. Elsewhere, even in their
> usual and legitimate form, they are a threat to peace this year. They may
> be the signal in one place, or many, for an attack on Roman Catholics –
> under colour of reprisal – and the match would be lit.[5]

Despite a clear wind of tension sweeping through the northern metropolis at
this time, life went on much as usual. The city's Grand Opera House was
staging 'The Wild Widow', direct from London's Lyceum Theatre, the
Hippodrome featured leading sopranos Nellie and Sara Kouns, a Grand Floral
Fete was due to open in the Botanic Gardens and the city's leading department
store, Robinson and Cleavers' summer sale was approaching its conclusion.
Those thinking of the future could purchase villas in the Woodvale area for

£1,000, or a 'superior' terrace house in Alexandra Park Avenue for £850, whilst thrifty artisans were likely to have been tempted by offers of houses for sale for £200 on the Grosvenor Road and £420 in Kimberley Street, off the Ormeau Road. And, of course, for those more concerned with the short-term, preparations for the Twelfth in the city's back-streets neared their climax.

The combination of a murky political climate and inclement weather on the Big Day – during the afternoon dark cloud give way to showers – did not deter what proved to be 'record gatherings in town and country – the most imposing on record'.[6] 'Elaborate precautions', including the positioning of 'strong military pickets' at main thoroughfares and the searching of motor vehicles on the city's approach roads, were taken to ensure that only the second full-scale Orange parade in the city since the tense summer of 1914 passed off peacefully. Not for the first time, nor indeed the last, would English reporters appear mystified by the scenes unfolding in front of them in Belfast. Castigating the 'anachronistic intolerance' of loyalists, the *Times* concentrated on the parade's alien nature:

> It is difficult for the inhabitants of this country to comprehend the peculiar psyche of Orangemen or to disengage the sterling qualities of the Ulster Protestant from the tradition of bigotry which he loves to honour … [of the Orange crowd]. Their mood is partly that of devotees and partly that of holiday-makers. For days before sentiment mounts towards a climacteric, and on the day itself, to the waving of banners and the beating of drums, the 17th century is reborn for a few hours.[7]

The Orange procession heralded the return to Belfast of Unionism's most popular leader, Sir Edward Carson. Despite a lengthy absence from Ulster's political scene, Carson had, as ever, his finger on the Orangeman's pulse, realising loyalist concern over the rising tide of republican violence elsewhere and potential economic problems in the Belfast shipyards. He also intended using his Orange audience as a sounding-board for his contention that the cream of the UVF should be utilised as a 'defensive' police auxiliary force. Fired up by the passion engendered by the flute bands and Lambeg drums, Carson again used a Twelfth platform to stoke up unionist ardour. Just as he had warned Asquith of the civil war threat posed by Irish home rule at an Orange gathering nearly a decade earlier, so now at Finaghy he took the opportunity to remind Lloyd George that loyalists had an alternative strategy to political action. He told his expectant audience:

> We in Ulster will tolerate no Sinn Féin ... [to the government]. We tell
> you this – that if, having offered you help, you are yourselves unable to
> protect us from the machinations of Sinn Féin, and you won't take our
> help, well then, we will tell you that we will take the matter into our own
> hands. We will reorganise.[8]

As always, Carson was concerned about maintaining Orange unity across the
social classes and in ensuring that working class Protestants resisted the temptation of moving away from sectarian politics, into a socialist movement.
Reminding his audience that Ulster was 'the real battlefield of Ireland', Carson
warned:

> The more insidious method is tacking on the Sinn Féin question and the
> Irish republican question to the Labour question ... What I say is this –
> these men who come forward posing as the friends of Labour care no
> more about Labour than does the man on the moon.[9]

The response of certain British papers to Carson's rousing speech was
predictably vehement in its tone. The *Manchester Guardian*, a long-time supporter
of the cause of Irish unity, condemned the Unionist leader for his 'barren, bitter,
hostile and provocative' speech, urging him to cease his 'railing accusations and his
appeals to his followers to arm and be ready' and instead apply himself to 'the
consideration of some real remedies.'[10] More surprising was the reaction of other
British broadsheets which had, during the home rule crisis, provided considerable
support and encouragement to Carson and his followers. In the changing circumstances of the post-war world, with its focus on facilitating self-determination,
Irish unionists were hopelessly abandoned and their pre-war 'minority' status had,
under the proposed terms of the new legislation, been replaced by a more dominant role.[11] The *Times,* a warm supporter of the Ulster Unionist cause during a
different political climate, warned the loyalist leader that 'the most serious consequences would accompany the execution of his proposal for the UVF to be
resurrected as a 'defensive' police force.'[12] Cautioning Carson that the British
public was 'not prepared to endorse any counter-provocation from the Ulster
Volunteers', the *Times* reminded loyalists that 'what was illegal in Connaught [was]
equally illegal in Ulster' and stressed that loyalism enjoyed 'no prerogative which
entitles it to defy the law'.[13]

Belfast's predominantly unionist press naturally interpreted the Finaghy
speech rather differently. Thus, Fleet Street criticism of Carson's Belfast speech

was condemned and the emphasis was switched from the inflammatory nature of their leader's speech to those extracts focussing on Sinn Féin's 'invasion of Ulster' and 'its crimes and propaganda.'[14] The *'Whig'* chose to paint a picture of two contrasting Irelands, and asked the wider audience to make its choice between two disparate societies:

> On the one side loyalty, peace, a passionate enthusiasm for all that Britain and Protestantism stands for; on the other, revolution, the ethics of the footpad and the assassin and the utter negation of all that the world ever considered religion to mean.[15]

However, genuine tension and a growing feeling of disillusionment and despair existed in Catholic Belfast. The previously carefree childhood of nine year old Jimmy Kelly was abruptly disturbed by the beating of a bath-tin by his young neighbour, Sam. According to Kelly, events in Belfast over that holiday period spelled 'the end of our happy, carefree days' and precipitated a sudden realisation that imminent danger would result in 'violence and terror overshadowing our play that lovely summer.'[16] Kelly recalls:

> It was the Twelfth of July, 'Orangemen's Day', and above the rattle of the bath-tin across the open fields from the direction of the distant Shankill Road came the dull menacing roll of big Lambeg drums, rising and falling on the breeze. Later that day I heard adults whisper that Carson, the great Protestant leader, had arrived from London and it was feared there would be trouble.[17]

Despite sharing such a concern, the *Irish News* had, on the eve of the parade, conceded that participation in the annual Orange pageant was 'a congenial habit very natural to anyone of normal gregarious instincts', especially predictable in a city 'bereft of the economic and cultural benefits of a labour movement.'[18] On the morning of the parade, the mouthpiece of northern nationalism had, in claiming 'the future lies with Nationalist Ireland', reverted to type.[19] The paper was far from complimentary about Carson's Finaghy speech, lampooning the Orange platform party as one more to be associated with 'a Punch and Judy display'.[20] The *Irish News* pursued a similarly sardonic approach in another article the following day when journalist Frank Harkin re-enacted the walk to the Field with cartoon characters 'Sammy' and 'Billy', who remarked, 'there's one thing we must give Dublin credit for; if they can't make sashes they can make good stout!'[21] Elsewhere in that edition of the paper, the Unionist leader was accused of shirking the issue, in the light of his decision to accept a form of home rule and castigated for scare-mongering by focusing on the utilisation of UVF resources.[22]

Within days the anxiety engendered by Carson's controversial Twelfth speech had been compounded by the breaking news that a senior Ulster-born police officer had been assassinated in Cork. Colonel Gerald Smyth, the Munster Divisional RIC Commander and a native of Banbridge, was shot dead by three IRA gunmen at the Cork Country Club. Smyth, a disabled war hero, had been a fervent critic of Sinn Féin and, along with District Inspector Oswald Swanzy (soon to be another victim of republican gunmen), had been involved in the killing of Tomas MacCurtain in the city in March. Smyth was probably targeted for his gung-ho approach to militant republicanism rather than, as perceived by many in Ulster, for his northern unionist background. He had endeavoured to lift sagging RIC morale at a time when the police found themselves increasingly in the front line of IRA attack. Addressing officers in Listowel, Gerald Smyth had urged:

> Now, men, Sinn Féin has had all the sport up to the present, and we are going to have the sport now ... you may make mistakes occasionally and innocent persons may be shot, but that cannot be helped, and you are bound to get the right participants sometime ... The more you shoot the better I will like you, and I assure you, no policeman will get into trouble for shooting any man.[23]

The Unionist press acknowledged that Smyth had been a vociferous opponent of Sinn Féin. The *Northern Whig* suggested the Divisional Commander had been shot because he had been 'in earnest in his resolve to meet Sinn Féin with its own weapons' and also because it was 'feared he would succeed in inspiring his police with his own spirit.'[24] The *Whig* maintained that the attack on such a senior policeman constituted 'a direct challenge to the British Government which, if it were not countered, would result in men despairing of Ireland altogether'.[25] Loyalists were further outraged when the southern rail crew assigned to transport the police chief's body back to his home town of Banbridge refused to do so. This anger boiled over, both in Banbridge and its neighbouring town, Dromore, after his funeral on 21 July, when there were reports of attacks on the small Catholic communities in both towns.

ORIGINS OF SHIPYARD EVICTIONS

It would be simplistic to imply that the violence which was to erupt in Belfast's streets that July merely represented the repercussions of a long-fermenting scheme to systematically eliminate Belfast's Catholic population. Obviously the orchestrators of the summer's attacks in the city's industrial heartland could not have predicted the assassination by republicans of a senior police officer nearly 200 miles away, nor the degree of venom in Carson's Finaghy exhortations. On the other hand, it would be disingenuous to suggest that the attacks in the city's shipyards and those in small, outlying towns, were merely spontaneous outbursts of anger generated by Sinn Féin violence, both in the south as well as inside Ulster's own boundaries. Indeed, the precise timing of the shipyard incidents – the day on which several thousand employees returned to work after their annual holiday – indicates a measure of preparation. The revival of the UVF around this time, the calls by Wilfred Spender and others for the reorganisation of the paramilitary force into a special constabulary, and speculation that there had been a build-up of arms caches in loyalist areas, indicate that some loyalists were, at the very least, cognisant of the need to be prepared for an imminent outbreak of communal fighting within their particular areas.[26] The sparks had been lit and were soon to be applied to the 'firewood', Belfast's mixed religious workforce, located in its industrial centre, the shipyards.

There was undeniably a sense of grievance amongst many loyalist ex-servicemen. Thousands of yard workers had joined the 36th Ulster Division and other Irish regiments during the war and their places in the shipyards had been taken by Catholics, both from within the city's boundaries and many from outside. When the war ended and the inevitable economic slump occurred, the 'returning heroes', encouraged by Lloyd George and others to expect a 'better tomorrow', were understandably aggrieved to be forced on to the dole.[27] Many of them felt they had a moral right to regain their former jobs. It was this belief they were simply reclaiming what was rightfully theirs which, from a loyalist perspective, justified the blatantly intimidatory tactics used to oust law-abiding Catholics from their workplace. Even partisan observers acknowledged the existence of 'a number of decent Roman Catholics who did not deserve this treatment', although they claimed these 'could not be separated from the others'.[28] Protestant ex-servicemen were not alone in feeling uneasy about their job prospects. An economic slump hit Britain during May 1920, resulting in a substantial increase in the numbers of unemployed and those forced to work shorter days.[29] As in any economic crisis, those with limited skills were most vulnerable and it was no coincidence that the groups actively engaged in intimidating Catholics and socialists from the workplace were apprentices and 'rivet boys', who were amongst the lowest paid workers, less likely to be unionised and, therefore, most insecure.

Another explanation of the industrial intimidation was its political dimension. Michael Farrell suggests that the campaign of expulsion was masterminded by those in high office within the Unionist Party, as a means of buttressing flagging support from the Protestant working class and identifying clear scapegoats, in the form of Catholics and socialists.[30] Cracks had been beginning to appear in the Unionist hegemony since the end of European hostilities and these fissures were perceived by loyalists to have been caused by 'disloyal' trade unionists and socialists. Unique solidarity across the sectarian divide had surfaced at the beginning of 1919, when engineering and shipyard workers campaigned, unsuccessfully, for a reduction in their working hours.[31] Although the four week strike was unsuccessful, hopes for the emergence of a thriving socialist movement in the city received a further boost when 13 Labour councillors were returned in the city's council election early in 1920.

Unionism had long been wary of the dangers posed by a strong socialist movement in the city. Carson had endeavoured to give working-class Protestants a voice in his pre-war anti Home Rule movement and the establishment of a pressure group, uniting trade unionists within a wider unionist movement, was established in 1918. The Ulster Unionist Labour Association (UULA) had branches in the east, north and south of the city and enjoyed the support of illustrious figures in the unionist movement, including Carson and mill-owner J.M. Andrews. Although enjoying political success in the 'khaki' election of November 1918, the UULA was never a mass membership movement, nor did it succeed in concealing divisions within the Unionist Party.[32]

Many nationalists believed that the UULA's promotion by the Unionist establishment and its involvement in the meeting which pre-empted the initial industrial evictions was indicative of an elaborate loyalist plan to precipitate an anti-Catholic onslaught in Belfast. A number of journals rejected the notion that the shipyard attacks were simply spontaneous reactions to political speeches or to the killing of senior northern-born police officers, like Smyth in Cork. The *Westminster Gazette* claimed it was 'common knowledge' in Belfast that plans had been 'matured at least two months ago to drive all Home Rule workers in the shipyards out of their unemployment', maintaining that the RIC were 'well aware of the scheme' and suggested that 'the question discussed by them was not would the attack come but when'.[33] Accusations involving the 'importing' of agents provocateurs from places like Derry, with the specific purpose of increasing tension in the workplace, were regarded as evidence of collusion between unionist leaders and workers. The *Irish News* observed how 'firebrands' from Derry had been brought in to Belfast to deliver 'inflammatory harangues' to loyalist workers.[34] Others believed that the intimidatory tactics employed in the shipyards had been sanctioned by the UUC who had come to the conclusion that expulsions had to be executed 'systematically' with 'unbelievable ferocity' in the yards.[35] Also, is was alleged that agitators had used the correspondence pages of the unionist press to stir up bad feeling amongst the Protestant working class. Certainly some anonymous exhortations to adopt a physical response to the IRA were made in papers like the *Belfast Newsletter*. An 'observer', writing in the letters' pages of the newspaper, lamented the prevailing 'apathy and stagnation' amongst loyalists, before concluding it was 'time that unionists roused themselves to act, because before very long it will not be possible to do anything.'[36] However, apart from such veiled threats, there is little evidence that grassroots loyalists were being publicly persuaded to join with other activists in specific militant action, nor is there indication of a concerted programme in industrial centres spearheaded by agents provocateurs. Although these anonymous 'calls to arms' did little to defuse tension on the eve of the marching season, they amounted to little more than sabre rattling. Therefore, whilst it's undeniable that the atmosphere in the city was tense and that security forces and citizens alike were bracing themselves for trouble, there is a dearth of evidence to support the theory that the Unionist Party was actively sponsoring a systematic programme of sectarian attack.

Whilst direct Unionist involvement in the industrial expulsions was unlikely, the reticence of their leaders to condemn the intimidation or to intervene in a proactive manner against those responsible for the industrial violence, undoubtedly gave moral support to those responsible. Thus, loyalist vengeance for republican subversion elsewhere in Ireland and the apparent acquiescence or sympathy of northern Catholics for that campaign, helped legitimise loyalist retribution in Belfast shipyards and factories. Carson was later to express his 'pride' in the actions of his shipyard 'friends' and in his Westminster speech in the wake of the expulsions, endeavoured to deflect criticism of such actions by suggesting that the desire of 'loyal citizens' to assist in the defence of their districts had been consistently ignored by those in authority. Carson argued:

The republicans are at war with England and there is a section of the
people in Ireland who say 'We are anxious to help you', but the government say 'we cannot allow you to help us' . . . I foresaw months ago from
information which came to me that there would be an attempt by Sinn
Féin to penetrate into Ulster. I foresaw that it would create a difficult
situation . . . I felt certain that Ulster people would not take it lying down
and I know they will not.[37]

Carson and his colleagues also referred to the stresses caused by Ulster's political uncertainty. Though legislation was being drafted which would create a
regional parliament and administration subject only to the Imperial Parliament
at Westminster, Unionists had accepted this begrudgingly, and their rank and
file, in particular, had serious reservations about its implications. They were
increasingly concerned by a growing coolness between themselves and their
former friends in the Conservative Party and British press, and by Sinn Féin's
apparently unassailable position elsewhere in Ireland. Unionists' political uncertainty and growing sense of isolation partly explains their subsequent reluctance
to condemn the intolerant actions of their co-religionists.[38]

   If one accepts the thesis that the unionist leadership had, through its alleged
employment of agents provocateurs and its encouragement of the UULA,
masterminded the industrial expulsions, one would also likely accept the argument that they also controlled the weaponry required for physical intervention.
Certainly the time and circumstances were favourable, given the worsening
political situation, the considerable arsenal which had been in loyalist hands
since the gun-running escapades six years before, and the comparative dearth of
firearms and, indeed, manpower of the IRA in the city during the first half of
1920. It is difficult to estimate the number of pre-war weapons still in prime
condition and in the hands of 'maverick' loyalists, as distinct from being subject
to the tighter discipline of the UVF, but easy access to such weaponry was
unlikely to have constituted a significant problem for 'rogue' loyalists.[39] The
availability of vast arsenals of pre-war, mainly German, rifles and handguns is
undoubted. Frederick Crawford admitted having half a million rounds of
ammunition in his bleach-works near Brown Square.[40]

'SHIPYARD CONFETTI'

Groups of workers, believed to belong to the Belfast Protestant Association (BPA), posted notices on the gates of Queen's Island on the morning of 21 July, as workers returned from their Twelfth holiday.[41] These posters called for a meeting of 'all Unionist and Protestant workers' during the lunch-hour outside Workman Clark's yard that day.[42] An impassioned gathering, consisting of up to 5000 workers, denounced IRA atrocities, especially the recent killing of Smyth in Cork, and demanded the expulsions of 'non-loyal' workers.[43] After the meeting had ended, a large mob, still 'high' on loyalist rhetoric, used sledge-hammers to force their way in to Harland and Wolff premises. Once inside, and armed with hammers, iron bars, wooden staves and, reportedly, revolvers, they roamed the vast concourse searching for potential victims.[44] Some workers had anticipated what was afoot and had left the premises at lunchtime, whilst other Catholics managed to suffer only verbal abuse before making a speedy exit. Many others were not so fortunate and for them the next hour was to prove a nightmare. Human dignity was of little importance in the identification of victims. To help determine the religious persuasion of individual workers, their undergarments were frequently torn open to see if these men were wearing rosaries or other Catholic emblems. The potential escape of workers had been made more difficult by the decision of Harland and Wolff's management to lock the main gates at Queen's Island which effectively trapped many workers inside the yard. As a consequence, Catholics came under direct attack and were severely beaten. Several 'non-loyal' workers felt compelled to swim across the Musgrave Channel, but whilst in the water were pelted by a fusillade of 'ship-yard confetti', consisting of iron nuts, bolts, ship rivets and pieces of sharp steel, and one worker who reached the upper side of the channel was driven back into the water. There was also the pathetic sight of non-swimmers struggling in the water, having unsuccessfully pleading their assailants for mercy. One Catholic worker recalled:

> The gates were smashed down with sledges, the vests and shirts of those at work were torn open to see if the men were wearing Catholic emblems, and then woe betide the man that was. One man was set upon, thrown into the dock, had to swim the Musgrave Channel, and having been pelted with rivets, had to swim 2 or 3 miles, to emerge in streams of blood and rush to the police in a nude state.[45]

Nationalist observers maintained that little effort was made by loyalist gangs to distinguish between republicans and those with recent service experience. The *Irish News* pointed out that several wearers of the Mons Star, one of whom had a silver plate fixed into his head as the 'memento of a serious and almost incurable wound received while doing his bit with an Irish Regiment' in France, were 'on the run' from the shipyards. The paper concluded that, although their service records were 'well-known', this did not 'save them from the common fate decreed by the originators of the pogrom'.[46] Most Catholics and socialists had been removed from the yards by the afternoon. At least 20 men had to receive hospital treatment and as they made their bloodied and weary journey home, the response in Catholic districts was a mixture of horror and rage. Jimmy Kelly, barely nine at the time, recalls the commotion which followed the shipyard expulsions:

> While on errand to Fleeton's shop at the Springfield Road corner I saw a fleet of cars and taxis conveying workmen with bloodstained bandages around their heads to the nearby Royal Victoria Hospital. These were the Catholic workers, beaten up and expelled from the two great shipyards on the Lagan.[47]

INDUSTRIAL INTIMIDATION

The following day the BPA and their associates turned their attention to several of the city's other industrial sites. Catholic workers were ejected from the Sirocco Works to the east of the city centre, with many of the expelled workers having 'to climb the railings and jump for safety into the backyards of adjacent houses.'[48] Other places where workers were compelled to leave that day included several linen mills, Musgraves, Combe Barbours and Mackies Foundry in west Belfast. Although none of the cases of expulsion that day, or in the weeks ahead, matched the spectacular evictions in the shipyards, most of Belfast's industrial centres were either visited by marauding gangs of intimidators, or in some cases, threats were relayed by work colleagues. Where expulsions were more obviously orchestrated, as in the case of the shipyards, internal 'policing' of those expelled was carried out by vigilante committees organised by the BPA, which monitored such cases, ensuring there were less opportunities for such victims to make an unheralded return to work. In smaller industrial units where infiltration of the BPA was less likely and sectarian tension amongst workers was compara- tively low, Catholics were frequently able to carry on working.[49] In other businesses, many employers promised to keep jobs open for valued Catholic workers who were advised to 'lie low' for a while. The expulsions were mainly inflicted by loyalists upon Catholic and socialist workers, but there were a small number of reported incidents where Protestants were also expelled from their place of work.[50]

Estimations of those intimidated from their workplace vary and completely accurate figures are impossible to ascertain, given the circumstances which meant that not all workers claimed relief from charity agencies.[51] However, the most likely number of those expelled was around 10,000, including several hundred female textile workers.[52]

Whilst the majority of expulsions appear to have occurred within the first few days, there were some cases where intimidation did not occur until well into the following month or even early in September.[53] From that period onwards, intimidatory methods tended to be restricted to verbal threats, though the implications of refusing to sign documents expressing 'loyalty' were fairly obvious. Nearly three weeks after the shipyard expulsions, a handful of long- serving Catholic workers at Dixon's Saw Mills in Milewater Road, ignored a threat to stay away from their work and also refused to sign the 'loyalty' docu- ment, which again resulted in them being forced to leave their work premises after a vote taken by their Protestant workmates.[54]

Other Catholic workers had to endure serious physical threats. One experi- enced employee in a mainly Protestant bakery owed his life to his employer. An armed mob visited the bakery but the manager hid him in an empty oven. However, the mob realised this Catholic employee was on the premises and posted a guard of six men at the gates of the bakery during the night. The next morning an angry crowd had gathered, promising to find the worker and 'do him in'. Fortunately sharp thinking on the part of the bakery manager saved the day. Hiding the petrified worker in a van, he drove it through the gates, informing the baying mob that he had been obliged to make a delivery himself due to the sudden, drastic reduction in the number of available drivers.[55]

The ambiguous position of industrial bosses and managers was reflected in another case at a big city firm whose 400 strong workforce contained about 10% Catholic workers. When these employees, already intimidated from their workplace, returned to the factory asking for a guarantee of protection before resuming work, the manager, pressurised by a deputation of 'loyal' workers, felt unable to guarantee their safety on his premises.[56] Other managers were equally impotent, advising harassed Catholic employees to stay off work for a time until 'things calmed down',[57] Owners or managers of larger firms or organisations which employed Catholics enjoyed more flexibility and were sometimes able to relocate their intimidated workers in factories or workshops closer to their own areas.[58]

Intimidation of Belfast's industrial workers was not restricted to Catholics. Other workers refusing to sign an oath of 'loyalty' were also considered targets and these were Protestant trade unionists, many of whom held senior office in their unions.[59] Superficially at least, this political rather than ostensibly religious targeting of victims might suggest that the sectarian thesis is inherently flawed. In other words, by failing to distinguish between Catholic workers and socialist ones, the expulsions could be interpreted as political rather than sectarian in their essence. It's certainly true that Protestant trade unionists were penalised in similar ways to Catholic workers, though there were fewer reported cases of trade unionists experiencing physical assault. Thus, 'rotten Prods', as they were labelled by loyalist gangs, were intimidated and expelled from their place of work, had threats made on their lives and experienced arson attacks at their political clubs.[60] Their plight was eloquently described by a Belfast Labour councillor at the national Trade Union conference. James Baird told his fellow delegates:

> Every man who was prominently known in the labour movement, who was known as an IPP-eer [sic] was expelled from his work just the same as the rebel Sinn Féiners. To show their love of the ILP, they burnt our hall in North Belfast. The Chairman of our central branch had to flee to Glasgow for his life. The secretary had to fly all the way to London. The district chairman of the AEU, a very moderate and quiet Labour man, was beaten not once but 2 or 3 times because he persisted in returning to his work. A member of the executive of the Joiners' Society was also expelled. He was not a Catholic, and he was also a moderate Labour man.[61]

Hatred aimed at such 'rotten Prods' was fuelled by propaganda emanating from a Unionist leadership which twinned the great 'evils' of Irish republicanism and Bolshevism. Whilst the linking of ideologically-motivated revolutionary forces with agents of Irish republicanism might suggest political naivety, there was a genuine feeling that such an alliance was responsible for fermenting the current turmoil. In a private memo, Sir James Craig warned Lloyd George that 'the Rebel plans are directed towards the establishment of a Republic hostile to the British Empire', maintaining that Sinn Féin were 'working in conjunction with Bolshevik forces elsewhere towards that end.'[62] Despite the partial success of such propaganda and the undoubted extension of intimidatory tactics towards Protestants expected of sympathising with the Catholic predicament, there can be little doubt that many such attacks were fuelled by raw bigotry. Another Belfast socialist, John Hanna, told the 1920 TUC conference of an extraordinary instance of bigotry, involving the sons of a Protestant yard worker forced from their employment on account of their widowed father remarrying a Catholic.[63]

In the absence of any 'official' aid from the Government, those Catholics expelled from work were reliant, especially in the early stages, on charity and support organisations.[64] Within days of their expulsion from the shipyards, representatives of at least 2,000 Catholic workers appointed a committee to organise the presentation of 'the full circumstances of expulsions' which would be presented to 'the executive of various unions and employers concerned'.[65] Registration offices were opened for 'victimised workers' at the beginning of August and this paved the way for the relatively smooth distribution of relief payments to the workers concerned a fortnight later. Those claiming were required to register, according to their trade, in halls with an estimated 2,000 enrolling.[66] The treasurers of the group responsible for organising the fund for Expelled Workers, in an advertisement in the nationalist press, stressed the 'dire need' of the expelled workers and their dependants, appealing not only for financial support but also directly to 'the Industrial World for Industrial Justice'.[67] Money soon began to 'pour in' for Catholics and a number of fund-raising events organised by groups such as the Ancient Order of Hibernians, which staged concerts in St Mary's Hall.[68] Supported by leading members of the local community such as Joe Devlin and Bishop MacRory, the group also widened its net and, from the autumn, appealed successfully all over Ireland, in Great Britain, France, North America and Australia.[69] Making the appeal to sympathetic external audiences had the dual purpose of raising funds swiftly and disseminating information about their plight.[70] This was achieved with considerable success, as the circulars of the Expelled Workers fund group compared the plight of their community with that of 'ravaged' Belgium in 1914, reminding their foreign audience 'it was not the Huns [who] did this'.[71] The fund's treasurers appealed to 'the freedom loving people of America for aid for our poor victims of insensitive and diabolical fanaticism', and begging their American audience 'not to let our people starve', the circular ended with an 'SOS across the seas for help for our persecuted people'.[72] The underlying premise of the fund's organisers was that everybody should be offended by this blatant attempt to deprive Catholic workers of the chance to eke out a livelihood. Their plea was a passionate one:

> Everyone has a right to live by his wages. If this Right is lost all is lost. If religious bigotry or political rancour, engineered by selfish and insidious capitalists is allowed to imperil the God-given Right the position of labour will be undermined.[73]

Inside a week the first payment to the expelled workers was distributed. Engineering workers were the first to receive payments at St Mary's Hall on 19 August, with other groups following them in the next few days. They were given claim cards relating to their trade with married men receiving additional payments.[74] The fund continued to operate even after the government's belated decision to issue benefits, with an estimated 8,140 still registered under the scheme by early October. These included over 4,000 heads of families and meant that over 23,000 were estimated to be benefiting from these payments.[75] This prompted the *Irish News* to suggest that 'pogromists are actually enlarging the sphere of their operations.'[76] However, despite the high number remaining on the Expelled Workers register, many Catholics gained employment either elsewhere or returned to work, frequently in a different location, once a calmer atmosphere was restored. Although this process could be a slow one, return to work for some Catholics was speedier. For instance, railway workers and fire officers expelled at the end of August were reported to have returned to work inside a week.[77] Less than a month previously the *Irish News* informed its readers that 'a number [of workers] have left, and are leaving the city for other centres where employment is obtainable'.[78]

Predictably Bishop MacRory was quick to allocate the blame for the violence to 'secret political and capitalistic influence' and to 'the unholy Carsonite incitement' to bigotry. He proceeded to argue in his letter to the treasurers of the Expelled Workers' Fund that the factories and the shipyards might have been temporarily closed in the light of events and that stronger denunciation of intimidation might have been forthcoming from the Unionist leadership. He concluded that 'the whole terrible business is a fine commentary on the precious Partition Bill'.[79] The bishop was especially perturbed by the fact that it was 'fellow workers' who had been responsible for the 'systematic' and 'deliberate' nature of the expulsions which made him 'despair of human nature.'[80]

Bishop MacRory's initial declaration of his 'pain' at the 'distress' suffered by his community reflected not only his closeness to his flock but also his political awareness. Lamenting the state Catholics found themselves in, Dr MacRory stressed the importance of 'nationalist Ireland' picking up the 'gauntlet' against their Unionist opponents. In another letter he wrote of Belfast:

> Until this city is taught that it depends on Ireland, there will be recurrent outbursts of bigotry here, and a standing obstacle to the settlement of the whole of the Irish Question. I believe this to be a providential opportunity, if properly availed of, for putting an end to both.[81]

Political representatives, especially those of a nationalist hue, despaired at the British Establishment's lack of urgency or even basic understanding of dealing with the causes and social consequences of the industrial expulsions. As Westminster discussed the Government of Ireland Bill, west Belfast's MP castigated the government's lack of realism and besought them to remember the fate of 'a quarter of the city's population'. Joe Devlin reminded his parliamentary audience of the real nature of the problem in Belfast.

> It is a story of weeping women, hungry children, homeless in England, homeless in Ireland. If that's what we get when they have not got their Parliament, what may we expect when they have that weapon with wealth and power strongly entrenched? What will we get when they are armed with Britain's rifles, when they have cast around them the Imperial garb, what mercy, what pity, much less justice or liberty will be conceded to us then?[82]

Initially at least, the Government disclaimed direct responsibility for events in the north. Whilst condemning the intimidation and industrial expulsions, the Irish Secretary, Sir Hamar Greenwood, sheltered behind the principle of political non-intervention in economic issues. Speaking to the Commons, Greenwood appeared to distance his administration from direct responsibility for events in Belfast. Greenwood argued he had 'no power to insist upon employers employing

Roman Catholics, Orangemen or anybody else' and that he was unable 'to compel one trade unionist to work alongside another.'[83] Within a matter of weeks the Government showed more urgency over the enduring nature of the expulsions, although this did not lead to measures which might have directly alleviated the plight of the city's Catholics. A leading civil servant, Sir Ernest Clark, was appointed on 15 September 1920 with a brief to provide a framework for the forthcoming Belfast administration.[84] By delegating on-the-ground responsibility to Clark, Greenwood could afford to appear to be more assertive in his approach. In a letter to Clark, he stressed as 'a matter of paramount importance that the Catholic workers in the Belfast area who had been expelled from employment should be restored and your most urgent duty is to get in touch with employers and leaders of public opinion and do all in your power to insure the restoration of normal employment.'[85] However, Clark's belief that the loyalists' intimidatory tactics would be short-lived was based on his interpretation that their behaviour was an emotional response to the expulsion of Protestant workers in the Derry dockers a few months previously and, of course, to the continuing IRA campaign in the north.

Although patently pro-unionist in his political attitudes, Clark did make an effort to calm the tension, speaking on occasions to various pressure groups, including the UULA and the Loyalist Vigilante Committee. On 21 September Clark encouraged the UULA representatives whom he met to persuade loyalist vigilantes in the shipyards to accept the return of Catholic workers. Nevertheless, the stumbling-block was to prove to be the proposal of a declaration of loyalty, renouncing support of Sinn Féin. This was to prove to be a Catch 22 situation for most Catholic and socialist workers. By refusing to sign, they were shown to be 'disloyal' to the monarchy. However, even those Catholics who were not followers of Sinn Féin would have been deterred both by this intrusion into their political beliefs and by the inevitable ostracism which it would produce within their own community. The dearth of Catholic workers' signatures proved to their cynical Protestant workmates that their initial doubts over the loyalty of Catholic workmates had been fully warranted. In the end, Clark was overtaken by the pace of events and the murder of two policemen at the end of September meant the elimination of any chance of a speedy return of nationalist workers.[86]

The Westminster Government initially refused to pay those workers forced out of their workplace unemployment benefit on the technicality that they had not lost their jobs, but were not attending their place of work due to issues related to trade disputes. Pressure from the Catholic hierarchy and political representatives and the extent of the hardship experienced by many Catholic families resulted in Westminster's reassessment of the benefits issue. The first payments to such workers started on 16 September (they were backdated to the beginning of the month). The rates distinguished between ex-soldiers and those who had not seen service, but did not differentiate between the various trades.[87] Praising Devlin's 'timely and effective intervention' in campaigning for such compensation for their misfortune, the *Irish News* described such payments as 'an important element in lightening the heavy burden imposed on voluntary effort by the present unparalleled state of things in Belfast brought about by the persecution of Catholic workers.'[88] Perhaps a factor in encouraging the decision by Westminster to provide financial assistance to destitute Catholic workers was the unleashing of an 'army' of dissatisfied workers, normally fully engaged at their workplace, onto the city's streets and a considerable number of disturbances and shootings were undoubtedly executed during normal working hours.

Owing to the systematic enforcement of the 'loyalty test' in many Belfast workplaces, inevitably the chance of a short-term return to work for many Catholics rapidly diminished. Indeed, it can be argued that numerous Catholic workers and their families would have been dependent on charity for most of two years until they had been fully reabsorbed into the mainstream workforce. In the meantime, many picked up work on a casual, 'odd job' basis within their own community, or took advantage of the Corporation's offer of jobs on its tramline reconstruction scheme. Others went further afield, taking on temporary work in places like Dublin or Glasgow.

Workplace expulsions, both in larger industrial units like the shipyards and linen mills and in smaller commercial concerns, were, therefore, the result of a fusion of factors which ignited a tense situation into a fireball. The encroachment of political violence into Ulster territory, the killing of northern police personnel, fiery political speeches by leaders responding to a tense atmosphere generated by the passage of the Government of Ireland Bill, the economic grievances of soldiers returning from war service to Belfast dole queues and the easy availability of a stockpile of weaponry combined to plunge Belfast into a prolonged period of darkness with only occasional chinks of light. Not surprisingly it was the east of the city, location of the first expulsions, which was to witness the initial blasts of violence.

Chapter 2

Trouble in the east

AFTERMATH OF YARD EVICTIONS

Word quickly spread around Catholic side-streets of the fate of their co-religionists who had just been expelled from the shipyards. Not surprisingly, the first response came from Catholics living close to the tram-lines which ferried the largely Protestant yard workers to their homes across the Lagan. Trams were attacked just after six that evening near Short Strand, where workers were dragged off vehicles and assaulted, some finding themselves disorientated in the warren of little streets at the city end of the Newtownards Road. Tramcars were also attacked in Cromac Street, just to the south of the city centre, where gangs pelted passengers with heavy rounded paving stones. Inside an hour, loyalist gangs had started to gather in the Donegall Pass area and a full scale riot broke out between them and nationalist factions in Cromac Street, where the police had to baton charge the assailants and fire blank cartridges to disperse them. Gunfire broke out as darkness descended and continued intermittently for several hours. Only essential family business could possibly have enticed people to risk such danger by stepping onto bullet-ridden streets. Margaret Noade's mother lay desperately ill in her bed in Cromac Street and she took the crucial decision to visit her. Around midnight, Mrs Noade (27), who lived at Anderson Street in the Short Strand, proceeded with her baby and a friend to make the 15-minute journey. She was struck by a police bullet as she turned in to Cromac Square and became one of the conflict's early fatalities.[1]

At the edge of Ballymacarrett lay the small Catholic enclave of Short Strand. The church serving this community, St Matthew's, was surrounded by the fiercely loyalist Newtownards Road and once the spark of violence had been ignited, it was inevitable that St Matthew's would become an inferno.[2] St Matthew's, aptly described as 'lying embedded in a vast area of the worst Orangeism', suffered greatly during the conflict, with an estimated 32 people from the parish losing their lives over the two year period of disturbances.[3] Hours after the industrial evictions on Wednesday 21 July, the Short Strand was in turmoil, a situation which was to peak during the next few days. During this time the church and its neighbouring convent, the Cross and Passion, as well as homes of ordinary Catholics, spirit groceries and public houses, were to be the objects of relentless aggression by rampaging loyalist mobs. The violence peaked the following evening. An arson attempt was made on the convent and a military detachment from the 1st Norfolk Regiment opened fire on a large loyalist crowd which had congregated in Bryson Street and was threatening to storm the building.[4] Nellie McGregor (20), of Frome Street, had been walking towards the city centre at around 9.30 p.m. with a friend, Samuel Faulkner, who lived in Dee Street. Discovering 'a great commotion in and about Bryson Street', they debated whether to continue their journey towards the city centre as the army were given the order to open fire on the loyalist mob. At her inquest the City Coroner, John Graham, heard the witness claim he had physically thrown Miss McGregor to the ground where both had stayed until there was a break in the gunfire. As they were getting up again, a military volley was fired from Bryson Street, seriously injuring Miss McGregor, who died from her wounds the next day.[5] Two other Protestants were fatally wounded, probably by military fire, during these riots. James Stewart, a teenager living in Scotland, who had been holidaying with relatives in Frome Street, was shot on the Newtownards Road, as was John Dole (24), of Prim Street. Mr Dole died of his injuries in hospital nearly three weeks later. The army were involved in another fatal shooting that evening, barely a mile away in the Cromac area. Albert McAuley, a Catholic from Stanfield Street, who was a well-known greyhound trainer and official at Celtic Park, was shot as the army opened fire on stone-throwing youths at Cromac Square.[6]

Catholics continued to be evicted from their homes and Catholic-owned business premises were destroyed by fire the following day, Friday 23 July, especially in the east of the city. Later in the evening a large loyalist crowd directed their anger towards the Cross and Passion convent, attempting to set it on fire.[7] A small detachment of police and military struggled to cope with the advancing mob and in their panic, opened fire on the crowd, injuring at least a dozen, three fatally. These were Mary Weston (29), of Welland Street, ex-soldier William McCune (39), from Clonallen Street, who had recently been demobbed and had just applied for a military pension, and teenager Susan Houston, who died from her wounds in hospital on 11 August. Desperate as the order to fire might have been, it did have the desired effect, bringing a degree of calm to the area. Indeed, the assertive nature of this early security force reaction to potential loyalist violence was in stark contrast to subsequent indecision and vacillation.

'GUTTED LIQUOR STORES'

One of the earliest targets for loyalist gangs in east Belfast was the predominantly Catholic-owned spirit groceries which, having licences to sell liquor as well as groceries, were the 'supermarkets' of their day.[8] Apart from being greatly outnumbered by Protestants in Ballymacarrett, managers and owners of such premises were also in the unfortunate position where some of their sales items were the prime prize of an already intoxicated, emotionally-charged mob. The scale of such attacks in east Belfast was staggering. Press accounts of the trouble suggest that at least 60 spirit groceries and a dozen pubs in the city were damaged inside 48 hours, and an estimated 75% of Ballymacarrett's 54 spirit groceries were damaged during this period. Most of the 14 fires attended to by the Fire Brigade on 22 July were on the premises of spirit groceries. Irresponsible elements in the local community, using the prevailing tension and the shopkeepers' different religious persuasion as an excuse, threatened and, in several instances, physically attacked these owners, raiding their shops before permanently damaging the premises. There were even reports of women and children rolling around in various states of drunkenness in a number of locations and of the military's failure to intervene when the stolen contents of these liquor stores were being openly passed around a braying mob.[9] Many of those who had either been involved in actual theft, or had been mere recipients of stolen items, were, it was acknowledged by community leaders, actively involved in the civil disturbances. Indeed, one such leader claimed that 'all[of the riots] were led by men more or less under the influence of drink'.[10]

The scale of the damage in Ballymacarrett was undoubtedly extensive. The *Irish News* noted the area's 'demolished' state and informed its readers that the district was 'nothing but a trail of smashed and looted shops, with the street strewn with broken glass, flour, flake meal, sugar and other contents of spirit groceries.'[11] The same edition carried a detailed report on the experiences of two owners of spirit groceries in east Belfast. It was noted that alcohol was taken from the stores and consumed by men, women and even children on the streets. Empty beer barrels were set alight following an attack on Patrick Shield's Foundry Bar, whilst the taps of those few remaining beer barrels in McGurk's ransacked spirit grocery in Bankmore Street were allowed, by the mob, 'to continue running until the contents of every barrel in the premises had been drained onto the floor, forming a copious stream, which flowed into the roadway and down the sewer'.[12] The loyalist press also condemned the 'melancholy spectacle' that was east Belfast, comparing the landscape of the Newtownards Road with the appearance of towns in Picardy following German attack and occupation during the Great War. The *Northern Whig* lamented:

> Smashed shop fronts, gutted liquor stores, burning debris in the side streets, pavements covered inches deep with broken glass, and fragments of demolished fittings would suggest that the street had been bombarded before being sacked.[13]

However, despite being 'appalled' by the extent of the damage in the east of the city – the *Whig's* correspondent suggested that 'Pussyfoot' Jackson, the leader of the American prohibition movement 'could not have effected [*sic*] greater havoc among the drink shops of East Belfast' – the paper endeavoured to minimalise the publicity damage by reminding their readers that the majority of Belfast's citizens would have 'to pay smartly for the two days recreation of a comparatively small number of rowdies.'[14]

Many of the owners of spirit groceries and other Catholic-owned businesses on the Newtownards Road had to flee their premises (this was inevitable as, in most cases, they lived above the shops), generally making the short journey to the already overcrowded, but welcoming, Short Strand. In a number of cases the threat of arson was enough, whether it came from smashed windows, written messages pushed through letter-boxes, or veiled verbal warnings, sometimes from those in responsible positions. Nora McMullan recalls such a visit:

> When I was 5 or 6, a police sergeant called at my father's spirit grocery in Calvin Street on the Beersbridge Road to tell him to get out as he was next on the 'B's list. We left the next morning. I stayed with my granny in the country, on a farm near Cullyhanna.

Catholics forced out of their businesses and homes also made the move across the city to the Falls Road, transporting their possessions as best they could, often reduced to staying, temporarily at least, with relatives or being put up in church halls.[15] As these 'refuges' were usually tiny, cramped, terraced houses containing large families, such displacement clearly 'added to the hopelessness and despair brought about by the pogrom'.[16]

Owners of such properties grew increasingly sceptical with both the agents of law and order and also the actual legal process. Thus, they complained about police failing to intervene as drunken mobs wrecked their properties and were also irate about the slowness of the legal system, the apparent dearth of sympathy from senior legal personnel and the lack of generosity they believed to be evident in the authorities' reimbursement of their losses. The bewilderment of Resident Magistrate Mr J. Gray over the ease with which looting of such premises occurred is revealing. Speaking in the city's Custody Court, Mr Gray enquired of the Crown Solicitor if the publicans concerned 'could not make some effort to protect their places' as he believed they 'all seemed to go away and leave the premises to the mercy of the mobs.'[17] With such a high number of claims for damages to property and business premises, it's perhaps not surprising that many claims involving publicans and the owners of spirit groceries damaged during the summer disturbances were not heard until early the following summer. Also, when individual claims were considered, claimants rarely anticipated receiving more than a third of their submitted claims. This is reflected in several cases detailed in the local press which also provide further insight in to the distress caused to the owners of spirit groceries and to their families. Experienced owners such as James Largey, who had run a spirit grocery in the Woodstock area for 17 years, received £950 for damages inflicted on his premises on 21 and 22 July, although his original claim was £2,715. Another long-serving spirit grocer, Francis Hoey, of Bentick Street, despite sustaining threats and recovering from earlier damage to his property, had it completely destroyed in August 1920 and received a mere £910 damages (he had asked for £3,000).[18]

Despite these horrific setbacks, many spirit grocers survived on account of their resilience and the availability of compensation (limited as it might have been). Nora McMullan's father was such a case. She recalls how, after being intimidated from their Beersbridge premises, the family eventually moved back to the city, but this time to the safer environs of Cavendish Street in the Falls area, where her father ran two spirit groceries, largely funded, she believes, from the compensation award he received for his property in the east of the city.

REDMOND'S 'PEACE PICKETS'

It was fortunate that there were calming influences in east Belfast, especially during the summer of 1920. One such voice of common sense and decency was John Redmond, rector of St Patrick's Church of Ireland parish in Ballymacarrett. The Revd Redmond, recently installed in his post, was already respected in the area, managing to combine sympathy for the economic and political predicament of his co-religionists with a broader concern for strong law and order in the city as a whole. Redmond's views of the origins of violence certainly coincided with those of mainstream unionism. He wrote about the significance of news of events elsewhere in Ireland:

> All this information and much more of its kind created intense indignation in Belfast. This was intensified by the fact that when thousands of men left well-paid jobs in the Belfast shipyards and other larger industries to join the Ulster Division, Sinn Féiners took the vacant jobs and were in possession of them when the Belfast men who survived the hardships and wounds of war came home and had to go on the dole … It was believed that, generally speaking, Roman Catholics here were approving the outrages being committed in the rebellion in the South and West.[19]

Redmond's fundamental concern was how to defuse the tension caused by the congregation of large crowds which spilled on to the Newtownards and Albertbridge Roads, almost daily that summer. He estimated that these approached 10,000, constituting about 20% of the area's population at that time and he was concerned their presence, largely due to curiosity, would 'hinder the work of the troops.'[20] Like other community leaders, Redmond was alarmed by the wanton looting and destruction.[21] He believed that the presence of locally respected men would deter what he considered to be a minority 'rabble' element from fermenting havoc on the streets of Ballymacarrett. Therefore, within a day of the initial disturbances, he had hastily assembled ex-servicemen at Albertbridge Orange Hall in an urgent attempt to deter rioting. Redmond argued that police forces were stretched on account of so many locally-based RIC members being called away to quell trouble elsewhere in Ireland and he was also aware that many local men, now back in civvies, had the benefit of recent military experience which could be harnessed by the civilian authorities. The ad hoc nature of Redmond's scheme was illustrated by his orders to the vigilantes or 'volunteers'. He later recalled:

> I asked them to march up and down the Newtownards Road and if they found a building threatened, to form up between it and the crowd. This they did for the rest of the evening till the crowds dispersed and no further breach of the law took place.[22]

Undoubtedly Redmond made a significant contribution to defusing the passions of local Protestants. Apart from instigating his vigilante groups, he took his message of self-control directly to workers during their lunch-break when tension increased again towards the end of August, appealing to his co-religionists not 'to play in to the hands of their enemies' and persuaded them to pass a resolution favouring the enrolment of yard workers as Special Constables.[23] Redmond's ability to calm nerves during uneasy situations was also apparent in his dealings with nationalists. A press report noted how a republican mob in Short Strand had started throwing stones at returning workers, but 'a serious situation was avoided through the timely intervention of the Vicar of Ballymacarrett who boldly walked out and appealed to the Sinn Féin crowd to desist.'[24] The effectiveness of the vigilante patrols was lauded in the unionist press, with the *Northern Whig* claiming that 'the greater peace [which] prevailed over the last two nights had been largely due to Redmond's volunteer patrols who have been able to do by persuasion what could not be done by other means.'[25] The *Whig* declared that Belfast owed 'a distinct debt to these public-spirited citizens whose numbers, we trust, will be reinforced by others'.[26]

Redmond's involvement with his vigilante forces during the summer of 1920 was to have long-term ramifications. It was the successful operation of his 'peace pickets' which persuaded those in authority to establish a new force to assist the police and army.[27] When the Specials were formally established in November 1920, Redmond was to claim with pride that the volunteers he had organised to contain rioters and looters on the Newtownards Road during that summer, were to become the nucleus of the Special Constabulary in Ballymacarrett.[28]

VIOLENCE RETURNS

Although tension in the east, like elsewhere in the city, was to subside for a few weeks and the security forces appeared to have control of the main artery in east Belfast, the Newtownards Road and the streets around St Matthew's Church, this did not ease the plight of those Catholics unable to return to the workplace. Some hope was provided by an on-the-surface conciliatory statement emanating from representations of Harland and Wolff workers in the Dee Street Hall at the start of August. In this, loyalist workers said they were ready 'to offer the hand of friendship to some of their Roman Catholic fellow workmen.'[29] This included Catholic ex-servicemen to whom they were 'ready

to show ... the same spirit as they had displayed towards them on the fields of
France and Flanders.'[30] In a bid to illustrate their genuine intention to distinguish between 'decent' Catholic workers and 'rebels', the representatives
discussed issuing 'loyalty' cards to such workers where they could sign their
loyalty to the King which would precipitate their return to work. Although
considered to be a magnanimous gesture and one which offered a modicum of
hope for the future, the 'loyalty' cards appeared to underwrite nationalist fears
that appropriate political allegiance was a prerequisite for the right to a job. At
the same time, intimidation of workers persisted and violence returned to the
city following the assassination of Detective Inspector Swanzy on 22 August.[31]

From lunchtime onwards on 25 August, there were 'widespread disturbances'
in the east of the city, on what was described as 'the wildest day' of violence in that
area.[32] Riots were reported in various parts of the Newtownards Road and
Mountpottinger, as well as Short Strand. Two young Protestants, James
McCartney, of Frome Street and Ethel Burrows, of Bright Street, were killed by
the army in the vicinity of Dee Street and several others were injured.[33] Twenty-
five fires were reported in the district and the Fire Brigade were stretched to cope
with the worsening situation. Catholic-owned spirit groceries and some families
again proved to be easy targets for loyalist gangs. The *Belfast Telegraph* reported
that in Dee Street 'a spirit grocery was fired, while in Pitt Street a huge pile of
furniture taken from one of the residences was set on fire and burned fiercely for
several hours.'[34] A further 'dastardly' attack was mounted on St Matthew's
Church by a large loyalist mob, though quick military intervention prevented
serious damage to the church.[35] The apparently premeditated nature of the
attack, an indication that the mobsters were being organised by ultra-right forces,
was propagated by the *Irish News* which reported that those besieging Seaforde
Street in the Short Strand 'seemed to have petrol in plenty and all the materials
necessary for carrying out systematic incendiarism, and they were also evidently
well-armed with revolvers.'[36] The *Northern Whig* chose to concentrate on smaller
scale nationalist misdemeanours and under-reported the serious disturbances
which had probably been started by loyalists. Their coverage of events focussed
on an afternoon attack on a Protestant school in Comber Street, during which
'stones were thrown and windows [were] broken', prompting the arrival of 'many
anxious parents' who escorted their children home.[37] There were also reports of
attacks on shipyard workers proceeding home around the Youngs Row area and
several trams containing workers were also subjected to attack.[38] Earlier in the
day, Catholic dock workers who had been intimidated from their shipyard jobs,

were set upon by their former colleagues, whilst they were unloading coal and several were severely beaten or thrown into the lough.

This pattern of events was continued the following day when Ballymacarrett again proved to be the focal point of the 'Unionist Mobs' Day of Destruction'.[39] Over 30 fires were reported and the violence erupted again in the early afternoon, continuing until late in the evening. The congregation of large crowds at a time when there would normally be less people out on the streets was mainly due, of course, to the expulsion of hundreds of industrial workers, many of whom now assumed a 'defensive' role in their neighbourhoods. There were petrol bomb attacks and shooting in the Seaforde Street area and machine-gun fire was heard on the Newtownards Road. Adverse weather conditions – in the form of heavy fog – thankfully curtailed violent activity on 27 August, though there were some minor disturbances in Ballymacarrett during the afternoon, including the burning of a maternity nursing home on the Newtownards Road.[40]

East Belfast was fortunate not to suffer the heavy violence experienced in other areas at the end of August and beginning of September. Although there were sporadic disturbances in and around Short Strand, only three more lives were lost. Riots broke out on 28 August between returning industrial workers and residents of Short Strand, resulting in the military firing into Seaforde Street. Several people were injured, including Francis McCann (55), of Chemical Street, who died after sustaining a serious leg injury. Three days later, there was another morning attack on Catholic dockers, believed to have been instigated by angry shipyard workers. On this occasion, firearms were used and one of the dockers, James Cromie (25), of Trafalgar Street, who had served in the Royal Navy during the war, was fatally wounded.[41] The only other fatality in the east of the city during this period occurred on 11 September following a breach of the curfew regulations. Catholic widower John Toner (50), a carter, was shot by a military patrol during curfew on the Newtownards Road, close to his Cable Street home. The army claimed they opened fire when Mr Toner failed to stop when requested and he died in hospital the following day. Although Ballymacarrett was not to witness serious street disturbances or widespread gunfire for another nine months, this first summer of the Twenties' conflict set the pattern for its remainder. In the case of east Belfast, its proximity to Belfast's industrial heart ensured it would be the fulcrum of some of its worst street violence and intimidation, especially that involving beleaguered Catholic residents of the Short Strand, Catholic small business owners increasingly isolated in predominantly loyalist districts and Protestant workers making hazardous journeys to and from their workplace.

Chapter 3

'The verge of bankruptcy'

THE FALLS ERUPTS

Although the initial violence occurred in the back-streets of the lower Newtownards Road where the small Catholic population was especially vulnerable to sudden onslaught, disturbances soon spread to more traditional areas of conflict, in the west of the city, and also in north Belfast. The intense, yet intermittent, nature of the disturbances, the more sophisticated range of weaponry available to civilian gunmen and the raw hatred of the opposing mobs were common characteristics of the violence. The scale of trouble across Belfast during the first three days of the conflict was unparalleled. The number of fatalities during this short period (approaching 20), the large number of people requiring hospital treatment (nearly 100) and the intimidation from both home and employment of thousands – what the *Irish News* described as 'a bloody carnival of bigotry' – exceeded the damage experienced in 1886, which had constituted the worst of the city's riots during the nineteenth century.[1]

In the early evening of 21 July, angry crowds of Shankill shipyard workers and their sympathisers, who had been stoned and assaulted on their way home from work, congregated on the streets bordering the Falls. Catholics also assembled at the edge of no-man's land between the city's two main western, arterial roads and military fire was employed as the tension boiled over. Two Catholics were killed and seven received hospital treatment for their injuries. Francis Finnegan (40), of Lower Clonard Street, was fatally wounded by a ricochet bullet fired by the army in Milliken Street and an ex-soldier, Bernard Devlin (20), of Alexandra Road West, was shot dead by the military near the Falls Road Baths as he returned from a dog-racing meeting at Celtic Park.

An air of tension prevailed throughout the city the following morning. Stone-throwing incidents were reported at the Sirocco works where there were cases of Catholics being evicted and spirit groceries were looted in Ballymacarrett. It was in west Belfast, however, that the worst of the violence was to occur. In the early morning there had been clashes on the Springfield

Road as tram-loads of Protestant workers arrived at Mackies Foundry. The police soon arrived to protect the workers from angry crowds and before long, baton-charged the Catholic protestors. A local priest, Reverend Pat Convery, sensing that police over-reaction might spark a major riot, stood in the middle of Malcolmson Street facing the policemen and demanded they should be recalled to their barracks. The order to do so arrived and an uneasy peace endured for a few hours. However, as darkness started to descend on the dangerous warren of streets between the Shankill and Falls (especially Bombay Street and Kashmir Road), reports began to circulate of Catholics being forced to leave their homes, as well as the outbreak of intermittent shooting. There was considerable dispute over the origins of this gunfire. The military authorities claimed they had simply been responding to sniping which had been directed at them from the Clonard area. Although Catholic clergy later rejected the Norfolk Regiment's accusation that the firing had come from the belfry of Clonard Monastery, it's likely that republican personnel were active in the area. Whilst IRA involvement in the early part of the conflict was comparatively low key, volunteers had been drafted into the city from other parts of Ulster, as well as from the south, and a variety of weapons, including Lugers, Lee Enfield rifles and Webley revolvers were readily available.[2] Thus, it has been suggested that police in the city were 'neither mistaken nor were they spreading alarmist rumours when they claimed there were members of the IRA in the district.'[3]

Many of the victims that evening appear to have been undeterred by the events of the previous day and they were to pay the ultimate price for their determination to proceed with their everyday business. Mackies' worker Henry Hennessy (48) was fatally wounded returning to his house in Ardilea Street, probably by a loyalist gunman and John Downey (20), from Roden Street, was killed by military fire as he visited his sister in Kashmir Road.[4] An ex-soldier, Joseph Giles, was killed in Bombay Street and machine-gun fire struck down another Catholic, Thomas Robinson (33) at the corner of Kashmir Road.[5] John McCartney (36), a Catholic from Lucknow Street, was a victim of the military shooting in Kashmir Road and succumbed to his wounds in hospital two days later. In the course of the evening the army, believing they were under attack from snipers directed fire into the grounds of the Redemptorist Monastery in Clonard. Brother Michael Morgan (28), a native of County Cavan and a member of the monastery for less than a year, had been cleaning a corridor on the third floor when he stopped to look out of a window. Father J. Kelly, Rector of the monastery, observed in a letter:

> Brother Michael happened to look out of the window of the top corridor near the edge of the stairs. He saw the soldiers deliberately aiming at him. 'My God, they are going to fire!' Scarcely were the words out of his mouth when a bullet from a Lewis gun stretched him dead … It is sad to think that an innocent, unoffending creature should be made the victim of Orange bigotry and cowardice.[6]

The fatally-wounded Redemptorist, struck twice in his throat, was eventually administered the last rites by Father Kelly, who had at first been unable to reach his injured colleague due to the relentless military barrage. The Rector responded angrily to a Press Association claim the next day that the military had merely been responding to sniping from within the monastery's grounds. Father Kelly maintained:

> No sniper could be in the tower or any other part of the building without my knowledge and I am prepared to testify on oath that not a shot was fired from the monastery either before or after we were attacked.[7]

This outright denial of clerical collusion with IRA volunteers was clearly a factor in producing the rare admission of Crown responsibility from the City Coroner at Brother Morgan's inquest a few weeks later. At this, it was determined that the monk's death had been 'entirely unnecessary for the purpose of suppressing the riot' and also that such a deed had been 'unprovoked by any person in the Monastery.'[8] The funerals of six of the Catholic victims of the west Belfast disturbances took place on Saturday 24 July, prompting a 'remarkable' response from the people of the Falls Road. After three days of the most bloody violence in living memory, they closed ranks to remember their dead. The *Irish News* vividly described the journey of the merged funeral cortege as it wound its sorry way to Milltown Cemetery:

> Along the whole length of the Falls Road onlookers were massed on each sidewalk, bare-headed and hushed as the remains were borne past, each of the coffins being almost hidden underneath the wealth of floral tributes from relatives, neighbours and friends. A reverential silence hung over the scene, coming as a vivid contrast to the people of the district, whose ears have been attuned during the previous few nights to the harsh

uproar of invading mobs and the terrifying punctuation of modern firearms.[9]

There were also Protestant casualties, especially in the Cupar Street area. At inquests into four deaths in this district, the army vehemently denied firing into these streets, suggesting the fatal bullets had been fired from the Clonard area. The victims were Alexander McGovan (25), of Tralee Street, William Godfrey (46), of Argyle Street, ex-soldier William Dunning (23), of Bellevue Street and James Conn (32), of James Street.[10]

With the notable exception of east Belfast, the level of violence dropped the following day. Although the weekend proved to be relatively quiet, there was an underlying edginess which was reflected in the outbreak of minor street disturbances and intermittent sniping on the Falls Road and in the north of the city. A loyalist crowd, encroaching on the nationalist Peters Hill, was baton-charged by police in Hastings Street. A more obvious military presence, including the employment of sandbags and barbed wire fortifications, was soon established, reassuring many people. Whilst the city remained quieter for the next few weeks, the first alleged case of a civilian being shot due to his failure to heed military instructions, occurred during the early morning of Sunday 25 July. Taxi driver David Dunbar, of Silvio Street in the Shankill area, failed to stop at a military post as he returned to his base in Carlow Street. Soldiers on duty at the post maintained that Mr Dunbar had jumped from his vehicle as it headed towards them, but his brother pointed out that the victim would not have been capable of such agility due to the effects of a war wound.

SHIFTING THE BLAME

Initial reactions to the disturbances predictably differed, both in their assessment of the causes of the violence and also over the allocation of culpability for the bloodshed. Official accounts of what had occurred were somewhat vague, with the establishment line being that there was little else they could have done under the circumstances. Remarkably, the Irish Chief Secretary focused on the damage committed by Sinn Féin elsewhere over the previous three years. Pressurised by Joe Devlin to address the more immediate issue of 'the organised attack on Catholic workers employed at Queens Island', he inferred few precautions had been taken in the light of Carson's Orange Day speech.[11] In a heated exchange, Sir Hamar Greenwood strongly refuted Devlin's criticism of the slow reactions of Belfast's military garrison:

> The general officer commanding the troops in Belfast has not got his headquarters on Queens Island. I repeat that everything has been done before the 12th July, on the 12th July, since the 12th July and now to preserve order in one of the most difficult areas in His Majesty's Dominions.[12]

The veteran nationalist parliamentarian, T.P. O'Connor, joined Devlin in castigating Carson whom he contended had been the cause of 'the bloodshed in Belfast' and whose speeches had 'sent many young men to death and mutilation.'[13] Carson stoutly defended his actions later in the debate:

> I will tell you what I said on the 12th July. I said we would not allow ourselves in Ulster to be trampled on by Sinn Féin. And we will not. I said further, that it was the duty of government to preserve Ulster from Sinn Féin ... I said that, if they didn't do it, we would be willing to help them ... If a man comes to strike you in the street, is it a crime to prevent him and knock him down?[14]

Greenwood's announcement of the creation of the post of a senior civil servant to assume specific responsibility for the northern area, illustrated growing British concern that as Ulster posed 'different' problems to the rest of Ireland, it would have to be administered accordingly.[15] Loyalist response to this news was lukewarm to say the least. The *Belfast Newsletter* insisted that the new appointment should have the 'full confidence' of unionists and that he 'must be none of the political charlatans who are advertising their nostrums of Devolution, Dominion Home Rule, or other Utopian scheme of 'Reconstruction'.[16] Just over a week later when Devlin again raised the plight of the expelled Catholic workmen, Greenwood's response appeared non-committal. He reminded the House that he had 'no power' to 'compel one trade unionist to work alongside another, against whom he has an antipathy.'[17]

There was considerable press criticism of the response from those in government to the events in Belfast and also of the unionist leadership for allegedly fermenting the discord. Some of these came from surprising sources. The *Times* criticised both the government and Carson's party, suggesting that the former were 'guilty of delay' and the latter were clearly culpable of 'obstructionism'.[18] Pro-unity journals castigated the government for being 'less interested in the suppression of crime than in the suppression of the efforts of the Irish to substitute a Government they do not like for one they do' and warned that Government of the dangers of 'staggering blindly towards an Amritsar'.[19] Nationalist condemnation of such indecision or obstructionism was not so surprising. However, despite its tone of profound disillusionment and grave concern, nationalist-owned papers had yet to develop the outright cynicism towards all governmental assurances on law and order issues, which was soon to become characteristic of their position. A leading article in the *Irish News* two days after the shipyard evictions suggested a 'charitable' view of the situation would be that 'grave and fatal' mistakes had been made by the authorities.[20] The paper's editorial asked:

> Has enough been done in the way of bloodshed to satiate for a time the Moloch of Bigotry and Hatred whose infernal appetite was deliberately reawakened by the conveners of the meeting held at the Queens Island on Wednesday?[21]

Nationalist politicians led the demands for increased protection of Catholic workers and residents and also called for 'justice' in speeding the arrest and prosecution of those responsible for the bloodshed and damage to property. Joe Devlin demanded:

> Are these men to be brought back to their employment and be protected there by the authorities and are those who seized them and endeavoured to throw them back into the sea to be brought to justice?[22]

Clerical leaders focussed more on exonerating their flock from blame, attempting to gain the moral high ground from the very start of the conflict. Beseeching his congregation to refrain from adopting a physical response, Dr MacCrory, the Bishop of Down and Connor, speaking at St Peter's Church on Sunday 25th July, argued:

> We have not been the aggressors, we have not begun this horrible business, we have been driven from our employment, robbed of our bread and [the victims] of religious intolerance and organised bigotry.[23]

Both the Catholic clergy and political representatives were convinced that the combination of a lethargic government response over facilitating the return of the expelled workers and their lack of entitlement to state financial support, posed a severe threat to the whole of the Catholic working class community. Indeed, it was speculated that unless prompt action was taken, a substantial section of the Catholic population would come 'face to face with starvation within a week in the great and prosperous city they have helped to create.'[24] Much of the talk in Catholic circles that summer reverberated around stories of removal vans and carts conveying the furniture and personal belongings of those intimidated from their homes and seeking solace in safer, if overcrowded Catholic areas.[25]

Loyalists interpreted events rather differently, preferring to contextualise the violence within the scenario of conspiracy and external threat. This had been at the centre of Carson's Finaghy speech on Sinn Féin malevolence and errors in governmental policy. They also targeted Joe Devlin for failing to denounce violence elsewhere in Ireland and for refraining from encouraging his followers to pledge their full support to the RIC. The *Northern Whig's* character assassination of the MP for west Belfast concluded:

> He [Devlin] can do nothing but indulge in wild diatribes, which we have heard over and over again about the wickedness of Protestant Belfast. The most sensible thing that men and women can do who are really anxious for peace is to ignore him, and to pursue the most profitable path of ceasing recrimination in the meantime and taking action to nip in the bud any recurrence of such scenes in the future. There is work here enough for any body.[26]

As noted earlier, the *Whig* had played down both the scale and significance of the events in the east of the city and instead warned the government that 'unless they reverse their policy and take effective measures for the suppression of lawlessness they may prepare for even more serious outbreaks of popular feeling.'[27] A more pragmatic unionist approach to the danger posed by prolonged sectarian disturbances was adopted by leading civic figures who had the task of dealing with such disorder. Lord Mayor William F. Coates assured his citizens that the authorities were quite 'determined to take the most dramatic measures to deal with disorder of any kind.'[28] He also implored people to be responsible and assist the authorities by 'using influence to prevent groups of people assembling in the streets, by counselling irresponsible youths to refrain from doing damage in any way and by advising the inhabitants in their own interests as far as possible to remain indoors during the evening.'[29]

Although Protestants did not experience ejection from work or home on anywhere near the scale which many Catholics had to face, some Protestants who worked in a mainly Catholic environment, such as in the docks, brewing industry and licensing trade, were edged out of their jobs. Many more found that, whilst they had a job to go to, their work place was not as safe as it had been and many were shot, beaten or intimidated on their way to and from work. Expelled Catholic workers put considerable pressure on factory owners to temporarily close their works. Fred Crawford noted how his firm was the only one in the district to remain open and said of the Catholic residents:

> They have raided several [factories] in the vicinity. They threaten to burn down our works because just now we happen to have no RC employees. They want to stop our men and women earning their wages when the RCs can't get into the mills and other places owing to their being closed.[30]

The swelling tide of British press disquiet over loyalist responsibility for street disturbances in Belfast surfaced again during the second outbreak of violence at the end of August. Writing in the *Daily News*, Hugh Martin outlined the scale of economic damage, stressing how 'practically the whole of this damage' had been inflicted on the property of Catholics, a campaign which had brought Belfast to 'the verge of bankruptcy'.[31] The *Daily Herald* was virulently anti-unionist in its condemnation of events. Its leader condemned 'the bloody harvest of Carsonism ... being reaped in Belfast', suggesting that 'the gangs who have organised the reign of terror are the very people who protest they are afraid that *they* would, under even partial Home Rule, be persecuted and denied religious liberty'.[32] The liberal *Nation* which had been, a decade before, a staunch advocate of Home Rule, called for the 'end of our Government of Ireland', suggesting that, 'after the pogrom of Belfast, we can only hope the end will be soon for we would rather see the Union Jack in different company from its promoters.'[33] Suggesting the strategy of the 'Orange army in Ulster' had been the 'clearance' of its area, the *Nation* also criticised 'the benevolent inaction of the British Government, and its refusal to sanction out of work pay to exiled and starving Catholics'.[34] Even traditional sources of sympathy were critical of what they perceived to be premeditated and one-sided attacks. The *Daily Mail* suggested the city was 'in its current plight' on account of the 'organised attempt' that was being made 'to deprive Catholic men of their work and to drive Catholic families from their homes.'[35] The *Times* too, had severe reservations, not only about the origins of such violence but also on the suggestion that the UVF should be recruited as an auxiliary force in order to quell such disturbances. The *Times* argued:

> The last remnants of moderate and constitutional opinion in Ireland would be destroyed and ... there would be only 2 parties left in Ireland, Orangemen and Sinn Féiners. Open civil war could scarcely be avoided.[36]

On the other hand, certain English papers maintained their support for Ulster's loyalists. The *Daily Express* focussed on the plight of Belfast's industrial workforce getting to work rather than that of besieged Catholics. The paper's Belfast correspondent noted that 'this morning workmen on their way to the shipyards had to face a terrible onslaught from isolated groups of Sinn Féin foes.'[37] The *Daily Chronicle* welcomed the increased security presence especially in Belfast's centre and advised its readers that 'the military are gripping the situation with a firm hand.'[38] A fortnight later the same paper condemned Sinn Féin's action of 'taking its campaign of murder and crime' to the north, arguing that such behaviour fully illustrated 'the disadvantages of keeping it up under the same system of administration as the rest of Ireland.'[39]

FLEEING THE TROUBLES

Street disturbances and industrial evictions were followed by many cases of Catholic residents being intimidated from their homes. Although this harassment peaked during the summer of 1920 and in May–June 1922, it proved to be a periodic occurrence over the two year conflict. Intimidation was more likely to happen in areas where a minority of one religion lived alongside a majority from another faith, or in streets on the fringes of an exclusively Protestant district. Intimidation could take a number of forms. These could have been verbal threats, accompanied by demands for instant removal, or perhaps warnings giving imminent deadlines for 'voluntary' removal, frequently accompanied by minor violence, such as window-breaking or physical abuse. On occasion it was more sophisticated and organised. Typed notices of warning were dropped through letter-boxes. One to an ex-soldier gave him a 'notice to quit' with the warning, 'Take notice to be out of this house before 7 o'clock on Wednesday 28th – a well wisher', which the *Irish News* claimed was 'a typical example of the "Notices to Quit" which are still flying broadcast about districts of the city where isolated Catholics had still the temerity to remain in their houses.'[40]

Once they accepted the inevitability of leaving their homes, the victims had to encounter the problem of removing their furniture and other possessions, often at short notice. The problems which many Catholics experienced, especially in July and August 1920, were compounded by the difficulties they had in persuading furniture removers to take their possessions to temporary accommodation, 'as instances had already occurred of attacks being made on furniture vans'.[41] The *Irish News* claimed that the result of such reluctance on the part of removal men was that 'many Catholic families have had to leave their furniture behind in distinctly hostile localities'.[42] Once they had made their hasty escape, neighbours often dragged furniture onto the street where it was either stolen or burned. However, a number of families were fortunate to return to their homes inside a week or two, when the situation had calmed down. Thus, inside a week of the first large-scale evictions, nationalist commentators were able to express their satisfaction on learning that 'the process of restoration is proceeding and that many families have already taken possession of their homes, sometimes with the assistance of the authorities'.[43] Those in authority also assisted in protecting those Catholics who briefly returned to recover their stolen goods which had subsequently been abandoned. Rare instances of a more proactive approach by the authorities did occur, particularly in cases where properties had been repossessed illegally. A Protestant, whose father had been the agent for a house in Clonallen Street off the Newtownards Road, was prosecuted in August for moving his furniture into a property which had been occupied by a Catholic family for nine years, following the 'flitting' of that family, who had been threatened by neighbours, to the Short Strand.[44]

The scale of such movement was considerable, especially during periods of severe disturbances. According to one report, extensive areas of the city were affected, and the victims had to be resourceful in dealing with their dire predicament:

> From all parts of the city where the pogrom has been holding sway furniture vans, donkey carts, hand-carts, and every make and shape of

'vehicle' were seen from day-break until a late hour last night going in all directions, laden with whatever of their household effects the people could rescue from the wreck of their homes.[45]

The initial wave of coercive attacks stretched to the limit the capacity of self-help mechanisms within the Catholic community. In Ballymacarrett where intimidation was rife, the pattern appeared to be for harassed Catholic families to vacate their homes on the Newtownards Road and stay, for a short period at least, with co-religionists in the Short Strand. Of course, this meant families had to be accommodated in small houses which were already overcrowded and, not surprisingly, such 'flittings' led to considerable congestion.[46] On occasion commonsense and mutual gain conquered over raw sectarianism. There were instances of Catholics exchanging houses with 'friendly' Protestants, who might themselves have been increasingly uncomfortable over being located in the 'wrong' area. John Boyd recalled his grandparents swapping their Beechfield Street home for a house previously occupied by a Catholic family in Portallo Street in the Castlereagh area. Boyd wrote:

> I was told that the Boyds had heard of a Catholic family who were scared of being chased out of their house which was in a Protestant area, and they wanted to get out before this happened. When grandpa and grandma heard of this they met the Catholics and agreed to switch houses because Beechfield Street was adjoining the small Catholic area of Ballymacarrett. This would be doing the Catholic family a good turn and doing themselves a good turn too.[47]

The Swanzy killing in late August 1920 again exposed the vulnerability of Catholics especially in places like east Belfast. Towards the end of the month it was claimed that 'hundreds of refugees from Ballymacarrett' were attempting to seek refuge elsewhere in the city.[48] An estimated 150 homeless families, especially on the Newtownards and Woodstock Roads, were in 'urgent need of shelter.'[49] Harrowing stories were told in the nationalist press of the unparalleled suffering of Catholic families compounded by the exodus of their co-religionists from towns close to Belfast during the late summer. Thus, the *Irish News* reported how Lisburn women and children 'tramp over mountains' to seek assistance in Belfast's St Mary's Hall and noted the irony of how some of these 'refugees' received temporary accommodation from the victims of the July disturbances.[50]

Reports giving dramatic accounts of the suffering of individual families, doubly hit by the loss of the chief breadwinner's job and being evicted from their home, filled the pages of the *Irish News*.[51] One especially sad cause involved a Catholic widow and mother of five children evicted from her Ballymacarrett home, who had just spent three nights in temporary accommodation and who was in dire financial straits on account of two of her three children of working age being expelled from their employment (the third was in the services).[52]

The 'flittings', or 'clearances', occurred intermittently over the next two years, especially in and around small Catholic enclaves such as Short Strand and Marrowbone. It is difficult to present precise and accurate figures of Belfast's 'refugee' population during this period, particularly on account of the temporary nature of some of this movement. However, it's likely that over 20,000 Catholics were displaced on at least one occasion during the conflict, with virtually whole streets of Catholic housing being destroyed by arson attacks.[53] Although many of them continued to live in the city, with several returning following brief sojourns especially in Dublin and Glasgow, others did not come back to the city of their birth, even after hostilities had ceased.[54] Many others who stayed in the city had to endure cramped, overcrowded conditions in temporary accommodation, provided by family or by the Catholic Church, for prolonged periods. Eviction of Catholics from their homes re-surfaced on a significant scale on the eve of the royal visit during the early summer of 1921. Many of those made homeless were absorbed into existing accommodation, Catholic clubs and a former pub which housed up to 50 people. Several small 'kitchen-houses' were reported to be catering for the needs of 20 people and 'with no beds, no furniture, no lighting and conditions of the utmost wretchedness, the plight of the occupants is appalling'.[55]

The Church came to the aid of many distressed Catholics in the city. For instance, following the initial outburst of violence in 1920, over 40 families were accommodated in St Matthew's School in Seaforde Street, with their furniture being stored nearby. The inequity of people having to surrender their homes and move elsewhere was highlighted by Bishop MacRory and the nationalist press. In a telegram on 27 July, the former reminded Belfast's Lord Mayor that it was his 'duty to see that no honest man, prepared to pay his rent, should be denied freedom as to where he may choose to live'.[56] The *Irish News* compared the 'sad sights' which were unfolding in Ballymacarrett with the plight of the Boers and Belgians in previous conflicts and reminded the authorities that those who had been forced out of their homes were 'tenants enjoying, under the law and in their relationships with property owners, all the rights and privileges conferred on the urban community by the various Rent Restrictions Acts'.[57] MacRory was, of course, active in promoting the cause of his flock in a number of ways, including helping to establish the Boycott Committee, encouragement of the conciliation committees established under the terms of the second Craig-Collins Pact in March 1922 and his role in helping to establish the Belfast Catholic Protection Committee. This latter committee concentrated on coun-teracting the pro-unionist propaganda which he and many others felt had reflected badly on the Catholic case. Much of this claimed the moral high ground, as well as berating those senior officials for their apparent inactivity. Thus, one statement issued by the committee blasted A.W. Hungerford, the UUC Secretary, for daring to claim that Protestants had also suffered in the conflict. With more than a hint of self-righteousness, the committee claimed:

> Not a single Protestant family has been rendered homeless in Belfast by Catholics. A very few have been put to temporary inconvenience by having to exchange homes with Catholics.[58]

The group also put direct pressure on the Westminster authorities, often point-edly ignoring Craig and appealing directly to Lloyd George and Churchill. A telegram sent by MacRory and the Catholic Protection Committee in April 1922 epitomised the desperation of Catholics in the city at this time:

> Belfast Catholics gradually but certainly exterminated by murder, assault and starvation, their houses burned, streets swept by snipers, life unbear-able, military forces inactive, special police hostile; Northern Government either culpable or inefficient. Your Government saved the Armenians and Bulgarians. Belfast Catholics getting worse treatment; last two days here appalling.[59]

Whilst the Catholic Church continually endeavoured to provide temporary relief and succour to its displaced members, it was clearly reliant, in the absence of state support, on external charity support for the homeless.[60] This came from American relief organisations, such as the US Committee for Relief in Ireland and the American White Cross fund which jointly provided nearly £2 million of relief payments to, in the main, Belfast Catholics. Therefore, by the middle of 1922, between £5000 and £7000 relief payments were allocated to Belfast

Catholics every week, with large grants being used to provide new housing accommodation for those burned out of their homes.[61]

Although the support mechanisms and relief payments provided by Church and charity groups proved to be invaluable for many Catholics, many others felt obliged to flee the city and seek support from friendly co-religionists elsewhere. Whilst this was often generous as well as timely in its nature, interest in the predicament of northern Catholics was variable. There had been an exodus of Catholics to the south of Ireland and the Clydeside area in Scotland from the earliest stages of the conflict, but this peaked in the early summer of 1922. Severe overcrowding was reported in traditional areas of refuge for harassed Catholics such as the Falls, with cases of eviction being reported from traditionally quiet areas such as the Ormeau Road and Ardenlee Avenue. The *Irish Independent* reported that 'wholesale evictions continue and whole districts are being cleared of Catholics'.[62] Many sought relief further afield. Over a thousand were believed to be receiving support in the Glasgow area, about half of whom were being sheltered and fed in church-halls. Dublin was another popular destination for Belfast's most desperate citizens. By the middle of June, 228 were being accommodated in a Dublin workhouse.[63] Another temporary base for Belfast refugees was the headquarters of the Orange Order in the city's Kildare Street, which had been requisitioned for this purpose by the southern administration. Fugitives from the north were usually met by Sinn Féin or Boycott Committee representatives at Amiens Street station and taken to destinations such as Marlborough Hall where they would be housed. They were the subject of much attention in the southern press at this time. At the beginning of June the *Irish Independent* wrote about the 'urgent plight' of these migrants and showed a picture of 'a little refugee ... proud of having brought her doll safely through the terror'.[64] Other photographs portrayed refugees picking flowers in the grounds of Marlborough Hall and being serenaded by an IRA man playing the accordion, under the caption, 'enjoying their freedom from persecution.'[65] Though there was considerable moral support for the plight of northern Catholics – a speaker at a support meeting in Dundalk said their sorry position 'would bring tears from a stone' – this did not always extend to practical support, such as attendance or expressions of unreserved support at public meetings.[66] This was particularly true in the Cork area, with accounts of 'unwanted' refugees being snubbed in the city and even the Mayor of Cork's appeal for financial support distinguished between refugee families and fleeing single men, even if they happened to be in the IRA. Speaking to a 'meagre' crowd, he said;

Belfast families must be looked after, but any young man coming to Cork must be asked why he was not in the army in the North and no one should be taken over as a refugee unless he had his discharge from the army, showing that his services were not needed.[67]

As Catholic eviction from Belfast homes peaked in May and June 1922, Sinn Féin's propaganda department listed examples and the extent of arson attacks on homes as well as evictions of families. In May about 150 Catholic families were forced to leave their homes in the north of the city (these evictions were mainly from Milewater, Jennymount, Weaver and North Derby Streets). By the end of the month about a half of this number of families were reputedly forced out of their homes, mainly in the west of the city, during one day (31 May).[68] Many of these 'refugees' stayed with relatives but an estimated 6,000 were still sheltering in temporary accommodation in Catholic schools and parochial halls by July 1922. Sinn Féin provided a factual summary of the heartache suffered by one Catholic parish in the city during the conflagration. Sacred Heart Church on the Oldpark Road, which served the Marrowbone community, had lost 17 members of the parish to communal violence, 244 families were expelled, 29 houses completely destroyed (mainly in Antigua and Sanderson Streets) and 57 houses damaged.[69] In the midst of the persecution and hopelessness some Catholics used their ingenuity and resourcefulness to circumvent their predicament. A government memorandum highlights the case of an estate agent's property in May Street which was occupied one evening by a Catholic family, who were allowed by the police to remain in the property for nearly two years, when it was bought by the Ministry of Finance.[70]

One can barely surmise what were the thoughts and feelings of those who were intimidated from their homes, in several cases shortly after the chief wage-earner had been forced out of the workplace. Clearly sheer desperation, raw fear of physical attack, as well as trepidation over an uncertain future, would have been their chief responses to what was happening around them. Other thoughts and issues might well have crossed their minds at this time. These would have included the practicalities of what to pack and what to leave behind and the mode of conveying their belongings often at a moment's notice; the disappointment and hurt over the threats or apparent indifference of previously cordial neighbours; and vague hopes of eventually being able to return. However, the 'daily procession of harried and tortured men, women and children' described in sympathetic southern journals cut little ice with apparently cold-hearted unionist columnists.[71] One report even claimed those seeking help in Dublin, Glasgow and elsewhere were rather 'fugitives from justice' who were 'now posing as persecuted Catholics.'[72] Yet it is likely that in many such evictions, neighbours were powerless to intervene even when they had previously enjoyed cordial relations with these victims.

ASSASSINATION, REVENGE AND THE START OF CURFEW

After a few weeks of comparative quiet, another shooting outside Belfast ignited widespread communal disorder within the city's own boundaries. RIC District Inspector, Oswald Swanzy, who had been accused by republicans of involvement in the killing of the Mayor of Cork, Tomas MacCurtain in March and had been transferred to the north, was assassinated by an IRA team led by Roger McCorley, as he left Christ Church Cathedral in Lisburn's Market Square on Sunday 22 August.[73] DI Swanzy had just attended morning service in the church and was making his homeward journey through unusually crowded streets, when he was attacked by four men who fired several shots at him. In a dramatic scene, the gang's escape was nearly thwarted by the intervention of a retired army officer and people leaving Christ Church. Such was the confusion that the driver of the taxi used by the IRA squad started to leave without its leader, McCorley, who was, in Keystone Cops style, being pursued by many people, including police personnel.[74] As McCorley dragged himself aboard the fleeing vehicle, the police were forced to abandon their pursuit of the assailants when one of the wheels of their own car fell off. The IRA members, correctly anticipating they would be intercepted in Belfast, dispersed outside the city. However, their driver Sean Leonard was arrested and eventually tried for Swanzy's murder.[75] The unionist press were indignant at the sacrilegious nature of the attack. The *Northern Whig* fumed:

> The murder was committed on a Sunday, when the minds of all professing Christians should be concentrated on the command, 'Thou shalt not kill'. The men who are carrying on this vile conspiracy have no regard for the laws of God or man.[76]

Retribution was soon forthcoming in the staunchly loyalist County Antrim town. At least 8 houses were burned down in Lisburn later that day and there were reports of Catholic families making a speedy retreat, mainly to the south (especially the Dundalk area). This 'tramp over mountains' continued for the next couple of days, when the *Irish News* reported there was a 'Catholic exodus' from the town which was 'at the mercy of incendiaries'.[77] Indeed, the destruction in Lisburn was compared to that of 'a bombarded town in France.'[78] Ten miles away in Belfast, feelings of tension returned, especially in the west of the city. The weekend of 28/29 August and the first couple of days of the following week proved to be particularly bloody. Excluding the attacks in Ballymacarrett, at least 25 people died within a five day period, with scores of others suffering serious injury. On Saturday 28 August, a crippled Catholic labourer, Terence Burns (36), of Massarene Street, received a fatal leg wound at Quadrant Street in the Albert Street area, whilst a young Protestant shipwright at Harland and Wolff, William Mullan, of Upper Meadow Street, was shot dead on a tram in Henry Street as yard workers made their way to work on Monday the 30th.

There was vicious rioting and gunfire in the Catholic enclave of Marrowbone, off the Oldpark Road, the following day. Six Catholics were shot dead during disturbances involving considerable gunfire from the nationalist residents of the area, loyalists in surrounding streets and the security forces. Henry Kinney (18), of Ardilea Street, was wounded in the chest and died later in the Mater Hospital, whilst a teenage neighbour, Thomas Toner, also succumbed to chest wounds. Owen Moan and John Murray, both of Glenview Street, also received fatal injuries, as did William Cassidy, of Glenpark Street. A neighbour of Mr Cassidy's, ex-soldier, Charles O'Neill (40), was shot in the chest on the Oldpark Road and died in hospital less than two weeks later. The inquest into these Marrowbone deaths determined that the army had not been responsible for all of the killings, declaring that in the case of Mr Murray, the fatal bullet had been fired by a rioter before the military's arrival on the scene. The jury's verdict was that the police and military had been 'justified' in firing at the crowd.[79] Also on Sunday 29 August, in the west of the city, two more young Catholics died following disturbances in the Townsend Street area. They were Robert Lynch (17), of Massarene Street and Patrick Gilmore (25), a soldier on leave at Campbell's Row, who were believed to have been shot by the army. A Protestant teenager, Henry Hobson, who lived at Cromwell Road in south Belfast and was a promising member of Distillery Football Club, was shot in the nationalist Millfield area and died later in hospital.

Early the following morning, Protestants were targeted on their way to work, especially those travelling through Great George's Street and York Street. John

Thompson (18), a driver from Henry Street and a young message-boy who had been reportedly watching the sniping, Robert McAlpine (11), of Little York Street, were both victims of nationalist snipers. Another casualty in this area was Samuel Colville (18), a riveter, who was shot dead in nearby Henry Street. IRA gunmen also claimed the lives of John Coard, a driller at Workman and Clark's yard, who was killed in the North Street area and Adam McClean, who was believed to have been the victim of a ricochet bullet in Southwell Street, near York Street. Grace Orr (23), of Edenderry Street, was shot in the Oldpark area and later died in the Mater Hospital. The situation was so serious in north Belfast that the tramcar service was suspended early in the day and consequently many businesses failed to open that day. Across the city in Sandy Row, an angry loyalist crowd which was attempting to wreck a Catholic-owned pub, ignored the military's order to disperse. The army opened fire and four people were shot, two of whom died later in hospital. They were Paul Chapman (31), of Matilda Street and Sandy Row grocer Robert Seymour, who had been shot whilst working close to his shop.

Tuesday 31 August inevitably produced a significant loyalist response to the previous day's events. The last day of the month witnessed not only the spread of rioting and burning of property across the city, resulting in six deaths, but also the introduction of curfew restrictions. Several loyalists rushed to Earl Street and started firing at its residents. Edward Burns (65), of Grove Street, was wounded and died later in hospital. To the west, Henry McCann, of Wall Street, was shot dead in Brown Street, whilst Protestant teenager James Mathers, of Hartley Street, suffered a serious leg injury, passing away in hospital three weeks later. The first curfew restrictions came into operation that evening and although there had been a considerable demand for their implementation, two more people died during this first curfew.[80] A Scottish Riflesman, Private Jamison, was shot patrolling on the Linfield Road, but as this was a staunchly loyalist area, the soldier's death was probably due to the accidental discharge of a military weapon.[81] Fred Saye (26), a Protestant engineer from the Donegall Road, was fatally wounded by a military patrol.[82] Despite these two fatalities, the new restrictions appear to have been effective in terms of clearing the streets, as this press report indicates:

> Deserted streets – the tramcars ceased running shortly before half past nine o'clock and at that hour strong parties of military were taking up their positions, and the barbed-wire barricades were being re-erected at

York Street and other points, while civilians were already hurrying home-
wards. At half past ten o'clock the streets in the centre of the city were
deserted, and the military patrols were very promptly moving about,
holding up such stray civilians as were still abroad.[83]

Another interesting feature of Tuesday's feverish activity in Belfast was that
horrific, violent acts were executed in the very heart of the city. Thus, panic
beset shoppers in the busy shopping area of Castle Junction when gunfire in the
area produced stampedes in the crowded thoroughfares of Donegall Place,
Royal Avenue and High Street. The *Irish News'* report graphically portrayed the
scene of panic in the hub of the city:

> Four o'clock is the fashionable promenade hour in the vicinity of the
> [Castle] Junction and the pedestrian traffic naturally included a large
> crowd of ladies out on shopping expeditions and afternoon strolls.
> Suddenly shots were heard from the direction of Castle Street and a wild
> rush occurred. People sprinted in all directions and crouched into door-
> ways and women raced frantically for shelter.[84]

There was no respite for Belfast's beleaguered citizens the following day, with
incidents occurring in the usual trouble-spots in the north and west of the city,
as well as in its centre. There were reports of early morning gunfire directed at
loyalist workers in the Peters Hill area. However, the serious attacks were to
happen later in the day in the Oldpark area, when four Protestants were killed,
at least three of them by IRA gunmen. Thomas Maxwell (38), a well-sinker, of
North Boundary Street, died from a leg wound sustained near Hartley Street,
whilst William McMurray (18), a shipyard worker, was also shot in the same
district and died in hospital two days later. Thomas Boyd (45), a labourer from
Northland Street, was shot in the throat and died in hospital the following day.
Controversy ensued over the killing of ex-soldier, James Cowser, from Benwell
Street. Cowser had allegedly been in a group of loyalists pursuing a Catholic in
the Oldpark area. This fugitive had run through a house in Clifton Park
Avenue, escaping over a yard wall. It was believed that the military opened fire
as he was clambering over the wall in pursuit.

Trouble spread to the west of the city. A 'determined onslaught' was reported
on the Falls around lunchtime on 1 September, as a large loyalist mob (some of
them believed to have been armed) made their way down streets linking the
Falls and Shankill, including Boundary, Percy and Dover Streets. Frederick

Hobbs (28), an ex-Navy stoker, who was intending to emigrate to Canada, was shot in the head as he stood at the door of his home in Boundary Street. Mr Hobbs later died in the Royal Victoria Hospital and a charge brought against Alexander Trainor, of Dover Street was subsequently dropped. Another Catholic, John O'Brien (45), from Kildare Street, was shot in the head, standing at the corner of his street in the Carrick Hill area and died in hospital the following day. However, the visibly heavier military presence, especially in central areas – a Lewis machine-gun was posted at the corner of North Street, as well as in the Oldpark and in the west of the city – improved protection for the city's industrial workforce (for many, armoured vehicles accompanied them on their journeys to and from work) and the imposition of curfew restrictions, resulted in a temporary reduction in the level of disturbances in the city.[85]

Just over three weeks later, an IRA attack on the RIC provoked considerable violence in the west of the city and ended the lull. Two RIC officers based at the Springfield Road barracks, Constables Leonard and Carroll, were on foot patrol on the Falls Road when they were approached near Broadway by a group of gunmen. The officers reportedly refused the command to raise their arms and the gunmen opened fire, killing Constable Thomas Leonard and seriously wounding his colleague, before making their escape.[86] Loyalist anger quickly boiled over, finding its retribution a few streets away. Early the next morning (26 September), four assassins with blackened faces and wielding rifles, knocked on the Falls Road home of Edward Trodden. Mr Trodden, who lived above his barber's shop, was a prominent official in the Irish Republican Brotherhood and the IRA were suspected of holding meetings in his shop. The sleeping family were roused by hammering at the door and the call, 'Military to raid' and realising their father was the intended target, persuaded him to allow one of his sons to answer the door. Eddie recalled with horror:

> I opened the door and when I saw them with rifles ready and blackened faces I shut the door again. They fired through the door . . . It just missed me. They seized my father saying he was to be arrested. I begged them to take me instead. They only let my father put on his trousers, showed him down the stairs, dragged him into the yard and shot him dead. Oh, it was awful.[87]

Inside an hour another two Sinn Féin members, John McFadden (24) and James Gaynor (24) would be killed in their homes on the Springfield Road, most likely by the same gang. During a debate in the House of Commons on 4 November, the local MP, Joe Devlin, informed his parliamentary colleagues that the 'uniformed' assassins had used an armoured vehicle in their journeys from one house to the next. Sir Hamar Greenwood emphatically denied that the assassins were members of the security forces but a government statement apparently distinguished between the killings of Trodden and McFadden by 'persons unknown' and Gaynor who, it was claimed, had been shot 'resisting arrest'.[88] The similarities between these attacks, their close proximity and timing heavily suggest that only one party was directly involved in the three attacks and therefore this endeavour by the authorities to distinguish between them damaged the authenticity of their overall claim. Despite official denial of police involvement in these attacks, they were regarded by nationalists as the first in a series of atrocities masterminded by Nixon and Harrison.[89] However, apart from that emanating from the Falls area, there was little sympathy for the victims, on account of the assault on the police officers and the victims' strong republican credentials.[90] This was reflected in the threat made to Devlin by a parliamentary colleague, Donald Thompson, that there were would be retaliation on Sinn Féin members if more members of the security forces were assassinated.[91] He was supported in this eye-for-an-eye approach by the *Daily Express* which praised the police for 'acting with promptitude', claiming there was 'evidence to show that plans had been drawn up for a concerted attack on the Police in the Falls district.'[92]

Predictably these incidents increased the degree of tension in the city and at least another six people lost their lives inside the next two days, despite an increased military presence on the streets and the reintroduction of suspended curfew restrictions on 27 September. Nationalists turned their anger on returning industrial workers and following serious rioting and sniping in the Marrowbone district, two shipyard workers were hit by IRA snipers. Frederick Blair (44), a prominent official in the Orange Order and a UVF drill instructor in north Belfast, and John Lawther (19), of Everton Street, were hit by sniper fire. Ex-soldier Blair died at the scene, whilst Mr Lawther, who had received a stomach wound, died on 11 October. Catholics were also caught up in the line of fire in north Belfast that day. A mother whose infant had just died, found her Glenpark Street home in the line of gunfire and had to make a hasty retreat, assisted by a neighbour who carried the recently deceased child.[93] The liveliest district in the aftermath of the Sinn Féin killings was predictably the Falls where, following street disturbances on 29 September, four Catholics were shot dead by the army. At the coroner's inquest into the deaths of Robert Gordon (18), Thomas Barkley (32), James Shields (19) and William Teer (30), it was declared that the army had been 'justified in firing on the crowd.'[94]

In this section it has been shown how street disturbances spread right across the city and the way in which some of the conflict's characteristics became evident in its earliest phase. Thus, whilst street fighting remained a vital element of the disturbances, prolonged gunfire and bombing soon became regular features of the violence. Also, the state's response to the early disturbances set the pattern for the conflict. These included the slowness of those in government to intervene, the lack of security resources which would lead to panic and disastrous consequences, security measures such as curfew restrictions which provoked mixed feelings from the community and the earliest incidents involving 'rogue cops'. Another early feature was the tendency, on both sides of the sectarian divide in Belfast, to pass the blame on to others. On the loyalist side, the large-scale intimidation of Catholics from workplace and home, coupled with a series of vicious sectarian assaults, was underplayed by politicians and journalists whose agenda remained the external threat and the weakness of others to contain or even condemn such a threat. Nationalists, probably on account of the unique pressure they found themselves under on a daily basis, felt unable to offer reassurances to loyalists who also felt besieged, and their clergy and politicians encouraged their people to seek solace in romantic notions of Irish nationalism and the moral sanctity of their position. Finally, the pace of events was set in the early weeks of conflict. As political and security tension continued elsewhere, it became rapidly clear that this would be no short 'war' or a brief series of localised incidents. Although the security forces would inevitably restore law and order, this would be short term in its nature, merely providing a lull for the whole community. This is what was to happen in the weeks ahead.

Chapter 4

Boycotting Belfast

THE BELFAST BOYCOTT COMMITTEE

Believing that little would come of their own verbal condemnations of the intimidation and expulsion of industrial workers in the city, representatives of Belfast's Catholic community, including businessmen, church leaders and Sinn Féin personnel, combined in setting up the Belfast Boycott Committee in August 1920.[1] They included IRA leader Frank Aiken, Ulster-born Sean MacEntee, a Sinn Féin representative in the Dáil Éireann, Bishop MacRory and the Reverend John Hassan, with an advisory Boycott Committee operating from St Mary's Hall in Belfast's Bank Street.[2] The committee realised that support for their cause needed to be swiftly harnessed in the south. A petition urging the Irish Parliament to back the request of northern Catholics for 'a commercial boycott' of Ulster was presented to the parliament on 6 August. MacEntee, realising the growing well of sympathy in the south for the plight of Ulster Catholics, stressed the last resort nature of his appeal and the reliance of the northern Catholic minority on the rest of Ireland. Referring to Belfast, he argued:

> Until this city is taught that it depends on Ireland, there will be recurrent outbursts of bigotry ... and a standing obstacle to the settlement of the Irish Question.[3]

MacEntee urged Sinn Féin supporters to withdraw their accounts from Belfast-based banks and to transfer these to southern ones. In demanding a tougher approach to be adopted towards the north, he was exposing genuine divisions in southern Ireland between those who were wary of becoming too closely embroiled in northern affairs and those, like himself, who demanded more meaningful intervention. The former group managed to defeat the motion in the Dáil, but the Irish government did agree on 11 August to support a boycott which confined itself to the Belfast banks and insurance companies. Inside a month, instances of supportive action were being reported all over the country. However, a combination of initial confusion over the aims and internal organisation of the movement and an ongoing uncertainty about how events might unfold in the north, resulted in an uneven start to the southern campaign. This is not to deny there was considerable sympathy for Belfast's Catholics. Although many southerners were far from convinced that economic sanctions would bring an end to the 'pogrom' or lead to a reinstatement of Catholic workers in the city's industries, others voiced the irrationality of political partition for a region whose economy they believed to be dependent on southern markets. However, it was not until early in 1921 that a proper organisational framework – in the form of a Department of Boycott – was established to move the campaign forward. The new Minister, Joseph MacDonough, reminded local authorities of the immediacy of the situation and also of their moral, if not statutory, obligations. He spelled out the urgent need for establishing committees in 'every town and village', maintaining that 'the necessity for the rigid enforcement of the boycott' was, 'now more vital than ever.'[4] A report delivered to the Dáil on 20 January 1921, claimed that over 80 local boycott committees had been formed in the south and west and that 'an effective watch' was being kept on the Amiens Street rail terminus in Dublin with the intention of 'detecting traders still receiving supplies from the north.'[5] However, the government admitted that 'very little can be done ... as the goods arrived without any trace of their Belfast origin.'[6]

THE BOYCOTT CAMPAIGN

Initially the majority of border incidents were reported inside Ulster's own boundaries (4 counties were affected in January 1921), but trouble had spread to 12 Irish counties by April and in the period between February and September 1921, incidents had been reported in 24 counties.[7] The number of local boycott committees rose to around 400 and MacDonough boasted in the summer of 1921 that, 'except in Antrim and Down, it was impossible for a Belfast merchant to sell as much as a bootlace in any other part of Ireland.'[8]

Firms breaking the boycott were fined and its 'policing' was conducted by the IRA. A boycott 'patrol' was operating on Belfast trains from early in 1921, with cargoes of bread and newspapers being destroyed and whiskey looted. Trains were halted just across the border, where they were thoroughly searched and goods either confiscated or destroyed. Such siding parties played a 'cat and mouse' game with the security forces and there were cases of areas which had recently been searched being chosen for raiding parties. One such example took place outside Drogheda on 9 May 1921 when a consignment of northern goods on its way to Dublin was damaged. An *Irish News* report gives a vivid insight into the fashion in which trains were raided:

> While the train was slowly proceeding up the incline, a number of armed men appeared and jumped on the engine. They compelled the driver and fireman to halt and stand by, and then approached the guard and procured from him his wage bill of invoices showing the forwarding station of the goods carried ... the raiders went systematically through the 50 odd wagons on the train and removed oil, cart wheels, drapery and tea.[9]

Typical small-scale attacks included the emptying of the contents of a Belfast salesman's car into the Erne at Ballyshannon, the rapid cancellation of orders for Belfast-manufactured goods by Sligo merchants and physical intimidation of Belfast salesmen, including one who was forced to leave Galway. Other examples of boycott interventions include the refusal to deliver Belfast merchandise even when it reached its southern rail terminus, the burning of identified northern goods in rail sidings, the looting of lorries, the threatening of commercial travellers at gunpoint and the confiscation of ledgers from offices suspected of continuing trade with northern firms.[10] Probably the most spectacular incident of the whole boycott campaign occurred in April 1922 when around 100 IRA volunteers raided a bonded stores in Dublin, before proceeding to destroy half a million gallons of Dunville's whiskey, worth an estimated £50,000.[11] At least one boycott incident proved to have fatal consequences. A large Dundalk drapery firm with strong Ulster connections was set alight during the evening of 27 August 1921 and it was believed three shop assistants who had been sleeping in the building, perished in the blaze.[12]

Due to Belfast's pivotal role as distributive centre for the rest of Ireland, the boycott's effect on Ulster's cross-channel trade was considerable. Many English firms which had used Belfast as their operations centre in Ireland, were unable to sustain normal levels of business. Therefore, by September 1921, Dunlop were advising their customers to transfer their orders from the city to Dublin or even Birmingham, whilst J.S. Fry and Sons were one of a number of English firms which refused to use Belfast as their base for Irish distribution of their confectionery goods.

An interesting feature of the boycott tactic was its failure to distinguish between the religious denomination or political allegiance of the owners of specific goods emanating from Belfast. Thus, although most northern industries were controlled by unionists, there were a number of trades and light industries which had traditionally been dominated by the city's Catholic community. It was probably due more to logistical factors rather than adherence to a strict, non-sectarian, principled approach which resulted in business across the sectarian divide being caught up in the boycott. Indeed, the Belfast Boycott Committee complained to MacDonough about the damage inflicted on the businesses of grocers, fruiterers and those in the boot and leather trades, many of whose members would have been Catholics. In one ironical case, a leading republican, Denis McCullough, had to close his bagpipes factory due to the financial repercussions of the boycott. As time passed, an increasing number of nationalists realised the benefits of modifying a policy which was proving to be self-defeating and some proposed a system of granting licences to firms sympathetic with both the principle of a return to work for the expelled workers and to the broader nationalist cause. However, such a proposal was unlikely to have worked, especially as it had to be implemented in Belfast, where sympathy for the tactic was limited.

Apart from the actual physical destruction of Belfast goods and the deterrent impact on its distributive trades, one of the main financial repercussions of the boycott, was the decline of banking business in the north. Banking transactions in Ulster were significantly reduced and several branches of Dublin-based northern banks had to close.[13] Pressures on banks with Belfast headquarters were, even from an early stage in the boycott, 'so acute that steps have been taken to ask the British Government to declare a moratorium against withdrawals.'[14] Again, it was the border areas which were especially, if not exclusively, affected. Pressure, in the form of public notices warning that the paper money of northern banks, including the Northern, Ulster and Belfast Banks, would become illegal tender from 14 July 1921, was emphatic. These posters also warned that 'any persons trading with [these] Banks will be severely punished and Bank Notes will be seized'.[15] An incident in a border town illustrates the widespread prevalence of threats made against provincial businessmen, especially for utilising the services of northern banks. An irate bank manager, James Newel, drew the attention of Sir James Craig and his cabinet colleagues to threatening notices, which had been 'widely circulated in this district'.[16] Calling for the government to get 'a move on to drive ... the southern Banks out of the North', Newel described the forfeit of business from northern banks to their counterparts in the south as a 'disgrace'.[17] Mr Newel also forwarded to Craig a copy of an anonymous threat made to businesses which traded with Belfast-based banks. It read:

> We understand you are one of those who still do business with the Northern Bank Company Limited. In doing so you are aiding and abetting intolerance. As long as workers are victimised and denied their primary right to earn their bread unless they submit to religious and political tests, the boycott of Belfast industries must continue. You are hereby requested to take this letter as due notification.[18]

The response of Craig's cabinet would hardly have placated Newel or his County Down banking colleagues. Minutes of a cabinet meeting indicate that they decided it would be 'inadvisable' to call a meeting with representatives of the local banks as they did not at that time possess powers to take appropriate action.[19]

Although several Sinn Féin leaders were lukewarm in their support of the boycott tactic, others believed that, by striking at Belfast's commercial operations, it would bring the unionist community to heel.[20] Eoin O'Duffy, speaking in the Dáil debate on the Treaty in January 1922, did not try to conceal Sinn Féin's economic blackmail:

> I know the businessmen of Ulster don't want separation because they fear economic pressure – the boycott gives them a taste of that [referring to bankruptcy cases in Belfast] ... With bankruptcy staring numbers of others in the face, they will see that the Northern Parliament comes to terms with the rest of Ireland.[21]

Much to the chagrin of unionists, the boycott tactic survived the truce which started in July 1921, but it was to end officially when the first Collins-Craig agreement was reached in January 1922.[22] The question of Catholic expulsions from the Belfast workplace formed the second article of this pact, in which Collins agreed that the boycott would be 'discontinued immediately' in return for Craig undertaking to 'facilitate in every possible way the return of Catholic workers, without tests, to the shipyards as, and when trade revival enables the firms concerned to absorb the present unemployed.'[23] Although this was welcomed by Belfast's merchant community, the likelihood of delivery from both sides was in doubt from the start. Sir James Craig was unlikely to have been in a position to accommodate thousands of unemployed Catholic workers in a climate of existing high unemployment, whilst they were unable or unwilling to confront those elements within the republican movement, which were keen on pursuing the boycott.[24] Not surprisingly, therefore, the pact wasn't implemented and the second agreement two months later did not directly address the boycott question.[25] In any case, Unionists argued that the boycott, if anything, increased in intensity following its official cessation. Dáil Éireann continued to levy fines, and encouraged their enforcement both by the armed hold-up of trains and lorries by IRA personnel and the physical intimidation of shopkeepers. Boycott posters continued to be printed and displayed both north and south of the border. Armagh shopkeepers reported cases of Sinn Féin intimidation and Dublin retailers complained about being pressurised into paying fines, even though the boycott had been officially terminated.[26] In April 1922, Craig pointed out that the degree of boycott activity was greater than it had been during the official boycott. The Unionist leader argued that 'interference with our trade has been greater than in the whole period when the boycott was officially countenanced, and damage has been done to Irish goods aggregate in value to many thousands of pounds.'[27]

'REFUSE TO BUY HIS GOODS ...'

Despite their vociferous condemnation of the Irish Government's organisation of a boycott, the Unionist establishment endeavoured to paint a brighter picture of the north's economic condition. They reminded their supporters that Belfast industries were not dependent on Irish markets for their outlets. However, the city's business community did not dismiss the impact of the boycott quite so lightly. A meeting of the Belfast Wholesalers, Merchants and Manufacturers Association in the spring of 1921, admitted they had been 'hit hard' by the boycott and reported how, in some areas, over 80 per cent of their trade had 'gone off'.[28] Six months later, the same group's President, John McCaughey told a meeting in the city that the government should 'extend to traders in this country full protection in the discharge of their legitimate business, in as much

as freedom of trade with many areas has ceased to exist through the illegal operation of what is known as the "Belfast boycott" and which is carried on by means
of violence and intimidation.'[29] Noting that Lloyd George had promised
protection for English traders who were being boycotted in Ireland, the organisation's spokesman 'respectfully' asked for 'the same protection to be extended
to us.'[30] Despite these genuine concerns, this association was reticent about
eking out revenge on their southern boycotters. The *Whig* praised the same
association for deciding not to boycott southern goods, and welcomed its decision not to adopt 'a policy of retaliation simply for the sake of "serving out" the
foolish and malignant people who planned the boycotting campaign.'[31]

A more proactive counter-offensive to the southern boycott was comparatively slow to emerge. A pressure group, the Ulster Traders Defence Association
(UTDA), was established during the second half of 1921. With accommodation
in Donegall Square and funding estimated at over £25,000, the UTDA was a
belated response by angry unionist merchants and businessmen to the southern
boycott. Advised by Craig to desist from acting directly against the southern
authorities, the group adopted an effective advertising and propaganda
campaign early in 1922. As violence escalated during the early spring, the organisation adopted a higher profile, posting numerous handbills and placing several
advertisements in the local press, urging Ulster people to refrain from
purchasing southern goods.[32] This sometimes involved taking whole page
advertising in the loyalist press, encouraging their readers to adopt the same
tactics which had been used against them for 18 months. One advert in the
Belfast Telegraph led with the headline, 'Ulster Boycotted – Refuse to buy his
goods as he refuses to buy yours ... Not a penny to the Boycotter!'[33] Other
adverts reinforced this tit-for-tat principle, condemning the fact that 'the products and merchandise of the people, who are manipulating the unholy
exclusion of Belfast and Ulster in the hope of throttling your industries still
come into the Six Counties area freely.'[34] Asking the question 'are you going to
allow this to continue?' the advertisement listed 40 different items of merchandise which Ulster people should refrain from purchasing.[35]

Unionist press reaction to the political and coercive nature of the boycott
campaign was predictably virulent. Describing the 'daily' burning and destruction of Ulster goods (it was claimed there were 'almost hourly' burnings in the
border town of Dundalk), the northern press lamented the fact that Dublin
wholesalers had been 'fined' for accepting Belfast goods with 'no efforts being
made by the Irish administration to intervene.'[36] The *Newsletter* interpreted the

boycott as an economic weapon motivated by a political bid by de Valera and his colleagues to 'coerce' Ulster Unionists into 'abandoning their principles'.[37] The paper described the boycott tactic as a 'reprisal', intimating it had been 'advocated long before the events which [are] supposed to have led to it occurred and its avowed object was to compel Ulster to come under a Parliament for all Ireland.'[38] Another editorial suggested that the central object of the boycott was to 'penalise' Ulster Unionists for their obduracy towards Irish unity, whilst the *Whig* maintained the tactic was 'an attempt to frighten us into abandoning the constitution set up by the Government of Ireland Act.'[39] A constant theme of press coverage was the comparative lack of impact which the boycott was having on the northern economy. One leader claimed that the boycott 'leaves the great staple industries of Belfast totally unaffected' and, in conceding certain trades were adversely affected, especially distributive ones, claimed such trades represented less than a tenth of the city's business interests.[40] The *Newsletter* pointed out that, as most of Belfast's trade was outside Ireland, it could not bring an 'economic disaster upon the city', suggesting that if the boycott proceeded and Ulster was 'eventually forced to retaliate', it would be found that it could 'do better without the rest of Ireland than the rest of Ireland can [*sic*] do without it'.[41]

'GESTURE POLITICS'

The rationale behind the boycott had been that economic sanctions would bring Ulster trade to a standstill and that this would make loyalists relent, both in their intimidation of Catholic workers and in their opposition to Irish unity. The sanctions did have an impact, especially in the short-term and in isolated sectors of the northern economy. Certainly the efficiency of the banks to operate effectively was severely tested and there was a considerable reduction in Belfast's share of the market in the rest of Ireland.[42] Also, as it was such an important centre for the distribution of raw materials and produce, Belfast's role as a distributive centre suffered, although this decline was also to have a negative impact on the economy of other parts of Ireland. Certain industries suffered disproportionately because of the boycott; these included distilleries, tobacco and bakeries. However, those who had masterminded the boycott had clearly underestimated the importance of Belfast's 'triangular' trade with Merseyside and Clydeside, and the economic collapse which they had been anticipating failed to materialise.

Apart from these economic ramifications, the boycott was singularly unsuccessful and even counter-productive, especially with regard to its broader aims.[43] Therefore, it failed to precipitate even a small-scale return of Catholic workers to the shipyards and other industries which had been, after all, its *raison d'être*. This was partly due to the obduracy of the city's Protestant community but it should also be seen in the context of increasing unemployment (a situation not helped by the boycott) and the perceived republican threat to northern territory. The boycott was also counter-productive in the sense that such economic intimidation by a larger state of its smaller neighbour was unlikely to entice the latter into a political union. Many Republicans were far from convinced about the tactic and, at least in the sense of failing to achieve its fundamental objective – the reinstatement of the city's Catholic workers – it was to be regarded as 'an utter failure'.[44] A leading member of Sinn Féin, P.S. O'Hegarty, admitted the boycott actually intensified feelings on both sides of the border, a position which inevitably led to stalemate. He later wrote of the boycott:

> it raised up in the South, what had never been there, a hatred of the North, and a feeling that the North was as much an enemy as England. It made Protestant Home Rulers in the north almost ashamed of their principles, and it turned apathetic Protestant unionists into bitter partisans.[45]

Another negative repercussion of the southern boycott was that, apart from accelerating a counter-boycott, the measure funded and orchestrated by Dáil Éireann 'spawned numerous sectarian boycotts in both parts of Ireland.'[46] As Dennis Kennedy has observed, the boycott accentuated unionist mistrust of their southern political opponents, whom they accused of orchestrating an threatening campaign aimed at forcing them into an all-Ireland against their will. Kennedy noted that the boycott 'heightened Unionist perceptions of the Dáil and the whole Sinn Féin movement as the enemy of the unionist community, determined to wreck the Government of Ireland settlement and to inflict hardship on people already suffering economic decline and unemployment.'[47] Such apprehension was compounded by the reluctance of the British administration to intervene, especially as they were endeavouring to woo Sinn Féin during the Treaty negotiations in the latter part of 1921. Some loyalists may well have enjoyed perverse satisfaction over the boycott's ultimate outcome. It was a 'boycott' incident which sparked Ireland's Civil War. In an atmosphere of escalating bad feeling between pro and anti Treaty forces in the south, Leo Henderson, the first director of the Belfast Boycott Committee and some colleagues set out to seize a fleet of cars imported from Belfast by the Dublin branch of Ferguson's. He was arrested by pro-Treaty forces, but subsequently the pro Treaty Deputy Chief of Staff, General J.J. O'Connell, was seized as a hostage. This led to the bombing of the Four Courts and, due to the inevitable escalation of violence in the south, the systematic enforcement of the boycott fizzled out.[48]

The boycott's success was, therefore, limited to a relatively few areas, most notably in the commercial and banking spheres. Here, the efficiency of banking operations was severely tested and considerable, in some cases permanent, damage was inflicted upon firms and industries in the city. Also, the considerable reduction in the city's share of the market in the rest of Ireland was 'the mark of the boycott's success.'[49] Thus, two years after the boycott had been lifted, the exports from Northern Ireland to the Irish Free State were barely half those of 1920 levels. However, this was offset by the damage done to Ireland's economic unity, especially in the context of Belfast's central role as a distribution centre for the rest of Ireland. Yet it is likely that the boycott was partially successful in raising the morale of the dispirited and besieged Catholic minority in Belfast. Although the confiscation and destruction of northern goods would have been openly applauded in the backstreets of Catholic west Belfast, many others were wary of the repercussions of such actions on the already vulnerable Catholic community in other areas of the city. Setting fire to northern produce in Dundalk rail sidings did not lead to the renewed employment of a single Catholic in Belfast. Indeed, smaller businesses relying heavily on southern trade, which were more likely to utilise Catholic labour, had to reduce staff numbers during a period of high unemployment. Whilst it would have been only the commercial community and leaders of industry who would have been directly affected by the boycott, there can be no disguising the fact that it produced a significant increase in tension and stiffened loyalist opposition to republican demands for Irish unity. The pursuit of a policy of economic partition by an administration actively opposed to political partition and the apparent reluctance of the British Government to confront Dáil Éireann over the boycott issue during a period of tense political negotiation, may not have directly resulted in disturbances on the Belfast streets, but they hardly assisted in lifting tension within the communities.[50] Placed alongside the fury caused by IRA incursions into Ulster, irreparable damage was done to north-south relationships. Increasingly frustrated and embittered loyalists took their vengeance on familiar targets in the Belfast ghettoes.

Chapter 5

'The dregs of the Orange lodges'

ESTABLISHMENT OF THE ULSTER SPECIAL CONSTABULARY

For many Catholics the Ulster Special Constabulary (USC), which was created towards the end of 1920, remains Ulster's historical equivalent of the Black and Tans. Indeed, there is a tendency by some to interpret the Twenties' conflict as basically the story of the excesses of the Specials.[1] This over-simplification both of the conflict and the role of the Specials has resulted in the fostering of several misconceptions relating to the involvement of the USC and has not helped understanding of the wider conflict. This section focuses on tracing the establishment of the Specials near the beginning of the hostilities in 1920 and on various differing reactions to its formation. Whilst it attempts to assess the legacy of the USC, it does not describe specific incidents involving the Specials, either as perpetrators or victims of violence, as these are addressed elsewhere in the book.

Calls for the creation of a 'reserve' police force to assist sorely-pressed 'regular' officers and military personnel had grown in their intensity, especially as the conflagration spread to Ireland's north. As has been noted, they were given an unofficial 'trial' by the Revd John Redmond on the streets of Ballymacarrett during the summer. Increasingly pressurised by growing demands within the loyalist grassroots for a more stringent security presence along the border and in Greater Belfast, Sir James Craig rapidly grew convinced that, with incessant demands for military assistance elsewhere in Ireland, not to mention existing shortfalls in the number of police officers throughout the island, the only short-term solution to the security problem in the north lay in the creation of a new volunteer constabulary which would provide vital back-up to sorely stretched security personnel. Such pressures came to a head during the first week in September, following the severe disturbances in the city the previous week. At a ministerial conference in London chaired by Bonar Law, the Lord Privy Seal, Craig maintained that urgent action was needed to address the rapidly-worsening situation in the north, stressing the fact that loyalists were 'losing faith in the government's determination to protect them and were threatening an immediate recourse to arms, which would precipitate civil war'.[2] Illustrating Unionists' growing distrust of Dublin Castle officials, Craig also requested the appointment of a senior civil servant to operate in Belfast. His main focus, however, was the creation of a special constabulary and at this meeting he outlined the proposed composition of such a force. Calling for the direct fusion of UVF personnel into such a reserve police force, Craig called for the setting-up of a 2,000 strong complement of full-time Specials:

> This force must be armed ... for a general duty within the six counties only. As far as possible the organisation should be along military lines. A reserve force of Special Constabulary should be raised from the loyal population which would only be called out for duty in case of emergency. The organisation of the UVF should be used for this purpose, as was done for raising the 36th Ulster Division when the war broke out.[3]

Unionist pressure on the cabinet continued during the following week, first with another call for a Special Constabulary the following day, this time from the UUC, and four days later by a deputation of grassroots unionists [including UULA members] who met Law and his colleagues in London. Inevitably the government conceded to such pressure, confirming the acceptance in principle of establishing both the Special Constabulary and a senior civil servant as an Ulster Under-Secretary, though the contentious suggestion of utilising the existing UVF framework in the creation of such a constabulary was conspicuously ignored.[4]

Although, on the surface at least, the swift Westminster reaction to Craig's demands might have seemed a sop to unionists, it was, as far as Lloyd George's administration was concerned, more a matter of pragmatism than acquiescence. The worsening situation in the rest of Ireland and reluctance on the part of Westminster to sustain a high military presence in Ulster meant they were attracted by a localised solution to the north's security problem.[5] Thus, financial considerations involving the shortage of troops and regular police in Ireland as a whole, but especially in the north, was the chief reason why this auxiliary force was raised. The announcement of the formation of the Special Constabulary did not require the introduction of any new legislation, as there was provision within existing legislation – the Special Constabulary Ireland Acts of 1832 and 1914 – which afforded local authorities the opportunity of raising a

Special Constabulary. Therefore, the order to use such legislation came from Dublin Castle on 22 October, being formally announced by central government on 1 November.

It was proposed that the new force in Ulster should be raised at county level and should be split into three sections, each of which would be armed.[6] The 'A' Specials were perceived as constituting a top-up to existing RIC strength in Ulster and they were to be armed, equipped, uniformed and paid the same as the regular police. This full-time force, aiming to muster 2,000 recruits, would consist, in the main, of former soldiers, earning around 10s. a day and executing security duties for six months at a time. A volunteer force of part-time constables, described as a 'B' Constabulary, were expected to carry out one night's duty approximately each week in 'home' territory (loyalists were, theoretically at least, restricted to policing their own areas), receiving expenses for 'wear and tear' (about £5 every six months). This category of Special Constabulary was initially given caps and armbands, though by February 1922 'B's were fully armed with rifles and bayonets and had been issued with uniforms. Lower profile tasks such as foot patrols, operating road-blocks and guarding buildings at night were deemed to be appropriate for this force, which aimed to recruit 4,000 men in Belfast alone. Many stipulations were given on the potential deployment and, more especially, on operational restrictions for the 'B' Constabulary. The main restriction on their use was that they could only proceed on armed patrol under the command of a regular RIC officer and that, whilst working under their own appointed officers, were subject to the orders of the RIC and in particular, Sir C.G. Wickham, the District Commissioner of the RIC in the north.[7] The less controversial 'C' category was envisaged as an emergency reserve force consisting of mainly older men. Like the 'B' group they received no official uniform or payment, apart from expenses, but were issued permits for firearms which could be used on duty.[8]

RECRUITMENT

Advertisements for Special Constables were printed in the local press on 1 November. The government called on 'all law-abiding citizens' between the ages of 21 and 45 to apply and 'assist the authorities in the maintenance of the order of the prevention of crime in the country.'[9] Enrolment forms were issued and processed via police stations. Select committees, consisting of J.P.s and retired officers, were formed in each northern county and were instructed to select 'only men of unquestionable fidelity and efficiency.'[10] This emphasis on loyalty was also reflected in the oath which potential constables had to undertake when they enrolled. It read:

> I do swear that I will well and truly serve our Sovereign Lord the King in the office of Special Constable without favour or affection, malice or ill-will, and that I will to the best of my power cause the Peace to be kept and preserved, and prevent all offences against the persons and proper-ties of His Majesty's subjects.[11]

Such a focus on loyalty and the promises of their trusted political leaders clearly assured UVF members that they would be warmly welcomed to the new constabulary. They were expected to apply en masse to the new organisation. In a memo to UVF company commanders, the leading officer in the UVF, Lieutenant-Colonel Wilfred B. Spender, felt he could 'confidently rely on the members of the UVF to do all they can to make the Special Constabulary forces a success' and added 'our Great Leader' could rely on volunteers for the new force to exercise their duties 'conscientiously and impartially, under discipline, and with that restraint towards those who disagree with us which has always marked the attitude of our Organisation.' Spender confidently added his expec-tation that there was 'no reason why the UVF should not furnish all the numbers required.'[12]

However, initial recruitment to the Specials, whilst relatively brisk in border areas such as Fermanagh, fell considerably short of the high expectations set by Spender and others. In Belfast around 750 men had been accepted as 'B' consta-bles inside a fortnight (half of these were ex-servicemen) and by May this had nearly doubled, to 1,480.[13] Yet senior figures within the UVF were a trifle concerned about the sluggish start to recruitment. Fred Crawford, writing shortly before Christmas to Colonel R.H. Wallace, County Grand Master of the Belfast Orange Order expressed his concern over recruitment figures, stressing that Orangemen 'must come out now or be very sorry later that they have been neutrals, when they see Nationalists filling the ranks of an *armed* force where they might have been.'[14] Several months later, loyalist fears over apathy within their ranks were verbalised more publicly and with increased desperation. In a leading article expressing concern over recruitment to the Specials in Belfast, the *Northern Whig* warned:

> It is foolish for loyalists to suppose that because they are in a majority in any district they are therefore free from the attacks of Sinn Féiners ... We would therefore appeal with all the earnestness at our command to every loyal man in Ulster who is fit for service to join one of the branches of the Special Constabulary ... Prudence and patriotism alike dictate that every Ulsterman capable of bearing arms should enrol in the Special Constabulary. Unless prompt steps are taken to stamp out murder and sedition we shall be compelled to go through the most terrible chapter in our chequered history.[15]

Such concerns over recruitment were not confined to the Special Constabulary. Three months after the RUC was established in May 1922, it still had only achieved a third of its proposed complement. The far from convincing recruitment figures were probably less to do with the apathy claimed by the anxious voices of unionism and rather more related to an understandable reluctance on the part of many civilians in joining a potentially dangerous organisation.

A divergence of opinion over the desirability of using large numbers of UVF personnel within the Special Constabulary clearly existed between, one the one hand mainland British politicians and military figures, and on the other local unionists and police chiefs. Sir John Anderson, joint Under-Secretary at Dublin Castle, agreed with General Sir Nevil Macready, the O.C. British forces in Ireland, about the wisdom of choosing potentially partisan recruits for a new constabulary force. Writing to Bonar Law on 2 September 1920, Anderson argued:

> We have ... tried the experiment of setting up an unarmed body of Special Constabulary in Belfast and even that has not been an unqualified success. On the first night three of the Special Constables were arrested for looting ... you cannot in the middle of a faction fight recognise one of the contending parties and expect to deal with disorder in the spirit of impartiality and fairness essential in those who have to carry out the Order of the Government.[16]

The perspectives of on-the-ground police chief contrasted sharply with those of Anderson and Macready, especially as concern grew over the escalation of violence emanating from 'the growth of unauthorised Loyalist defence forces'.[17]

An internal police memo from Colonel Charles Wickham, the most senior police chief in the north, written a year after the formation of the USC, was intercepted by Sinn Féin and 'leaked' to the press. In his letter, Wickham did not countenance 'facing down' the illegal forces of the UVF, but rather promoted 'the desirability of obtaining the services of the best elements of these organisations', especially within the 'C' category, where he felt they could be turned into 'regular military units.'[18] The British political establishment was alarmed by this apparent endorsement of the principle of utilising a paramilitary force for the purpose of recruitment to a new, supposedly inclusive, police force and northern unionists were hard pressed to defend such thinking. Unionists claimed that this merely reflected their endeavours to control increasingly impassioned sections of the Protestant working class and was rather a method of staving off possible civil war in the north. Such explanations were drowned by nationalist claims that this plan merely underlined loyalist attempts to prepare a substantial force to suppress the minority community in the north.[19]

'WELL-DISPOSED CITIZENS'

Responses to the announcement of the creation of the Special Constabulary were, apart from some unionist self-satisfaction, far from welcoming. At Westminster, Joe Devlin, not for the first time in his career, voiced the genuine fears which many of his constituents had about the new proposals. Suggesting that the decision to create the USC would actually make the situation in the north worse, he warned the Irish Chief Secretary, Sir Hamar Greenwood:

> If I had the power . . . I would . . . organise special constables to fight your special constables. The Chief Secretary is going to arm pogromists to murder the Catholics . . . The Protestants are to be armed, for we would not touch your special constabulary with a 40 foot pole. Their pogrom is to be made less difficult. Instead of paving stones and sticks they are to be given rifles.[20]

Although they afforded space within their columns for Special Constabulary recruitment notices, the *Irish News* was no less dismissive of the proposal than Devlin and his colleagues. A leading article in the paper interpreted the proposal as part of a wider campaign by the British government to 'emphasise and embitter the artificial divisions between two integral parts of an indivisible and hitherto undivided country.'[21] Mocking the government's appeal to 'well-disposed' citizens to offer their services as Special Constables, the *Irish News* dismissed the suggestion that such an appeal was genuinely inclusive, warning those supervising such a scheme that 'not a Nationalist in all broad Ulster will dream of offering himself as a "candidate" for admission to the new force of Janissaries.'[22] The paper went on:

> The 'citizens' who are 'well-disposed' towards Partition, Carsonism, Ascendancy and Pogromism are welcome to a monopoly of Sir Edward Carson's 'standing army'.[23]

Public opinion in Britain, hardened as it was against unionism following the sectarian attacks in Belfast, was deeply concerned about the establishment of a reserve force. Even right wing organs, previously sympathetic to the unionist cause, had severe reservations, and in some cases, outright hostility. The *Times* questioned the logic of the government's decision, suggesting 'such action would produce the most disastrous results'.[24] The *Daily Mail* attacked the notion of volunteer armies in Ireland, quizzing the logic of the decision to arm 'well-disposed citizens', which they suggested, raised 'serious questions of the sanity of Government'.[25] The paper had serious reservations about the potentially tragic consequences of arming an exclusively Protestant force, composed in many cases of individuals and groups who had been to the fore in the summer disturbances:

> A citizen who is 'well-disposed' to the Government, is from the very nature of the cause, an Orangeman or, at the very least, a vehement anti-Sinn Féiner. These are the very people who have been looting Catholic shops and driving thousands of Catholic women and children from their homes.[26]

Other consistently critical observers of unionism turned their venom on the proposal. The *Westminster Gazette* suggested that many of the attributes of eligibility for membership of the USC equated to 'all the eager spirits who have driven nationalist workmen from the docks or have demonstrated their loyalty by looting Catholic shops' and concluded that the proposal was 'quite the most inhuman expediency the government could have devised.'[27] The liberal weekly, *Nation* also described the decision 'to arm the Ulster Volunteers' as 'the most amazing' of the government's decisions and, referring to the large number of ex-soldiers involved in the Catholic exodus from Belfast, condemned Lloyd George for 'telling these thousand homeless soldiers that he is going to make the men who turned them out into the police of Belfast.'[28] Closer to home, a provincial paper forecast that such Special Constables would be 'nothing more and nothing less than the dregs of the Orange lodges, armed and equipped to overawe Nationalists and Catholics.'[29]

Support for the USC was, in the main, restricted to the loyalist press. Unionists felt that the proposals indicated the government's acceptance that only a more rigorous security policy and increased numbers of security personnel would further the cause of peace. The *Belfast Telegraph* informed its readers on how the force would police the Belfast area, suggesting that the object of the 'B' force was to 'relieve the troops from some of the police duty which they are presently called upon to perform'. In its conclusion the *Telegraph* claimed that the force 'should perform a very valuable adjunct to the regular forces of the Crown', as well as proving to be 'an additional safeguard for the protection of the lives and property of the citizens'.[30]

SALVATION ARMY MEN?

The first 'A' Special patrol in Belfast took place before Christmas 1920, with the first 'B' patrol taking to the city's streets six weeks later on 4 February. Although the dreaded Special Constabulary was established comparatively early in this conflict, their presence in the city was not, despite the legend, particularly prominent until its latter stages. Following the Truce in July 1921, the USC was to immobilise, only to resurface towards the end of September following further violence in the city and a promise by the Dublin headquarters of the IRA to 'protect' the Catholics of Ulster.[31] With the Belfast administration assuming responsibility for law and order on 22 November 1921 and the peaking of violence during the first half of 1922, the Specials were increasingly in the fore-front of the action, especially in the border areas. This is reflected in the number of officers killed and wounded, with the majority of fatalities occurring during this period within rural areas.[32] Physically attacked by the IRA and verbally assaulted by politicians and journalists, the lot of the Special Constable in the early 1920s was far from happy. The official historian of the organisation, Arthur Hezlet noted:

They had to do their ordinary job as well and missed their night's sleep when on duty. Their main role was guarding, walking and patrolling and they spent a night a week out in all weathers. When on patrol they were always in danger of an ambush and could never relax. Even when off duty they were liable to attack on their homes, and unless they had firearms of their own, were without protection.[33]

Frustration over failing to catch the perpetrators of violence and boredom caused by the rather mundane nature of much of Special policing were features of the Special's experience. Writing to his mother in London, a young Constable, Edmund Duffin, bemoaned the fact that, following a Mills bomb attack on the Ulster Club, 'nobody as usual was caught.' Describing his first duty as a Special Constable, Duffin wrote:

> I did my first duty on Monday night and found it dull work. I went on patrol with a policeman round Cavehill Road district and except for moving on a crowd of youths who congregated at Fortwilliam Park in the evenings … we had no excitement. I then did sentry go for two hours outside the barracks and Dermot Campbell and Smiles arrived triumphantly with a curfew prisoner. We got a cup of tea at 11 and then started off with a Sergeant and policeman all round the Fortwilliam area and I got home rather weary at 2.30 a.m. Fortunately it was a fine night and we are allowed to smoke after curfew. We have a belt, baton, revolver, cap and armlet and look rather like Salvation Army men.[34]

Acclaimed by many for the effectiveness of their increasingly front line role in 1922, the USC also rapidly became an anathema to many others, especially within the Catholic community.[35] A disproportionate number of fatal attacks, both in Belfast and in outlying areas, were executed by the Specials.[36] However, as members of the USC were required to operate from regular police barracks and accompanied them on patrols, any corrupt officers intent on breaking the law were likely to be a mixture of police personnel, rather than simply Special Constables.[37] Whilst many officers were undoubtedly over-exuberant and sometimes sectarian in their approach to Catholics, one would be hasty in suggesting that the majority of them were gun-toting desperadoes. Most of them were genuinely motivated by a desire to protect their community and were unlikely to have been involved in shooting or severely beating Catholics.

However, it is also true that a sizeable minority of them, if stopping short of using their weaponry, mistreated Catholics and behaved in an overtly sectarian manner. Therefore, whilst it might be difficult to accurately assess the degree of culpability of the Special Constabulary for specific incidents during this period, there can be no disputing the degree of trepidation which they produced amongst the city's Catholic population. Graphic accounts of the alleged misdemeanours of Specials abound in the nationalist press and some are referred to elsewhere.[38] Jimmy Kelly recalls the Specials he encountered near his Falls home as 'swaggering louts' and proceeds:

> About 8 p.m., after several hours boozing, the Specials issued forth [from the Beehive Bar] swinging their rifles, and into their Lancias and caged armoured cars for a night of fun 'shooting up' the area and teaching the Fenians a lesson. Speeding along Beechmount Avenue they fired volley after volley up the long streets where neighbours gossiped and children played. As they fired at random, women and children ran in terror or dropped down out of sight in the little gardens. Door after door slammed shut and in spite of the bright summer evening, nobody risked going out, even though the official curfew was not due until 10 p.m.[39]

CRAIG'S MIDWIFE

Not surprisingly, historians' interpretations of the legacy of the force founded in November 1920 differ considerably.[40] B.A. Follis reminds us that the Special Constabulary can not be used as a scapegoat for explaining communal strife, nor should its role in helping to contain the level of violence be underestimated. Follis maintains that the Special Constabulary was established to 'help maintain the public peace after serious public disorders between two communities' and was rather 'a product or symptom of the divisions and not the cause'.[41] A more emotional assessment of their achievement is provided by Arthur Hezlet, who emphasised the 'very small' number of reprisal cases relating to the USC on RIC files, arguing that the force behaved with 'great restraint'. Indeed, Hezlet went on to claim the USC were 'more responsible for saving N Ireland from anarchy than either the army or the RIC'.[42] Other writers, whilst not contesting the pivotal contribution of the USC in reducing levels of disorder in Belfast, also emphasise the fact that such success was 'largely accountable to systematic repression, spearheaded by the Specials'.[43] However, despite his condemnation of the force's 'strong predilection for pursuing Catholic rather than Protestant miscreants and the unionist involvement of errant members and units in illegal reprisals', David Fitzpatrick conceded the Special Constabulary's 'crucial part in suppressing violence and subduing the northern divisions of the IRA'.[44] Brian Griffin also acknowledges the 'major role' played by the Specials in defeating the IRA in Ulster, but reminds us that in so doing, its long-term legacy was only to 'increase the sense of bitterness and alienation which most Catholics felt towards the new northern state'.[45] Griffin proceeds to castigate the involvement of individual Specials in reprisal attacks and points out that 'these killings, if not condoned at the highest levels of the security apparatus in N Ireland, certainly were neither adequately investigated nor punished by USC commanders, the RUC, or the N Ireland or British authorities'.[46]

Probably the most damning indictment of the Special Constabulary comes from Michael Farrell, who argues that as the British government willingly financed the USC, this amounts to an official sponsorship of Craig's controversial force. However, as Follis points out, the British administration were far from happy about the funding and only conceded to Craig's request after consideration of wider British interests, especially the exorbitant cost of military replacements for the Special Constabulary and political uncertainty relating to the likely findings of the Boundary Commission.[47] Farrell also claims that the USC were engaged in 'a significant number of reprisal killings as well as widespread petty and not so petty harassment of Catholics'. His conclusion is perhaps more reasoned. He maintains that the evidence suggests 'many of their officers knew what was going on and if they did not actually encourage it, did not do anything to prevent it.'[48]

Certainly the record of the Special Constabulary, especially in its formative years, was a chequered one. Whilst few will dispute its success in dealing with violence in Ulster, many will point to disquiet over the manner in which this was achieved and at what cost. Defenders of the force may, with some justification, attribute some of its shortcomings to 'external' failings, including the considerable delay in handing over security powers to the new northern administration and the uncertainty and undermining of confidence which this produced.[49] The ongoing political uncertainty relating to the new administration in Belfast and to the Boundary Commission, aligned to problems about channels of communication between political and administrative authorities in London, Dublin Castle and Belfast as well as between the military and police in the north, did little either to lift the morale of serving policemen, regular or USC, or that of the population of the new state.[50] However, this should not camouflage the fundamental image problem suffered by the new force and the breaches of discipline committed by a small number of police personnel, albeit not solely from the Special Constabulary. Whilst its infamous reputation was the product of an amalgam of rumour and truth, the consequences of this were profound. Although they were essential for ushering in the safe birth of N Ireland, their reputation as the pariahs of the Catholic subconscious, was to mitigate against the development of the new state. Thus, Craig's 'midwife' was to disappoint in its immediate post-natal care.

Chapter 6

Lull in the storm

QUIETER DAYS

The city was to experience an extended period of comparative calm, which, apart from a few significant incidents, was to prevail for nearly six months. Thus, there were only four cases of people being fatally wounded in terror attacks in Belfast during the final quarter of the year.[1] Despite the welcome response to a prolonged period of comparative tranquillity, the city remained tense and intermittent street disturbances and sniping were reported in a number of areas. A heavy security presence and the repercussions of curfew restrictions were the main explanations for this reduction in the level of violence. This in itself did not precipitate an overnight return to normality. Whilst many of the centres of entertainment doggedly remained open, the last trams to the suburbs left at nine in the evening, with all places of entertainment closing half an hour later. Therefore, by 10.30 p.m., a *Daily Express* reporter noted how the city's streets were 'deserted except for parties of police with carbine slung on shoulder and revolver on hip, and posts of soldiers in steel helmets with bayonets fixed.'[2]

This underlying tension, influenced by events elsewhere in Ireland and sparked off by apparently trivial events, resulted in two brief, but bloody, outbursts of violence in separate districts during October. On Saturday 16 October, a Catholic who had just been evicted from his home in a loyalist district of north Belfast was, despite being accompanied by police and a soldier, attacked by a mob. Though there were no serious injuries, the nationalist response was swift. Many Catholics, some of them reportedly armed, returned to the area but were thwarted by the arrival of a military vehicle. Although they managed to contain the situation for a short time, large crowds of loyalists attending a football match at Cliftonville's Solitude ground were fired upon by nationalists. Military reinforcements arrived and in crossfire between the military and nationalist gunmen, three Protestants were killed. They were John Gibson (52), a riveter from Bryson Place, ex-soldier William Mitchell (25), a shipyard plater, from Downing Street, who had just returned from inviting his mother to the christening of his baby and Matthew McMaster (39), a shipyard stager. The latter case was especially tragic. Mr McMaster, a father of eight and another former soldier with experience of both Boer and Great Wars, had been returning from the match at Solitude. In his rush to get his children to safety, he was struck by a military armoured vehicle and crushed.[3] Just over a week later, following the death of hunger-striking Cork Mayor, Terence McSwiney in London's Brixton Gaol, a flag-waving altercation involving republicans in Short Strand led to disturbances in the Foundry Street area. During these, a Protestant rope-works labourer, Joseph McLeod (22) from Church Street East, received gunshot wounds to his head and died on his way to the Royal Victoria Hospital.[4]

November and December were even more tranquil. Notwithstanding an outburst of violence in Derry on 7/8 November, the north's premier city was fortunate in not experiencing a single major shooting incident or widespread rioting. This is not to deny that Belfast's citizens felt completely at ease with one another. Minor disturbances were reported in the Old Lodge Road and Clifton Street area on the afternoon of Sunday 7th November. There were also disturbances in the Lepper Street area and windows were broken at a school in Duncairn Gardens on 17 November. An example of the delayed danger caused by street disturbances was the tragedy which occurred at a spirit grocery in the Beersbridge Road area. The Catholic-owned premises at the corner of Hanbury and Canton Streets had been wrecked in recent violence, but on 9 November, an outside wall suddenly collapsed, killing a boy playing beside it and injuring three others.

'LICKING OUR WOUNDS'

The city's Catholic community used the lull in violence to contemplate the enormity of the events which had occurred since the summer and to plan for what promised to be even more difficult days lying ahead. Although partly reassured that the boycott campaign was gathering momentum in the border areas and in parts of the south, the city's minority community's natural capacity for self-help was being sorely tested by financial problems aggravated by industrial expulsion and eviction from homes. Their spiritual leader, Bishop MacRory, was aggrieved by the victimisation his community had to suffer and admitted his deep anguish at such persecution. He lamented that 'every day brings me powerful evidence of the widespread and bitter destitution'.[5] Not only was the bishop coming to terms with the extent of economic distress being experienced by his flock, but he was also growing increasingly irritated by the lack of governmental progress in addressing the practical dilemmas posed by Catholics' continuing exclusion from their workplace. In a letter to the committee of the Belfast Expelled Workers' Fund, he asserted that, seventeen weeks after the initial exclusions, the authorities had 'not moved a finger ... to have our victimised workers restored to their work.'[6] Condemning the 'intolerant claim of the Belfast bigots' that 'only workers of certain religious or political brands should be afforded the opportunity to earn their living as contrary to all principles of trade unionism', MacRory attested they would 'continue to protest until it [the pledge] is withdrawn'.[7]

Realising that such destitution could not be speedily eliminated at home, Bishop MacRory turned his attention to foreign audiences. In a Christmas appeal to Cardinal O'Connell, the Archbishop of Boston, Bishop MacRory reminded American Catholics that approximately 10,000 of their co-religionists in Belfast, along with 40,000 dependents, still did not have jobs or even access to unemployment allowances. In a letter rich with political undertone, MacRory begged his American colleague:

> Fully 50,000 Catholics are now on the verge of starvation in my Diocese which is no longer in Ireland, not even in Ulster, for that historic province has been mutilated, but in the Nameless Satrapate made up of the six amputated counties. Could your Eminence see your way to make known the dire straits of my persecuted people to the generous Catholics of America?[8]

Poignant appeals such as this were clearly effective in reaching a wider, more sympathetic external audience, and a substantial number of contributions, mainly from America, was reaching Belfast's Catholics early in the conflict. Apart from external aid, Belfast Catholics helped each other. The Society of St Vincent de Paul staged a Christmas dinner and cinema entertainment for an estimated 10,000 children at St Mary's Hall on Christmas Day. However, the generosity of co-religionists both in Belfast and further afield could only partly address the repercussions of recent expulsions. Therefore, as harsh wintry weather emerged, many Catholic homeless were plunged into abject poverty. The plight of such homeless could be a harrowing experience for the onlooker:

> On a winter's night in the first year of the pogrom a witness passing through Cupar Street told how his attention was drawn by the feeble lighting emerging from the charred remains of what was once a house. Inside a tallow light was burning; a pot holding a fire was suspended from the roof, some 4' or 5' from the ground, and about a dozen men or women were hanging about it. One could notice in the dimly lighted corners children asleep on the straw patches – wood had been provided by a charity organisation.[9]

Although loyalists were relieved by the subsidence in violence, they were still concerned by political developments and events elsewhere in Ireland. Therefore, the unionist press diverted the attention of their readers to other issues, including the economic boycott of Ulster, recruitment to the Special Constabulary, the progress of the Government of Ireland Bill and also to events outside Ireland, including the opening of the Tomb of the Unknown Soldier at Westminster Abbey. With the absence of local 'horror' stories, the *Belfast Telegraph* devoted substantial column inches to 'Dublin's Day of Horrors' when 28 people were killed and to the series of IRA arson attacks in Cork during December.[10] Scape-goating extraneous enemies like Sinn Féin was an essential ingredient of unionist propaganda and the *Newsletter* castigated both 'the murder gang under de Valera's control' and the British government for conducting negotiations with 'outlaws against civilisation.'[11] The repercussions of the activities of such 'outlaws' for those living in the north was constantly emphasised in the loyalist press, where it was trumpeted that the new northern police auxiliary force, the Specials, would form 'a very valuable adjunct to the regular forces of the crown', as well as providing 'an additional safeguard for the protection of the lives and prosperity of the citizens.'[12] Another concern for loyalists was threats directed at both Protestant workers who were free to earn their weekly wage and and factory owners for staying open whilst a substantial number of workers were prevented from carrying out their duties. Fred Crawford was one such businessman. His Millfield factory was 'the only firm who have kept open in the district' and threats to burn it down were received. Some of Crawford's workers were handed revolvers for their own 'protection' and the UVF chief, who had himself been threatened on several occasions, ensured he was always alert to possible attack. He wrote in his diary:

> When going through their [RC] district I keep my automatic pistol handy and a sharp lookout for strangers and if I see strangers loafing about I immediately push back the safety lever on the pistol and get my hand on it in my pocket that I can have it out in a moment.[13]

LLOYD GEORGE'S CHRISTMAS BOX

The people of Belfast and Ulster were to receive a seasonal present from the British premier. The Better Government of Ireland Bill, which was to underpin the framework of partition, passed its Final Reading in the House of Lords on 23 December.[14] The 'Partition' Bill, as it was dubbed by its opponents, had been introduced in the Commons nearly ten months before and its parliamentary passage had been long and contentious. The British administration, anxious to produce a compromise political solution to the Irish crisis, believed that nationalists would be more prepared to accept two Irish parliaments, rather than simply exempting Ulster from the legislation. They also promised that, by granting fairly extensive local powers to each of these new parliaments they would, in effect, be absorbing themselves from future culpability for specific events. Ulster Unionists, likely to reign supreme in a parliament bereft of active nationalist or republican representation, were persuaded into accepting that such an institution would be beneficial for their own interests. The legislation contained many of the features of the third home rule bill which had been introduced to the Commons in April 1912, including the transfer of responsibility for many services from Westminster to the new regional parliaments in Dublin and Belfast, and the subordinate status of these administrations to the Imperial Parliament.[15] Westminster was to remain responsible for many significant 'excepted' areas, including the Crown, foreign policy, external trade, the armed services, the Post Office, coinage, income tax and customs and excise duties on manufactures were to continue to be paid into the British Consolidated Fund.[16] At the same time, control over a plethora of areas, including law and order, local government, education, agriculture, industry and local trade, was delegated to the local administration.

What was different about this new measure was the application of home rule to six counties of the Ulster province, an area which had previously, of course, been most vociferous in its opposition to such a principle. Now Belfast was to have its own parliament, elected under the single transferable voting system of proportional representation and implicit within the legislative and constitutional nuances of this complex statute was the principle that Ireland would eventually be united within the monarchical state.[17] One of the most controversial features of the bill, especially as far as loyalists were concerned, was the Council of Ireland clause, which from their perspective, suggested that the bill might be regarded as erecting a 'bridge' which would lead towards ultimate Irish unity.[18]

Untypically this flurry of political activity towards the end of 1920 was accompanied by a decline in sectarian violence. However, the degree of interest which Belfast's citizens had in the political debate surrounding the impending legislation was high. As the details of the new bill were unravelled, deconstructed and carefully packaged by the propagandists of various parties, people's attitudes to the forthcoming political changes and new institutions were also to be modified. Therefore, loyalists' initial apprehension about a political package appearing to offer what they had consistently opposed and the apparent abandonment of over 100,000 southern unionists, was gradually replaced by a grudging acceptance of the proposed legislation, accompanied by a belief it was their 'duty' to do so. It was this mood of obligation and political compromise which was to prove to be the public face of unionism's defence of the legislation although other, more altruistic, factors were also important. Many loyalists gradually realised the true potential of the bill and how it might bolster their position. The brother of the new northern premier, Captain Charles Craig, gave voice to some of these points in Parliament during debates on the bill. In upbeat mood, Charles Craig argued:

> We would much prefer to remain part and parcel of the United Kingdom ... But we have many enemies in this country, and we feel that Ulster without a parliament of its own would not be in nearly as strong a position as one in which a parliament had been set up, where the executive had been appointed and all the paraphernalia of government was already in existence.[19]

The proposed measure met with a markedly more hostile response from nationalists. Joe Devlin was convinced about the 'abandonment' of the new state's Catholic minority, arguing the region's estimated 340,000 Catholics would be placed 'at the mercy of the protestant majority in the North of Ireland.'[20] The west Belfast representative suggested that they would be the obligatory sacrifice on the alter of political compromise. Referring to the considerable powers to be invested in any unionist administration, Devlin asked:

> What will we get when they are armed with Britain's rifles, when they are clothed with the authority of government, when they have cast round them the Imperial garb; what mercy, what pity, much less justice or liberty, will be conceded to us then?[21]

In an earlier parliamentary debate, Devlin had condemned the 'ridiculous' nature of the bill, castigating its designers, especially Lloyd George, for 'changing the geography of Ireland.'[22] This was a theme developed in the columns of the nationalist press, especially after the bill became law. The *Irish News*, in its initial response to the new legislation, queried the word 'better' in its title, arguing it was rather 'a plan devised by unscrupulous politicians to assassinate Ireland's Nationality.'[23] The paper's editorial alleged 'a more ghastly "Christmas gift" was never thrust on our Nation', but ended more optimistically, suggesting the 'glorious vision of Irish unity would yet become an actual achievement'.[24] Sections of the British liberal press also expressed concern over the precarious position of Ulster's Catholics, interpreting the act as a legislative 'sop' to unionism. The pro-unity *Nation* argued that the bill had been designed to meet 'the aggrandisement of the Ulster Unionists' and denounced the measure for providing 'no protection at all' to the large Catholic minority in the region.[25] However, other papers were more optimistic about the prospects of the new legislation. The *Times* was keenly aware of the significance of the new Act and said the 'indifference' which it produced in Great Britain was 'wholly out of keeping with its great and far-reaching importance'.[26] The *Times* editorial concluded on a cautiously optimistic note:

> If, therefore, in the new circumstances of Ireland, the mood of her people should soften, the new Act may prove, far sooner than could have been expected six months ago, the basis on which a lasting settlement can be built.[27]

Other British papers were also supportive of the new legislation, although their rationale for doing so differed from that of the *Times*. Some editorials called for the combination of a forceful security policy throughout Ireland with a more conciliatory approach to settling its political problems. Thus, the *Daily Chronicle* backed the measure largely on account of its belief that it would end violence, especially in the south and west of Ireland. During the Bill's final stages in the Lords, the *Chronicle* maintained 'the sooner it becomes law, the better for peace in Ireland', as the proposed legislation promised to 'cut away . . . from under the feet of those in the southern provinces who seek their ends by violent means.'[28]

'Relief' and 'thankfulness' were the chief loyalist responses to the Bill's passing.[29] The *Belfast Telegraph* compared it favourably with the pre-war home rule legislation, saying the threat of the latter would 'no longer haunt us' and also expressed their 'thankfulness that the right of Ulster to separate treatment and to be arbiters of her political testimony is now recognised in fact and by Act of Parliament'.[30] Ordinary loyalists were confused by the creation of a rather grandiose parliamentary system with its imperial trappings and whilst they retained confidence in their political leadership and the increased power they would inherit under the new constitutional arrangements, there was a growing feeling that the military threat posed to Ulster by the IRA was more immediate and real than any political uncertainty. The *Irish News* were dismissive of the legislation, suggesting that any rejoicing over the 'dismemberment' of the Act of Union would be muted as 'the undoing of this crime of 1800 has been accomplished by the commissioning of a still more odious deed.'[31]

Real Christmas presents soon harnessed the attention of a Belfast public, reassured to some degree by the decline in street disturbances. The big city stores latched on to the changing mood of their beleaguered public and, funding several pages of advertisements in the local press, proudly announced discounts of up to 25% on a range of practical Christmas gifts.[32] Elsewhere, Anderson and McCauley were selling boys' overcoats for 25s. 6d., whilst the suburban firm, Prices, were reducing the cost of winter underwear in their Mountpottinger storerooms.[33] At the other end of the price range, the Royal Avenue based International Fur House proudly proclaimed they were selling beaver furs at 45 guineas and 'large skunkwrap caps' between 35 and 70 guineas.[34] As Christmas approached, Belfast folk, whilst remaining ever-vigilant, proceeded to converge once again on the busy shopping thoroughfares of their compact centre, eagerly searching for appropriate presents for their loved ones, not to mention those ever elusive bargains. The people of Belfast were able to enjoy the seasonal pleasures of visiting Father Christmas at Robinson and

Cleavers, watching a Chaplin movie in a picture-house or taking in a pantomime at one of the city's numerous theatres or music-halls. On their way home, as their tram eased its way past the brightly illuminated City Hall, the angelic singing of carols by school children would have cheered their hearts and eliminated any lingering doubts over the possible return of political and communal conflict.[35] Belfast, like the rest of the world, was at peace with itself.

1921

'To Forgive and Forget'

'... I appeal to all Irishmen to pause, to stretch out the hand of forbearance and reconciliation, to forgive and forget, and to join in making for the land they love a new era of peace, contentment and good will.'

King George V,
opening the Northern Ireland Parliament, 22 June 1921

Chapter 7

Return to reality

MURDER IN RODDY'S BAR

Despite the significant reduction in the level of violence during the last quarter of 1920, there had been genuine feelings of apprehension and concern permeating throughout the entire community. People had made a conscious effort to enjoy Christmas and the annual sales attracted the usual high numbers of customers. The Bank Buildings proudly announced 'multitudinous bargains' awaiting their customers, whilst the Robinson and Cleaver sale was also boasting reductions of up to 50% and 'record bargains' galore.[1] However, especially in the evenings after Christmas, the city became quieter, primarily because of curfew restrictions which 'wrapped the streets in silence'.[2] On New Year's Eve, the streets were busy until ten o'clock but were deserted long before midnight. Sirens were sounded as the Albert Clock struck twelve and at the Salvation Army Citadel in York Street, an all night prayer vigil was held. The *Belfast Telegraph* lamented the 'strenuous and strange times' Belfast's citizens were living in, observing that neither 'the solemnity of the midnight hour in the watchnight service nor hilarity in the streets were possible.'[3] Despite its cautious welcome to the new legislation and the reduction in the levels of street violence, the *Northern Whig's* advice to its readers was not to 'discard the vigilance and the unity that have hitherto characterised them.'[4] The mood of the *Irish News* was gloomy as it described the start of the New Year as 'opening for Ireland about as sadly and gloomily as the year that began twelve decades ago.'[5] Although major disturbances were averted, the city was not completely trouble-free. Two policemen were fired at on the New Lodge Road on New Year's Eve and a disorderly crowd, reportedly singing republican songs, were dispersed in York Street on New Year's Day.[6] However, the more relaxed atmosphere resulted in the Belfast public diverting its attention to pending increases in tram fares and the reported reduction in profits for the city's Harbour Authority.[7]

This relatively calm start to the year was to be a protracted one, with only two major, related incidents occurring during the first two months of 1921.

These happened towards the end of January and the first showed the IRA's capacity for accurate intelligence-gathering and execution of daring attacks was still potent. Daring it certainly was, occurring close to the Musgrave Street police headquarters. Three members of the RIC's Reserve Force, attached to the Phoenix Park Depot in Dublin, had been sent to Belfast where one of them, Constable Gilmartin, was due to give evidence at a trial involving an IRA man accused of killing a RIC officer in Tipperary two months previously. The three officers were staying at the Central Railway Hotel, known locally as 'Roddy's Bar' and a popular stop for commercial travellers, which was situated at the corner of Townhall Street and Oxford Street. No doubt reassured by the hotel's proximity to the Musgrave Street barracks, the southern policemen retired to their rooms during the mid evening of 26 January. Shortly before ten o'clock, five men who had been drinking in a 'snug' near the bar, made their way up the stairs to the top floor where the RIC officers were asleep. Forcing their way into the officers' rooms, several shots were fired, with Constables Thomas Heffron (26) and Michael Quinn (20) dying instantly. The attackers forced their way past startled drinkers in the bar and made their escape. A barman ran the short distance to the police barracks to raise the alarm and the seriously injured Constable Gilmartin was rushed to the military hospital at Victoria Barracks.

The unionist press were furious about the 'premeditated' nature of the attack, hinting that the officers' movements had obviously been spotted by hotel patrons or barstaff and information duly passed on to the IRA.[8] The *Northern Whig* gave voice to the 'great indignation' which was being felt by many loyalists that 'such a cold-blooded murder of responsible officers of the law should have taken place in loyal Belfast.'[9] That evening the *Belfast Telegraph* also condemned the 'cold-blooded atrocity' which they affirmed had been 'deliberately planned' and 'perpetuated with that thoroughness which has come to be associated with the Sinn Féin campaign of assassination.'[10]

The loyalist response was swift. A few hours after the hotel murders, a chemist's assistant, Michael McGarvey, who was lodging at a house in Bray Street, off the Crumlin Road, was shot dead in his bed. Three assailants had used a latchkey to gain access to the house and, ignoring the calls of Mr McGarvey's Protestant landlady, Mrs Morgan, opened his door and shot him three times. The distraught landlady rushed to his aid screaming, 'You have murdered the boy!'[11] Within a short time a police detachment arrived in Bray Street and removed the body. An interesting feature of this murder was the way in which rival papers concurred on its premeditated nature and its likely links to the RIC killings a few hours earlier. The *Northern Whig* noted how Armagh-born McGarvey had been 'done to death with such thoroughness as to suggest complete knowledge of the victim's habitation and his movements'.[12] Nationalist opinion, however, had considerable reservations both about the origins and accuracy of such 'knowledge'. A belief that certain police officers, seeking revenge for the 'Roddy's Bar' attack, had been responsible for the Bray Street murder surfaced during the McGarvey inquest at Victoria Barracks on 23 March. At this, Mrs Morgan described the 'leisurely' departure of the three assassins from her house and how, ignoring her screaming, they had met up and chatted with another group of men on the Crumlin Road before leaving in a car. This suggested to many that the assailants perceived themselves to be above the law and rumours circulated that senior police personnel, including Richard Harrison and John Nixon were involved in this attack.[13]

Whilst serious violence was not to reoccur until March, there were several robberies and occasional street disturbances at this time.[14] One such 'audacious hold-up' occurred in Divis Street where six men stopped the work of phone-repairers, stealing their kitbags.[15] Of more serious concern was an incident a few days later when shipyard employees were attacked leaving their work. According to the *Northern Whig*, 'a rather serious riot', involving revolver fire and stone throwing, occurred in the Dock Street area, where it was alleged the confrontation commenced.[16] Although army vehicles eventually arrived and soldiers dispersed the crowds, sporadic disturbances continued intermittently until curfew.

'ANOTHER IRELAND IN THE NORTH'

During the break in the violence, unionists were able to turn their thoughts partly to events elsewhere in Ireland and also to making plans for the difficult times which inevitably lay ahead. Although there were relatively few security incidents in Belfast during the winter months, there was considerable activity elsewhere and the loyalist press was scathing in its criticism of the perceived orchestrators of such violence. Attacks on police near Newry, the killing of a police auxiliary in Dublin, the shooting of a RIC officer and a postman in County Armagh, a number of shootings in Cork and Dublin, the killing of 7 policemen in County Clare and 4 other security fatalities towards the end of the month confirmed unionist fears that their enemies had not disappeared.[17] The

particular plight of the Protestant minority in Ireland's south-west was highlighted by the case of a County Cork farmer, John Bradfield. The *Belfast
Telegraph*'s report, 'Cork loyalists' peril', described how the Bandon farmer had
been 'tried' by republicans and found 'guilty' of intention to provide information about the movements of republicans to the Crown forces. The report
detailed his final predicament:

> It now transpires that two days before his death Bradfield was visited by
> six men in military uniform whom he took for being British. He enter-
> tained them to tea, and, in the course of conversation mentioned a
> forthcoming ambush which had come to his knowledge. These men
> have turned out to be Sinn Féiners in disguise.[18]

The suffering of Protestants at the hands of the IRA elsewhere in Ireland
proved, of course, to be an issue of considerable concern to Belfast unionists. A
few months later, the *Telegraph* reported on an exodus of hundreds of Protestants
from southern Ireland to Canada, Britain and Ulster. Noting how they had
received countless letters from southern loyalists who wrote 'with sad hearts [to
say] that they had arranged to leave the country', despairing of how 'intimidation, coercion [and] violence have been employed against them.'[19] Estimations
of the scale of the intimidation on their kinsmen in the south abounded in
unionist circles. One loyalist propaganda pamphlet claimed, early in 1921, that 'if
the figures of removal of Protestants during the past six months were known they
would cause a sensation'.[20] Attention was also drawn to the plight of those loyalists, closer to hand, who had been forced to relocate following the summer riots.
Whilst the bulk of people evicted were mainly Catholic, the organisation of a
fund to alleviate hardship amongst working class Protestants indicates that such
intimidation was not completely one-sided. A Loyalist Relief Fund, co-ordinated
by a Joint Committee representing the Ulster Unionist Labour Association and
the Ulster Unionist Council, was formed on 19 January 1921 and inside 48 hours
had received 762 applications for assistance.[21] In the absence of direct republican
activity in Greater Belfast, the unionist press devoted generous space to allegations of a 'plot', involving Sinn Féin and Germany during the Great War. Details
of duplicity between the Kaiser and Sinn Féin leaders in 1916 were released to the
press in January and the *Belfast Telegraph* maintained the revelations 'speak for
themselves as to the complicity of Sinn Féin and its active and guilty relationship
with Germany at a crucial period in the war.'[22]

Politically it was quite an eventful winter for Belfast's loyalist community. They continued to digest the implications of the Government of Ireland Act, with unionist papers attacking, in turn, southern hostility to the recent legislation and the reluctance of northern nationalists to participate in the new parliament. The *Northern Whig* incredulously suggested that 'one of the first results of setting up an Ulster Parliament and its successful operation will be to make Southern Ireland begin to ask whether it is not cutting off its nose to spite its face in persisting in its present insane attitude.'[23] In another of a series of leading articles devoted to the recent legislation, the *Whig* castigated the reluctance of the nationalist leadership to participate in the new northern Parliament, promising that such a new body could 'go forward and do its work whether the Nationalist electorate co-operates or stands aside, and we cannot imagine any section in Ulster itself who are in any doubt about the matter.'[24] Unionists also started turning their attention towards the selection of a leader who would inevitably become Prime Minister of the new state. Ill health meant that Sir Edward Carson, the natural choice for the new post, was ruled out of consideration. Speculation over the new job intensified on the eve of Carson meeting UUC representatives in London on 25 January. The *Northern Whig* appeared to accept that 'a break with the past might be in the offing'. An editorial said of Sir Edward:

> However he decides he may feel assured that he will always have the affection and gratitude of Ulster, just as we ... do not doubt that in one capacity or another his help and guidance will always be at our disposal in the future as in the past.[25]

Carson was to visit Belfast early in February to formally resign his leadership of the UUP. He addressed an enthusiastic meeting of Duncairn Unionists in the north of the city and his visit was welcomed with 'genuine pleasure and satisfaction' by his audience and Belfast's loyalist community.[26] In his Duncairn speech, Carson referred to the violence in the south of Ireland and compared the two parts of the island:

> What is going on in the south and west of Ireland almost makes a man ashamed of being an Irishman ... But thank God, there is another Ireland in the North [cheers] – another Ireland which sees that its closest, its truest interests are bound up with Great Britain.[27]

Unlike the clamouring in the loyalist press, both the 'old' and the 'new' leadership of the Unionist Party urged for the emergence of a new spirit of reconciliation to accompany the new political institutions. Speaking to the UUC in Belfast, Carson urged his colleagues to ensure that Catholics had 'nothing to fear from the Protestant majority' and, in urging them to 'win' over political opponents, he exhorted them to 'give the same rights to the religion of our neighbours.'[28] His future successor as leader of the Unionist party, Sir James Craig, speaking a few days later at the Belfast Reform Club, also made an apparently genuine plea for tolerance in the new parliament instigated by the legislation which he claimed was proving to be 'a brilliant prospect' for Ulster. Craig reminded his audience:

> Remember that the rights of the minority must be sacred to the majority and that it will only be by broad views, tolerant ideas and a real desire for liberty of conscience that we here can make an ideal of the Parliament and the Executive.[29]

'THE SO-CALLED ULSTER DIFFICULTY'

Nationalists were, of course, not persuaded by such rhetoric, and instead used the breathing-space afforded by the improved security situation to regroup and exhibit their own political muscle. A series of 'unprecedented' meetings were staged in venues such as St Mary's Hall and the Tivoli Cinema in west Belfast on Sunday 13 February. Speakers included Joe Devlin, who suggested they should 'spurn the temptation to yield up our confidence in our nation's glorious future or to shed a scintilla of the courage that has brought us through the trials and perils of the past.'[30] In a more positive vein, the West Belfast M.P. reminded his audience that nationalist organisation in the city had 'never been in a better condition than at the present.'[31] However, he was also concerned that his supporters should not be complacent nor react in a fitful manner to events in the rest of Ireland. Speaking at a convention of Ulster nationalists organised at St Mary's Hall on 4 April, Devlin urged his supporters to adopt a more aggressive approach so that 'whatever happens in the 26 counties from North Donegal to South Cork, we must prepare to take our own part in the struggle against the destruction of our country which is to be waged in the North East.'[32] Whilst Devlin and his supporters had to contemplate the practical consequences of political separation, de Valera and his southern colleagues perceived the recent legislation to be a temporary irritant and therefore focussed on attacking Britain's culpability for such a measure, rather than empathise with northern nationalists who would soon have to endure its repercussions. Speaking to American journalists at this time, de Valera surmised:

> The so-called Ulster difficulty is purely artificial as far as Ireland itself is concerned. It is an accident arising out of the British connection and will disappear with it. If it arose from a genuine desire of the people of the North East corner for autonomy, the solution proposed would be the obvious one. But it is not due to such a desire-it has arisen purely as a product of British Party manoeuvring.[33]

The nationalist press combined a critical attack on the Unionist leadership with a clear statement of its political hopes for the future. Although the *Irish News* informed its readers that 'Carsonism' had 'vanished nominally', the Irish people would have 'bitter reason to regret its invention and its baleful existence for many a trying day to come.'[34] Part of this Carsonian legacy, what they described as 'anti Catholic bigotry', would form the 'basis of the appeal' of unionism to the electorate in the forthcoming election. The paper forecasted that the 'right Orange' parliamentary candidates would observe 'the hand of the Pope in every suggestion that the Ascendancy does not approve.'[35] A month later, the same paper was to clearly articulate its political position, asserting 'we stand for *Ireland undivided and free*, and that it is not a policy of destruction but the only form of constructive patriotism that some men in this country can sanction and support.'[36]

SPRING VIOLENCE

The IRA again showed their capacity to strike unexpectedly when they murdered three police auxiliaries in the city centre on 11 March. Constable Walter Cooper, originally from Surrey, Constable Robert Crooks from Cornwall, and Constable John McIntosh, from Inverness, had arrived in the city the previous day from Gormanston with the task of driving military vehicles back to their depot.[37] At around 8.30 p.m., while on foot patrol in Victoria Square, they stopped near the Empire music-hall to talk to a girl, Agnes

Murphy. At that moment, the three auxiliaries were approached by up to five gunmen who fired at them several times. Constables Crooks and McIntosh were killed instantly and Constable Cooper died of chest wounds in the Royal Victoria Hospital two days later. Two civilians, Miss Murphy and Alexander Allen were also injured in the shooting and Mr Allen, a Protestant, of Austin Street, died later in hospital.[38] Predictably there was a heavy military response with raids on homes and pubs the following day in search of weapons. Although there were no reprisal attacks, minor skirmishes were reported in the Short Strand during the next two days.

Although loyalists proclaimed stronger allegiance towards the regular police and the new Specials than they did for 'mercenary' forces like the Black and Tans, the shooting of these officers clearly hightened anxiety in the city. This was evident in the Great George's Street area on 19th March. Minor disturbances led to the shooting of two men around teatime the following day.[39] One of these was John Graham (35), a Catholic from Emily Place, who was seriously wounded and died in the Mater Hospital on 21 March. Mr Graham was believed to have been sitting in his home when the disturbances started and rushed out to fetch his children who had been playing in Great George's Street. A few minutes later he staggered back to his home, having sustained a severe abdomen wound. He was taken to hospital in a fire tender which had been called to the scene. At his inquest, it was concluded that his injuries had been received during the rioting but not from shots fired by the police.

Trouble was to flare up again in the York Street area following news of the shootings of two Protestants in Rosslea, County Fermanagh, on 22 March and, more locally, following Mr Graham's funeral the following day. Street disturbances were quickly followed by an exchange of gunfire which led to the death of Annie Jamison, a Catholic from Moffat Street and the wounding of Robert McCracken who lived in Vere Street. The former had been shopping when she was struck in the head by a bullet which many believed had come from a loyalist area. Mr McCracken was wounded going to her aid. However, it was two Catholic brothers, George and John McKeown, of Grove Street, who were accused of Miss Jamison's murder.[40] Despite the charged atmosphere which followed news of her death, the authorities managed to restore an uneasy calm to the district, mainly by sustaining a constant vehicular presence in the area until curfew. However, rioting was renewed on 24 March in Vere Street, with the IRA reportedly 'invading' the district, continually firing from North Queen Street. Although there were no further injuries, a Special

Constable had a lucky escape when he was shot in this area, but bullets passed through his tunic.

Wintry weather spoiled the holiday period for many but at least it cleared trouble-makers from the streets and the city enjoyed relative peace during the early Easter break.[41] However, tension was still prevalent in the city's side-streets and republican activity was far from muted. Therefore, a military sentry was slightly wounded guarding the entrance to Crumlin Road gaol and a bomb exploded in the Springfield Road police barracks during the evening of 13 April, fortunately claiming no casualties. Routine robberies continued to be committed by the IRA, though not all of these proved to be successful. A 'daring daylight robbery' was attempted on the Falls Road during the afternoon of 5 April.[42] Five armed men held up a Corporation wages clerk who had £600 in his possession, but they were thwarted by the official's 'stubborn refusal' to hand over the wages and the timely arrival of a couple of detectives. Three of the would-be 'highwaymen' were arrested after a car chase across the Bog Meadows.[43] Sectarian tension was also evident in the east of the city where there were reports of street 'invasions' into the Short Strand, with shooting breaking out in Foundry Street where a teenage boy suffered an ankle wound. The reduction in the levels of violence increased the temptation for some to breach the curfew restrictions. This was possibly the case with Charles Nicholson, a 28-year-old Protestant, who was killed on the Albertbridge Road on 20 April. Mr Nicholson had been 'lifted' by the security forces during curfew hours and it was claimed he had fallen from the cage-lorry and been crushed under the vehicle's wheels. A verdict of 'accidental death' was later recorded at the inquest, but it was suggested that the evidence of military personnel had been contradictory.

Widespread violence returned to the city during a weekend towards the end of April. Another spectacular IRA attack on auxiliary policemen was mounted in the city centre during the evening of Saturday 23 April. Two English-born Tans, part of a detachment of 12 based in Sligo, were patrolling in the city centre which was crowded with weekend revellers, shortly after nine o'clock. Two men approached them in Donegall Place, near the corner of Fountain Lane and opened fire on the officers. The IRA gunmen ran back towards Fountain Lane but a passing RIC detective fired after them. Shots were returned by the auxiliaries' assailants and in the crossfire tram passenger Ruth Galston and pedestrian Thomas Kennedy were wounded. Cadet Ernest Bolam (34), originally from Kent, died at the scene and his colleague, Cadet John Bales (23), another ex-soldier with a distinguished war record and a native of Norfolk, died in the Royal Victoria Hospital the next day.[44] The *Irish News* report of the shooting illustrates the utter confusion and horror caused by such outrages in city streets. It read:

> The loud reports of the revolvers, coupled with the shooting of women, caused a stampede of the multitudes of people in Donegall Place, Castle Street and the adjoining thoroughfares and by-streets. The section of the crowd in Donegall Place, nearest the point where the shooting took place rushed in all directions, and, regardless of the passing vehicular traffic, endangered their lives in seeking shelter in shops or on board passing trams.[45]

The response of the security forces was swift. Police and the unfortunate auxiliaries' colleagues dashed up Royal Avenue, and motor vehicles were stopped and houses raided during the early curfew hours. Direct retaliation for the killings of the Tans was carried out inside three hours, probably by the gang of 'rogue cops' associated with Inspector Nixon.[46] In this particular instance, the victims of the revenge attack were not randomly selected. Both of the brothers who were targeted in this raid had strong republican connections.[47] The murder gang, four strong and wearing trench-coats, called at 64, Clonard Gardens in the Falls area just before midnight. Patrick Duffin (28), a teacher at St Paul's School and his brother Daniel (24), an unemployed clerk and IRA officer, were the only members of the family not in bed as they opened the door.[48] At least six shots were fired into the brothers' bodies as they stood petrified in the kitchen. Another brother, John, was brushed aside by the gunmen and found his brothers dying downstairs.[49]

Soon after the lifting of the curfew restriction a crowd gathered in Clonard Gardens. DI Ferris, a Catholic RIC officer, and soon to become a victim of violence himself, had requested the removal of the bodies by the police but was advised this would not have been well received by a growing, hostile crowd. Instead, the police removed a dog from the house, one which was familiar to many in the waiting crowd. This animal, which had been cowering behind furniture in the kitchen, was said to belong to Christy Clarke, another Catholic policeman to be subsequently targeted by republicans. For the crowd gathered around the Duffin home, this identified a clear link in the attack. The following day, the *Irish News* asked the question, 'Who owned the dog?' declaring they found its presence in the Duffin home a 'mystery', but concluded, 'the inference is that it accompanied the men who shot the brothers.'[50] Thousands attended the brothers' funerals on the morning of Wednesday 27 April. The coffins, draped in tricolours and accompanied by marching ranks of the IRA, proceeded down the Falls Road, past Divis Street and made its way up the Antrim Road towards the family graveyard in Glenravel, County Antrim. A sizeable number of clerics defiantly joined IRA volunteers at the front of the cortege. Bishop MacRory gave the graveside oration and in an apparent endorsement of the republican campaign, assured the young men's grieving father, 'You should be a proud man to have reared such splendid specimen of Irish manhood.'[51]

Thus the upbeat mood and hopes of peace initiated by the prospect of political stability in the New Year, had been sustained for a period of several weeks. However, despite the absence of violence on the city's streets, the apprehension in both communities was palpable, fuelled as it was by political developments, such as the Government of Ireland Act. Consequently it was only a matter of time before the targeting of police led to tit-for-tat loyalist killings and a dashing of those emotive sentiments expressed during the season of goodwill. The dismantling of these hopes was followed by a hard-nosed realism fostered by the proximity of elections to a new Parliament. Again, the necessity for political change denied a divided community the opportunity of a prolonged breathing-space.

Chapter 8

Election fever

FOR BETTER GOVERNMENT?

The Better Government of Ireland Act, which had received the Royal Assent on 23 December, came into effect on 1 May. A central element of this legislation was the election of a Northern Ireland Parliament, which was to be conducted under a single transferable voting system of proportional representation. For unionists, backing a devolved administration seemed to be the antithesis of what they had held most dear, namely the governance of their area by Westminster, and persuading them otherwise proved to be a challenging task for their leaders. Thus, personal assurances from unionism's most revered figures proved invaluable and denials of betrayal were a regular feature of campaign speeches. Addressing an audience at the Ulster Hall on 10 May, the Unionist leader vowed 'never to desert' the Ulster people, assuring them he would 'never bow the knee to treachery or allow a whisper of "Republic" to enter my thoughts'.[1] Sir James Craig's considerable reputation at grassroots level proved to be instrumental in assuaging the fears of loyalists, appealing as he did to ideals such as 'devotion to the Throne, close union with Great Britain, pride in the British Empire and an earnest desire for peace throughout Ireland.'[2]

Although unionism remained solid on the constitutional issue, managing to avoid the disharmony of their opponents, the loyalist 'family' was by no means the homogeneous movement it had been during the halcyon period of the anti Home Rule campaign a decade previously. Whilst ostensibly a consensus of opinion was preserved, there were significant ripples beneath the surface, notably at grassroots level, about Sinn Féin's enduring campaign of terror and bewilderment at their leader endeavouring to sell a political package which he and his colleagues had for so long opposed.[3] The loyalist press did their best to absolve their leader from blame and suspicion, shifting the focus to other, 'guilty' parties. The *Northern Whig*, not for the first time, expressed its annoyance at the dearth of support for the unionist cause emanating from Great Britain. It complained about 'bored and weak-kneed British Unionists' who found the Irish question 'an awful bore' and pondered if Sinn Féin 'might not be quite so stiff-necked as the Ulster people made out and who thought the Ulster Unionists could be just a bit bigoted.'[4] Surely the *Whig* felt, the 'steady descent towards crude savagery' on the part of Sinn Féin would help 'even these people see things correctly.'[5]

A big fear amongst loyalist pundits and politicians was the prevalence of apathy which endangered unionist success at the polls. Some doubted if unionists were aware of the potential afforded by a new parliament and likely unionist administration. Being responsible for determining their own fortunes appealed to Ulstermen weighed down by what they regarded as the wicked intentions of others. A letter-writer to the *Northern Whig* asked if his fellow unionists realised that 'henceforth we are to be held solely responsible for our actions.'[6] However, much of the Unionist election material concentrated on traditional targets such as republicanism, the Catholic Church and socialism. Condemning the decision of socialists to stand in 4 of the Belfast constituencies and urging loyalist voters to 'have nothing to do' with these Labour candidates, the *Belfast Newsletter* suggested that 'socialism in Ireland stands for revolution and for the establishment of an independent state, just as [does] Sinn Féin.'[7] Over a week later the same paper again warned loyalists against the 'peril' of apathy, suggesting its likely consequence, a Dublin Parliament, would be 'literally without any safeguards for the protection of our religious and civil liberties against the dominant influence of the Roman Catholic Church in that Parliament.'[8] Other journals reminded their readers that, in associating itself with the economic boycott of Ulster produce, the southern press had scant regard for Belfast. The *Telegraph* condemned the attempts of papers like the *Irish Independent* to 'fan the flames of bitterness' against Ulster, which it had described the previous day as 'Ireland's enemy', urging its readers to 'realise it was their duty to beat Belfast'.[9] Condemning the Irish press for its one-dimensional application of the term 'intolerant', the *Belfast Telegraph* fumed that 'they lecture us on toleration and show their own tolerance by destroying our goods and worse.'[10]

Election 'fever' was especially evident in the working class quarters of loyalist Belfast. Thus, whilst the upper and middle classes 'clothe themselves in white and board the trams that take them to the cricket-grounds and tennis courts', loyalist workers were ready to sacrifice their more limited leisure time to participate in demonstrations and meetings arranged to arouse support for unionist candidates.[11] Utilising the invaluable network afforded by Orange lodge and marching bands, and setting off from the traditional loyalist vantage point, Carlisle Circus, just north of the city centre, large numbers of working men congregated for such an occasion on Saturday 7 May. A cacophony of sound, stemming from brass, flute and Lambeg drum-led bands drew an admiring audience of women and children. Gradually three large banners were unfurled on which were emblazoned the names of the unionist candidates for North Belfast, together with such exhortations as 'Vote for Union, Home and Empire!' Ex-soldiers, don't betray your colleagues who shed their blood!'[12] The march proceeded down side-streets and along the Shankill Road, before winding its way back to Clifton Street and Peters Hill. The onset of steady rain 'could damp neither bands nor enthusiasm and the police presence determined that there would be no untoward "incidents"'.[13] This type of meeting, with its popular 'mix' of familiar Orange tunes and cultural symbolism with more topical political slogans, was just one of several organised in Belfast during the election campaign. The unionist press and politicians ensured that the political temperature remained high during the lengthy run-up to polling day. The various papers did their 'duty' particularly towards the end of the campaign, by reminding their readers of the basic issue at stake – what they described as 'the British Empire and loyalty on the one hand, separation and disloyalty on the other' – and rallying them around the veracity of 'a sane Imperialism.'[14] On the final full day of campaigning, Unionism's icon, Sir Edward Carson visited Belfast to rally his troops. In the Assembly Hall on 22 May the ageing Unionist leader warned that 'every loyal man or woman who fails to vote, without good reason, is aiding and assisting our opponents to destroy all that has been handed down to us and which we are bound to preserve.'[15]

'UNNATURAL AND UNNATIONAL' PROPOSALS'

In contrast with this united campaign presented by Unionists, the pro-unity voice of the north's minority community was stifled, to a large degree, by internecine bickering between Devlin's United Irish League (UIL) and Sinn Féin. Despite nationalist opposition to the new Parliament, Catholic clergy and political leaders regarded the election as representing a barometer of Catholic feeling on recent constitutional developments, and the former especially pleaded with their flock to exercise their democratic right. On the eve of the election, Bishop MacRory warned northern Catholics of the potential long-term repercussions of Catholic apathy and division over recent constitutional developments:

> The character of your children's education and with it, perhaps, their eternal welfare, may depend on the result of this election. Hence, all differences between Sinn Féiners and Parliamentarians ought to be flung aside for the moment in the face of the common danger.[16]

Indeed, from the start of the campaign, MacRory and other key Catholic leaders had been demanding a semblance of nationalist unity, but this had only been partially achieved by an electoral pact between de Valera and Devlin.[17] This pact allowed for an agreed number of candidates in each constituency and for the transfer of preference votes between Sinn Féin and the UIL. Although this agreement was intended to avoid a splitting of the anti-partition vote, it was a little restrictive for some of Devlin's colleagues, who were obliged to implement a strict abstentionist policy towards the new parliamentary institutions.

Between them, Sinn Féin and the UIL fielded over 30 candidates, with several leading republican figures being nominated for mainly 'border' constituencies. They included de Valera in County Down, Collins in County Armagh, Arthur Griffith in Fermanagh and Tyrone and John MacNeil in County Derry.[18] Whilst they tended to warrant fewer paragraphs in the local press than Devlin's group, Sinn Féin ran an active campaign with several meetings organised both in Belfast and rural areas.[19] There were brief reports on a Sinn Féin election meeting in St Mary's Hall on 9 May and a large Armagh republican gathering addressed by Michael Collins and Frank Aiken on 23 May.[20] Like Devlin's nationalist colleagues, Sinn Féin attacked the principle of partition at every opportunity. Sean MacEntee addressed an open air audience in Smithfield Square on 22 May, asking his followers if they had ever witnessed such a 'paradox' as 'the cutting of a country in two in order to unite the people.'[21] De Valera's campaign combined an 'inclusive' approach involving both 'orange' and 'green' traditions, with a more aggressive, vote-winning line, which distinguished between Sinn Féin's gung-ho approach and nationalism's more accommodating one. Thus, Eamon de Valera maintained that those who voted for Sinn Féin would 'cast your vote for nothing less than legitimisation of the republic, for Ireland against England, for freedom against slavery, for right and justice against force and wrong here and everywhere.'[22]

De Valera had also been active on the diplomatic front during the election period. Less than three weeks before polling day, he had met Craig at Dublin Castle in a hastily-arranged meeting instigated by Lloyd George. The intention was to produce an agreement which would dramatically reduce the level of violence across Ireland. Concerned voices were raised in the north at Craig's acquiescence in travelling south, but the *Belfast Telegraph* advised its readers 'not to be alarmed' by the previous day's meeting.[23] The *Morning Post* also acknowledged the legitimacy of loyalist concern over Craig's meeting with de Valera at such a sensitive time, but concluded that, by trying to 'save the faithful remnant of south of Ireland Protestants ... being murdered by the friends or followers of de Valera,' Craig's decision to proceed with the talks was 'a horrible necessity.'[24] Predictably, their encounter had a negative outcome. Although they outlined their respective positions, the likelihood of even minor compromises being agreed was always slim and the respective leaders duly returned to their electioneering.[25]

In their election address, the UIL candidates condemned the 'rashly conceived, insufficiently considered proposals, which they dismissed as 'a trumpery expedient'.[26] Stressing that the partition option had not been high on the unionist agenda either, Devlin's party castigated the very principle of partition which they claimed meant 'National suicide'. The manifesto proclaimed:

> There is no thoughtful man – Nationalist or Sinn Féiner, southern unionist or Ulster Covenanter – who does not realise in his inner consciousness that the setting up of a legislative divorce between the 6 Counties and the 26 is fraught with evil alike to the North East corner and to the rest of the country. The proposal is as unnatural as it is unnational.[27]

Joe Devlin was one of the busiest speakers during the campaign. Standing both in west Belfast and Antrim, he travelled the length and breadth of Ulster in his efforts to deliver the maximum nationalist turn-out on Election Day. He addressed a crowd estimated at around 6,000 in Belfast's Mill Street on 12 May and four days later a 'magnificent' meeting involving another large audience in Derry 'cheered [him] to the echo'.[28] Perhaps Devlin's most eloquent speech of the campaign was delivered to an Ancient Order of Hibernians meeting in Ballycastle. At this, he criticised what he believed to be the unethical character of the British government's proposals and he made a passionate plea to Ulster nationalists to display in full their opposition to partition. He argued:

Providence has fashioned this land to be one and indivisible. Ireland is one, not by directive of England, but fashioned out as one race, with a single purpose and an inspiring ideal, and we are going to make an earnest, a powerful and a triumphant fight against this sacrilege upon our nation.[29]

If Devlin concentrated on the 'unnatural' nature of partition, then some of his UIL colleagues focused more on condemning their opponents' election programme. Barrister T.J. Campbell, standing in east Belfast, addressed several lively meetings, maintaining that unionists possessed 'no programme worthy of submission to progressive, free-spirited men.'[30] Attacking their lack of concern for the poor and elderly, Campbell expressed his fear that 'if the working classes were gulled by these men's catchwords about the Pope, the way would be easy to make the Ulster Parliament a citadel of capitalism and reaction.'[31] Generous press coverage was also devoted to other nationalist meetings addressed by Campbell and Frank Harkin (who was standing on north Belfast) in Oldpark, Ardoyne and Celtic Park. As ever, Devlin's views were echoed by the *Irish News*, which concentrated on the 'bankruptcy' of the new parliamentary institutions, reasserting their view that 'abiding Peace' would only be obtained when 'freedom was won.'[32] On the eve of the election, the paper made an emotional appeal to its readers, urging them to register their vote against partition:

Whoever shrinks from inconvenience, unpleasantness, or actual peril, is unworthy of the sacrifices made and the sufferings endured by the men who fought and died for Ireland.[33]

A LOYALIST LANDSLIDE

Ironically voting had been arranged to take place on Empire Day, Tuesday 24 May. As has been noted, election 'fever' was especially prevalent in the city's loyalist areas. The *Belfast Newsletter* suggested that 'never at any period within the recollection of the present generation has there been such a profusion of flags or such a wonderful manifestation of patriotic feeling.'[34] In London, the *Daily Telegraph* described the election as 'the most extraordinary in Ulster's history' and reported 'unprecedented scenes' in Belfast where, it claimed, 'most districts were experiencing 90% turnouts.'[35] The paper's correspondent observed:

Crowds were waiting for the polling booths to open, and at many of them [were] long queues of voters ... and decorated motors with the loyalist colours, flashed to and fro in great numbers.[36]

Craig did his best to dissuade loyalist apathy and to remind them exactly why they should vote, on the eve of the election. He implored his supporters:

Do your duty. Let no one stand aside. The cause is sacred and worthy of every personal sacrifice. Rally round me that I may shatter your enemies and their hopes of a Republican flag ... The eyes of our friends throughout the Empire are upon us. Let them see that we are determined as they to uphold the cause of Loyalty.[37]

The nationalist press, on the other hand, focussed their attention on the distasteful features of Election Day. The *Irish News* condemned the intimidation of electors in several areas, alleging that 'thousands of Catholic voters were forcibly and brutally prevented from exercising the franchise.'[38] Examples were given of such intimidation, including shipyard workers loitering and threatening outside polling stations in east Belfast, where bullying was at its worst and a nationalist agent who was assaulted with an iron bar on the Woodstock Road. Reports were also provided of nationalists being kicked and threatened with knives outside polling stations on the Newtownards Road, taxis containing nationalists being stoned and gunfire being directed at a taxi driver on the Falls Road.[39] There were also allegations of widespread personation occurring at several polling stations, again especially in east and west Belfast. Therefore, there was a shared feeling amongst many Catholics that the events of Empire Day constituted 'a mockery of a free election'.[40] Unionists disputed the extent of such alleged misdemeanours, whilst Sir Ernest Clark, who had been appointed Assistant Undersecretary the previous September to help pave the way for the new northern administration, concluded that those cases of intimidation and personation had been practised by both sides and had little effect on what proved to be an emphatic result.[41] In the same correspondence, Clark also acknowledged the central role played by the Specials in guarding polling stations, suggesting that without their contribution, the instances of personation at the polling-booths and violence in the surrounding streets, would have been considerably higher. Certainly the turn-out of Specials on duty during the election was on an unprecedented scale. Fred Crawford, a Specials

Commandant in the city at the time, noted in his diary how in one police station 180 'B' Specials turned up for duty on 24 May.[42]

Seventy-eight candidates stood for the 52 seat legislative assembly, with several being returned unopposed in their constituencies. Of these, 40 were Unionists and with the return of all loyalist candidates, Craig enjoyed unparalleled success. Despite a few individual successes, the other parties were less happy with the election outcome. Although fielding more candidates and gaining a marginally higher share of the vote, Sinn Féin returned the same number of candidates (6) as the UIL. The bleakest fate of all befell socialist groups which failed to return any of their 5 candidates. The election turnout had been a massive 89% of the new area's 380,000 electors, which indicated the success enjoyed by those politicians, journalists and clerics who had warned against apathy during the election build-up.

Despite their initial uncertainty over the new electoral system and, indeed, the new Parliament, fear of Sinn Féin violence and the constant reassurance that they were voting for 'a safe pair of hands' in the form of Craig, had resulted in an unexpectedly high loyalist turnout. The unionist press barely disguised their jubilation at the election's outcome. Dismissing nationalist claims that intimidation had tarnished unionism's 'great victory', the *Belfast Newsletter* declared that the day had 'passed off without any serious disorder.'[43] A couple of days later the *Newsletter* turned its venom on those critics, maintaining that 'no degree of misrepresentation or abuse about imaginary intimidation and terrorism, no ingenuity in argument, can minimise or explain away the significance of such a sweeping victory.'[44] Unionist gratification at the discomfort of their political enemies, Sinn Féin, and their anti-partition allies, the UIL was, therefore, profound.[45] Nationalist papers, unsurprisingly, took a different stance on the election outcome. Apart from condemning the 'disgraceful' election day scenes, the *Irish News* blamed the 'stale and ineffective' nationalist and republican party organisations, suggesting that disharmony between Sinn Féin and the UIL was a significant factor in explaining the disappointing election result for anti-partitionists.[46] Indeed, there had actually been street disturbances between supporters of these groups in the Seaforde Street area of Short Strand during an election meeting and a pro-Union reporter gleefully observed they had rioted 'with as much vigour as though the opposition were loyalists, and there was much sniping with revolvers.'[47] Although realistic in their assessment of the nationalist defeat, the *Irish News* attempted to divert their readers' attention to the undoubted personal success of Joe Devlin, who had been returned both in west Belfast and

Antrim. Describing his victory parade in west Belfast as 'a wonderful sight', the report went on to paint the picture of celebration on a crowded Falls Road where marchers waved green and gold flags and spectators looked down from open windows on the triumphant nationalist procession. In his speech, Devlin was upbeat about the future for Belfast's nationalist community:

> Belfast has never been false to Ireland. She was never truer than she was today. [*cheers*] We will go on defending the fight, fighting for our principles, promising peace with honesty and ultimately succeeding in the great life work for which we have laboured in common – the freedom of our country and the happiness of our people![48]

A VIOLENT BACKDROP

Whilst a heavier than usual security presence prevented large scale riots and prolonged violence which would have proved an unwelcome back-drop for the run-up to the election, a number of security incidents did occur, intermittently, throughout May. These involved both loyalists and the IRA, who, as internal memos indicate, were increasingly active at this time. Republican activities ranged from significant operations such as an attack by 12 armed men from the 'D' Company against police on the Springfield Road on 17 May and an attempted break-out from Crumlin Road jail on 3 June when a gang of 4 dressed in police and military disguise, nearly succeeded in 'springing' a republican prisoner, to smaller scale operations including an arms raid on a house in Florenceville Avenue in the south of the city on 10 May, the 'commandeering' of a typewriter from the offices of the Prince of Wales Fund on 22 May and the shooting of an 'enemy' transport mule in Donegall Street on 28 May. There was also concern in the Dublin headquarters of the IRA at the absence of military discipline on the part of 'juniors' in Belfast, following a robbery in the city for which 'no authority was ever issued' and Belfast republicans were reminded that there was 'no such thing as prize money, legitimate or otherwise.'[49]

May was to claim 7 lives and witnessed several serious injuries. During the early evening of Saturday, 7 May, Detective Inspector Ferris, of Springfield Barracks, who had been the investigating officer in the Duffin case, was leaving St Paul's Presbytery following a meeting with parish priest, Father Convery, when he was attacked by three gunmen in Cavendish Street. A report by the

Belfast IRA confirmed their involvement in this 'special operation' which had been executed by its 'B' Brigade, and claimed there was 'every reason to believe that men under the command of DI Ferris were implicated in the murder of the Duffin brothers and therefore the responsibility rested with him.'[50] Four shots were fired, striking Ferris in the neck and stomach. The gunmen, believing the police officer's wounds to be fatal, hastily escaped through Dunville Park.[51] The following morning, disturbances broke out after Sinn Féin representatives were spotted making collections for their election campaign outside St Patrick's Church. Following mid-morning Mass in the Donegall Street church, shots were fired, with one man receiving hospital treatment for a thigh injury and a number of arrests being made. Stones were thrown at a police vehicle by a crowd at the corner of Upper Library Street and a woman was knocked down in the melee. Shots were fired to disperse the crowd.

A couple of days later, Alfred Craig (24), a Harbour Constable, was shot dead guarding the Ship Street entrance of the western approach to York Docks. Craig, who was newly married and a former member of the Royal Inniskilling Fusiliers, had reportedly intervened earlier in a row involving members of a ship's crew and there was a widespread perception that the attack was 'mysterious' and not necessarily sectarian in its nature. This interpretation was noted with some satisfaction in a republican report of the attack which noted 'the impression here in the city that the IRA [was] not concerned with this shooting'.[52] The IRA memo reveals that this operation was planned and executed by republicans, probably in an endeavour to add to their relatively depleted weapon arsenal. The IRA's account of the attack read:

> ... an attempt was made to disarm a Special Harbour Constable at Belfast Docks by men of D Coy. When covered he immediately put up his hands, but as one of the men was about to disarm him he dropped his hands and clutched the [IRA] man around the throat. Our man pulled the trigger of his revolver but it misfired twice. Another of the party then fired, shooting the Special dead. The men were unable to obtain the revolver and retreated.[53]

There was a gradual intensification in the level of violence as the election drew closer. Although this did not result in loss of previous, or indeed subsequent, bouts of violence, it undoubtedly did little to defuse tension levels in Belfast. On 16 May, Mary Ann Carroll, a teenager from Carntaul Street, was shot in North

Queen Street by a sniper believed to have been operating from Henry Street and she succumbed to her wounds a week later. The following day, another Catholic teenager, Philomena Burns, of Upton Street, near Wall Street, was shot standing by her front door and died in hospital on 6 June. Later on 17 May, bombs were thrown at a police lorry on the upper Springfield Road. The next evening was also eventful, especially in the east of the city. A loyalist parade, involving Orange bands and ex-servicemen, took place at the Oval football ground in Ballymacarrett, where Sir James Craig inspected Great War 'veterans'. An Orangeman who had been walking on a west Belfast 'feeder parade', was shot by a republican sniper. George Walker (19) of Eighth Street was wounded whilst marching in Beverley Street and died of his wounds over two months later. Rumours of this shooting spread like wildfire through the loyalist ranks and tension was high, as the main parade made its way to the Oval. There were allegations of shots being fired in the air as they were passing the Short Strand area, but the main trouble flared up after the meeting had ended. Most of the crowd appeared to heed the advice of their leaders and returned to the city centre via the Albertbridge route. However, a sizeable minority did not, choosing instead to approach the city centre via the Newtownards Road and the Short Strand. A Catholic ex-soldier, John Smyth (29), who had been wounded serving with the Royal Inniskillings, was hit by gunfire as he crossed the Newtownards Road. Mr Smyth, a Corporation worker, who lived in Seaforde Street, fell across the tramtracks and, on account of prolonged gunfire, it was some time before assistance could be provided. Mr Smyth was taken to a house in nearby Khartoum Street, where he died shortly afterwards.[54] Disturbances flared up after this incident and a teenager, Anthony Cavanagh, of Tomb Street, was wounded. Although this trouble was quickly quelled, disturbances reoccurred the following evening in the same district.[55] This time, turmoil followed anti-partitionist meetings in the Short Strand. Four people suffered gunshot wounds, including Lena Kelly (13), who later died from her injuries.

Serious disturbances were avoided in the vital days running up to polling, but another Catholic victim was claimed on Wednesday 25 May, the day after the election. Thomas Reilly (39), an ex-serviceman, was returning from a game of cards with friends when he was struck by a sniper's bullet as he and his son approached their Butler Street home. However, the comparatively low fatality count for what was considered to be a month fraught with considerable tension, was seen by many as a sign for optimism for the future. Unfortunately such hopes were to be dashed in the months ahead.

Chapter 9

'Stretching out the hand ...'

'BEFLAGGED AND BESMIRCHED'

The first sitting of the new Parliament took place on Tuesday 7 June, within a fortnight of the elections. The swearing-in of the new representatives took place in the Council chamber of the City Hall.[1] Local journalists were divided over the degree of significance which was to be attached to the occasion. The *Irish News* advocated that there was 'no enthusiasm' for an event which they contended 'no one wants and which must be amended without delay.'[2] The unionist press described in detail the scene as large crowds congregated in Donegall Square waving Union flags and cheering the Lord Lieutenant, Viscount FitzAlan, as he drove past in a carriage on his way to the City Hall.[3] Rather ominously, military armoured vehicles, with engines running, were stationed in 'strategic positions' in side-streets around the City Hall for an event which loyalists clearly regarded as a ceremonial *hors d'oeuvres*.

With nationalists and republicans absenting themselves from the inaugural meeting of a new Parliament bereft of socialist representation, the Lord Lieutenant was, in effect, addressing an all-unionist body. In spite of this reality, FitzAlan emphasised the 'high hopes' which many in the British establishment had for the new body which he believed would mark 'the beginning of an era of political reform and progress, industrial development and peaceful, orderly government.'[4] These hopes were reflected in much of the British press with the *Times* describing the creation of the new assembly as 'a long and irretraceable step in the right direction' which they believed would, 'despite all obstacles ... ultimately achieve an Irish peace.'[5] However, certain organs on the left had reservations about the new Parliament. The *Daily News* feared it would entrench itself 'behind its bigoted Orange barricades with the blessing of Imperial authority.'[6]

Contrary to the wishes of his security chiefs, it was decided that Northern Ireland's Parliament would be officially opened by the king. As was noted in the last chapter, violence escalated during the run-up to the elections the previous month and continued throughout the first half of June. Consequently fears spread that the protection of the royal party could not be guaranteed. However, the king's political advisors believed that the royal visit to Belfast and the monarch's delivery of a carefully-scripted plea for reconciliation, could offer a modicum of hope for all of Ireland, and not just for Ulster.

The respective communities had contrasting expectations for the visit. Ulster Unionists saw the royal trip as an indication that the British connection had actually been strengthened by the recent legislation. On the morning of their visit, the *Belfast Newsletter* confidently proclaimed that the trip would signal to 'the whole world that our acceptance of the new status in no way weakens the link between us and the Crown, and that the gift of self-government under our own Parliament, does not depreciate our connection with Great Britain and the Empire.'[8] The paper's confident hopes for the visit reflected their conviction in the reciprocal nature of Ulster loyalism. It proudly proclaimed:

> We still remain in full possession of all the rights and privileges of citizenship of the United Kingdom and of subjects of the King. Therefore we welcome King George and Queen Mary today not only out of loyalty to their persons and to the Crown and Constitution, but because they have graciously set the seal of their Presence upon our new Parliament and thereby brought it in visible among the Parliaments of the Empire which acknowledge their rule.[9]

Nationalist Belfast, on the other hand, saw things rather differently on the eve of the royal visit. Focussing on the plight of Catholics made homeless following violent attacks in west Belfast the previous week, the *Irish News*, the day before the arrival of George and Mary, led with the headline, '150 Families homeless-victims of Orange Intolerance and Bigotry'.[10] The paper proceeded to suggest that those in authority in the city had got their priorities wrong:

> Belfast today is beflagged and festooned, streamers are flying from many houses and shops, bunting yields to the breeze and gives colour to a city which boasts of its loyalty to the King – and yet gloats at its bigotry. But if Belfast today is a beflagged city, it is also a besmirched one. For them [the Catholic homeless] Wednesday will pass as one more day of suffering and anxiety.[11]

The Bishop of Down and Connor, Dr MacRory, also bemoaned the 'simply intolerable' conditions which these homeless Catholics were having to endure and questioned the rationale behind the royal visit. The Bishop suggested that the King's advisors had made 'a great mistake in asking the King to go out of his way to signify special approval of an institution which was set up in defiance of the determined opposition of more than four fifths of the Irish Nation.'[12]

Loyalist Belfast had been eagerly awaiting the arrival of the Royals which would provide them with the opportunity of exhibiting devotion to their monarch, not to mention the chance of enjoying additional loyal celebrations in July. It had been nearly 20 years since the last visit of a monarch to the city and the unionist citizens of Belfast were determined to savour every fleeting moment of the royal presence. The King's visit stirred many memories for Robert Preston who was 13 at the time. He recalls that a 'rehearsal' was arranged shortly before the royal visit, which was indicative of the degree of anxiety surrounding the imminent regal arrival and the organisers' steely resolve that the day would pass off without major incident. Robert remembers watching the rehearsal at Shaftesbury Square and seeing the 'King's' coach turn there, before proceeding down Great Victoria Street. He recalls 'A' Specials, in their distinctive uniforms, lining the streets and other officers checking premise-holders' identity in buildings along the route.[13] For the big day itself, Robert's family had made special plans:

> We stayed overnight in Bangor so we could see the 'Victoria and Albert' steaming up Belfast Lough, near Sydenham I think it was. The Royal Yacht was accompanied by six destroyers, three on each side, and it got a salute as it entered Musgrave Channel. We got a tram into the city and watched the royal procession going up Great Victoria Street from the vantage point of the first floor of the factory my Dad worked at in Bedford Street.

Preparations had been going on since the visit had been announced and nowhere was this more evident than in the little 'kitchen' houses on the Shankill Road and Ballymacarrett. The new premier's wife recorded the excited anticipation amongst Belfast's working class in her diary. Lady Craig observed:

> The King and Queen have the most wonderful reception, the decorations everywhere are extremely well done and even the little side streets

that they will never be within miles of are draped with bunting and flags, and the pavements and lamp posts painted red white and blue, really most touching, as a sign of their loyalty. Imagine Radicals in England thinking they would ever succeed in driving people like that out of the British Empire or wanting to.[14]

'A RIGHT ROYAL DAY'

Amidst this frenetic atmosphere of anxiety and fervour the Royal Yacht sailed up Belfast Lough during the mid morning of Wednesday 22 June. The weather was fine, if a little overcast, and several women would suffer heat exhaustion in the crowded Belfast streets later in the day. They received a noisy salute from the quayside guns and steamers' horns, landing at Donegall Quay around 11.30. As the King and Queen Mary disembarked, a Boys' Brigade band struck up the National Anthem. Harry Currie, then a Staff Sergeant in the 9th Belfast Company (attached to Fitzroy Avenue Presbyterian Church) was chief drummer in the band and believed he was the first person to exchange eye contract with the king as he disembarked.[15] George and Mary were met at the docks by Craig and transported in an open landau up the city's High Street and along Donegall Place to the City Hall. Thousands of people, many of whom had arrived hours before the anticipated regal appearance to ensure good vantage points, lined the royal route, and their infectious enthusiasm helped create a carnival-like ambience. A reporter recorded how the city's industrial heartlands had come to a standstill:

> All business was suspended for the day. At the shipyards there was an almost uncanny silence; the whirr of machinery ceased in the mills and factories, shops, offices and warehouses were closed; and the children revelled in the luxury of a holiday which, owing to its vivid association, will remain with them as an abiding memory.[16]

For youngsters in the enormous crowds, the wait seemed interminable and the royals' passing by an all too brief climax. George Morrison, perched in his father's arms, recalls a particularly clear view at Cromac Square, and Sam Jamison remembered the deafening roar of the crowd intermingling with the distinctive chimes of the Albert Clock. The security presence was unprecedentedly tight, with over a thousand troops and police positioned over the mile-long route. Lady Craig noted in her diary that 'luckily it was not very far, and precautions had been taken of every description, trusted men in each house, and on every roof top, and the closest security of all in the houses and of course in the streets too.'[17]

Their arrival at the City Hall was marked by a fanfare and, not for the first time that afternoon, a lusty rendition of the National Anthem.[18] Around noon, George and Mary were escorted to specially-designed gilt thrones, and, after prayers, the King delivered a stirring plea for peace and reconciliation in Ireland as a whole. The King implored the assembled representatives:

> I speak from a full heart when I pray that my coming to Ireland today may prove to be the first step towards the end of strife among her people, whatever their race or creed. In that hope I appeal to all Irishmen to pause, to stretch out the hand of forebearance and conciliation, to forgive and forget, and to join in making for the land they love a new era of peace, contentment and goodwill.[19]

Historians have stressed the statesmanlike, conciliatory nature of the monarch's speech, but it received a mixed reaction from the Belfast public. Certainly Unionists were pleased. The high emotions aroused by the royal visit undoubtedly contributed to what might be regarded as uncharacteristic generosity of spirit in the positive responses of many loyalists to the King's request for reconciliation. Thus, the *Belfast Newsletter*, in celebrating the memory of 'a right royal day in the city', pledged to combine loyalty to the Crown and the constitution' with an obligation to 'dealing out even-handed justice to all creeds and classes.'[20] Nationalist opinion, however, expressed its disappointment with the royal address. This had, it was claimed, 'utterly falsified' the widespread hope that the monarch was 'to figure as the bearer of glad tidings' and instead one could detect 'the tainted hand of Lloyd George in every sentence.'[21]

After the official opening of Parliament in the City Hall, the royals made the short journey to the Ulster Hall in Bedford Street, where an adoring audience of loyalists awaited them. Here, 'unforgettable' instances of fealty were expressed when the audience 'could not contain themselves, breaking in to singing the National Anthem at a moment when it was not on the official programme.'[22] This fervour not only surprised a sceptical and mildly neurotic royal entourage, but also delighted the royal couple. A court correspondent noted how the King had been 'deeply touched by the fervour of his triumphant welcome' and observed that his wife had, at least on one occasion, been 'seen to be smiling through happy tears'.[23] However, the shadow of violence hung over the whole event. Besides the colossal security presence, it was deeply etched in the minds of the main participants. Consequently, when the brief visit passed off without major incident, unionist joy was unsurpassed. This was understandable, given the considerable misapprehension prevalent amongst the King's security advisers. Such concern was illustrated by a regal aside to a greatly relieved premier at the quayside. Just before he boarded the Royal Yacht, George told Craig:

> I can't tell you how glad I am I came, but you know my entourage were very much against it.' J replied, 'Sir, you are surrounded by pessimists; we are all optimists over here.'[24]

The King's decision to visit Belfast was warmly appreciated by its loyal citizens. This 'gratitude' was expressed by the *Belfast Telegraph* which claimed the royal trip had 'struck a chord in the hearts of his loyal citizens' and the King's personal bravery and conciliatory address also gained applause in the British press.[25] The monarch was not the only person whose reputation was bolstered by the five-hour royal sojourn. Loyalists, perturbed by the recent shift in Fleet Street opinion – from the pre-war stance of relative sympathy for the plight of Ulster Unionists, the 'underdogs' of the Irish situation, to a harsher perception of loyalists as the 'blockers' on the road to political progress – were delighted both by the positive tone of media coverage of the royal visit and by their assessment of the pivotal role played by Sir James Craig throughout the whole trip.[26] A *Daily Chronicle* correspondent wrote about the Unionist leader's 'fine reception' as he arrived to meet the King, adding:

> He has been an outstanding figure of course in today's ceremonies ... He is a man of character rather than subtlety. He is ready with a plan and goes straight to his object, disregarding cross-currents and side issues. A man of great common sense, he has much of the nature of General Botha. It may be added that he has as difficult a part to play as General Botha, but his friends believe he will succeed.[27]

However, Ulster's Catholic population did not share in this eulogising of George V or Craig, instead voicing criticism of the political and constitutional symbolism of the King's speech, which the *Irish News* regarded as representing merely 'the official promulgation of partition.'[28] Though the same editorial had conceded that, at least in terms of its impact as a spectacle, the royal visit had been 'an undoubted success', its frank assessment of the real essence of the visit could not have been blunter. The paper's headline the following day was unequivocal; 'Four Hours of Pageantry and Feasting; Verbal Flummery; Not an Honest Word of Hope.'[29] Those Catholics still working in the city's offices and factories generally stayed with their families and friends in their own districts throughout the day of street partying which they were not expected to join. Loyalist celebrations merely intensified nationalist feelings of isolation as they mulled over their predicament. Indeed, some Catholic institutions did not even formally recognise the occasion. Jimmy Kelly, 9 years old at the time, was a pupil at St Paul's School on the Falls Road and was rather peeved to discover his school was not closing for the day!

As has been noted, loyalist euphoria over the royal occasion largely accounts for the relatively heady language of 'fairness' and 'reconciliation'. The *Belfast Telegraph* was upbeat, suggesting that Ulster was 'turning her face eagerly and hopefully towards the dawn' and assured its readership that the new provincial government would 'accord the same rights and privileges as its duty to all classes and creeds.'[30] The inclusivity of the new administration was also stressed by Craig in Parliament the day after the King's visit. Promising that his administration would be 'absolutely honest and fair in administering the law', the new premier promised that 'every person inside our particular boundary may rest assured that there will be nothing meted out to them but the strictest justice.'[31] Craig's assurance that his government would be 'cautious in our legislation' and 'absolutely honest and fair in administering the law' personified the mood of optimism and conciliation which predominated the early speeches.[32] Whilst this could not camouflage nationalists' disappointment with the content of the King's address to the northern Parliament, there was a hope, especially from within Whitehall, that the conciliatory tone of the monarch's speech would pave the way for political negotiations between the British administration and Sinn Féin.[33] In the meantime, Unionists contented themselves with the realisation that their 'self-sacrifice' in accepting a parliament which they had not campaigned for, had been recognised by their monarch and government.[34]

THE BLOODY SEQUEL

Barely 48 hours after the pageantry and joyful celebrations in the city, the IRA exhibited its response to the pleas of George V. Realising the heavy security in the Belfast area mitigated against the staging of a spectacular attack on the royal party, republicans planned a low-risk operation aimed at relaxing military personnel returning from Wednesday's ceremony in Belfast. During the morning of Friday 24 June, a military train carrying nearly 120 soldiers and over 100 horses was destroyed by an IRA bomb 'team' at Adavoyle, near Bessbrook, close to the border. This train, the last of a convoy of three troop locomotives, was carrying a detachment of 10th Royal Hussars officers and their horses to Dublin where they were scheduled to catch a Holyhead-bound ferry. Frank Aiken's team had captured workers on the railway line and planted bombs between the sleepers, before lying in wait for the approaching convoy. The devices were detonated a safe distance from the track and several carriages of the train were catapulted down a steep embankment. The Hussars had formed the King's cavalry escort during his visit and 4 soldiers were killed and 20 more injured. In addition, 2 civilians and 80 horses were killed in an attack which undoubtedly lifted the morale of republicans throughout the island.[35] Some security personnel had a fortunate escape. Hugh McIvor, a recent RIC recruit, recalled how a slight delay in Belfast had saved his life and those of his colleagues:

> We had to march to the Great Northern [Railway] and just as we went in, the train tooted and they wouldn't let us through. So we caught the next one. But the train we should have been on was bowled over, horses and all killed. We were lucky.[36]

Loyalist reaction was unanimously virulent and condemnatory in its tone. The following day the *Belfast Telegraph* lamented:

> The diabolical outrage on the Great Northern Railway yesterday is apparently the answer of Sinn Féin to the King's appeal for peace in Ireland. It is saddening to think that some of the gallant soldiers who but a few hours ago escorted their Majesties the King and Queen through Belfast will, a few hours hence, be borne through our streets to their last resting-place.[37]

George and Mary's visit would have been regarded by many in the city as an interlude, a chance for the wider community to draw its breath, before political developments and communal violence would once again grasp their stranglehold over the everyday lives of Belfast's citizens. This is not to suggest that June was a trouble-free month. Indeed, apart from the military fatalities on the Belfast–Dublin train on 24 June, another 14 people lost their lives and over 70 received hospital treatment due to violence in the city during June. Also, the tense atmosphere in Belfast which had pervaded throughout the election the previous month persisted, manifesting itself in sectarian attacks on vulnerable individuals and IRA arson attacks, specifically aimed at motor and engineering firms acting as agents for the security forces.[38] However, discounting a decidedly bloody three day spell in the middle of the month, the city experienced comparatively few major security incidents.

The three day spell occurred just over a week before the arrival of the royal couple. Loyalist passions were roused by a Seamus Woods-led IRA attack on three police officers on the Falls Road on 10 June. At lunchtime Sergeant James Sullivan, Constable James Glover and Constable Hugh Sharkey were patrolling in Cupar Street near the Diamond Picture House when they were approached by 6 men who fired about 40 shots at them. Sergeant Sullivan managed to return the fire, but all 3 officers were hit, Glover fatally. The latter, a 31-year-old Antrim-born officer with a distinguished war record, was based at Springfield Road barracks and was suspected of having links with the Nixon gang.[39] He was hit four times, and clutching his back, staggered into the Falls Library, from where onlookers assisted him across the road to the Royal Victoria Hospital (he died there nearly three weeks later). Constable Sharkey received treatment for a neck wound and an elderly pedestrian, William Donnelly, was also treated for a leg wound. Inevitably edginess following this daring assault boiled over on the Falls later in the day. Just before curfew, lorries of auxiliaries toured west Belfast and reports of 'indiscriminate' firing were greeted with loud cheering, a few streets away on the Shankill Road. John McKay was wounded in Cupar Street and there were reports of Catholics, who had been arrested by police, being dragged from their lorries by a furious mob in Conway Street. The *Irish News* declared:

> Terror-stricken men, women and children fled for their lives in all directions, seeking places of safety wherever they could find them. Scores, if not hundreds, who were considerable distances from their own homes

found refuge in the homes of other people, and were compelled to
remain there for the night.[40]

The following evening attention veered back to the north of the city. A serious
riot broke out around teatime in the Dock and North Thomas Streets district.
Rival crowds hurled stones and revolver fire was exchanged. A bomb was
thrown into the mainly Catholic Dock Street, killing Terence McGinley, from
North Thomas Street and injuring 20 others, including William Kane, who lost
a hand in the explosion.

In the early hours of Sunday 12 June, an apparently orchestrated attack on
three Catholics was executed in the north of the city. Armed men attired in
police uniform and utilising motor transport, visited several homes during
curfew hours. In each of these attacks, the assailants requested people by name,
though in the majority of cases, intended victims were either not at home or
else managed to make speedy escapes. Three young men were not so fortunate,
however. The first victim was Alexander McBride (30), a native of Ballycastle,
and a successful North Street publican. Mr McBride, married for barely a year
and the father of a newly-born child, lived in a villa at Cadogan Drive, a prosperous avenue off the Cliftonville Road. A lorry pulled up outside the McBride
residence around 1 a.m. and, hearing banging at his front door, Mr McBride
opened his bedroom window. On hearing it was 'police on duty', he opened the
door and was told by his visitors to get dressed as he was required for an identification parade. His wife, increasingly anxious at his plight, enquired where he
was being taken and was far from reassured by the reply, 'Hollywood Barracks'.
When she tried to intervene she was told they were 'not the murder gang' and
that her husband would soon return. The lorry made its way up Oldpark Road,
Ballysillan Road and on to Ligoniel Road. Shortly after daybreak, McBride's
bullet-ridden body was discovered just off the Ballysillan Road.[41] Later that day
as DI Nixon called at Cadogan Drive, Mrs McBride allegedly identified him as
the leader of the gang which had called at her home earlier that morning.

Barely 20 minutes after Mr McBride had been whisked away, William Kerr
(26), a barber was described by neighbours as 'a very religious lad', was sleeping
at home on the corner of the Old Lodge Road, when there was loud knocking
at the front door. Kerr, a member of the Ancient Order of Hibernians and the
Irish National Foresters, was initially protected by his sister who had opened the
door, offering to take his place. She was bluntly informed she would never see
him again and he was taken away in their lorry. His body was found later that

morning in a lane known locally as 'Dan O'Neill's Loney', off the Springfield Road. Callers at Mr Kerr's barber shop that morning found it closed, with the notice, 'Closed in consequence of the death of the proprietor, murdered by the Crown forces of England', pinned to the door. Inside another ten minutes the murder gang was to call at the Ardoyne home postman Malachy Halfpenny shared with his mother and two sisters in Herbert Street. Mr Halfpenny had, along with his four brothers, served in the army and had been wounded during the war. When the gang pulled up in a blueish-grey motor lorry, his mother refused to open the door, but the gang, which reportedly contained a man with an English accent, broke in, threatening to shoot her. Halfpenny was dragged out and his body was found after daybreak in the Ligoniel area, close to Mr McBride's. He had numerous bullet wounds on his body and it was alleged he had also been tortured.[42]

A few days later, Joe Devlin, in an unsuccessful bid to force an adjournment debate in the House of Commons on these killings, asked the Irish Chief Secretary to explain why the motor vehicles involved in the attack had not been intercepted by the police during the curfew, which had been in operation at the time of the attack.[43] He proceeded to make allegations that the assassins actually emanated from the ranks of the security forces, demanding to know 'who but the forces of the Crown could have rampaged the whole city at 1 o'clock in the morning, stop at 3 houses and murder men in the presence of their families?'[44] A passionate Devlin demanded of Greenwood:

> Do I understand you to rule that it is not a matter of definite, urgent public importance that the forces go out at 1 o'clock in the morning to 3 different places – that they go into the homes of peaceable citizens, drag them out of their homes, and murder them and then we are told in this House that there is no redress?[45]

During the evening of these murders in north Belfast, severe rioting erupted in both the York Road and Kashmir Road areas. A Castlederg-born Special, Thomas Sturdy, who was based in Court Street barracks, was shot dead sitting in an armoured lorry in Dock Street.[46] Continual sniping was reported from the start of the curfew period, with gunmen believed to have been operating from upstairs windows and skylights. Another victim of this sniping was Thomas Mallon (51), who was killed when a bullet entered through the window of his North Thomas Street home. Retribution for the killing of S.C. Sturdy was swift. Patrick Mulligan (24), a dock labourer, was shot dead in his Dock Street home just after 10. A large number of men in Specials' uniforms were accused of breaking into Mr Mulligan's house and of shooting him as he tried to hide in a shed. The same assailants were most likely responsible for the murder shortly afterwards of another Catholic, Joseph Miller (25), of New Dock Street. Mr Miller was dragged from his bed and, despite the protestations of his wife and mother, was shot in the street. By a tragic quirk of fate, his mother, who was injured in this attack, died in a separate incident a few months later.[47] In the west of the city, sniping was also heavy around Kashmir Road in particular. Six people received gunshot injuries and Hugh Jenkins, who was an ex-serviceman from Emerson Street, was killed by a nationalist sniper.

No rioting was reported the following day (13 June) but 'an undercurrent of unrest prevalent in the disturbed areas of the city' was observed by a journalist and sniping occurred in Vere and Meadow Streets.[48] Another Protestant, Joseph Blackburn (39), from Hillman Street, was hit by gunfire directed from North Queen Street and he died in the Royal Victoria Hospital ten days later. On Tuesday 14 June, there was another flare-up on the city's 'bullet-swept streets', especially in the west which was in 'a veritable state of siege in the evening even after curfew.'[49] Gunfire lasted for over five hours and was believed to have been aggravated by an attack on Specials removing the body of their colleague from the Royal. The police returned fire and teenager Kathleen Collins, knitting at her front door in Cupar Street, was hit by a bullet and died shortly afterwards in the Mater Hospital (her sister was also seriously wounded in this attack). The disturbances were so severe that the Falls Road tram service was suspended and several businesses closed early. A shop girl on the Springfield Road had a fortu-nate escape when a bullet embedded itself in the fourth layer of ham which she had been lifting. Not so lucky was young William Fraser, of Mayo Street. William (12), a Protestant, had left home to search for a younger sister returning for her tea, and was shot by a sniper operating from the Falls.[50] Ex-soldier Hugh McAree (30), a Catholic, of Sackville Street, was also fatally wounded as he bravely went to the assistance of the dying boy.[51] Although serious disturbances were not to reoccur for another few weeks, instances of intimidation, mainly involving Catholic families, persisted for several more days until the eve of the royal visit.[52] As many as 150 families were pressurised out of their homes during June. An especially poignant case was that of Patrick O'Hare, a soldier in the Connaught Rangers. Whilst home on leave, O'Hare was dragged from his Urney Street home and threatened with execution if he did not leave.

The successful security operation surrounding the royal visit proved conclusively that 'blanket' security could significantly reduce the chances of widespread terror attacks from occurring and could usher in prolonged periods of relative quiet. However, as the subsequent attack on the military train, increasing IRA activity in the city and the apparent freedom of movement enjoyed by loyalist murder gangs all proved, underlying tension on both sides was still high and constantly ready for exploitation. Thoughts of peace and reconciliation inspired by King George V's address were rapidly replaced by more familiar ones of fear and suspicion.

Chapter 10

Stemming the tide?

BELFAST AND THE TRUCE

Shared pragmatism, rather than any lasting mood of reconciliation engendered by the King's June visit, led the respective sides to meet to formulate an agreement bringing to an end the 18-month Anglo-Irish war. Following two days of talks in Dublin between the Commander-in-Chief of British forces in Ireland, General Sir Nevil Macready and the IRA's Chief of Staff Richard Mulcahy, a truce was signed on Saturday 9 July.[1] This promise of a cessation of IRA violence across the whole of Ireland was perceived to be mutually beneficial for both Sinn Féin and the British Government.[2] Lloyd George's willing acceptance of a truce reflected his administration's increasing concern that military stalemate, accompanied as it was by a potentially astronomical security bill, was weakening British public support for such a commitment in Ireland. The IRA, who desired a ceasefire as evidence of British goodwill before their political representatives entered negotiations, had also been drained by the long war against the British, especially in terms of maintaining levels of military personnel, as well as accessing sufficient weaponry and ammunition.

Under the Truce, there was an agreement that movement of military personnel and open targeting of Crown forces, civilians, or pursuit of IRA personnel and arms would be curtailed. In the north, recruitment for both the new police force and the Specials was frozen and, along with the delay in the transfer of police powers to Belfast, Unionists felt they were being sacrificed on the high altar of political pragmatism. In other words, the scaling-down in security within N Ireland and the comparative impotence of Craig's administration in dealing with violence on their capital's streets, had been deemed to be an inevitable casualty in the termination of the wider Irish war.[3] The cruel irony of the July Truce and the de-escalation of violence elsewhere in Ireland was that it heralded a particularly vicious summer orgy of violence in Belfast, both in the west and other parts of the city. It also illustrated that the northern crisis was different from the situation in the rest of the country and that while the rest of

Ireland enjoyed a period of relative peace, the increased fears and suspicions of northern unionists – intensified by the signing of the Truce and commence-ment of political negotiations in London, not to mention the rumours of redeployment of the IRA – were close to boiling over. An attack on a police patrol in west Belfast within 24 hours of the signing of the Truce elicited the city's response to this official announcement of peace. Within a week, over 20 people had lost their lives and scores were injured.

The main gripe of unionists and much of the British press, was that Sinn Féin could not be trusted in implementing their side of the agreement, specifically with regard to the movement and training of military personnel in the north. Their perception, therefore, was that republicans were merely using the Truce as a breathing-space and an opportunity to redeploy forces from the south and west in the north.[4] Although many republicans, including Eamon de Valera, were wary of the forthcoming political negotiations, there was a consensus within republican opinion that the truce offered 'a welcome opportunity for rest and regrouping rather than a pathway to constitutional settlement.'[5] Belfast Cabinet papers indicate the new administration's fear that Sinn Féin were 'using the present truce to improve their machinery in the northern area' and their increasing awareness of the imminent escalation in republican violence.[6] Others stressed the view that the timing of the truce was far from being ideal for Ulster. The *New Statesman* noted a certain degree of irony in such timing, with a cessa-tion of hostilities being declared at a time when the north was 'in anything but a peace-making mood.'[7] The journal declared that both of the extreme factions in Ulster were exhibiting their full fury at this time:

> Sinn Féin has demonstrated its power to hit her [Ulster] by the economic boycott and also by carrying the war into her territory, and the average Orangeman, if not the wiser of his leaders, is prepared to sink all other considerations for the satisfaction of demonstrating that she can hit back.[8]

Also, the coinciding of the implementation of the truce with the main public holiday in the north was a potential disaster from the security viewpoint. Lillian Spender, wife of Sir Wilfred, wrote that the truce 'couldn't have come at a more difficult time with the Orange celebrations and holiday throwing crowds of youths-of the most irresponsible age – on the streets', resulting in 'inevitable retaliation' at the activities of the IRA.[9]

The Truce provided the IRA, especially its under-strength northern branch, with the opportunity of drilling, training and extending its arsenal.[10] Police reports in August and September indicated both an upsurge in support for the IRA and provided evidence of the drilling and training in the north shortly after the signing of the Truce. For instance, there was an IRA camp at Torr Head in County Antrim in August, and also at this time, a review of 200 west Belfast republicans at Hannastown in the hills above the city.[11] This hardly eased the fears of both the local authorities and the unionist population that republicans were using the truce to improve their machinery in the north for subsequent attacks. With the lifting of curfew restrictions from 12 July and the chief responsibility, at least temporarily, for security resting with the regular police, there was considerable consternation within the ranks of the RIC as to whether they could cope on their own. Another insertion in Lady Spender's diary illustrates the uncertainty over the exact responsibilities of law and order agencies. She wrote of the frantic comings and goings of her husband:

> W[ilfred] spent the rest of the day ... fixing up a meeting in the City
> Hall for this morning, of representatives of the government, the military
> and the city, to get the whole matter settled, as to who's to be responsible
> for the safety of the city, and what part the military can and will play.[12]

The authorities were clearly disturbed by the upsurge in support for the IRA and especially by the manner in which the 3rd Northern Division were utilising the Truce period to reorganise. However, internal correspondence indicates the financial predicament of northern republicans and also their problems accessing arms and ammunition. A letter from divisional headquarters to the Chief of Staff in Dublin claimed that the Belfast Brigade had 'never at any time been in a very sound financial situation' with an estimated three quarters of their volunteers unemployed.[13] Roger McCorley begged the Dublin leadership to reconsider weapons supplies for the north, claiming that 'up to the present I have received no arms from GHQ and if our programme is to be carried out after the Truce I would require much assistance in this line.'[14] Another note from the 3rd Division supremo to the Chief of Staff in Dublin indicates the concern the divisional leaders had about keeping nationalist hotheads under control, especially during the Truce periods. A specific example of such problems occurred when a volunteer, who had been endeavouring to extinguish a fire started by a nationalist mob, was 'beaten up' and it was 'only with difficulty that extra volunteers managed to prevent the mob from cutting the hosepipes of the Fire Brigade in its attempt to extinguish the flames.'[15]

Despite republicans' problems in acquiring sufficient weaponry, the authorities in Belfast were increasingly perturbed by the movements of leading Sinn Féin and IRA personnel in their area. Especially prominent was Eoin O'Duffy, a senior IRA staff officer who had been appointed Sinn Féin truce liaison officer in the city. An internal RIC report early in September suggested that O'Duffy's comments had 'only the result of inflaming feeling already high enough on both sides' and condemned his 'continuing propaganda' against the Specials in particular as being 'unjustified and untrue.'[16] The report recommended that the time had come when 'representations should be made in Dublin as to the desirability of withdrawing him and replacing him with another liaison officer more discreet and tactful.'[17] O'Duffy, whose statements featured on a regular basis in the nationalist press south of the border, claimed that loyalists were determined 'to make an impossible atmosphere for the truce' and also accused the police of distributing revolvers and ammunition to Protestants in the Grove and Vere Street area and of deliberately firing into Lancaster Street.[18]

MIDSUMMER MADNESS

As the holiday period approached, the rest of the city was initially spared the outrages which were occurring in the west. However, relatively minor disturbances occurred on the Eleventh night, when an Orange parade was attacked in the York Street area and shooting was reported in the Short Strand. The parades went ahead as scheduled, with a predictably heavy security presence. The *Belfast Telegraph* triumphantly proclaimed that, despite the recent violence, there had been 'no abatement of loyalist enthusiasm' and warned that no matter what negotiations were going on elsewhere, Orangemen were not going to be 'pawns in any political game' but rather were increasingly determined to 'hold with traditional tenacity to their birthright as Britons and to their privileges within the Empire'.[19] Apart from intermittent shooting in the North Queen Street area, the Twelfth evening was pretty quiet, largely on account of the decision to keep curfew restrictions. However, this area experienced an escalation in trouble the following day. In the early morning two policemen were fired at and shortly after noon nationalists exchanged gunfire with loyalists. Disturbances soon spread to 'the whole area between North Queen Street and York Street,

revolvers freely being used, before the police managed to quell the disturbances.'[20] Five people were wounded in the Harding Street district. A
26-year-old Catholic mill worker, Maggie McKinney, was killed near her home
in Balkan Street.

The following day, Thursday 14 July, proved to be bloody, though not quite
on the scale of Sunday's violence. Most of the incidents were concentrated in
the north and east of the city. During the early afternoon there were disturbances in Short Strand, with three people suffering gunshot injuries and two
others receiving severe beatings. Over in Garmoyle Street, close to North
Queen Street, a shop was bombed. That evening the trouble was more widespread and two people died from their injuries, with another 30 being
wounded. Margaret Walsh, a Protestant teenager doing a message in York
Street, died from sniping coming from the direction of Little George's Street
and a Catholic, Patrick McKenna was shot outside his home in Lepper Street.
Sniping reoccurred the following day when the little streets between York Street
and North Queen Street were described as 'a veritable inferno.'[21] Casualties
included unionist politician William Grant and a couple of police officers in
Little George's Street, including D.I. McConnell. A young Catholic labourer,
Bernard Mooney, of Spamount Street, was killed visiting a friend's house in
Lepper Street (it was alleged that he had been shot from the upstairs window of
a house opposite). On the other side of the city, a pub belonging to one of the
McMahon family was looted and set ablaze in Templemore Avenue, and there
were instances of sniping and looting elsewhere in the east (a pawn shop was
cleared on the Castlereagh Road).

Most of Belfast enjoyed a prolonged period of comparative peace from mid
July, with increasingly strident unionist calls for the removal of an 'unnecessary'
curfew being ignored by the authorities.[22] However, a number of isolated acts
of violence, including one in an unlikely location, occurred during the first half
of August. The 'fashionable quarter' of Knock had been relatively sheltered
from the disturbances of nearby Ballymacarrett, but experienced a bizarre
incident on 5 August.[23] Constable Thomas Keane, who had been patrolling in
the area, stopped two suspicious-looking men in Earlswood Road, when one
pulled out a revolver and wounded the officer in his leg. During a street chase
through what would have been unfamiliar territory for the west Belfast
assailants, one of them, Francis Joseph Crumney accidentally wounded the
other attacker. Police reinforcements arrived and arrested Crumney, although
his colleague, Freddie Fox (19), from Durham Street, died in hospital the

following week. Also that day, a Protestant cabinet-maker, Charles Green (42), of Lincoln Avenue, was fatally wounded during a robbery at his College Court business. A more traditional venue for attack was the docks, where two men suffered gunshot injuries in an affray at Queen's Quay the next week. There were also two bomb attacks in the north of the city. The more serious occurred in Tyrone Street, near Clifton Street, during the evening of 21 August, when a Mills hand-grenade was thrown into a crowd of bystanders, injuring six, two of them children.

Tension increased in north Belfast towards the end of the month. A home in Nelson Street had been bombed by a loyalist mob on 27 August, causing the *Irish News* to condemn Craig's silence on the incident and to argue that 'men inflamed with murderous rancour can walk abroad bomb-laden and fling explosives into the homes of sleeping citizens with perfect impunity.'[24] Inside a couple of days more successful missions were executed, resulting in two deaths and ten injuries. A Protestant teenager, Thomas Rafters, of Shandon Street, was shot in North Queen Street and Colin Fogg (42), a shipwright from Lawther Street, was fatally wounded by a nationalist sniper in Lepper Street on the New Lodge Road. Fortunately an unseasonable hailstorm succeeded in quickly dispersing the gathering crowds, hence giving the snipers less targets. However, the violence was renewed the following morning in the North Queen Street area. Even before daybreak 'at irregular intervals the sound of isolated shots stabbed throughout the dark stillness, and few of the residents obtained much sleep.'[25] The firing flared up again with 'renewed vigour' and favourite targets for the gunmen were people going to work.[26] Although the military had brought a temporary cessation to the violence, it was to re-emerge near teatime in the North Queen Street, New Lodge Road and York Street areas. Stephen Cash, a 68-year-old labourer, of Sussex Street, and William Kennedy (36), of Grove Street, were shot dead in the New Lodge area, and two other Protestants, Annie Watson (5) and William Smith (28), from the Old Lodge Road, were fatally wounded in attacks close to North Queen Street.[27] Tension and intermittent gunfire persisted throughout that evening (30 August) and three Catholics died from gunshot wounds in the same area. They were John Coogan (40), of Valentine Street, Thomas McMullan, a 34-year-old barman from North Queen Street and Charles Harvey (39), a labourer from Columbia Street, who died from his injuries the following week. There were two further Protestant victims of the violence that evening. Henry Robert Bowers, a 21-year-old labourer of Cambridge Street, was shot in the York Street area, whilst Samuel

Ferguson, from the Donegall Road, was shot by an IRA gunman returning from the City Cemetery. There were reports of yard-workers being attacked on their way home from work (near Curtis Street), republican gunmen firing into city centre crowds in Donegall Street and Royal Avenue and a pedestrian, Evelyn Hamilton, was seriously wounded in Academy Street. During curfew hours that evening, there was intermittent firing, with a policeman receiving gunshot wounds and ambulance crews, especially those based at Central and Whitla Street stations, were kept busy.[28] The next day, Wednesday 31 August, brought a fresh wave of violence, leaving 7 dead and at least 36 others injured. As early as noon, the Royal Victoria Hospital had treated 13 gunshot victims. Most of the violence was contained in the central and northern areas of the city, where four Catholics died. Alice Duff (60), a housekeeper, died of a stomach wound in the Mater Hospital, sustained near her home in Academy Street. William McKeown, a 18-year-old labourer of Lancaster Street, was shot in the head during mid morning disturbances around the same time as Richard Duffin (50), a Turkish baths attendant, was shot in North Queen Street. A carter, Thomas Finnegan (53), from Keylands Place, died from a head injury sustained as he was walking along Garmoyle Street.[29]

Belfast was tense as it prepared for the funerals of the victims of the late summer bout of terror. Expectations of a return to a period of calm were not helped by the killing of a Shankill Road teenager on 1 September and the bombing of a house in Boundary Street, where a number of people received minor injuries two days later. However, greater deployment of military personnel was influential in precipitating a relatively trouble-free fortnight. It was a familiar battleground, Vere Street, in between North Queen Street and York Street, which saw the re-emergence of violence on 15 September. Street rioting that afternoon ended in two more being shot in Cross Street and a couple of days later, three more people received gunshot wounds in Vere Street. The trouble in this area climaxed during the weekend of 17–18 September. Violence flared up on Saturday in Garmoyle Street, between Corporation and Whitla Streets, around ten that evening and the gunfire and bombing spread towards the main York Street thoroughfare. Tramcar passengers got embroiled in this shooting, with 'bullets flying about in all directions, some rebounding off the sidewalks or ricocheting along the streets' and due to the great danger, women and children were 'almost hysterical with fright.'[30] Bombs were thrown into Little George's Street near the curfew hour on the Saturday night, though no serious injuries were reported. There were no major incidents during curfew or for most of Sunday, but after teatime on the Sabbath, firing was again reported in Vere Street, this time with fatal consequences. Maggie Ardis, a Protestant from Bute Street, was visiting friends in Vere Street when a bullet from an IRA sniper passed through her head before striking her companion, Evelyn Blair, also 22 and a resident of Vere Street. Miss Ardis died instantly, whilst Miss Blair died shortly afterwards in hospital.[31] A curfew was called for 8.30 that evening in the North Queen Street and York Street areas. Although the evening was relatively quiet in the north of the city, some disturbances were reported in the Short Strand area that evening and within a few days the east of the city was to erupt in widespread violence.

The source of the trouble was the targeting of over 30 Catholic workers relaying tramlines on the Newtownards Road, who had been beaten by loyalist gangs. Tram services were quickly suspended and street rioting spread. A Protestant, Samuel Robinson (53), of Madrid Street, was crushed by a military vehicle. Also, a bomb exploded in Foundry Street during the mid evening and shooting was reported in the maze of little side-streets off the Newtownards Road and in the Short Strand. The *Belfast Telegraph* noted that the police were 'taken by surprise' and that military reinforcements were required to clear the streets.[32] During the next morning, Saturday 24 September, sporadic shooting was reported in the same area but the weekend's most serious violence occurred during the late afternoon and evening of the following day, when, again, the most serious incidents occurred in eastern Belfast. Disturbances were reported at 4 p.m. when a Special Constable was attacked and there were reports of firing from the Short Strand into the Newtownards Road. Street-fighting between Catholics and Protestants also occurred and stones were allegedly thrown over a roof towards a mob of loyalists advancing towards the Short Strand. There were conflicting reports about the origins of a bomb which exploded on the Newtownards Road tram-lines, killing 2 Protestants and injuring over 20 others. Unionist papers suggested the bomb was simply lobbed over the top of the Short Strand rooftops and into the baying loyalist crowd, whilst the *Irish News* suggested the bomb had originally been released by an 'invading force' of loyalists, but on failing to explode, had simply been returned by nationalists. The *Telegraph's* reporter noted the 'cheering' which went up from the nationalist quarter as the bomb exploded, killing teenagers James McMinn, from Reid's Place and Alexander Harrison, of Fraser Street. The report described scenes of 'indescribable confusion' which followed the expulsions, noting how the 'groans of the injured, mingled with the shrieks of frightened women and the cries of children' combined in producing 'a heart-rending and never-to-be-forgotten scene.'[33] A parish priest recorded in his diary the 'continuous' nature of the shooting around St Matthew's Church. Father Fullerton wrote:

> The Church and Presbytery were attacked, the front door and stairs had several bullet marks. The Lodge was burned and while a crowd of loyalists were cheering and singing around the burning house, a bomb (that came from nowhere) exploded in their midst, killing 4 [sic] and wounding many. Since the explosion the shooting has ceased and everything is quiet.[34]

There were other victims of what was described as 'Sunday's night of Terror.'[35] An IRA member, Murtagh McAstocker, of Moira Street, had been leaving St Matthew's Church after confession when he was attacked and badly beaten by a loyalist crowd which had entered Seaforde Street. The victim was shot but the hostility apparently did not end there. When an ambulance arrived to take away his body, it was surrounded by a loyalist crowd which gave 'an incredible display of savagery'.[36] The problems surrounding McAstocker did not even end with his killing. An ex-IRA man of the time remembered his funeral as 'massive' and claimed 'the British military drove armoured cars through the ranks of marching mourners to try to break up the funeral cortege.'[37] Declaring they 'didn't succeed though', the veteran republican recalled 'an IRA firing party at the graveside and shots [were] fired over the grave at Milltown.'[38] Also, in the Seaforde Street area of Short Strand that evening, Eliza Kelly (34) was killed by a stray police bullet as she was sitting in her home, during disturbances in the area. Elsewhere in the city that Sunday, George Berry, a 26-year-old Protestant, from Shore Street, was severely wounded when a bomb was thrown through his window, passing through the fanlight, with splinters injuring seven people in the room. Mr Berry, a former soldier, was struck in the neck and shoulder and died in hospital several days later. That common response of the authorities to bouts of unrest – the quick injection of military reinforcements and an increase in the frequency of military patrols – was warmly applauded by the *Belfast Telegraph* which claimed this had been 'one more emphatic justification' of their conviction that 'strong and prompt action' was 'the one readily effective method of dealing with outbursts of lawlessness'.[39] Despite the return of a more peaceful atmosphere which was to generally prevail for several weeks, the funeral procession of Protestant victims of the east Belfast bombing on Wednesday, 28

September provided trouble-makers with another opportunity to take revenge.[40] As the cortege of Mr McMinn and Mr Harrison was passing along the Donegall Road to the City Cemetery gunfire from the Falls was directed at the mourners. John Orr (32), of Derwent Street, was killed and three others were wounded. Also that day, sniping was reported in a number of districts, including Ardoyne and Nelson Street.

THE WILD WEST

Although one of the distinctive characteristics of the Twenties' conflict was the fact that it was not restricted to the west of the city, Belfast's sectarian cockpit remained the most consistently hostile and bloody of its districts.[41] This was due to the close proximity of large numbers of Protestants and Catholics, with interface areas proving especially tense. Unlike today, the Shankill area was densely populated and similar in size to the Falls, with other areas of west Belfast, such as the Grosvenor Road, also containing significant numbers of Protestants. However, for many Catholics west Belfast proved to be the only safe haven during a period when many were intimidated from their homes in mainly loyalist districts. Whilst the Falls area was already seriously overcrowded and a regular battleground, the district's long-established Catholic community promised sanctuary for beleaguered refugees from other districts. Yet at times, such as the summer of 1921, recent Catholic migrants to the Falls must have questioned their decision in seeking refuge in such a volatile area.

The start of a traditionally difficult month, was heralded by the killing of a Special in Newry and troops being fired at in the Markets area of Belfast. Loyalists in west Belfast joined with brethren in other parts of the city to commemorate the fifth anniversary of the Somme battle and the unionist press carried their usual stories about the unfurling of Orange arches and other preparations for the Twelfth.[42] Serious disturbances in the border region spread to the city on 6 July when an IRA squad operating from a nationalist district of west Belfast was probably responsible for carrying out an attack on police in the city centre.[43] Two RIC officers, Constables Jim Galvin and Henry Conway, both based at Glenravel Street barracks, had been on early morning traffic duty at the corner of Union Street and Little Donegall Street, when they were approached by a group of men from Library Street. Constable Galvin (26), originally from County Limerick, was attacked and disarmed before being shot and Constable Conway was wounded as he tried to draw his revolver. The planned nature of the attack was illustrated by the deliberate confusion caused by pedestrians who jostled passers-by, thereby creating an escape route for the assailants. The fatally wounded Constable Galvin, who had eight years' service in the RIC, was believed to have retrieved his revolver and fired a number of shots at his attackers as they escaped in the direction of Carrick Hill. Constable Galvin died shortly afterwards in hospital, where his colleague was also rushed in a serious state. The *Belfast Telegraph* reporter noted:

> The injured man was visited by his sister, who is a milliner in a Belfast shop. There was a pitiable scene as he was being conveyed from the ward to the operating theatre. Neither brother nor sister could speak, but tears flowed freely as the elevator disappeared with its burden.[44]

Although there were no major retaliatory attacks on Catholics in the wake of this police killing, unease in the city intensified.[45] Early in the morning of 8 July, police conducted searches of the Union and Stanhope Street area but were deterred by the large number of 'scouts' blowing whistles to warn IRA volunteers of their presence. Instead of moving freely, as anticipated, along deserted streets, the police found themselves involved in an hour-long gun battle with an estimated 15 IRA gunmen and had to call for reinforcements.[46] The spark for Belfast's 'Bloody Sunday', on the 10 July, was the attack on police at Raglan Street, off the Falls Road, late the previous evening. Rev. Hassan described this as an improvised attack by local residents, but most observers with local knowledge believed that police in armoured cars, who had been contemplating a raid, were lured into an ambush situation.[47] The daring nature of the Raglan Street attack might not have been typical of IRA activity in the city at this time, but it did indicate the presence of a significant number of active republican volunteers in west Belfast several months before their campaign 'officially' commenced. A 2nd Lieutenant in the local 'D' company of the IRA, speaking many years later, gave an interesting insight into IRA activity and especially the planning of such attacks. The republican veteran claimed that as many as 14 armed men were in position before curfew and had their normal recitation of the Rosary before being alerted by the banging of bin lids and the sounding of whistles in the Loney district. The company made their first sortie down Raglan Street, seven on either side of the road, around 11.20 that evening, crossing Albert Street and into Nail Street, but it was a false alarm. The next warning, half an hour later, proved to be a genuine one. Sean Maclomaire's detailed account of the attack on the Crossley tender is a vivid one:

> The tender came slowly: when it got 10 feet from Peel Street, the captain opened fire. I was about 15 or 16 feet off it when the 14 guns roared. A second volley was fired into it. Bullets were firing all the time and I emptied the rounds of my revolver into the tender. The firing lasted a full 10 minutes. The captain got round behind it. I and three men made the move through one house, over the wall and into the next street as we prepared to storm the tender. We came up to the tender. Our men were still firing as we got to the corner and Jack Donaghy shouted for us to look out as our bullets were hitting where we were. I gave the order to go back. When we went along the street the firing had stopped. We turned a corner, then a shout in a southern brogue, 'Halt! Hands up!' Jack Donaghy opened fire with his 'Peter the Painter'. Three policemen fell, 1 killed and 2 wounded ... We made our way to Albert Street – all the people left their doors opened – until we reached a house in Baker Street where we all gathered in case we were needed in the street again.[48]

Constable Conlon (33), a native of County Roscommon but stationed at Springfield Road Barracks, was shot in the neck and died instantly.[49] Two other police were seriously wounded, but survived the attack. They were Special Constable Charles Dunn and Constable Edward Hogan. In addition, the armoured car was destroyed and the IRA claimed they had suffered no casualties. In a follow-up search of the area, police found 1,000 rounds of ammunition and a German rifle in a house in neighbouring Ross Street. Despite the surprisingly light police casualties sustained against an enemy firing from close range with many weapons, the attack proved to be a major fillip for republican morale in the city and a ballad was devoted to the attack.[50] Part of this went:

> Oh, I'll tell you a tale of a row in the town
> When a lorry went up and it never came down
> It was the neatest oul sweetest row you'd ever meet
> When the boys caught the Specials down Raglan Street.
>
> They came cursing and swearing as always before
> And they swore they'd walk knee deep in Sinn Féin's gore

> But ours was the bullets those bould boys did meet
> And they ran like Hells Blazes down Raglan Street.[51]

Inevitably west Belfast was at the centre of much of the violence the following day. In the week after the Truce, over twenty people lost their lives in the city, 70 were seriously injured and over 200 houses were seriously damaged or destroyed, leaving a thousand homeless. On that fateful Sunday alone 16 were killed, including 11 Catholics, and 161 houses destroyed. Gunfire was intense and continuous from mid afternoon on the Shankill and Falls interfaces, with eyewitness reports of gunmen operating from the roofs of windows and street corners in these tightly packed streets. A tramcar was struck by snipers' bullets, and although there were no casualties, the service was discontinued. Rival crowds congregated on the main arteries of west Belfast, the Shankill and the Falls, and in the little side-streets linking them. Many of them had been watching the return of Orangemen in the late afternoon from a church parade in the Ulster Hall when gunfire had been directed at the stampeding crowd. An hour later, attacks were reported in an area stretching from the city centre right into the Shankill and the Falls, with reports of a soldier being wounded by gunfire in Upper Library Street, firing in Upper North Street, directed at police from Millfield and Carrick Hill (as well as the Old Lodge Road). Fierce gun-battles, involving machine gun and rifle fire, as well as the deployment of handguns and hand grenades, was reported in the Falls and Cullingtree Road area. One report suggested that a loyalist mob 'several thousands' strong, made 'a sudden and terrifying rush' in to streets on the Falls and noted that 'many of them carried petrol, paraffin, rags and even small bundles of wood.'[52]

During the evening 14 calls were made for the Fire Brigade and apart from the fatalities, another 40 people were injured. All the loss of life occurred in the west of the city, with at least 4 of the Catholic victims being ex-servicemen. Alexander Hamilton (21), a former member of the Inniskilling Fusiliers and Henry Mulholland (49) had both been shot in Cupar Street which experienced heavy violence and fires that day. Another ex-member of the Fusiliers, James Lenaghan (48) of Locan Street, was killed at the corner of Derby Street and the Falls Road, whilst Daniel Joseph Hughes (50), of Durham Place, an ex-member of the 7th Leinster Regiment, was shot in the Durham Street area. Frederick Craig (22), of Turin Street, who had served in France, was shot walking down Clonard Street, whilst two other Catholics, Bernard Monaghan (70), of Dunville

Street and William Tierney (56), of Osman Street, were killed at their doorstep
and in living-room respectively. Two fathers lost their lives desperately trying to
bring their children safely home. James McGuinness, a 35 year old mechanic,
had set off to fetch his child from Townsend Street but was shot dead near
Durham Street, whilst Daniel Hughes (28), of McCleery Street, was killed
rushing back towards his home, reputedly by a sniper operating from
Spamount Street. Patrick Hickland (46), of Hamilton Street, was beaten and
shot by a marauding loyalist mob in Boyd Street, whilst another Catholic
victim, Patrick Devlin, of Quadrant Street, who had been shot in Albert Street,
succumbed to his injuries the following April.

   Although Catholics on the Falls and Grosvenor Roads took the brunt of the
attacks, 5 Protestants also lost their lives that blood-soaked Sabbath. A 12-year-
old boy, William Baxter, of Argyle Street, was shot by a nationalist sniper as he
was making his way to Sunday School in Ashmore Street during the early afternoon, whilst another youngster, Ernest Park, of Moyola Street, was probably
killed by the same sniper, as he carried a kitten to a neighbour's home. David
McMullan (19), an apprentice fitter and keen footballer, was shot in the
Lawnbrook Avenue area, and a 50-year-old tailor, William Mullan, from James
Street, was shot and died shortly afterwards in the overstretched Royal Victoria
Hospital. Even the sick were not spared. Francis Robinson (65), of Brown Street,
had been lying ill in bed when fierce gunfire erupted in the Millfield and Peters
Hill area. He was hit in the head by a number of bullets which entered his upstairs
front window and these were later confirmed to have been police bullets.

   The curfew regulations which had been relaxed as a consequence of the
Collins truce, were reinforced the following day (11 July) in grim anticipation of
the imminent Orange marches. Whilst there was a decrease in the intensity of
the violence on the eve of the big Orange parade, there were further outrages
and three more fatalities in the city. A 45 year old Protestant haulage contractor,
William Brown, was killed by a nationalist sniper in David Street, whilst James
Ledlie (19), of Plevna Street, was killed trying to help rescue a friend's furniture.[53]
A young Catholic girl, Mary McGowan, had been crossing the street outside
her home in Derby Street with her mother, when they were shot at from a security force 'cage' lorry which had been patrolling what was described by locals at
the time as a quiet area. The inquest jury noted that the Specials had fired the
fatal bullets at the 13-year-old and suggested that 'in the interests of peace' the
Special Constabulary should not be solely deployed to police Catholic areas.[54]
The Twelfth celebrations were not, at least in the west of the city, accompanied

by the anticipated bouts of violence. The day after the parades the funerals of several of Sunday's victims of terror passed off without major disturbances. As with other funeral processions at the time, the local community came to a virtual standstill in respectful memory of those killed in the troubles. The *Belfast Telegraph* noted:

> The whole way from Albert Street to Milltown Cemetery where the interments took place, was thronging with a tremendous crowd of sympathisers. Blinds were drawn in all private dwelling-houses and places of business, and all work was suspended until after the passing of the funerals.[55]

Violence in western Belfast, in particular, eased after the loyal celebrations and did not reoccur on a significant scale until the end of the following month. Due to the unfortunate location of the City Cemetery, Protestant funerals provided an ideal opportunity for nationalist gunmen to attack loyalist mourners. Two Protestants attending funerals lost their lives inside a month and several others were wounded. On 30 August, Samuel Ferguson (42), from the Donegall Road, was shot whilst leaving the City Cemetery and, as noted earlier, several mourners at the funerals of those killed in the east Belfast bombing at the end of September, were hit by nationalist gunfire, with one of the injured, John Orr dying of his wounds. Four other Protestants died in violence in the west of the city during this period. In the most controversial case, Leopold Leonard (55), a French-polisher by trade and a prominent Shankill Road Orangeman, was shot dead as he walked along Peters Hill on his way to work in the early morning of 31 August. The shooting was not an isolated attack, accompanied as it was by onslaughts on tramcars containing loyalist workers. Yet nationalists were indignant at the verdict of the inquest jury which concluded that Mr Leonard's death had been 'inflicted by a member of the IRA acting in concert and under general orders.'[56] The *Irish News* naively recorded that there was 'not a tittle of evidence to support that statement', suggesting that the verdict was based 'on opinion [and] not on evidence.'[57] That evening a 5-year-old child, William Johnston, of Louisa Street, was shot in the neck by a sniper firing into the Brown Street district of the Shankill and he died in hospital nearly three weeks later. The following evening a teenager, Walter Campbell, from Silvio Street, was shot in the stomach during gunfire in the same area and died shortly afterwards. Also, an elderly Protestant, Thomas Lee (70), from Manor Street, was crushed by a military armoured vehicle on 31 August.

The following month there was considerable intimidation of workers, both Catholic and Protestant, in the west of the city. These included Catholic tramline workers who were forced to leave their jobs on the spot after the cemetery shootings and Catholic workers at a Donegall Road timberworks. Protestant workers were also harassed leaving Murphy's Brickworks on the Springfield Road and a mill in Flax Street. Though these attacks were frequently spontaneous, they were no less vicious or deadly in their results. Assailants were often persistent as well as deadly, but in one case, at least, they were thwarted. Towards the end of September a Sandy Row carter, John Johnston, was attacked near Durham Street, and received medical attention in the nearby Royal Victoria Hospital. On leaving he was again attacked by a gunman whose weapon jammed. Two more Catholics died during this period. In a case reminiscent of earlier 'murder gang' atrocities, Derry-born Francis James Bradley (26), a labourer living in McCleery Street, was shot, probably by a 'B' Special, in West Street at Peter's Hill on 31 August. Reports that a raucous, allegedly drink-sodden group of Specials, who had just cleared Molloys' pub at Brown Square and had drawn up a cordon outside, had started firing at Bradley as he passed by them, were noted in some papers.[58] Also that evening, another young Catholic, James McFadden (16), of Malvern Street, died from a chest wound following disturbances in Wall Street.

As one might imagine, everyday life in west Belfast at this time, especially on the main interfaces between the Shankill and the Falls, was difficult but people tried to conduct their lives as normally as possible in tense times. For Catholics it was a period of financial difficulty caused by sudden loss of wages and severe overcrowding. Strangers were viewed with the deepest suspicion on both sides of the sectarian divide and people restricted their movements in the main to their own areas.[59] Workers carrying out essential repairs to services and helping to maintain tram services were especially vulnerable and many paid with their lives for this devotion to duty. Although the authorities realised their responsibility in protecting those workers brave enough to venture in to threatening areas like west Belfast to carry out specialised repairs, it still did not diminish the fear of potential attack. Robert McElborough worked as a gas fitter during the conflict and recalled being sent to the Falls to 'cut off a number of meters in streets that had been set on fire'.[60] McElborough recalled the dangers associated with this task:

> One street on the Falls Road was my most dangerous job. A block of 6 houses were set alight and when the fire brigade fixed their hoses on the

water main the snipers cut the hose pipes with their bullets. I was warned by the brigade and the police of the danger I ran with these snipers, but for the danger of the meters exploding I would have backed out but I knew if the fire got a hold the service pipes in the houses there would be some trouble getting out. However, with the assistance of the Lancia police car, I was able to remove these meters and cap the service pipes.[61]

Whilst relationships between the nationalist community of the Falls and the RIC had been comparatively good before the Troubles started, suspicion and mistrust, especially of the Special Constabulary, soon deepened. Allegations of Specials periodically invading nationalist areas such as the Falls in their lorries and running amok, abound in republican folklore.[62] Although a distinction must be drawn between alleged and actual misdemeanours, it would be unwise to belittle the genuine fear generated by the behaviour of some Specials. Jimmy Kelly recalled what it was like lying in bed listening to activities going on in the street below:

> At night we were sometimes awakened by the noise of a raiding party . . . First there was the rumble of a heavy lorry as the vehicle slowed to a halt outside. Its headlights cast shadows on the window blinds as we lay quaking, listening to heavy foot-falls approach. They stopped at a house a few yards from us on the opposite side. Then came the sound of fists pounding on the door followed by a crash as they burst in. Many foot-steps ascended the stairs and we could hear shouts and screams as if a struggle was going on. Then again the noise of feet on the stairs as if 1 or 2 men were being manhandled. The door slammed closed and the engine of a lorry started up and soon it was moving out of the street.[63]

A feeling of 'us against them', fine-tuned by a strongly critical tone adopted by the Catholic hierarchy, pervaded throughout the minority community, adding to its sense of cohesion and unity of purpose. An inhabitant of English Street remembered a reliable Falls warning system related to an approaching security presence:

> Women would have got out of the top windows and do you know those big old-fashioned gramophones, well they would have . . . shouted through them and they'd have binlids, bells, whistles, everything.[64]

Other examples of 'helping the boyhos' included leaving doors ajar for escaping volunteers, extinguishing gas lamps just before curfew to deter Specials from making such raids, banging dustbin lids and using multi-coloured torches to warn activists of approaching security forces, 'lending' houses for meetings or the assembling of volunteers, and for the storage of weapons.[65] Not far away in west Belfast, but on the loyalist side of the Grosvenor Road, gunmen in and out of uniform were familiar sights on the street. Eddie Steele remembered seeing a Special running down his street with a revolver in his hand telling him to get indoors and also a pair of local toughs peering round a street corner with smoke still escaping from their revolvers.

Yet it was the delicate balance between a community determined to carry on with everyday life despite the close proximity of civil unrest which most accurately encapsulates the atmosphere in west Belfast during the early 1920s. D. Curran aptly described the Falls at this time:

> In the main business thoroughfare most of the shops were open as usual, the trams were running and there was little to indicate the deadly strife in progress elsewhere. Yet streets within a stone's throw could only be entered at certain periods at grave risk. The sharp crack of revolvers, punctuated at times by the louder reports of rifle shots were heard while the rattle of machine-guns indicated that the military were taking a hand in the deadly game.[66]

Overcrowding, enduring unemployment and unprecedented poverty, a heavy and frequently insensitive security presence and the constant threat of physical danger posed by gunmen and bombers operating both from within and outside the warren of little streets between the Falls and Shankill, may not have been the unique experience of the west Belfast populace, but these fears were perhaps most keenly felt in those districts. During the summer of 1921, the city's most infamous killing-fields had again claimed many lives and yet more suffering and destruction lay ahead for the residents of both the Falls and the Shankill.

MAKING SENSE OF IT ALL

The loyalist press mocked the 'Day of Truce' which followed the signing of the truce. In condemning the violence which erupted in the city during the early hours of Sunday 10th July, claiming at least 14 lives and injuring over 50 more, the *Belfast Telegraph* bemoaned that 'anything occurring in Belfast at the moment' would be 'blamed on the Orangemen and 12th celebrations.'[67] However, the *Telegraph* assured its readers that 'loyalists and Orangemen had nothing to do with yesterday's trouble' which had been planned and carried out 'by Sinn Féiners'.[68] Despite the main Orange parade in the city passing off without major incident, the language of the unionist leadership was noticeably more virulent than it had been for the royal visit a few weeks previously. Craig, whilst adhering to his promises of 'peace' and 'reconciliation', also emitted an ominous anti-republican warning. He reminded the city's Orangemen:

> How can we ever forget what has been done to our kith and kin in the South of Ireland? It's a hard thing, but I say this on behalf of the whole Ulster people that we are prepared now and today to say, 'No Republic, no tampering with Ulster, never. We are going to enforce peace if it does not come naturally.[69]

A constant theme of loyalist press coverage was the stress on 'defending' their community. A couple of days later the *Belfast Telegraph*, in a leading article entitled 'The Peril of Belfast', whilst condemning the 'reckless manner' of the city's gunmen, suggested that the resulting 'feeling of irritation' had inevitably led to some loyalists doing 'their best to protect themselves with the limited means at their disposal' and their conclusion was that 'frankly we do not see much prospect of peace till these gunmen are rooted out.'[70] Sinn Féin was a frequent target for unionist venom. Early in August, the *Newsletter* declared that republicans were 'still under the delusion that Ulster can be intimidated or coerced, directly or indirectly.'[71] However, in the same article, the *Newsletter*, in a more conciliatory vein, suggested that if Sinn Féin succeeded establishing a just administrative and justice system, they 'will go far to gain the confidence of the people of the North, and may within a reasonable time, gain it altogether.'[72] More familiar, forceful criticism of de Valera's claim that Sinn Féin didn't intend using force against Ulster was soon to be employed by the same paper. In a hard-hitting editorial, the *Newsletter* asked:

> What have they been doing for two years? They have sent out their flying columns throughout Ulster murdering loyal citizens and burning property, robbing Post Offices, and cutting telegraph and phone lines, and

1 Rioting in central Belfast

2 Manning the barricades at North Street

3 Military on duty in north Belfast

4 'C' Specials patrolling on the Albertbridge Road

5 City Hall gathering; the first meeting of the Northern Ireland Parliament

6 Road-block in the southern suburbs

7 Searching pedestrians after the assassination of William Twaddell

8 Police escorting IRA prisoners along Great Victoria Street

9 The Model School in Divis Street destroyed by arson

10 'Falls firebugs' strike at Donegall Quay

11 'Collecting ammo'

12 Smiling for the cameras after a police raid

13 Seizure of a Falls arms cache

14 Curious bystanders gather during city centre sniping

15 A Lancia patrol-car ventures down York Street

16 Police patrol in Little George Street

17 Specials on duty

18 Soldiers accompany a republican funeral procession

committing other outrages – all of them ordered by de Valera and his ministers. Yet these are the men who say they do not contemplate the use of force. Let no one in Ulster trust them. They fully intend to do all the damage they can.[73]

The loyalist press also complained that 'all the advances and concessions' made during negotiations with republicans were 'upon one side, all the obstinacy and refusal upon the other', warning the government that it was time for them to realise that 'peace in the present mood of Sinn Féin is impossible.'[74] Apart from their fears that British politicians would ignore their rights and desires at the expense of placating those of the majority on the Irish island and to save the truce south of the border, the unionist press were also embittered by press attacks from across the water. The *Belfast Telegraph* angrily denied claims in the *Daily News* on 31 August that unionists had been the 'aggressors' in the late summer violence, and asked a number of rhetorical questions:

> Was it 'confessed Orangemen' who fired upon shipyard workers going to their day's toil? Was it 'confessed Orangemen' who fired out of Gresham Street and brought down a father and son? Was it 'confessed Orangemen' whose revolvers were blazing on Springfield Road?[75]

The *Daily News* had not been alone in laying the blame on loyalists for the late summer bout of madness. The *Westminster Gazette*, suggesting that loyalists had concocted 'a deliberate and well-planned attempt' to 'provoke a riot', focussed on tension around Mackies in the Springfield area, rather than North Queen Street which saw the most serious outbreak of trouble, to illustrate their point.[76] Describing how Mackies' employees and other workers went down the Springfield Road on trams from one of which 'bolts and stones were rained on people standing at street corners', the *Gazette* concluded that such a 'deliberate' attack by tram passengers 'naturally incensed the residents and large crowds flocked down to the Road.'[77] Both the *Gazette* and the *Daily Chronicle*, albeit to a different degree, castigated the security forces for not giving enough protection to the public. The following day the *Gazette* suggested that the armed Catholic response in the north and west of the city was not surprising because the 'police and military didn't give adequate protection' and suggested sinister motives on the part of the security forces in ensuring that 'nothing was being done to protect the nationalists who were being shot in their own streets.'[78] The

Chronicle also pointed out that the police were unable, without military support, to cope with the intimidation of workers both in the north of the city where textile workers had to leave their place of work through a hastily-made hole in a brick wall and at Mackies Foundry where workers were attacked.[79] Although the *Guardian* conceded that 'both sides must bear responsibility' for the violence at the end of the month, they insisted that 'the blame for beginning the trouble lies at the door of the Orangemen.'[80] There was also some political support for Sinn Féin amongst the British press. The *Nation* sympathised with de Valera's position, claiming that Sinn Féin was 'well within the sphere of negotiation' and that it was Ulster which, 'as always', was 'the obstacle to Irish peace.'[81] The *Morning Post* was one of the few papers to actually depict loyalists as oppressed, arguing that the purpose of the attacks in the city had been 'to provoke Ulster to reprisals and so put her in the wrong'.[82] The *Post* went on to remind Lloyd George and other politicians negotiating with Sinn Féin that Ulster 'should be treated with the honesty, courtesy and loyalty she has ever shown, even under provocation, towards England.'[83]

The nationalist press covered several contentious issues during the summer especially during the lull in violence at the start of August. Condemning the comparative lightness of prison sentences given to rioters, including a six month jail sentence meted out to three men robbing a shop in Garmoyle Street, the *Irish News* warned that 'only a stern demonstration of the rigours of the law can stem the current of disorder which . . . has left parts of the city looking as if they had been overrun by an invading horde of savages.'[84] Another subject of considerable debate was the ongoing plight of those forced out of their homes and jobs. On the anniversary of the industrial expulsions, the *Irish News* deplored the fact that there was a 'general acceptance of the situation as normal' and 'a condition of things which would not last 6 weeks in any civilised city in the world is taken as rather natural and inevitable in Belfast after 12 months, during which Catholics have been living from hand to mouth in the generous aid of sympathisers from all over the world'.[85] Several weeks later, another editorial lamented a situation where 'thousands of ex-servicemen are tramping the streets of the city day after day, despairingly searching for work that is not to be had.'[86] Some had highly imaginative solutions to this problem of Catholic unemployment. Francis McArdle, a civil engineer in the city suggested, in a letter to Bishop MacRory, that 'the only real solution to the problem' of expulsions was 'to establish opposing industries.'[87] In particular, Mr McArdle urged the financial backing of an industrial engineering scheme which would involve the purchase of a three-acre site, with foundry buildings and equipment costing over £50,000 and employing a workforce of around 500, with the hope that workers 'would agree to contribute a portion of their earnings to the expelled fund, so that from the very beginning the drain of the White Cross Fund could be greatly reduced'.[88]

The *Irish News* combined its stance of claiming the moral high ground in terms of its monopoly of suffering, with an emphasis on the sanctity of the ideal of a united Ireland. Thus, disingenuously asserting that 'not a shred of evidence' existed as far as the identity of the policemen's assailants was concerned, the *Irish News* urged nationalists in the city to 'close up their ranks' and to practise 'restraint and prudence'.[89] In its Twelfth Day report the *Irish News* described in detail the toll of damage and suffering felt in Catholic districts over the previous weekend, of areas 'swept by machinegun and revolver fire' and of 'lorries and armoured cars laden with men equipped for battle' driving through the streets but apparently unable to prevent civilians forcing the 'unhappy residents of more than 200 houses out into the bullet-swept streets' and to eventually escape 'unscathed and triumphant'.[90] Despite the moral indignation of such articles, the *Irish News* was not averse to underlining its political solution to such problems, declaring at the end of the same leading article, 'the dawn may seem long in coming, but it will come and the light of Liberty will bless a united Ireland.'[91]

The very different interpretations of the street violence, as well as the scapegoating of opposing factions, should not disguise a shared recognition that, far from representing a turn down the road towards peace, the events of that summer rather represented a worrying increase in militant activity on both sides. Far from ushering in an interval of calm, the post-Truce period actually witnessed a significant increase in the level of street violence, illustrated by three especially frenetic bouts of blood-letting during the summer. Whilst there would be a slight reduction in the number of security incidents during the last part of 1921, the mood of non-conciliation which had been evident in this midsummer period continued, and along with the inevitable escalation in political activity, Belfast people felt far from optimistic about the future.

Chapter 11

A false dawn

The last quarter of the year brought a mixture of comparative peace, high profile political activity culminating in the signing of the Treaty in London, the formal transfer of security powers to the new northern administration and sporadic street violence, including a particularly bloody 4 day spell late in November when nearly 30 lives were lost. Although the state of security in particular areas was more likely to have been determined by the degree of local tension provoked by specific incidents in the immediate district than by political negotiations or the killing of policemen elsewhere, it was not coincidental that when political activity was low-key, the level of communal violence in Belfast was also reduced.

Whilst there were no fatalities recorded in October, security incidents were noted in the local press almost on a daily basis. The first weekend in the month was 'a fairly quiet' one with 'a few isolated cases of assault', armed robberies in Albert and North Queen Streets and a baton-charge on stone throwers at the Shaftesbury Square end of Donegall Road resulting in minor injuries for two policemen.[1] On 3 October, John Bell, of Station Street, who had been suspected of being a Special Constable, was attacked by an armed gang whilst visiting his mother in Lepper Street. Attempted bombings and sniper attacks continued throughout October. A bomb was thrown at worshippers leaving a Protestant church on the evening of Sunday 4 October and the following day a Mills bomb was thrown into a house in Great George's Street which, although owned by Catholics, contained predominantly Protestant lodgers. Fortunately this bomb failed to explode. Sniping from Meadow Street into North Queen Street was reported on the same day and inside 48 hours armed gangs carried out four raids (three of which were successful) in North Queen Street, Atlantic Avenue and Duncairn Gardens. Other cases of violence that month included a 'sensational' incident, with modern resonance, outside Catholic churches, where two IRA dissidents were chained to the railings of St Patrick's Church in Donegall Street and St Paul's Church in west Belfast, and the harassment of Catholic pupils and teachers at a school in Conway Street.[2] On 10 October, a familiar target for attack was again chosen. Tram workers, on this occasion Protestant ex-servicemen reconstructing track near Foundry Street off the Newtownards Road, were warned to leave their work and when they didn't, were fired at shortly afterwards. They eventually resumed work under military protection. Over a week later, the press reported a renewal of shooting in the city with a teenager, Maggie Courtney, receiving gunshot wounds in Stanhope Street. Also, on 19 October, a policeman was struck by a missile near Henry Street Barracks, whilst a fireman, James Johnston, received a foot wound at Nelson Street. On the same day, there were reports of further intimidation of sections of the Gallaher workforce and the assault of a newsboy in Clifton Street. As the month drew to its close, there was a robbery on business premises in Upper Library Street.

Leading Unionists took advantage of the lull to condemn others for their failure to stem the tide of violence. Transfer of security powers to Belfast was obviously going to take time, and the intervening period was to prove a difficult one for the agencies of law and order. Speaking to a group of Strandtown Unionists in east Belfast, the Minister for Home Affairs, Richard Dawson Bates claimed he was 'more like a King without a Kingdom', pointing out that the responsibility for security still lay with British officials in Dublin Castle. Bates testily argued that these officials, 'with the excuse of the Truce, had fettered the hands of the military and police authorities in Belfast'.[3] At grassroots level, such frustration with the absence of strong measures taken against the perpetrators of violent actions, was difficult to contain. Following attacks on workers' trams during this period, Fred Crawford noted in his diary: 'My tigers are very difficult just now to keep in hand: in fact except the Ulster government does not get some force up to meet present emergency there will be trouble that they will not be able to cope with.'[4] Whilst sharing his colleagues' frustration over co-ordination of security policy, Craig was also obliged to represent Ulster's interests at the forthcoming London conference. Announcing on 4 October that he would be attending the conference, Craig assuaged concerned right-wingers within his party by suggesting refusal to attend might prove to be harmful to loyalist interests.[5]

As the London conference opened, the British press again turned their attention to the Ulster question. Hard-line stances were taken by the *Daily News*, with Hugh Martin focusing on the 'Orange terror' in Belfast which he maintained had been 'the main feature of the recent violence', and by the pro-Union editor of the *Spectator*, J. St Loe Stachey, who described the 'spirit' of Belfast as 'practical' rather than 'bigoted or unmerciful', warning that the 'strain' of republican violence and external political pressure upon the loyalist community was on the verge of becoming 'intolerable'.[6] Most papers distanced themselves from the position of the rival parties in Ulster, with even pro-union journals like the *Express*, whilst pledging its support for 'maintaining the fundamental rights of Ulster', reminded its readership that Britain would 'not permit the fate of this or that village or district to stand in the way of the settlement of the infinitely greater question of Irish peace.'[7]

Once the conference had opened, Craig felt compelled to reassure loyalists who were concerned that, in the eventuality of it breaking down, a concerted republican onslaught would be made on the north. His political opponents condemned the Northern Ireland Prime Minister after he addressed an UULA meeting in east Belfast during the middle of October, for 'openly lending himself to the infamous plot against the public welfare devised by [the] inventors of the flaming falsehood' of such an attack.[8] South of the border, Dáil Éireann's official organ, the 'Irish Bulletin', in denying the existence of such a plan, alleged it was Craig's supporters who had been 'the only party in Ireland which has indulged in bloodshed and destruction' since the signing of the truce three months previously.[9] In his response, the Ulster premier reminded Sinn Féin that Ulster could 'only be won' and 'never coerced', also refuting their claim that the violence was one-sided, by naming several instances of republican-initiated violence, including recent incidents, such as the Vere Street killings and attacks on Protestants attending funerals of other victims.[10]

With the temporary reduction in the number of security incidents, the local press turned its attention towards other conflict-related stories, including the boycott, the enduring plight of those banished from work and home, and the progress of compensation claims. The growing dissatisfaction of local businessmen at Lloyd George's reluctance to intervene in the boycott dispute and disquiet over the lack of protection afforded to northern traders was expressed during meetings of the Belfast Wholesale Merchants and Manufacturers Association. Northern nationalists also condemned the boycott, but reminded their unionist opponents that it 'arose directly from the illegal, brutal, violent and murderous interference' of Catholic workers to 'earn the price of daily bread for themselves and their families'. The *Irish News* and went on to criticise this pressure group, none of whose members had 'uttered a word in protest or deprecation up to this hour.'[11] City councillors met representatives of those Catholics thrown out of work, at the City Hall on 3 October. Desperate pleas for intervention and grim forecasts of 'dire starvation' were made by republicans, including Miss Mary Galway. Criticising the 'captains of industry', the 'merchant princes' and 'impotent' City councillors, the *Irish News* forecast that Belfast's trade could be revived 'within a week if the political salary-bugs and noisy bigots place the public will before their own selfish interests and senseless prejudices.'[12]

Although the contributions made by charity groups such as the American Committee For Relief in Ireland failed to solve the problems caused by such immediate poverty, they were certainly of great assistance to the most desperate. By October the White Cross Society had distributed about £100,000 in weekly payments to the families of those evicted in the industrial expulsions the previous year.[13] Meanwhile, the plight of other victims of the conflict was being, albeit belatedly, addressed. The enormous and ever-growing number of riot claims had inevitably resulted in a considerable backlog of cases, many dating back to the previous summer, and an estimated 2,700 claims for damages still had to be heard in the city's courts by October.[14] Many claimants were to be disappointed when their cases were eventually heard. Unrealistic sums were claimed and consequently many victims of violence were to be dismayed by the subsequent decisions of the court. In awarding a paltry £13 10s. for a claim of nearly £1,000, Deputy Recorder John Leech remarked that the settlement was 'a good deal below the original claim, which was nothing unusual, for wild claims were often put in that court.'[15]

'EAST, WEST – HOME'S BEST'

Although major street disturbances were not to erupt again until late November, the tension caused by the Treaty negotiations in London and increasing communal feeling from the middle of November (especially in the Short Strand, where there were reports of shooting and a bomb thrown in Seaforde Street), indicated that a fresh bout of violence was imminent. A strange incident was reported in the local press early in November. Following a police raid at Kent Street, off Royal Avenue in the city centre, a Protestant, Arthur Hunt was discovered in a workyard described as 'a Sinn Féin prison' where he had been 'incarcerated, under sentence of death'.[16] The authorities' decision to relax the curfew restrictions on 8 November (the start of curfew was put forward to 11.30 p.m.) seemed, in the light of subsequent events, to be misguided and premature. On the 19 November prolonged riots broke out both in the east of the city and in York Street, where 3 people were shot and another 4 casualties were reported in Ballymacarrett the following day.

The next three days (21–24 November) proved to be the bloodiest for some time, with at least 24 fatalities and 91 injuries being recorded. Shipyard workers were attacked on their way to work on the morning of 21 November, with rifle and revolver fire raking the district for a considerable time. William Hanna (40), a Harland and Wolff painter – an ex-member of the Royal Engineers who had been gassed at the Somme – died after being shot in the head at the corner of Foundry Street on the Newtownards Road. Gunfire from the Short Strand also claimed the life of Robert Graham (50), who was shot in the Beersbridge area, on his way to the Electric Station where he worked as a crane-driver (Mr Graham died in hospital four days later). A third Protestant worker lost his life proceding to his place of work that morning. Shipyard worker Henry Stirling (25), of Clandeboye Street, who had been walking along the Newtownards Road when he was felled by a sniper operating near Bryson Street, died over six months later. Following the arrival of police at the scene of the attacks, gunfire resumed, albeit at a reduced level but street assaults and ferocious stoning continued unabated in the Youngs Row area where a house was wrecked and some shops were set alight on the Newtownards Road. Around tea-time a Catholic barman, James Hagan (22), who worked at the Turbines public-house in Station Street, disobeyed the orders of a gunman who fired both at him and a colleague. Mr Hagan died shortly afterwards in hospital from a head wound. Violence got worse in the north of the city from the late afternoon and with the onset of darkness, sniping became heavy, especially in Little George Street. Just after eight o'clock, Andrew James Stewart (22), a Protestant, was shot dead in Earl Street, as he returned from work. The *Irish News'* response to the previous day's violence and the proposed transfer of security responsibility was one of weary, ironical acceptance. It noted:

> Men walked the streets of East and North Belfast last evening, carrying rifles in their hands and bandoliers on their shoulders; they took up 'vantage points' at their leisure; they fired volley after volley into the streets and houses where Catholics and Nationalists live. W*hy not*?[17]

'A day and night of terror' followed, with at least 10 people losing their lives and over 50 receiving serious injuries. Rioting, shooting and bombing outrages were common in what the *Belfast Newsletter* labelled the city's 'Big Day of Terror'.[18] In the east, a bomb was thrown into the grounds of St Matthew's Church and an attempt was made to burn the sexton's house. Andrew Patton (32), a Protestant from Saunderson Street who had a distinguished war record, died from injuries sustained in the disturbances which followed and nearly 40 others were injured. Earlier in the day gunfire had been directed at shipyard workers during their lunch-break. Unlikely victims of this shooting were two Protestant clerks working in their offices at the Bridge End Labour Exchange. Both of these office workers, William McMordie (22) and J.P. Keating (28) died from their injuries. A besieged shopkeeper likened the 'continuous rattle' of gunfire to 'thunder' and, referring to the four hour gun battle, concluded there must have been 'a little arsenal of rifle and revolver ammunition in the network of streets between Bryson Street and Bridge End.'[19] Elsewhere in Ballymacarrett, Neil and Kathleen McConvey died after a stray police bullet burst a gas main in their Thompson Street home. Mrs McConvey ran a spirit grocery in Thompson Street and her young assistant, Minnie Kelly, who had been lodging with them and who was due to visit her family in Draperstown, also succumbed to the gas fumes. Also that evening, another east Belfast spirit grocer lost his life. Patrick Malone, died from a chest wound after a group of men shot him in Beersbridge Road shop.

Gun attacks had been reported in the York Street and North Queen Street districts from early in the morning, though the arrival of an armoured car from Victoria Barracks brought a brief calm. However, yet another spirit grocer, Patrick Connolly, was shot in his Duncairn Gardens shop and died the following day. An early morning bomb attack resulted in several people suffering minor injuries in Henry Street. Bertie Phillips (25), was fatally wounded by a sniper as he endeavoured to escort a terrified woman to safety and the ex-Royal Navy man had to lie without assistance as gunfire continued unabated in Molyneaux Street, off York Street. Another tragic case involved a distraught father looking for his son at the height of the shooting. There were several other incidents in Belfast that day. Agnes Stewart, of Little George Street, and a policeman were injured by gunfire and an ex-soldier, Patrick John McNally, of Park Street, who had made a quick journey to the corner shop, was shot dead in Stanhope Street (a police car had been seen in the vicinity at the time). Fortunately several employers let their workforce out early to avoid them running the gauntlet at tea-time. The bloody events of Monday 22 November coincided with the transfer of security responsibility from Westminster to the northern administration, but despite loyalist clamour for such an action, there was no short-term unionist rejoicing.[20]

A more practical immediate step was taken by the authorities, with the revision of the city's curfew regulations. Bill-boards and press notices coined the slogan 'East West-Home's Best', warning people not to venture out on the streets at night.[21] This, along with a heavier security force presence in troublespots, meant a reduction in the number of violent incidents the next day. However, several people were either seriously injured or lost their lives, with the worst cases occurring in the York Street and North Queen Street districts. Four Catholics were fatally wounded in the north of the city. Foreman Patrick Brunton (38) was fatally wounded in Dock Street by a sniper believed to have been operating from Corporation Street, Ellen Bell (70) was killed at lunchtime in Great Patrick Street, Michael Spallen (27), a sculptor, was shot dead crossing Little George Street and Margaret Jane Millar (48), of Dock Lane, who died the following day from a chest wound. There were also reports of looters being shot in separate parts of the city (North Queen Street and on the Woodstock Road), a publican was wounded in York Street, four people received minor gunshot injuries following an outburst of gunfire in Royal Avenue and, despite the increased protection afforded to workers by heavy-armoured vehicles and caged lorries on their journeys to work, there were further reported cases of sniping.

Further carnage occurred the next day (Wednesday 24 November). Trouble flared up at the funeral of Andrew James Patton when Catholics were attacked as the cortege passed down York Street. A Catholic youth was shot and a spirit grocer in the area had a lucky escape when he was fired at. Not so fortunate was John Kelly who owned a spirit grocery in Ohio Street, off the Crumlin Road. A single gunman entered his shop, which had been attacked several times previously and opened fire on Mr Kelly who was talking to a customer, Thomas Thompson, also of Ohio Street. The latter, a member of the Orange and Masonic Orders, went to the aid of Kelly and was fatally wounded for his efforts. John Kelly's son, Eugene, who was in the store, also received fatal injuries (he died in hospital the next day). This was a rare example of cross-community help and common suffering. However, any chance of the former spreading soon evaporated on account of an attack on a Shankill tram later that day.

ATTACKS ON WORKERS' TRAMS

Travelling across the city, especially on trams operating on permanent lines and bearing clearly designated destinations proved to be a dangerous activity for many of Belfast's workers at this time. Many were the victims of frequently serious physical abuse, usually executed by gangs interested in identifying victims of a different religion, and there were also cases of fatal shooting attacks, frequently committed by loyalist gunmen. Although security force protection was sometimes provided, especially near key road junctions during peak times, it was clearly impossible for them to give round-the-clock protection to tram passengers. Not that the authorities were complacent about such threats. The Belfast City Trams Department used ingenuity to combat the growing number of attacks on their vehicles by fitting heavy wire-mesh around trams. This kept out some missiles thrown at the vehicles, such as bottles and stones, and reduced the damage of more deadly missiles, including Mills bombs and hand-grenades.[22]

Workers' trams passing through or near nationalist areas on the periphery of the city centre were inevitable targets for attack. There were two serious bomb-ings within a 48 hour period during the latter part of November. Returning yard workers on the packed 62 Oldpark-bound tram were, at about six o'clock on the evening of 22 November, close to Mitchell's Distillery in the Corporation Street area, when the motorman observed a group of men standing in a dimly-lit Little Patrick Street. A few moments later he felt the impact of an enormous explosion accompanied by a brief outburst of gunfire. The floor of the tram collapsed and its glass sides smashed to pieces. Confusion reigned on the vehicle, although some alert passengers and pedestrians gave chase, albeit losing the culprits in the maze of side-streets. Three people lost their lives in this attack and there were several other casualties. Two friends who commuted to the Workman and Clark yards from their home in Comber, died instantly in the attack. They were William Cairnduff (40), who died of blast injuries and his younger townsman, James Rodgers, the son of a RIC sergeant, recently widowed, who died from gunshot wounds. Another worker, Robert Nesbitt (17), of Josephine Street, died a few days later from his injuries. The *Northern Whig* reported that 'the cries and moanings of the wounded [were] harrowing in the extreme' and went on to describe the attack as 'an outrage comparable in its unspeakable atrocity with the worst that has been committed in various Continental countries by Nihilists and other enemies of mankind.'[23]

A remarkably similar and even costlier attack was executed two days later. As noted above, 24 November had seen less rioting and gunfire in the city, but a workers' tram bound for the Shankill proved an irresistible target for republican bombers lurking in the 'no man's land' area around Berry Street in the city centre. As it proceeded along Royal Avenue, a member of a group of bystanders loitering outside a shipping office at the corner of Berry Street, approached the tram and threw a bomb into the vehicle. Despite a horrific toll of dead and injured, the crowded nature of the tramcar confined splinters to a small radius, thereby reducing the number of seriously injured. Four people died and nearly thirty were injured. The fatalities were all middle-aged 'bread-winners'. They were Richard Graham (42), of Beverly Street, a Harland and Wolff foreman, Jeremiah Fleming (54), of Glenvale Street, a joiner at the shipyard, Robert Johnston (41), of Westmore Street and Thomas Rodgers (66), of Northumberland Street.[24] A number of people chased the bombers and two men were held by a crowd but were subsequently released by police. A press report described the 'terrible scene' as the 'poor fellows' were carried into the Royal Victoria Hospital. It said:

> Their begrimed faces, soiled and oily from their day's work, were smat-tered with blood and blood was flowing from their wounds. Their dungarees were also saturated with blood and with their clothing torn in places by the force of the explosion and the fragments of the bomb.[25]

Although murder and mayhem continued the following day, it was not on the same scale as the previous 72 hours and proved to be the end of this brief yet bloody period. Clearly the increased security presence on the streets – 'armoured cars with military in charge and Crossley tenders containing armed police patrolled the city all day up to midnight' – was a major factor in the reduction in the level of violence. However, it was not sufficiently tight to deter two murders from taking place in the city around teatime on 25 November.[26] Harbour police were easy targets for armed gangs, using guarding relatively remote premises on their own. For the IRA, the perpetrators of such attacks, such targets had the dual attraction of an easy 'uniform' hit and the chance to add to their depleted weaponry. Harbour Constable John McHenry, a popular officer with 30 years service, was found dying in the Milewater Road area, having been shot six times. Also around this time in the north of the city, a Catholic shopkeeper, James McIvor, was shot dead outside his shop door in Little Patrick Street. The neighbour he was chatting to was also wounded.[27] Spasmodic attacks, sometimes with fatal consequences, continued to occur during the last few days of the month. On 29 November, a loyalist bomber approached Keegan Street and lobbed a Mills bomb into the nationalist quarter.

Shrapnel struck Annie McNamara in the throat and killed her. Early the following morning, in what some regarded as a reprisal attack, Alexander Reid (48), a Protestant, was shot dead going to work in the shipyard. Mr Reid, who had been forced out of his East Street home the previous summer, had been waiting for his son outside a tobacconist's shop on the city side of the Ormeau Road (where he lived) when he was hit by a Cromac Street sniper.[28] In other attacks the following day, a young Catholic barman was shot on the Lisburn Road and a shipyard worker narrowly missed death in Russell Street, whilst a bomb exploded in Berry Street near the city centre.[29]

DECEMBER DEVASTATION

The culmination of the Treaty negotiations early in December resulted in increasing tension which boiled over on a couple of occasions, although not to the degree of mid November.[30] An attack on a police car was reported on 7 December and a man was arrested following disturbances in North Queen Street the same day.[31] There had been 'much rejoicing' in nationalist areas once the news of events in London had reached them and the *Northern Whig* reported how 'bonfires [were] lighted, Sinn Féin flags flown ostentatiously – many of them [were] removed by police'.[32] Some shooting incidents were reported during the next weekend, although serious injuries were minimal. A police officer was shot on Saturday 10 December and there were reports of firing in the docks area the same evening. Two people were shot in north Belfast the following day, with the focus of attention shifting to the east of the city on Monday, with reports of a woman receiving an arm injury on the Newtownards Road and shots being fired into a shop on the Woodstock Road.

There was an escalation in violence the following day when three people were wounded, one on the Newtownards Road and two in Marrowbone. One of the latter, Michael Crudden, of Oldpark Road, was returning home from evening mass at the Sacred Heart Church with his brother and was walking up Glenview Street, when he was fatally shot by a lone gunman.[33] Inevitably the workers' trams on the Oldpark Road were a renewed target for snipers the following morning and later that evening there was gunfire in the Marrowbone, York Street and eastern parts of the city. The same areas were tense the next day when two bombs exploded in the Marrowbone, although there were fortunately no casualties. A fatal shooting in the Ormeau Road that evening underlies the degree of fear which many people, especially 'strangers' to an area, had at this time. Gunfire was heard in Ormeau Avenue and shortly afterwards Bernard Shanley's body was found, with a gun by his side. At his inquest his solicitor suggested that on account of the 'Wild West' condition of affairs in the city, this had resulted in an 'unprotected people driven to arm in their own defence.'[34] The following evening a police lorry was raked by machine-gun fire in Seaforde Street and there were also reports of sniper fire in the Docks and Ardoyne areas.

Four people were to lose their lives on Saturday 17 December. A well-known local boxer, Walter Pritchard (30), of Malcolm Street, was one of a gang laying down new tram-tracks on the Newtownards Road, when a sniper from the Youngs Row part of Short Strand shot him in the head.[35] Sniping and rioting continued in the Short Strand district and two other people died there later that day. John McMeekin (41), another Protestant, of Lower Mount Street, was shot during these disturbances and his body was found lying in Malcolm Lane.[36] Tram services, especially in east Belfast, were hastily curtailed after these and shopping in the city centre were uncharacteristically light for the weekend. A Catholic ex-soldier, Edward Brennan (22), a carter from Short Strand, was visiting his mother when he became the victim of a sniper operating from the Albertbridge Road. Mr Brennan died from a head wound. Elsewhere in east Belfast men entered the Ravenhill Road shop of Frances Donnelly and shot her in the stomach. Mrs Donnelly, a Catholic, died two days later.[37] Although increased military patrolling and an earlier curfew hour undoubtedly helped ease tension especially in the east, violence continued, albeit on a smaller scale, with three more people losing their lives before the end of the year. Two off-duty Catholic barmen, Charles McCallion (30) and Donegal-born Hugh Kelly (28) were shot in separate attacks in Millfield and York Street. Both men failed to recover from their injuries. Shots were fired at a pub on 20 December and an elderly Protestant carter, John Wilson, was shot on his way to work the following morning. Mr Wilson (71), who was hit in the leg, was found near Youngs Row and died in hospital nearly two weeks later. Armed robberies were also reported on the same day and a bakery worker was wounded in Eliza Street, near Cromac Square on 21 December.

A mystery killing, motivated either by sectarian jealousy or feuding, occurred just two days before Christmas, when a wealthy Protestant publican, William Armstrong, the owner of the busy Union Jack pub on the Newtownards Road, was shot dead by gunmen lying in wait on his return to his luxury Strandtown villa. The proceeds of the evening's business (£733) remained unopened and Mr Armstrong, hit by four bullets, died as his wife came running to his aid. Earlier that day another attempt to kill homeward-bound workers on a tram-car – this time near Durham Street off the Grosvenor Road – narrowly failed when the bomb failed to explode. A deputation of disgruntled industrial workers expressed their dissatisfaction with the quality of protection they were receiving directly to the Lord Mayor and Police Commissioner. It was to no avail. Even on Christmas morning the gunmen were active when an attempt was made to kill two policemen on duty near Cupar Street in the west of the city and one of them had to be detained in hospital.

The holiday weather proved to be unseasonably mild, as Belfast citizens enjoyed their brief Christmas break, pondering over the chances of the Treaty bringing peace to Ulster. True to form, the respective newspapers had different explanations for the pre-Xmas upsurge in violence. The *Northern Whig* believed that the IRA's return to the 'warpath' was 'not accidental', warning that these disturbances were 'the work of men who want to see Belfast and indeed, the whole of the Six County area, reduced to a condition of chronic anarchy.'[38] The *Irish News'* leading article on the same day, however, implied that like those in Marrowbone constituted 'an organised campaign of extermination', complaining that residents in Catholic areas frequently had to face 'double' attacks, initially from loyalist gunmen who 'rain torrents of bullets into the streets and into the homes of victims' before Crown forces 'reswept the same streets with rifle and Lewis-gun fire.'[39]

The last major incident of the year occurred in the afore-mentioned Marrowbone district. Two days after Christmas, an 'exchange of gunfire' in the early morning between police and nationalists resulted in the death of Catholic ex-soldier, David Morrison, of Mayfair Street, and the fatal wounding of a police officer. Constable Francis Hill (32), a native of County Leitrim with 12 years' service, had been commanding a patrol of Special Constables on patrol on the Oldpark Road when they saw a suspicious group of men at the corner of Gracehill Street. Gunfire was exchanged and the constable was hit (he died in military hospital over three weeks later). It was alleged that Mr Morrison, later revealed as an IRA officer, was shot as he was running away from the police. The claim that he had been firing at the police was denied by his family, who maintained that he was shot at his front door as he prepared to attend morning Mass. Prolonged sniping followed this incident and the noise was 'deafening'. The Oldpark tram was suspended and houses near the Cliftonville

Road were riddled with bullets, but with the exception of a dairyman's horse, there were no other reports of injuries. Sporadic violence returned to the area the following day and there were also reports of shooting on the Falls Road and trouble near St Matthew's Church in Ballymacarrett.

Reflecting on a year which had witnessed over 100 fatalities and several hundred injured, the *Northern Whig* pointed to the changing nature of the violence which was not just the 'party riots' of previous years, where 'stone-throwing and hand-to-hand fighting had been largely replaced by sniping and bombing.'[40] As the New Year beckoned those reflecting on recent events on Belfast's streets or political developments in London, would hardly have been convinced that the city had experienced the worst of the carnage. Instead many braced themselves for the Armageddon which they feared would engulf them in the weeks and months ahead.

Chapter 12

'Mind yourself . . .'

CLOSE ENCOUNTERS

Belfast in the early Twenties was undeniably a dangerous place in which to grow up. Young people were especially vulnerable in an atmosphere of civil unrest, and casualties involving the young were high.[1] Although any one of Belfast's citizens was liable to become embroiled in the disturbances, especially whilst travelling through the city or on business in its centre where many outrages occurred, the bulk of the unrest happened in working class areas away from the city centre. Whilst children were from time to time the deliberate targets of assassins (as in the Weaver Street attack), more often or not they became ensnared in the violence. Many would have been aware of neighbours or friends being shot or bombed in their districts and specific incidents would live long in their memories. John Parkinson, growing up on the Grosvenor Road in volatile west Belfast, recalls how his friend's sister became a helpless victim of a sniper's bullet:

> A sister of my friend, Billy Brown, was sitting in the front room of her house, round the corner from us on the Grosvenor Road, when a sniper's bullet hit her in the spine. Our parents talked of nothing else for days, warning that this could happen to any of us. We didn't need their warnings after a while, because when she finally came out of hospital she was confined to a wheel-chair.

Others recall how it was close encounters with gunmen and bombers which made the most impact upon them. Christy Robinson remembers retrieving a sniper's bullet which had lodged in a wall directly opposite his Durham Street home, and also being amazed by the rapid spread of fire, following a bomb attack on a shop in Telford Street. Jimmy Kelly still associates 'unbearable' volumes of noise with 'bad nights' in the city, especially on the Falls Road where he grew up. He admits longing for periods of calm, no matter how tense these might have been, following days of incessant gunfire. For Jimmy, the 'nightmare' especially involved 'lorries roaring up the street at one in the morning, the thundering at the door, the raised voices in the streets and the engines running on the big vehicles outside'. Jimmy also recalls a 'pitched battle' raging for hours near his Beechmount home, between 'B' Specials and IRA snipers firing across fields at the back of his home.[2] Despite the intervention of a military armoured vehicle, 'sporadic shooting continued all night, as we lay for safety beneath the windows, fearful of the crossfire.'[3] The results of such frenetic activity were, thankfully, not always tragic. Kelly remembers:

> Shocked and bewildered by it all we children fell asleep towards midnight, worn out by fear and trembling. We awoke in the early morning light to the desultory crack of revolver fire but it died away by breakfast time. When at last we issued forth expecting to see the streets littered with bullets we found nothing, but a few pock-marked walls. Only one person, a male 'staller' [a meths or 'blowhard' drinker] had been wounded at the local brickyard.[4]

John Parkinson noted that sustained sniper fire usually resulted in an increase in the volume and speed of traffic proceeding up the Grosvenor Road. He has vivid memories of the injured being ferried, not only in ambulances, but also in motor taxis, vans and carts, by despairing relatives to the Royal Victoria Hospital at the top of the road. Bread and milk deliveries were frequently interrupted or even curtailed by prolonged sniping, and as a youngster he was occasionally caught unawares by the outbreak of gunfire. When this happened, John felt compelled to adopt the favoured safety tactic of many at that time, namely running 'low', especially whilst within sniping distance of trouble spots, such as Albert Street.[5]

Even when the consequences were not always serious, attacks on parents or friends impacted significantly on impressionable youngsters. Such assaults or instances of intimidation frequently occurred when they were travelling through 'alien' territory on their way to work or conducting urgent family business. Christy Robinson recalls how his mother was upset after she had her face slapped returning from her mill on the Falls Road and was concerned about making such a daily journey for months afterwards. Physical or even verbal intimidation often resulted in protracted personal inconveniences, especially those involving journeys to and from work. Whilst security force protection was periodically provided on arterial roads, those taking deviations across potentially difficult side-streets, had to reassess the wisdom of such decisions, as well as sharpen their resourcefulness in improving their personal safety. Norman Douglas's father and uncle had to walk from the Ravenhill Road to the Sirocco Works, opting to go through the nationalist Short Strand to reduce their journey time. On one occasion they were assaulted and Norman's uncle ended up in hospital. After this, the brothers decided to take the longer, but safer, Mountpottinger route.[6] Norman's eldest brother, who worked at Mackies on the Springfield Road, was also threatened going to work and, successfully combining self-preservation and ingenuity, improvised a sling and a baton-shaped wooden truncheon, with a long piece of lead placed on the top. Intimidation of workmates by one's co-religionists often saddened their colleagues, testing, though not necessarily permanently damaging, those relationships. John Parkinson's father, Frank, was greatly annoyed when fellow joiner, John Green, from the Springfield area, was intimidated from his employment at the shipyards. Frank used to travel in the same tram as John and they often shared sandwiches.[7] Not everybody had to run the gauntlet to work. At this time Sarah O'Hare worked as a doffer in the Jennymount mill near North Derby Street. She experienced few problems, crossing some difficult areas on her way to work and once there got on well with her predominantly Protestant workmates.[8]

However, it wasn't just getting to and from work that posed problems especially for those who had to execute their professional duties in the open. Gas-fitter Robert McElborough recalled the taxing work conditions which he encountered whilst mending broken gas lamps in the Short Strand area:

> It was the snipers on the roofs and back windows who were the danger. Anyone seen on the streets within the range of their gun was a target. And they found out later through the press what side they belonged to ... My only dread was when I was standing on the ladder, putting up a lamp, bullets that I suppose were meant from me went though the lamp reflector. I brought some of the lamps back to the workshop and my workmates had many discussions on my narrow escapes.[9]

Everyday social movement was seriously affected during these troublesome times. John Parkinson's mother was stopped on the Falls Road on her way to visit a sick sister on the Shankill by residents who realised she was a stranger and were interested in her intentions. Even elementary school pupils experienced the harrowing experience of being intimidated and threatened by gangs of older boys. Patrick O'Donnell recalls such an occasion:

> My most frightening experience at this time was being stopped by a gang of Protestant youths as I left my school in Donegall Street. They took me around a corner and told me if I didn't say 'To hell with the Pope', I would be duffed up. I'm afraid I had to agree to their request, though now I can only smile at the irony . . .'[10]

Incidents such as these clearly had the result of reinforcing one's suspicion of the 'other' side and acted as a dire warning for gullible youngsters.

Catholic families were more liable to be affected by sudden change such as an overnight exodus of relatives, neighbours and friends. Sarah O'Hare recalls other Catholics moving into her Markets district and seeing lots of strangers congregating in her neighbours' already crowded homes.[11] For others living in 'hostile' areas, increasing tension frequently led them to make a rapid, and sometimes permanent, move from their area. Nora McMullan's family, besieged in loyalist east Belfast, temporarily sought shelter with relatives in Cullyhanna and on their return to Belfast, relocated to the Catholic parts of the west of the city. Like Nora and Jimmy Kelly, Sarah O'Hare recalls her street in the Markets being raided by the Specials, although neither she nor her family felt directly intimidated by the security forces.[12] Concerns and fears which did exist in nationalist districts often had the effect of reinforcing the cohesion of such beleaguered communities. This could manifest itself in a variety of ways. Religious unity was frequently expressed at the scene of tragedies involving members of the minority community. One of Jimmy Kelly's abiding memories of those terrible Twenties' days was standing transfixed by Murphy's brickyard at Daisy Hill in west Belfast, as a large group of Catholic women, rosaries wrapped around their hands, prayed at the spot where a Catholic had been shot the previous evening. Practical support for families of prisoners or republicans 'on the run' was often given by shopkeepers, who allowed them to 'live on tic' until their men resurfaced. Also, the residents of the little 'kitchen' houses in the maze of back-streets in the Catholic ghettoes invariably knew when an operation was imminent, ensuring that volunteers' escape could be facilitated by doors left ajar, or via holes made in side walls. Whilst tales of horror, beatings and shootings spread like wildfire around the nationalist areas, 'black' humour was also evident, helping to lift the gloomy tension a little. Nora McMullan recalls how the drunk husband of her mother's friend received an unannounced visit from a group of 'B' men. They soon discovered a locked trunk in his bedroom and demanded for it to be opened. The host, slightly the worse for wear, shouted to one of his obstreperous children to bring a hatchet so he could accede to the police request. However, the Specials quickly reassessed the situation, preferring to make a speedy exit, at the expense of discovering an arms cache!

MOVING AROUND

Trams, exhibiting distinctive destinations and mainly transporting people of one particular religious persuasion through 'hostile' districts, were easy and regular targets for those determined to maim and kill.[13] Since attacking trams offered a better chance of a quick getaway than incursions into adjacent areas, as well as providing clear identification of potential victims' religious status, tram travel could be a most dangerous activity. Even a Saturday afternoon visit on the tram to the safety provided by 'neutral' city centre stores tested the nerves of schoolboy Jimmy Kelly:

> The old red and yellow coloured tramcar swayed, whined and groaned over the rails down the Falls Road. There were certain danger points when it passed Cupar Street, Conway Street, Northumberland Street and Dover Street; long Streets leading from the Falls to the Shankill. Across these streets at moments of tension the report of rifle fire rang out as snipers on both sides opened up. The tram speeded and clanked past these streets as the driver crouched down on the deck behind the controls. The passengers took their cue and huddled down on the floor which the Tramways department thoughtfully provided with a carpet of straw. There were always audible sighs of relief when the neutral Castle Junction hove in sight.[14]

At night the trams were especially susceptible to attack and Norman Douglas vividly recalls his trepidation returning home with his mother from a church service in Great Victoria Street, when the lights on his tram car were suddenly cut following sniping from the Short Strand and they, as well as the other passengers on their Ravenhill tram had to lie flat on their stomachs. John Parkinson, who had just started an apprenticeship at Harland and Wolff, had to make a daily journey from Distillery Street off the Grosvenor Road, to Queen's Island. He too, remembers the 'nightmare' of having to 'duck' on passing hazardous areas and says his mother discouraged him from using the trams on account of their dangers (except when it was wet). Apart from numerous bombings and shootings directed against drivers, passengers and tramline workers, there were also several cases of tram passengers receiving severe beatings. George Morrison recalled seeing Jimmy Clawson, from a well-known Ballynafeigh horse-breeding family, being thrown from the top of a workers' tram after attempting to pacify a nationalist gang.

The curfew regulations were unpopular with many sections of Belfast's population, especially its business community. There was, as has been noted, variation both in the hours of curfew restriction and in the districts covered by the emergency legislation, depending on the levels of violence within particular areas. Many people found themselves trapped when disturbances erupted, with their degree of distress ranging from minor inconvenience to a family tragedy.[15] Recalling curfew, Ena McKenna suggested that the penalty for breaking it was 'certain death', even if on account of her tender age, she was unlikely to be out during the evening.[16] With children these restrictions were especially tiresome in the summer when they were unable to take full advantage of the long summer evenings. Norman Douglas found it difficult to accept returning home from his games of football and cricket in the Ormeau Park an hour in advance of the curfew when it was still light. Parents, unsurprisingly, were anxious that their children should be back home some time before curfew started and failure to do so produced hastily-arranged search parties and harsh admonition when the 'nomads' eventually showed up.[17] Eddie Steele recalled one such summer evening when over-exuberance resulted in his arriving home five minutes after the start of curfew, only to receive a tongue-lashing from his father. Quite often it was the heavy footsteps of patrolling policemen in that hour before the start of curfew which chased youngsters off the streets and back indoors. John Boyd remembered reluctantly having to curtail his games around a totem pole in Chatsworth Street, near Templemore Avenue in east Belfast, or when playing football with a hanky ball in nearby Lord Street.[18] Getting home from the city centre before the start of curfew could prove to be problematic, especially if one deviated from one's schedule. One evening, Mary Thompson, who had been given tickets by her grandmother to see a show with a friend at the Ulster Hall, decided after the show ended to visit another friend whose father, a police sergeant, had recently transferred to a station near the Technical College.

Anxious parents were relieved to find them in 'residence' at a city centre barracks.[19]

Occasionally the frustration at not getting to sleep made children restless and more willing to take risks. George Morrison, about 11 at the time, shared the attic of his Rushfield Avenue home, off the Ormeau Road, with his brother and remembers spending hours in bed, watching and listening to the flashing and rattle of gunfire coming from the Markets and Short Strand. One night he slipped out of his house during curfew:

> I crept along a wall at the corner of Rushfield Avenue. The firing was fierce that night and 3 or 4 bullets hit the far side of the wall near where I was crouching. After a few moments I peeped over the wall and saw a patrolling tender going up the Ormeau Road towards the end of the trolley-bus line at Galwally.[20]

The unpredictability in the timing of violence in the city often resulted in people becoming entrapped in threatening situations and being forced to seek shelter in shop doorways, safe houses, or in other buildings. While this was usually the most sensible course of action to take given the circumstances, it did little to ease the nerves either of the besieged or anxious relatives looking at the clock at home. This was especially true with youngsters trapped by sniper fire. Sam Jamison was a regular member of the Sinclair Seamen's Church Sunday School and remembered how gunfire in neighbouring North Queen Street and Garmoyle Street prevented him and his sister leaving the church at the end of morning service. The young Jamisons, like many other parishioners, had to seek sanctuary in the church and could only return to Whitla Street in the late afternoon. George Morrison's family walked into a nightmare situation when they arrived back in Belfast after a summer holiday visiting relatives in Scotland. On arriving at the docks they discovered that, due to unrest in the Cromac Street area, there were no landaus or trams running up the Ormeau Road. Their ordeal was just beginning:

> We decided to walk over the Albert Bridge and up the Ravenhill Road. My father tried to hail a taxi, but on hearing machine-gun fire, the driver failed to stop. Bullets just missed us as we tried to cross the main Ravenhill Road and we were grateful when a door opened for us. We were given welcome cups of tea but I was anxious about how we were

going to get home. A Lancia car came around the Albertbridge Road corner but although they stopped, the police were not allowed to give us a lift home. Fortunately a tram arrived soon afterwards and we went up to South Parade, before getting off with all our baggage and walking across to the Ormeau Road. This upsetting experience did little for my mother's ailing health.

COPS, TOMMIES AND FIREMEN

Memories of security force activity and even individuals loom large in the memory of many people. Ena McKenna recalled the 'aftermath' of raids conducted by the 'B' Specials, stressing the 'awful fear and atmosphere and lack of trust', and remembered how two families she knew were 'completely wiped out, murdered in their homes.'[21] Jimmy Kelly also recalls how he was petrified when these 'swaggering louts' received their monthly payments, and how the sight of barrels of Guinness being rolled across the road from Paddy Hynes' pub and into the Beehive bar near his home, was a 'danger signal' to local residents.[22] Kelly's description of their behaviour later that evening gives an insight into Catholic fear of the Specials:

> ... after several hours' boozing, the Specials issued forth swinging their rifles, and into their Lancias and caged armoured cars for a night of 'shooting up' the area and teaching the Fenians a lesson. Speeding along Beechmount Avenue they fired volley after volley up the long streets where neighbours gossiped and children played. As they fired at random, women and children ran in terror or dropped down out of sight in the little gardens. Door after door slammed shut and in spite of the bright summer evenings nobody risked going out, even though the official curfew hour was not due until 10 p.m.[23]

Even Protestants were not always impressed by the appearance or demeanour of some Specials. Christy Robinson remembers them being significantly smaller and 'more scruffily dressed' than their regular police colleagues and also recalls the time they nearly battered down the door of a Catholic neighbour, who had managed to evade them by clambering over his back wall. Norman Douglas also recalls how a group of 'C' Specials stationed at a jam factory in Park

Avenue, used to regularly smash the locks on the gates at the Ormeau Park in their haste to apprehend nationalists in nearby Cromac Street. Norman remembers the strains of the Sash ringing out just after the start of curfew, when they would smash the locks, which saved them the inconvenience of walking round the Lagan embankment in their approach to Cromac Street.

Having a father serving in the police was a strain for young children who were constantly worried about him not returning safe from his daily shift. Paddy O'Donnell recalls his father serving as a RIC officer in the city at the time, though he was naturally reluctant to tell his young son what security problems he had to encounter. Paddy recalls his father was an ardent nationalist who was dismayed by the establishment of the RUC in 1922. Thus, his father declined the chance to join the new force when it assumed responsibility for policing in the north and eventually became a tax official. Attitudes to the army were quite similar to those which Catholics held in the early phase of the more recent conflict. Hostility was noticeably deeper towards the Specials and though wary of military personnel, Catholics did not fear them as much as they did the police.[24] Indeed, affection was sometimes conveyed to characters amongst the ranks of the military. Jimmy Kelly recalls how a young lieutenant in the Norfolk Regiment, with an aristocratic, charming manner, clipped moustache and dry laugh (which warranted him the nickname 'Ha ha') charmed many Falls residents who were sorry when he was recalled to England and the Specials took his place:

> Many stories were told about his coolness in awkward situations ... Women terrified by some inexplicable shooting used to cry out with relief, 'Oh thank God, here comes Ha ha. But now 'Ha ha' and his men were being recalled by their masters in London.'[25]

Although Belfast's citizens quickly accustomed themselves to the army's presence, they were still a source of curiosity amongst the young and with strangers.[26] Christy Robinson, barely 10 at the time, remembers hearing the unmistakable sounds of military reveille and couldn't resist clambering up the wall at 'Inst', where the Norfolk Regiment were stationed, to observe them hastily completing their morning ablutions.[27] Visitors to the city often took a while to adjust to the heavy security presence. Eddie Steele recalled an American uncle visiting his family in west Belfast. Asked to accompany his relative – attired in an expensive suit, all fours and a Stetson hat – young Eddie froze with embarrassment as his uncle strode up to a military vantage point at Leeson Street and asked the bemused Tommies if he could inspect their 'mighty fine rifles.'[28]

Growing up in Twenties' Belfast might have been dangerous, nerve-wrecking and restrictive in so many ways, but they were also exhilarating times. Glimpses of both gunmen and the military in action, hearing the rumours about the latest exploits of the 'boyhos', and eagerly collecting conflict 'souvenirs', must have made an impact on impressionable Belfast youngsters. Jimmy Kelly used to draw pictures and share detailed technical information about the workings of Webley revolvers and rifles such as 'Peter the Painter', with his school friends in the fields above Beechmount. The natural curiosity of the young often resulted in the rapid learning of invaluable lessons. Christy Robinson recalls observing a police funeral in the west of the city, which was followed by the outbreak of stone-throwing. Seeking sanctuary, he hopped on to the back of an army vehicle, but quickly dismounted on spotting a body lying in the corner.

A bullet or piece of shrapnel would earn a boy the full attention of his chums for many a long summer's evening. Also, it would lead to the swapping of yarns about the exploits of IRA volunteers and where they were reportedly hiding.[29] Rumours abounded about gunmen on either side. Fierce competition developed between the various paramilitary groups in neighbouring districts. Jimmy Kelly recalls the savage rivalry which existed between the murder gangs of Albert Street and Northumberland Street in the west of the city, whilst Sam Jamison also remembered rumours about the infamous 'Buck Alec' Robinson and trilby-donning loyalist gunman, Davy Duncan.[30]

Despite the warnings of their parents, children's natural curiosity often led them into dangerous predicaments and, judging by the large number of young people tragically involved in shooting and bombing incidents, those fears appeared fully justified. Therefore, many parents banned their children from playing outside their homes, especially during twilight hours. Nora McMullan had such orders, but during a quiet spell she was tempted into playing outside and, on hearing gunfire in her district, had to hastily return home. John McKenna lived on the Springfield Road during these years and remembers the excitement of running past the Falls Road Baths and down Conway Street which were 'lively spots' at the time. One morning on his way to school, John spotted the door of a police cage-car slightly ajar. He recalls:

> I peeked inside, and saw a peeler with a mop clearing away pools of congealed blood from the floor and sides of the car. He caught my eye

and told me where to go in no uncertain terms. I turned to my friend and told him that the 'B's had been busy last night as one or two poor fellas around here must know to their cost.

Sam Jamison's 'Troubles' childhood was singularly exciting, due to the character of his 'home', the Whitla Street Fire Station, near the city centre. Several of Sam's uncles worked for the fire service and were based at stations on the Shankill, Albertbridge and in the Marrowbone and Sam, 11 at the time, vividly remembered living with 10 other families in the station where his father was Assistant Chief Officer. Like other children living in troublesome areas, Sam was constantly reminded to be careful in his movements, especially during his daily journeys to school. He attended Bingham's School in Duncairn Gardens and when tension was rife, he had to 'commute' to school via the Limestone Road in an ambulance based at the fire station. The children of fire officers were normally confined to the station premises but despite this curtailment in their movement, their immediate environment was a most exciting one. Sam recalled:

> My father and his colleagues were very busy during the Troubles and were called out to many fires caused by incendiary devices. They were even shot at on occasions. It wasn't easy for us either. You see, the families of fire officers lived in the station and we had to play out in the yard at the back. The station also housed ambulances and it was an exciting place to be at this time, what with fire engines rushing to put out fires and the ambulances bringing in the bodies of those shot or blown up in the disturbances. They used the station as a temporary morgue and our mothers frequently had to chase us youngsters away when they were laying out the bodies.[31]

AT PLAY

Despite the riots and disturbances raging in the city at this time, children were still able to exhibit a degree of normality in their everyday lives, managing to play together in comparative harmony. Eddie Steele and John Parkinson remembered playing together, sometimes with Catholics, on the Bog Meadows or in Falls Park and Dunville Park.[32] They enjoyed long summer evenings on the Meadows, playing football and cricket and catching stickleback in jam-jars. However, most of the time they played on the streets within their own area of west Belfast. They recalled:

> The girls used to play hoop games in the streets. We would play football, often in our bare feet, crigging [*sic*] our toes, but it was fun. We organised a league of street teams and our team, Distillery Star, was a 'mixed' one. There were, you see, a few Catholic families living in and around Distillery Street, including the Barretts, whose parents owned the 'Celtic Bar' at one corner of our street, the Bradys, the McDermotts, whose father was a police officer based at the Springfield Barracks and the Lynches, who owned the 'Distillery Bar' on another corner of Distillery Street.[33]

John and Eddie often attended football matches at nearby Grosvenor Park which sometimes involved southern teams, but although these matches passed off peacefully, other games with more partisan supporters often led to street disturbances between the rival fans either before or at the end of the match. Sam Jamison remembered being dissuaded from following his favourite team, Linfield, after an outburst of gunfire and grenades directed at the trams of Linfield's large loyalist following on their way to an Irish League game at Solitude in the Cliftonville area of north Belfast.

For many children, the spread of street disturbances meant they had to reassess what they did in their spare time. Sarah O'Hare, at an age when she was keen to go out to dances and shows, was restricted by the disturbances and with an abundance of free time, perfected her crocheting techniques. Like many of her friends, Sarah invited chums to her home and sometimes visited them in different, safer areas. Occasionally John Parkinson would escape from the danger lurking on city streets and help a local milkman on a Saturday morning. They would set off early on a cart and proceed to Drumbo where they would pour milk into jugs and collect cheese in containers.

Summer was an exciting time for children old enough to ride a bicycle and escape the dangers of Belfast for a while. John Parkinson recalls a bicycle shop in McDonnell Street between the Grosvenor Road and Albert Street, where a youngster could hire a bike at 6*d.* an hour and set off on a Saturday, heading for the Lagan toepath to Lambeg or even Lisburn, or along the Antrim and Down coasts to Whitehead, Carrickfergus, Groomsport or Bangor.[34] Christy

Robinson also eagerly anticipated the challenge of a long day's cycle ride along the coast. Like other children at this time, he had friends from the 'other' side. Indeed, his best friend was Jacky Kelly, a Catholic who played with him in the streets and on the Bog Meadows, where Jacky earned a reputation for his culinary skills, roasting very welcome sausages for his chums, exhausted after their games of football and cricket. Christy recollects:

> I remember waiting one Sunday lunchtime, rather anxiously I'll admit, outside the Clonard Monastery where Jacky was attending Mass. We eventually got together and set off cycling on two speed gear bikes to Kilroot. Mind you, some of the hills were steep, and on a hot summer's day, the sweat would fairly lash off us.

Others also recall close relationships with children of a different religious persuasion. Jimmy Kelly recalls his anguish when his friend, Sam Graham, one of the few Protestants in his street, was intimidated from his Falls Road home.[35] Norman Douglas insists that even during the conflict, these friendships survived considerable strain. One of the few Catholic families in his area, the Nultys, were very popular with their east Belfast neighbours. Indeed, Mrs Nulty often prepared lunch for him and her son, Peter, a tram driver, who used to banter Norman and his friends as they chased his tram on their way to school in the morning. Several of the people interviewed remembered receiving sporadic police escorts to and from school, usually after habitual name-calling between rival crowds of schoolboys had precipitated more serious stone-throwing incidents.[36] Although some children living in 'mixed' areas continued to defy the odds and carried on playing together, many more were discouraged from doing so by parents concerned about how others might perceive such friendships.

Street disturbances and the obligatory curfew regulations not only curtailed the opportunities to enjoy city centre shows and picture-houses, but also adversely affected the activities organised by various youth organisations.[37] Harry Currie was a junior officer in the 9th Company of the Boys' Brigade, based at Fitzroy Avenue Church, whilst Christy Robinson and John Parkinson were members of the 44th Christ Church Company. They remembered how the police had to provide protection during church parades and how BB officers gave permission for boys to change into their uniforms in the church hall, following the molestation of some members in the streets near the church.

Eventually the disruption caused by such intimidation and curfew regulations resulted in the curtailing of many BB meetings during the Troubles. Although some of their routine meetings, especially in west Belfast, were adversely affected by the disturbances, special excursions still proceeded as normal. Christy Robinson recalls Christ Church Sunday School organising trips to Bangor during this period, with the only inconvenience being a two mile hike to the railway station (a result of the suspension of trams). Only a few working class children enjoyed extended breaks from the Belfast disturbances. John Boyd's father was an engine-driver and he recalled being dropped near Ballynahinch Junction at the start of his summer holidays. He stayed there on a farm with the Spratts, who were friends of his father and remembered enjoying the freedom of space and comparative sanctuary offered by the countryside (even if he had to endure daily contact with their rather aggressive turkeys!).

The relatively brief duration of the city's conflict and the intermittent periods of calm meant that, apart from those experiencing personal tragedy, the Twenties Troubles would not have had a life-defining impact upon Belfast children. Yet few of them, especially those in the city's predominantly working class areas, would have been unaware of the unique crisis unfolding in their midst, given the heavy security presence, patrols and searches, the constant rattle of gunfire and thud of explosions, emergency curfew regulations and the endless warnings of anxious parents. Indeed, personal experience of such incidents often proved to be exhilarating and ready anecdote material with which to impress their own grandchildren. However, it would be inaccurate to suggest that children's lives were dominated by the disturbances to the extent that they were confined to their own homes for two years. As in subsequent conflicts, it was more about making the best of a difficult situation, so neither school nor play was completely sabotaged.

1922

Armageddon Beckons

The Troubles, 1922

The Troubles came; by Nineteen-twenty-two
we knew of and accepted violence
in the small street at hand. With curfew tense,
each evening when that quiet hour was due,
I never ventured far from where I knew
I could reach home in safety. At the door
I'd sometimes stand, till with oncoming roar,
the wire-cage Crossley tenders swept in view.

Once, from front bedroom window, I could mark
black shapes, flat-capped, across the shadowed street,
two policemen on patrol. With crack and spark
fierce bullet struck the kerb beneath their feet;
below the shattered street-lamp in the dark
blurred shadow crouched, then pattered quick retreat.

John Hewitt, 'Kites in Spring' (1980)

Chapter 13

Political pacts and street squabbles

SIGNING ONE'S DEATH WARRANT

Following the King's reconciliation speech in June and the signing of the Truce on 11th July, the push towards political accommodation between the various parties, especially those in Dublin and London, intensified considerably. Although a more peaceful, albeit temporary, climate was being created by externally-interested parties, this mood of optimism and desire for the creation of a more conciliatory atmosphere to facilitate fruitful political negotiations did not extend to Belfast, especially amongst its majority community. This can not be simply explained away as loyalist intransigence or a bullish desire to be party-poppers. Unionists did not believe republican declarations of truces, nor were they happy with a Westminster administration which, from their viewpoint, appeared to be more concerned about bringing a speedy settlement to the wider Irish problem than providing promises of protecting their precarious position in the north.[1] Northern nationalists were also far from reassured by developments outside Ulster and their position was increasingly threatened by unionists' growing feeling of political betrayal and desertion. In this section, I shall examine how these shared feelings of betrayal and besiegement were exacerbated by political subterfuge and negotiation, especially in the six month period between the late autumn of 1921 and the spring of 1922. The effects of these feelings upon levels of street violence and tension in Belfast during this period will also be explored.

On 14 July Eamon de Valera led a Sinn Féin delegation to London for exploratory talks and had four lengthy meetings with Lloyd George inside a week. These formed the framework for the subsequent Irish conference and also involved the tentative offer by the British of dominion status for Ireland. Meetings between another Sinn Féin delegation led by Griffith and Collins but significantly excluding de Valera, and involving British ministers, including Lloyd George and Churchill, started on 11 October.[2] The main areas for discussion were Ireland's constitutional status, the question of sovereignty and the particular issue of the oath of allegiance. It was this question – Irish people remaining subjects of a monarch, rather than the question of Ulster and partition – which dominated discussion, soon proving to be a major stumbling-block. There were seven plenary sessions during the conference, with much discussion also taking place in the various sub-committees. Representatives returned to Dublin with a draft document which was swiftly dismissed by de Valera's cabinet. On their return to London, the astute Lloyd George, aware of tensions within Sinn Féin and the effect weeks of tiring negotiation were having on the Irish delegation, turned the screw on Griffith and Collins. Reminding them of his own political predicament Lloyd George brought matters to a head on 5 December.[3] Dramatically holding two letters destined for James Craig – one containing articles of agreement between Irish republicans and the British government, and the other outlining Sinn Féin's rejection of the oath of allegiance and their refusal to come in to the Empire – Lloyd George suggested that there would be 'war in three days' if he was forced to send the second letter. Giving the Irish delegation until ten that evening to reach a decision, Lloyd George advised them to 'decide whether you will give peace or war to your country.'[4]

The Anglo-Irish Treaty was signed at Downing Street during the early hours of 6 December. Collins, later to defend it in a fierce debate in the Dáil, believed the terms to be the most nationalists could realistically expect to obtain, but he also fully appreciated its deadly personal implications. In a letter he noted:

> Think – what have I got for Ireland? Something which she has wanted these past 700 years. Will any one be satisfied at the bargain? Will any one? I will tell you this – early this morning, I signed my death warrant.[5]

Although it was the fourth article, specifying the undertaking of an oath of allegiance to the monarch on the part of Free State representatives which was to concern party colleagues of Collins and Griffith back in Dublin, northern interest was, not surprisingly, focussed on the issue of partition. However, Article 12 of the Treaty succeeded in ensuring the Ulster question would be sidelined. If, as expected, the Northern Ireland Parliament refused to join with the Irish Free State within a month, a Boundary Commission would be established to determine alterations in border zones. Whilst the Commission's terms of reference were especially vague, many nationalists surprisingly accepted it at face value. The *Irish News* claimed 'Ireland as a whole has welcomed the

Agreement with a spirit of hope and goodwill.'[6] Like Collins and his Treaty colleagues, the paper believed the agreement invested in the Dublin Parliament almost complete independence in domestic affairs, including fiscal autonomy and control over police and army.[7]

De Valera and his supporters, who were to warrant the nickname of 'irreconcibles', pointed to what they believed were several weaknesses of the agreement, including the oath of allegiance of Irish representatives to the British monarch, its remaining in the Empire and the provision of naval facilities for the British. Southern representatives debated the Treaty for nearly a month in the Dáil before the Irish Parliament approved it on 8 January by a narrow majority (64–57 votes). This resulted in Arthur Griffith becoming President of the Irish Free State and represented the planting of the seeds of civil war. Eamon de Valera and most other opponents of the Treaty, were primarily disturbed by its failure to deliver an Irish republic, rather than its failure to produce a united Ireland.[8] De Valera dismissed Collins' assertion that the Treaty 'offered freedom to achieve freedom', declaring:

> I am against this Treaty because it does not reconcile Irish national aspirations with association with the British Government. I am against this Treaty because it will not end the centuries of conflict, between the two nations of Great Britain and Ireland.[9]

One of the few exceptions in the Dáil debate to emphasise the Ulster question rather than that of sovereignty was northern-born Sinn Féin representative Sean MacEntee, who castigated the Treaty because it 'perpetuates partition' and hence the 'slavery' of Irish people, especially in the north. In an emotional speech MacEntee argued:

> I would not traffic in my nation's independence without, at least, saving my nation's unity. I would not hand over my country without, at least, securing the right to protect my countrymen.[10]

Northerners followed the Dáil debates with interest. Most Belfast Catholics appeared to support the Treaty and were hopeful it would be adopted by Dublin. Self-preservation was fundamental to such a view. Eoin O'Duffy warned the Dáil that rejecting the Treaty would result in further 'callous, cold-blooded murder' in the north and reminded those who intended to vote against the Treaty that they had 'a very grave and solemn responsibility before them' when they did so.[11] Near the conclusion of the Dáil debate, the *Irish News* again gave the Treaty unqualified support, maintaining it offered Ireland its best chance of national freedom:

> The national will has been made manifest. Those Deputies of Dáil Éireann who have deliberately resolved to defy it are with-holding from the Irish people the right that British Governments and military power had forcibly denied to all generations of Irish men and women since Henry II left Dublin in 1172.[12]

Northern nationalists felt confident that the all-important 12th article of the Treaty, that pertaining to the Boundary Commission, would compel Craig to ultimately choose between entering an all-Ireland state or the ignominy of leading a dramatically-reduced northern assembly. British supporters of constitutional nationalism also believed that this ambiguous clause would ultimately result in a united Irish state. C.P. Scott advised Ulster Unionists to 'make terms with [their] fellow-countrymen', but added that, even if they did not, 'the Ireland of the future is secure' and that it was 'certain it will in due course involve the whole of Irish territory.'[13] In Belfast, even the majority of republicans joined with nationalists in supporting the Treaty. Such support owed more to pragmatic factors such as the safety of the minority community in the city than it did to any political or ideological dogma.[14] Appreciating the vulnerability of their own position, the city's Catholic population clearly re-assessed the extent of likely political support and threw their weight behind the Collins camp.

Initially at least, Unionists attempted to distance themselves from the constitutional negotiations which were proceeding in London. The brother of Northern Ireland's premier suggested these were 'a matter which did not vitally concern them' (the northern administration), but admitted unionist concern that powers invested in the new northern government, especially in the security sphere, were being delayed in their implementation, due to Westminster fears that Sinn Féin negotiators in London would be offended.[15] Captain Charles Craig told the Commons that Lloyd George 'should hand over these powers to the Ulster Parliament at the earliest possible moment' and denouncing the 'intolerable' security dilemma facing the local administration, he said there was 'no doubt that these powers ... would have been put into our hands long ago if it had not been for the Conference.'[16] This concern was reflected in a series of northern Cabinet discussions late in November 1921, devoted to assessing additional security priorities.[17]

Also, Craig had a number of formal meetings with Lloyd George during November at which he expressed Ulster Unionists' total opposition to any constitutional format involving an independent and united Irish state and a desire for the same offer of dominion status which was being suggested regarding the south, to be extended to Ulster.[18] Although unsuccessful in this claim, Craig did extract a pledge from Lloyd George that N Ireland's right to refute involvement with any notion of unity would be respected. The growing disillusionment of Ulster Unionists at this time is also reflected in a straining of their relationship with erstwhile friends in the Conservative Party. Carson was especially offended by the Treaty settlement which went completely against his own ideal of the whole of Ireland being united within the United Kingdom. Turning on former colleagues like Birkenhead, the ageing ex-Unionist party leader, in his maiden Lords speech, reflected on the demise of their relationship:

> I was fighting with others [Tories] whose friendship and comradeship I hope I will lose from tonight, because I don't value any friendship that is not founded upon confidence and trust. I was in earnest. What a fool I was! I was only a puppet, and so was Ulster, and so was Ireland, in the political game that was to get the Conservative Party into power.[19]

His colleague, Sir James Craig, was more critical of Liberal figures in the Cabinet and in a letter to Austen Chamberlain, warned of a loyalist backlash, as 'many already believe that violence is the only language understood by Mr Lloyd George and his Ministers.'[20] The more pragmatic approach of Craig and his ministerial colleagues should not disguise a concern they shared with Carson over the loss of sympathy for unionists, who increasingly appeared to be the blockers of what most Englishmen regarded as the 'solution' to the Irish problem, and especially over the resulting increase in their isolationism. Craig also adopted a more aloof and distant response to the completion of the Treaty negotiations. Speaking in the Belfast Parliament, he told his colleagues:

> The South have decided that they can do better separating from the great Mother of the Empire, that they can do better by isolating themselves and becoming what they call a Free State. We, on the other hand, say

No. We can do better for ourselves and for the Empire by maintaining
the closest connection between Great Britain and ourselves ... and I pray
[to] God as I have anything to do with it we shall remain steadfast in the
true faith.[21]

However, the response of the loyalist press to the ongoing political negotiations, the signing of the Treaty and its political aftermath, proved to be a mixed
bag of curiosity and bewilderment, smug indifference, bullish condemnation
and growing acceptance. The beginning of the border talks was described as
'mysterious negotiations' by the *Northern Whig* which turned its wrath on the
response of the British press to the unionist dilemma.[22] Their leading article
made no apologies for Ulster's 'plain-dealing folk' refusing to make 'bargains'
and for not entering into 'partnerships with Sinn Féiners' whom they described
as 'leopards who would not easily change their spots ... and become in the
twinkling of an eye purring, amiable fireside tabbies.'[23] Cautious backing for
Craig's decision to keep in touch with Lloyd George during the conference,
condemnation of Sinn Féin's 'sham truce', and a sharp reminder both to the
Unionist leader and his party of the need to 'preserve undiminished all the
rights and privileges which the Act of 1920 has conferred upon it', were the
main features of loyalist coverage of the early phase of the London negotiations.[24] However, as the talks in the capital progressed, the *Newsletter* grew
increasingly suspicious of Lloyd George's motives and by the middle of
November were describing events as constituting a 'conspiracy', noting how the
British premier had been 'terrorised by the murder gang'.[25] Following the declaration of the Treaty the loyalist press devoted copious space to both its content
and the parliamentary debate which followed in London, Belfast and Dublin.
The *Northern Whig* reported Lloyd George's assurance to Ulster Unionists that
no coercion would be applied to Ulster and gave detailed coverage to pro-Craig
rallies in the city, at the Assembly, YMCA, Wellington and Grosvenor halls.[26]
However, the *Newsletter* described Westminster's ratification as being 'the
betrayal of Ulster', whilst the *Northern Whig* a few days previously had detected
'a strong and growing opinion that the Treaty should be ratified.'[27]

The unionist press was keen to exploit divisions within the republican movement over the Treaty. Indeed, there is a certain amount of truth in the
suggestion that loyalists warmed a little to an agreement which had the
welcome effect of dividing their opponents. Gloating over the stark divisions
evident during the Dáil debate on the Treaty, the *Northern Whig* sardonically

suggested that the leader of the dissidents in the Irish Parliament, Eamon de Valera, was putting 'a spoke in the triumphal car in which Lloyd George is prematurely posing as the central figure of the great historical tableau, Britannia and Hibernia Reconciled: the Welsh Wizard's Greatest Feat.'[28] Inside a few weeks, following the Dáil's narrow acceptance of the Treaty, the *Belfast Newsletter* had clearly started to warm towards an agreement which it had denounced before Christmas. Towards the end of January, the *Newsletter* said:

> If we can take it as evidence that the Provisional Government of Southern Ireland is prepared to adopt an attitude of goodwill towards the Government of N Ireland over these matters of government and administration in which both are now involved, then we say with certainty that the agreement is a source of satisfaction and is likely to turn out a blessing to the whole of Ireland.[29]

'HANDS ACROSS THE BOYNE'

Despite the crucial nature and timing of the Treaty negotiations they had not, of course, directly involved northern representatives and Westminster realised the urgent need to bring together the respective leaders of the northern and southern administrations. Churchill brokered meetings between rival leaders Michael Collins and James Craig and for a short time at least the fulcrum of the Irish question moved away from Belfast's desolate, volatile streets to the calm, salubrious surroundings of the Colonial Office in London's Whitehall. Following considerable rumour and speculation back in Belfast and two days of intensive negotiation in London, the first pact was signed on 21 January. Broadly speaking, this offered Ulster the termination of the southern boycott of northern goods in exchange for the restoration of expelled Catholic workers and the removal of religious or political tests by Belfast workers. There were five clauses in the January agreement, referring to issues such as boundaries, a Council of Ireland, the future of political prisoners and the Irish railway network, but by far the most important was the second.[30] This was significant because it committed the two leaders to political compromises which, in reality, they had little chance of fulfilling.

The response of the press on both sides of the Irish border and in Britain to the pact was generally favourable. Although the impetus for such an agreement had come from politicians outside Belfast and there was still considerable suspicion in the loyalist heartlands, the unionist press 'welcomed' the breakthrough in London, arguing it constituted 'evidence of a desire to co-operate for the common sense of Ireland.'[31] Another editorial pursued the Craig line, denying the suggestion that the pact constituted 'a first step on the way to the incorporation of Ulster in an all Ireland parliament' and suggested the 'mass of opinion' on the issue would 'approve of what had been done and sustain it in action.'[32] The *Newsletter* suggested if the agreement signified that southern politicians were 'prepared to adopt an attitude of goodwill' towards colleagues in the north, then it would prove to be 'a source of gratification' which would be 'likely to turn out a blessing for the whole of Ireland.'[33] In London, the *Times* believed the pact would prove to be 'a sensible business transaction.'[34] Although other mainland papers gave unqualified support for the pact, this was sometimes accompanied by a conviction that there was a new political agenda underpinning relationships between Britain and Ireland. Thus the pro-unity *Manchester Guardian* concluded that the pact was 'proof that the essential unity of Ireland in practical affairs and interests has already begun to be recognised', whilst the *Daily News* asserted that the pact indicated that Britain 'in effect, steps out of the North as she has already stepped out of the South.'[35]

Nationalist papers were even more forthright in expressing their belief that Irish unification had been brought closer by the agreement. Dismissing Lloyd George's Government of Ireland Act and the 'failure' of partition, the *Irish News* commented that the legislation reflected the inability of 'wise men who have recognised the fact [of failure] are laying the foundation of re-union', whilst the Dublin-based *Irish Independent* expressed its support for a pact which would prove to be 'a great and decided advance towards Irish union.'[36] However, despite its political satisfaction with the agreement, its leading article, 'Hands across the Boyne', appealed for a conciliatory approach:

> ... when the outlook is thus unexpectedly brightened let no one seek to gain party ends by the things that have passed: rather a recurrence of the discord, strife and riot which have brought discredit upon the name of that great city, and let the spirit of hate and jealousy be replaced by tolerance and brotherhood.[37]

The idealism inherent in the terms of the pact and the unrealistic nature of its promises were not going to be easily delivered, given the prevailing unease in the city. Within a fortnight violence in Belfast was to sharply rise, culminating in several of the most horrific murders in the city's history. However, the lack of progress in the days and weeks after the signing of the January pact did not go unnoticed by political leaders. Failure to implement the pact and the fear of escalating violence prompted another meeting between Collins and Craig at Dublin Castle on 2 February.[38] Although a range of issues were discussed, including the boycott and the position of expelled Catholic workers, the main focus was on the Boundary Commission, over which there was a considerable difference of opinion. Whilst there were few signs of progress between the respective political leaders north and south of the border, some hopes were raised by Craig's meetings with wealthy Catholic businessmen, Raymond Burke and Hugh Dougal, who were attempting to encourage middle-class Catholic support for the unionist administration. The emphasis in these discussions was on ways in which the police force might prove to be more acceptable to the minority community and several of their proposals – including the possibility of a 'mixed' Special Constabulary force and the establishment of a Police Advisory Committee – formed the basis of the March Pact. As noted elsewhere, March proved to be another bloody month in Belfast and the moral outrage which swiftly followed the McMahon murders prompted Churchill to hastily summon Craig, Collins and their colleagues to Whitehall on 29 March.

'PEACE IS TODAY DECLARED'

Craig travelled on the overnight ferry to Liverpool on 28 March and made his way down to London the following morning. The talks between British Ministers and the delegations led by Craig and Collins lasted nearly two days before the 11 point pact was issued from the Colonial Office on 30 March. The pact had been quickly drafted in a frantic bid to defuse the escalating violence in Belfast and a growing conviction that reforms in the security sphere would boost nationalists' confidence in the new state's institutions which would, in turn, result in a reduction of the levels of republican violence in the north. Churchill, like many of his British colleagues, had been especially disturbed by the Kinnaird Terrace attack the previous week and a consequence of this empathy for their predicament was a clear feature of a document which underlined the need for encouraging Catholic participation in emergency security organisations. Indeed, the pact, despite its failure to be implemented and its conception as an interim arrangement, was unique in its emphasis on protecting the nationalist community, in itself an acknowledgement of the heavy toll of Catholic dead during the city's recent violence.

The pact, therefore, was a more elaborate version of the January arrangement, but was 'equally ineffectual'.[39] Its first statement – 'Peace is today declared' – reflected the over-optimism of Churchill rather than the hard-nosed realism of Craig and its second clause, in which the two governments undertook 'to co-operate in every way' to eliminate violence in the north, was also unrealistic, given their very different aspirations.[40] The specifics of the pact make more interesting reading than Churchill's comparatively feeble attempt at statesmanship. The third and most controversial clause focussed on arrangements for reorganising the police in Belfast, with suggestions that Specials employed in mixed districts should be composed equally of Catholics and Protestants, that all police on duty should be in uniform and officially numbered, arms searches should be conducted by mixed forces, official records should be kept on the issuing of guns and ammunition from police barracks and an Advisory Committee, containing Catholic representation, should be established in order to assist the selection of Catholic recruits for the Special Constabulary.[41] Another proposal advocated the establishment of an equally-weighted committee 'to hear and investigate complaints as to intimidation and outrages', with such a committee having 'direct access to the heads of the Government.'[42] Other clauses included the eventual establishment of a court for 'the trial without jury of persons charged with serious crime', a promise to hasten the return of those expelled from their homes, the speedy release of political prisoners and the issuing of a £500,000 grant from London to the Northern Ireland Ministry of Labour 'to be expended exclusively on relief of work, one third for the benefit of Roman Catholics and two thirds for the benefit of Protestants.'[43]

The pact was welcomed right across the political spectrum in Britain and on both sides of the new border, though reaction in unionist circles was slightly more guarded.[44] The *Irish Independent* voiced its view that the agreement had 'brought satisfaction and relief' in Belfast and it was regarded within the Catholic community as 'a pleasant surprise.'[45] In a rare compliment to his political adversaries, Bishop MacRory expressed his belief that the pact had been 'conceived in a new spirit which does them [unionists] credit, and which seems to promise recognition of our rights.'[46] Belfast's daily nationalist paper applauded 'this co-operation between Irishmen' and suggested 'the achievement of great and beneficent objects rests the whole country's best and surest hope of redemption.'[47] Guarded optimism was the mood, however, of the *Northern Whig*, which concluded that the announcement heralded 'the promise of brighter and better days for Ireland', but warned its people 'may have to lament one more bitter disappointment.'[48] Both the *Belfast Newsletter* and the *Belfast Telegraph* warned of the agreement's ambiguity, with the latter describing it as 'not entirely self-explanatory.' However, the *Telegraph* warmed to the pact, admitting it contained 'the germ of peace, and if nourished and cherished it will yield in due course the full harvest we all desire.'[49] Perhaps it was the *Belfast Newsletter* which was most cautious, especially when it lamented 'concessions' on the one side, 'only that of the Northern Government.'[50]

Grassroots unionist opinion did not take so kindly to the pact and it was only Craig's powerful grasp over his community which prevented him suffering any lasting damage. General Wilson, appointed as a military advisor by Craig a few weeks previously, was wary of it and hard-line representatives such as William Coote, James Cooper, Robert Lynn and Samuel McGuffin ensured he would remain accountable to his party's rank and file. Fortunately for Craig, he didn't have to deliver what amounted to considerable concessions, especially as the IRA campaign of violence and the economic boycott actually intensified. The virulence of dissenting voices from within the Unionist Party had clearly annoyed the Northern Ireland premier's wife. Lady Craig warned that 'if Ulster does not want moderation and fairness, she might expect J. to resign and make way for the extremists, and then they would jolly well stew.'[51] A few days later she moaned 'how I wish sometimes he had stayed in England, where he is so much appreciated.'[52]

THE QUICK DEMISE OF CONCILIATION

Perhaps the most original feature of the pact was its acknowledgement of the role 'responsible' Catholics could play in endeavouring to improve law and order standards in Belfast. This was reflected in the provision within the agreement to establish two committees. Although both of them were to disintegrate within a few weeks, they briefly provided a forum for the expression of Catholic grievances, especially welcome in a political environment where active Catholic participation was absent.[53] The minutes of one Police Committee meeting held at the Scottish Provident Buildings in the city centre illustrate the problems faced by the authorities in trying to encourage Catholic recruits for the Specials. One of the representatives, the Revd Murray, announced that he intended resigning from the committee on account of two of its Catholic members being arrested and also due to a recent attempt 'to assassinate both myself and colleagues by forces of the Crown.'[54] Both he and another clerical representative on the committee, Father Laverty, maintained that persecution of Catholics would mitigate against the already slim chances of their joining the Specials. Laverty suggested that the issue of families being 'reinstated' in their own homes was of more immediate concern to the Catholic community , maintaining this could be achieved 'without Catholic Specials' and would be regarded as 'a sign of good faith on the part of the Northern Government.'[55]

Both committees were inherently flawed which was primarily due to their limited powers and a lack of trust between Protestant and Catholic members of the respective committees.[56] Membership of the bodies was evenly divided with Catholics sitting on the 12 member Conciliation Committee, but the groups had purely advisory roles and there was a feeling they had been established for cosmetic purposes and for calming down irate nationalists.[57] Optimism for both committees was high in the first few weeks after the pact was signed but it soon evaporated. Although the Conciliation Committee met within a fortnight of the agreement, the *Irish News* remained pessimistic over its chances of success, pointing to the tendency for 'party capital' following each security incident and the real need to discover 'the whole truth in relation to each successful crime'.[58]

Informal liaison between influential Catholics and politicians both in Belfast and London survived the demise of such committees. Thus, the back door diplomacy of Burke and his friends continued and they met Churchill in London to express the growing sense of persecution felt by northern Catholics.[59] However articulate and persuasive Raymond Burke and Hugh Dougal might have been, they were not representative of the wider Catholic community on account of their wealth and position, not to mention their qualified support for the new northern administration. This support, prompted by commercial optimism, contrasted sharply with the desires of ordinary Catholics who were more influenced by day-to-day matters affecting their personal safety and livelihood.

Michael Collins was quick to express his concern at the lack of political urgency devoted to the March Pact. Inside a month of its signing, he bitterly complained to Craig claiming that the latter was the leader of 'an authority [on] whose territory the members of the greatest Church in Christendom, which enjoys the protection of all civilised Governments, are harassed and persecuted in the most appalling fashion by armed mobs, who are apparently not interfered with in any way by your police and military.'[60] In his reply, Craig denied the allegations about security in his area, reminding Collins of his own responsibilities regarding the IRA. He also addressed Collins' comments about facilitating the return of Catholic workers, arguing this was 'a matter no government would undertake' because there was 'no law ... whereby a workman can be compelled to work alongside another.'[61]

On the surface at least, the pacts of early 1922 reflected the growing desperation felt by all three administrations and a belief that the violence and the resulting political instability both inside and outside the boundaries of Northern Ireland could be defused by meaningful negotiation. Thus, the pacts were evidence of the recognition by the various parties of the fears and grievances of their opponents, and a shared commitment to eke out a lasting political compromise which would, eventually, result in a de-escalation of violence on Belfast's streets. Therefore, the unthinkable happened, with political enemies meeting face-to-face and making, however reluctantly, compromises. The reality of the situation was that, although such meetings confirm growing British frustration and disillusionment, especially with the unionist leadership's failure to stem the violence, the degree of genuine commitment on the Sinn Féin and Unionist sides was debatable. Whilst the first pact asked for both parties to compromise, too many unrealistic demands were made of each side. In such an atmosphere of hope, any reservations about its terms were unsurprisingly shelved, resulting later in mutual criticism when the terms were not seen to be applied. Thus, Craig was condemned for not directly helping the return of Catholic workers and Collins was criticised for failing to implement the boycott terms and for his ambiguity towards the IRA's northern campaign. Yet their motives were not totally cosmetic. Collins was never keen on the boycott strategy and endeavoured to use his counsel, if unsuccessfully, to remove it, whilst Craig, despite the unrealistic expectations stated in the pact, encouraged loyalist workers to accept the eventual return to work of Catholics. The context for the second pact was different in that increasing pressure was being applied on Craig and his representatives. The high level of violence in Belfast during March 1922 acted as the barometer for determining the context of the political talks in London, with Catholics able to claim the moral high ground.

Chapter 14

A winter horror land

NEW YEAR BRUTALITY

With curfew restrictions firmly in place, the New Year was seen in relatively peacefully by a reduced number of restrained revellers. Despite their feelings of insecurity over the likely reaction of the gunmen to the recently signed Treaty, most Belfast people harboured relatively optimistic hopes for the year ahead. Certainly life went on much as before. The seasonal pantomime 'Babes in the Wood' was pulling in packed audiences at the Opera House and the Alhambra was showing Charlie Chaplin's latest movie, 'The Kid'. During the day crowds were flocking to the shops' annual sales, with men's tweed suits selling for a mere 26s. 3d. at James' in Lombard Street and 'model' hats retailing for 21s. at Brands in the Ulster Arcade. However, the city was brought back to reality during its opening evening when the short-lived taste of normality turned sour.

Not for the first time it was the York Street area, just north of the city centre, which saw the renewal of violence. At around 10.30 on New Year's evening, gunfire raked the area. Two young Catholics, Hugh Corr (14), of Little Patrick Street, and Samuel Campbell, an infant of 21 months, died in the same incident in Nelson Street. Young Corr had been visiting his aunt when he was shot in the head, with the bullet ricocheting into the abdomen of the infant who had been lying in his mother's arms. Both children, victims of gunfire emanating from Great George's Street, died within the next two days. These tragedies and the renewed violence obviously changed the mood of Belfast's citizens, but the *Belfast Telegraph's* report of the York Street violence had an amusing twist. Apparently an ice-cream seller appeared in the predominantly loyalist Sussex Street part of York Street, attempting to sell his wares on a typically raw winter's day, but a gang of shivering youths chased him towards North Queen Street, where he resorted to hiding under his cart to avoid gunfire coming from this nationalist quarter. The *Telegraph* noted his dilemma and how, 'on the one side were the youths who objected to his making things colder than they already were, while on the other he could hear the crack, crack of revolvers.'[1]

Gunfire returned to the district the following day when another three people died of gunshot wounds. In the morning, the first military fatality, Private E. Barnes, of the 1st Norfolk Regiment, was shot in Dale Street at the corner of North Queen Street and around the same time a Protestant, Alexander Turtle (22), of Mountcollyer Street, was shot in the head by a military patrol near Nelson Street.[2] Around 4 p.m. that day a Catholic butcher in York Street, John Murphy, was serving in his shop when he was attacked by three gunmen. Mr Murphy died in the Mater Hospital three weeks later and his brother Francis, who tried to escape from their assailants, received gunshot wounds to his legs. Violence increased the following evening when there was widespread firing, much of it military, in the York Street area and disturbances around St Matthew's Church in east Belfast.[3] It was estimated that up to 50 shots were fired at any one time when the firing was at its worst in York Street. Alleging that the sniping had started in the nationalist Lancaster Street, the *Belfast Telegraph* stressed the problems the security forces had in apprehending the miscreants:

> Machine guns were turned on the streets and armoured cars lumbered about dispensing showers of lead, but it was much like getting an elephant to catch a mouse. No sooner had the cars passed them the firing was resumed behind them and this game of hide and seek was continuing up to curfew.[4]

Further to the west of the city that evening a Catholic painter, John Gribben (28), returning to his Arnon Street home, had stopped at a shop on the corner of Kildare Street in the Carrick Hill district. Around this time, police from Brown Square Barracks had been fired at in this area, and soon afterwards Mr Gribben died from a head wound. By tragic irony his cousin, Maggie McVeigh, had received a minor injury during trouble in this vicinity and shared an ambulance with the dying Gribben. Security forces regained the initiative the following day, although there was some rioting on the lower Newtownards Road and Short Strand, during which a Protestant teenager, Albert McCrea, of Roundhill Street, was shot dead by the army. The *Belfast Telegraph* blamed Sinn Féin for the violence saying they had 'prophesised trouble when the responsibility for the maintenance of law and order passed into the control of the Northern Government', and that there was 'a plot to keep the city in a state of constant ferment with a view to dismantling the Government.'[5]

Leaders of both communities were anxious to dissuade curious bystanders from hanging around scenes of potentially violent encounters. Pleading their readers to 'keep away from street corners', the *Belfast Telegraph* urged for them to 'assist the authorities in every way possible', adding that 'if there were no human targets snipers would not waste their ammunition.'[6] Despite such commonsense appeals for greater vigilance, congregations of bystanders were to remain throughout the conflict and indeed were also evident in more recent bouts of violence.[7] This was hardly surprising, given people's natural curiosity and, especially in close-knit working class communities, the existence of a genuine sense of collective responsibility. Therefore, it was part of working class culture to spend prolonged periods chatting outside front doors and on street corners, which naturally made them easy targets for snipers. Yet there were several instances of more irresponsible loitering and displays of 'moral support' for the security forces in certain loyalist areas and in the city centre. Christy Robinson remembers as a youngster in west Belfast nipping in at the front of a crowd watching a gun battle between nationalist snipers and the police and the cheers of a crowd watching a gunman who was seen falling off a roof.[8]

Violence heightened during the weekend, most notably in the west of the city, where there were several reports of shooting and bombing, three deaths and many serious injuries. It was not, however, confined to the west of the city. The body of a former soldier and visitor to the city, John McDonough, from County Cavan, was discovered by the security forces late on Saturday 7 January in Lower Meadow Street, off Duncairn Gardens. Sudden indiscriminate firing was heard in the Divis Street area around teatime the following day, following which William Allwell, a Catholic teenager, who had been visiting a friend in Townsend Street, was shot dead and Elizabeth Brady, of Coates Street, seriously wounded. Percy Street, which ran from Divis to the Shankill Road, was particularly dangerous in the early evening and Bridget Devlin (50) was struck by gunfire as she made her way to Mass, dying in hospital a few days later. Police were fired at in Conway Street and North Howard Street and a bomb was thrown into Downshire Street, off the Grosvenor Road. Heavy shooting was reported in the Marrowbone district the following evening when teenager Maud Maguire from Ardilea Street, was shot in the hip. Gunfire was also directed at a tramcar in the north of the city and at a pub on the Crumlin Road.

The next day, a married couple who had been standing at their front door in the mainly nationalist Hooker Street, were singled out for attack by a sniper and they were hit by three bullets. The loyalist press gave copious coverage to this 'awful crime' which resulted in Andrew Anderson and his wife leaving five orphans. The victims' home – 'a scene of desolation' – was visited the following morning when harrowing details of the attack and its aftermath were recorded, including the pathos of 'a milkless breakfast'.[9] At their funeral three days later, a large crowd congregated well in advance , blinds of neighbouring houses and local shops were closed out of respect and the 'terrible and sudden nature of the crime and the pathetic circumstances of the five little ones proved the theme of general and sympathetic discussion.'[10] This attack on a Protestant family living in a mainly Catholic street indicates that such incidents, although occurring significantly less frequently than those perpetuated by loyalist gunmen and bombers, were far from being one-sided in their nature. Further attacks on workmen's trams occurred that morning (11 January) as city-bound trams passed Ardoyne Junction. The motorman had noticed men loitering near the street corner and immediately picked up speed which meant that the bomb which they had thrown exploded towards the rear of the vehicle, rather than at its centre. It was claimed that a large number of men had been involved in the attack and that jeering women from the Ardoyne had expressed their disappointment at the relatively low number of injuries sustained in the attack. Alfred Shippen, a Thomas Street grocer, was wounded on his premises and a handful of women were injured in separate gun attacks in Leopold Street and on the Newtownards Road. Another cold-blooded murder took place later that evening in the west of the city. Just before 11, Mary Hogg (40), who lived at Fifth Street between the Falls and the Shankill, was shot dead by gunmen who called at her door and asked her husband if they could speak to her.[11]

Disillusionment with the far from assertive response of the authorities to the mounting levels of violence grew in its intensity. Also, the city's religious leaders were more prepared than their political counter-parts to acknowledge their own community's culpability for many of the attacks.[12] A joint statement by the Moderator of the Presbyterian Assembly, W.J. Lowe, Bishop C.T.P. Down and the President of the Methodist Church, W.H. Smyth, urged that, although Protestants had 'not been the original aggressors', they should desist from criminal acts, admitting that 'members of the community belonging nominally to our churches have been involved in these outbreaks of violence.'[13]

There was also evidence of growing frustration at the legal system and its failure to adequately protect Belfast's citizens. The judiciary was criticised for its 'lenient' sentences with most of the few people apprehended receiving comparatively short custodial sentences.[14] The verdicts and opinions of coroners' courts were also regularly recorded in the columns of the local press. In an editorial, the *Belfast Telegraph* noted inquest verdicts which had been 'strongly critical' of the authorities for 'failing to take effective measures to preserve the peace of the city.'[15] At the same time, the loyalist press were quick to support security forces in their quest to ensure more efficient apprehension of trouble-makers. Apart from the irritant of curious bystanders mentioned earlier, the police and army had been thwarted on several occasions by snipers utilising empty or business premises for their attacks on them, and decided to conduct an information campaign in the local press. The military commander with overall responsibility for Belfast, Major-General Cameron, informed Belfast's citizens of his special powers which would enable him to 'evict all persons occupying buildings from which firing takes place, close such buildings or destroy them and arrest any individual owning or occupying premises from which firing takes place or found in them.'[16]

As noted, an increasing number of attacks, several of them fatal, were mounted on people either on their way to work or when they were at their workplace. This category of 'easy' target was appealing to gunmen as in an age of high unemployment many citizens had little choice but to face the possibility of gunfire or a bomb attack, especially whilst passing through hostile areas. At least such workers only had to face the dangers proceeding to and from work each day. Corner shop owners, publicans or barmen and those whose work meant they were constantly on the move through dangerous thoroughfares, such as tram-drivers and carters, had no respite as the tension caused by the possibility of imminent attack was ever-present. Economic necessity often conquered any fears over personal security. This was the case with Robert McElborough, a Protestant Corporation gas-worker, who had been assigned to repair lamps in the Short Strand area around this time. He recalled:

> I had the feeling that like Uriah of the Bible I was being sent to the front line. The people living in this area did not want the streets lit as they said they were a target when they were on the streets, and felt more secure from bullets in the dark, but the military who were patrolling this area insisted that the lamps be lit ... My first morning [was] with a handcart full of lamps;when the boy who was with me came to the end of the bridge which led into this area he refused to go any further and went back to the workshops. I don't blame the boy, but the fact that I had a wife and family and was threatened with dismissal if I refused to do this work, I would have given it up.[17]

'A MATCH TO A POWDER KEG'

Although the winter meetings involving Craig and Sinn Féin leaders had ensured that the atmosphere in Belfast would remain tense, there had been a distinct reduction in the level of violence since mid-January. Thomas Gray, originally from Dromore in County Tyrone, was shot in the back by a young gunman as he served in O'Boyle's Bar on 6 February and died the following day.[18] Another Catholic lost his life in the ever-dangerous Cuper Street. Teenager Patrick Hannigan had been chatting to a couple of girls during the early evening of 9 February when he was shot by two loyalist gunmen. However, as the city's populace drew their breath, events outside their environs precipitated the next vicious spell of sectarian in-fighting which was to result in nearly 50 fatalities in February, 31 of which were to occur during a three-day spell in the middle of the month. In a clearly orchestrated IRA operation along the Tyrone and Fermanagh border, 42 loyalists were kidnapped, an event which led to the immediate mobilisation of Specials in the border region, and a fierce denunciation of the kidnappings in the unionist press which clearly did little to lift the tension.[19] The *Belfast Telegraph* asked if Sinn Féin had 'any realisation whatsoever of the exasperation and provocation which such lawless acts involve, and the risks which they necessarily occasion in a moment of wild passion to their own co-religionists within certain areas of Ulster?'[20] The language of the *Belfast Newsletter* was even more vitriolic. Its leading article condemned the 'audacious act of war against the British Crown', blaming Sinn Féin for 'an act which, if perpetuated by an alien people, would be visited with retaliatory violence.'[21]

A couple of days later, Saturday 11 February, a patrol of 16 'A' Specials, less than half of whom were armed, travelled by train from Newtownards camp to Enniskillen via the small County Monaghan town of Clones in the Free State.[22] Clearly local republicans had a tip-off that the police group would have half an hour wait for a connecting train.[23] Panic prevailed for what seemed an eternity at the small rural station which had been busy at the time. Noting how four trains had been stationary at the time of the attack, the *Irish Independent* described how the train's occupants, 'in order to escape the flying bullets, flung themselves on the floors of the carriages and screams could be heard from the frightened lady travellers who became hysterical and rushed from the station.'[24] The IRA commander, Matt Fitzpatrick, who had boarded the train demanding the Specials' surrender, was shot dead and a vicious gun battle ensued, during which 4 policemen were killed and 9 others wounded.[25] The press universally condemned the 'unprovoked' attack at Clones Station, with the *Glasgow Herald*'s vivid report describing how 'the upper part of the platform was bespattered with blood, luggage was strewn about in all directions and many of the passengers, men and women, were in a frantic state.'[26] The *Times* too condemned the attack, labelling it 'a dastardly outrage', but opinion in the south tended to shift the blame on to the authorities in Belfast and London.[27] The *Irish Independent*, referring to an incident which had occurred a few weeks previously when 'members of a football team' were intercepted by security forces and detained, suggested that the responsibility for 'this regrettable tendency rests on the shoulders of those who have sanctioned the act of the Special Police in arresting the Divisional Officers of the IRA who were merely passing through 'Northern' territory to attend a football match in Derry.'[28]

The effect of these events 100 miles from Belfast should not be underestimated. Eamon Phoenix has described the Clones attack as 'a match to a powder keg' and although some violent incidents had occurred before the attack, once news filtered back to Belfast of events along and across the border, the atmosphere rapidly worsened.[29] Over 30 people died in the city between 12 and 16 February, over half of whom were fatally wounded during one day, the 13 February. Shooting had returned to Belfast's streets on the morning of Saturday 11 February, most notably in and around York Street, and was renewed more heavily on the Old Lodge Road in the evening. Margaret Page, a 42-year-old Catholic, was tidying up the stock in her North Queen Street corner shop when she was shot dead by what witnesses described as an extremely youthful gunman. News continued to filter back from Clones the following day and there were several shooting incidents during the evening of 12 February in the York Street, North Queen Street, Millfield, Townsend Street and Dover Street areas. Some churches closed in the evening and many worshippers soon changed their minds about attending services in those which had opened. There were three fatalities. A Protestant teenager, David Boyd, was shot standing at the corner of Hanover Street and the bodies of two Catholics were found in close proximity to Millfield, following heavy 'B' Special activity in the area just before midnight. The victims were William Tennyson, of Cavendish Street and James Mathers, of Jude Street, and a couple of hours later, Peter McNelis (28), a barman, was shot dead in the Markets district. That day, Monday 13 February, was to prove to be the bloodiest of the winter, despite the adjustments made to the curfew regulations (now 11p.m.–5a.m.). Gunfire was reported to have been directed at men going to work in the vicinity of Dale and Vere Streets early in the morning. Two Catholics, Francis Neary (40) and James Gregg (50) were shot dead in Kildare Street, whilst two Protestants James Brown (23) and ex-soldier, Ben Lundy (21) suffered the same fate near North Howard Street following gunfire directed from the Falls. A Catholic publican, Patrick Lambe (53), who had managed the 'Blacksmith's Arms' pub in York Street for over 20 years, was shot dead at lunchtime when several armed men stormed into his premises.[30]

Violence intensified during the evening, especially in the north of the city, with the *Telegraph* claiming 'the constant rattle of rifle and revolver shots' could be heard all over the city at times.'[31] People hurried home from their day's toil, so that 'by the time curfew hour approached, the main arteries of the city were deserted'.[32] Anthony Sadlier, a Catholic teenager, from Tyrone Street, was shot dead in an alleged case of mistaken identity, whilst Joseph Brown (50), of Regent Street, was another Catholic victim of loyalist gunmen. Mary Robinson, a Catholic teenager from Lancaster Street, received a stomach wound following shooting in York Street and died the following day. Two Protestants were also shot dead in the north of the city. Carter William Law (20), from Prospect Street, was shot in the stomach whilst leading his horse near Clifton Street and died the following day. Shore Road man Johnston Crothers (25), who had served as a machine-gunner in the 51st Highland Division, was killed near Little Patrick Street, as he returned from a visit to the grave of his girlfriend's father in Carnmoney.

The worst single incident on a day of extreme blood-letting occurred in Weaver Street where a bomb killed 6 and injured nearly 20 others, most of them children. Weaver Street, connecting North Derby Street and Milewater Street, was a Catholic street surrounded by the overwhelmingly loyalist Shore Road, and was an easy target for attack. Indeed, several children had been injured in a bomb attack several months previously in nearby Milewater Street, and with the border tension and killings of north Belfast Protestants Johnston Crothers and William Waring, such an outrage was more likely to occur. Children had been enticed onto the streets for skipping and other games by unseasonably mild weather and were happily engaged playing traditional street games when the bomber struck.[33] Their happy mood was caught in the *Belfast Telegraph's* evocative report:

> The beautiful moonlight night and sharp nip in the air had brought the youth from all the houses in Weaver Street into a common bond in the

centre of the thoroughfare for amusement. A rope was procured and soon a skipping school was in full swing and this, accompanied with the shouts of the buoyant revellers, spelled of nothing but the happiest enjoyment.[34]

The playful, delirious atmosphere of their games was abruptly broken when two loyalists threw a bomb from the corner of Upper Derby Street into the crowd of playing children and the bomb instantly exploded.[35] Two children Mary Johnstone (11) and Catherine Kennedy (15), who like most of the victims lived in the street, died instantly. Four of the injured were to succumb to their injuries. Elizabeth O'Hanlon (11), who had several brothers and sisters injured in the blast, died the following day, as did Rose-Ann McNeill (13), and two women, Margaret Smith (53) and Mary Owen (40), from Shore Street, were also to die of their wounds inside the next couple of months. The destruction and suffering caused by this large bomb – 'one of the largest ever used during disturbances in the city' – shocked the whole community.[36] The tragedies were, of course, personal and the suffering was compounded by the tightly-knit nature of the little Catholic community with many children belonging to large families. Martha O'Hanlon (13), many of whose family had been caught up in the huge blast, spoke to a reporter from her hospital bed. She said:

> I did not know I had been wounded until I tried to rise, and I felt the pains all over my body. The bomb made a terrible noise and people were crying and screaming. I did not see anyone as I was too much engaged in the fun of skipping. There were a terrible lot of wounded and two ambulances had to be got to take us to hospital … My wee sister, who was also wounded, died in this place last night.[37]

The sense of outrage was, at that time, unsurpassed. Leading British politicians were shocked at the scale of the attack and especially by the fact that children were chosen as the victims. In a telegram to Michael Collins, Churchill described the bomb as 'the worst thing which has happened in Ireland in the last three years' and attacks such as these unquestionably lost unionists support in Great Britain.[38] However, the real impact was in the Catholic ghettoes of north Belfast, where a genuine sense of fear endured. The severity of the situation prompted Dr MacRory to send a telegram to Lloyd George the following day. In this, the Catholic bishop pleaded for military reinforcements:

> For the past few days Belfast [was] again given up to terrible lawlessness. Since Saturday about a dozen Catholics shot dead, some in their own houses and over forty wounded, several it is feared fatally. No adequate protection here for Catholics. Military urgently needed on the streets.[39]

The psychological damage inflicted by such outrages, if anything, exceeded security statistics and the Armageddon warnings of Catholic bishops. The Weaver Street attack undoubtedly did irreparable damage to many young people in an age before such problems were fully appreciated. Although Sarah O'Hare lived in Catherine Street in the Markets district, she was a frequent visitor to Weaver Street where her cousin Katie Kennedy lived. She recalls:

> My cousin Katie had just started working in a mill. She lived in Weaver Street where we sometimes visited her and the rest of the family. One night she was skipping in her street when a bomb was thrown from North Derby Street. She and several other children I had met were killed or seriously injured. Her father John was a big, fine, religious man but despite his faith, he never got over the waste of such a young life.[40]

DEFENDERS OF THE PEOPLE?

Though evidence of IRA activity in the city can be traced back to the summer of 1920, it was in the first half of 1922 that the IRA was busiest in Belfast. Whilst specific actions of republican paramilitaries are considered in detail elsewhere, a number of central themes pertaining to the role of the 3rd Northern Division will be considered here. These include an analysis of its structure and relative strength during the conflict, a brief outline of the stages of its campaign and an attempt to assess its degree of significance. Just as it would prove to be in the late 1960s, the IRA and its political organisation Sinn Féin, was under strength and in a subsidiary position to constitutional nationalism in the city on the eve of the 1920s' conflict. The United Irish League had 18 branches, with over 6,000 members, in Belfast and the Ancient Order of Hibernians had over 25 branches. On the other hand, there were only 9 Sinn Féin clubs in the city and even Seamus Woods, who became the Commanding Officer of the 3rd Northern Division in 1922, admitted they had the active support of barely 10% of the Catholic population at that time.[41] Estimates of the size of the IRA in the city vary from 500 to just under 1,000, but Austen Morgan's consideration that, in numerical terms, they were 'insignificant nationally' is an accurate one.[42] Although there were several IRA operations in the city during the last months of 1920 and the first quarter of 1921, it was not until after internal restructuring in May 1921 that the republican campaign gained momentum.

The 3rd Northern Division, under the leadership of Tyrone-born Joe McKelvey, consisted of three brigades covering each of its areas, Belfast, Antrim and North Down. From the start, the 3rd Northern suffered a variety of disadvantages, including cumbersome administrative structures, unique operational problems, weak liaison with Dublin, the quality of many of their volunteers, – some regarded them as 'Hibernians with rifles' – problems in trying to restrain sections of their community from indulging in blatant sectarian retribution, and, most especially, the procurement of arms and ammunition. For the first year of the conflict, the IRA in the city was not properly armed and it was largely due to the breathing-space offered by the Truce and Collins' own commitment to the plight of northern Catholics that there was a gradual improvement in this area. Indeed, by the first half of 1922, the Northern Division was only second in terms of its arms and munitions to the Cork division (it possessed over 600 rifles and 5 machine-guns).

There were three broad phases in the 3rd Northern's campaign. Initially there was a period of improvisation as northern republicanism reacted to the shipyard expulsions and street disturbances. This reaction tended to take the form of spasmodic shooting attacks on security forces and on Protestants, as well as robberies to fund arms. A more active role was assumed from the spring of 1921, and especially following the signing of the Truce. The formal structuring of the IRA in the city and the desperate need for a more proactive response from it, in the wake of political initiatives and British security toughness, made this inevitable. The final phase of republican activity came after the Treaty, which ushered in a frenetic four month spell of IRA shootings, bombing, arson and political assassination, which also proved to be the culmination of their military involvement.

As has been noted, the small, disparate, group of republicans on the Falls Road, the Short Strand and in the north of the city, had been caught on the hop by the outbreak of trouble in July 1920. Although most of the casualties caused by the initial outbreak of sniping in the west of the city were probably the victims of police and loyalist gunfire, republicans were also undoubtedly involved, especially in the second outburst of serious disturbances in the late summer. Until the spring of the following year, the IRA's Belfast brigade were mainly involved in an improvised and intermittent campaign of arson attacks on business premises and robberies, especially directed against post offices, with the aim of procuring arms and ammunition for the enormous task which undoubtedly lay ahead of them. To keep up their profile in their own communities, they also periodically targeted Crown forces in the city. The drawback of this tactic was the normally virulent retribution extracted by loyalists and 'rogue' policemen. Therefore, the killings of a RIC officer on the Falls Road at the end of September resulted in the assassination of three Sinn Féin men in the west of the city and an attack on RIC officers staying overnight in a city hotel produced a counter assassination of a Catholic early in the New Year. Significantly a similar attack on three Black and Tans in the city centre in March produced no major revenge attacks, although another killing of auxiliary police officers precipitated the killing of the Duffin brothers in April.[43] Another killing of a Belfast police officer, James Glover, on 10th June sparked reprisal attacks on three Catholics in north Belfast.

IRA activity in the city increased during the second part of the year on account of a number of factors. These included the formal structuring of the 3rd Northern Division in May, the acquisition of more weaponry and, most especially, the signing of the truce between the IRA and Crown forces which paved the way for northern republicans to consolidate their position. In the north, the Special Constabulary and other forces took a noticeably less proactive security role, and the more relaxed atmosphere provided the opportunity for increased drilling and arms training, some of which were led by leading figures in the south including Dan Breen.[44]

One interesting internal repercussion of the signing of the Truce had been the appointment of a senior IRA staff officer, Eoin O'Duffy, as a liaison officer in Belfast.[45] O'Duffy's official role was to act as a link between the IRA and the British military in the north. Stressing that republicans would refrain from sniping attacks except in self-defence, O'Duffy operated from St Mary's Hall, near the city centre, from mid July 1921. In effect, the hall became Sinn Féin's headquarters in the city and was used as a multi-purpose centre, especially important for intelligence gathering and the bureaucratic co-ordination of the northern republican movement. O'Duffy's role, and indeed Sinn Féin's use of the centre, came to an abrupt end on the evening of 18 March 1922, when a joint raiding party of RIC and Specials thoroughly searched the hall. Although no IRA personnel were on the premises, a small arsenal of weaponry was seized and several revealing documents were uncovered during the extensive police search. These included detailed information about IRA personnel in the city and a list of the names and addresses of Special Constabulary members, especially in west Belfast and York Street. The northern IRA was not to be the same after this raid.[46]

Both sides uncharacteristically agreed on the significance of the Truce. Junior Home Affairs Minister, R.D. Megaw, conceded that the IRA had 'never become really active' until they had benefited from 'the protection of the so-called Truce', which he believed to be an 'instrument' used by 'a hostile army' aiming to 'overthrow' Craig's Government.[47] Seamus Woods also regarded the post-Truce period as a halcyon period for the 3rd Northern Division. Writing to Richard Mulcahy in Dublin, he stressed the effect the truce had had on the Catholic population of Belfast who 'practically all flocked to our standard.' Woods claimed that in the six month period between the signing of the truce and the Treaty, 'the perfecting of our organisation, training and equipping had been pursued with great earnestness on the part of all officers and men … a large number of recruits were taken on.'[48] The fatal shooting of a RIC officer, Thomas Conlon, in Raglan Street shortly after the Truce started, marked an escalation of IRA activity in the city.[49] This took the form of sniper attacks on Protestants proceeding to and from work and, in many cases, gunmen invaded the workplace. Shipyard workers were a favourite quarry of republican gunmen, frequently as they proceeded to work past the Short Strand, but workers were also targeted in trams in a variety of locations, especially in the city centre and north Belfast. Such attacks suggest that, rather than being merely a reactive, defensive force at this time, the IRA were quite prepared to engage, where possible, in aggressive actions against Protestant civilians, as well as targeting members of the security forces.[50] The attacks on workers' trams were blatantly sectarian and intensified hard-line unionist opinion, precipitating in turn further attacks on Catholics. Sean Montgomery was one republican with considerable misgivings about his involvement in an especially nasty attack in Royal Avenue in November 1921. He later wrote:

> Things were getting very bad so orders were given to bomb two shipyard trams, one was done in Corporation Street in the early part of the week. In Lancaster Street I was approached by Alf Mullan. He could not get anyone to cover him as he had orders to do two trams. I asked him if it was an order and he said it was so I went with him. We went to the York

Street face of the Belfast Co-op. An armoured car came along so we moved to Winetavern Street. While waiting a policeman who knew Alf told him to get from hell from there as he was on duty, so we went off to Berry Street and in front of the Grand Central Hotel he did the job. I covered him. As we ran down Berry Street we ran into the OC of the unit. He told me to put the gun that I had in my hand away. Off we went again up Francis Street to safety. Well there was a bit of a stink about it.[51]

The signing of the Treaty 'ushered in a new phase for the northern IRA', one which catapulted northern republicans into their most active phase of the conflict, but which was to result in its nemesis.[52] Although a small number of northern republicans, most notably Joe McKelvey, sided with 'irregular' forces during the Irish Civil War, the dispersal of northern republicans from Northern Ireland during the second half of 1922 defused the chances of the northern movement being destroyed by internal strife, like many divisions elsewhere in Ireland. This is not to say that the Treaty was a godsend for Belfast republicans, as many were soon to suffer demoralisation. This was caused by a shift in the focus of republicans elsewhere in Ireland and the massive haemorrhaging caused by internal division over the Treaty, not to mention the sheer superiority, both in terms of manpower and equipment, of the Crown forces.

Michael Collins had a special affinity with northern republicans. Though this was partly motivated by pragmatic considerations – especially the need to curb the drift of Belfast activists to the anti-treaty faction – his commitment to the plight of its besieged Catholic population was genuine.[53] It was this which prompted him to establish a secret group of 'Belfast Guards' to protect Catholic areas, on 22 February, (it was to disband in August). The force consisted of 72 men (including 12 officers) from the Northern Division who were to be paid £3 a week. Collins avoided publicising the new unit to prevent jealousy and further internal division amongst the city's volunteers. Though they were cheered by Collins' outspoken comments on their behalf, Belfast nationalists were far from reassured by the wider republican movement's level of interest in the north, and especially in their particular plight. Thus, apart from moments of crisis, the Ulster issue was rarely raised in the Dáil Éireann, and, as a leading Belfast republican pointed out, the decision by Sinn Féin to delay an election in the south on the Treaty question, plunged northern Catholics into greater uncertainty. Dennis McCullough argued:

Whilst they were making up their minds on the Treaty their people in
the north were being murdered day by day. They could not stand up to
the terror in Ulster unless they had a united organisation behind them.[54]

It is more tempting to view the 3rd Northern Division's concerted campaign
of May and June 1922 as their recognition that this constituted a last throw of
the dice in the North, rather representing a firm belief that they had a serious
chance of dismantling the British infrastructure in Northern Ireland. A step-
ping-up in their campaign can, indeed, be traced back to the border
kidnappings of loyalists and the Clones incident in February (see above). Police
barracks, railway stations and the houses of aristocratic Anglo-Irish Protestants
were the subject of frequent arson attack, with the IRA achieving some short-
term success in the form of spectacular incursions, such as the Belleek incident
early in June. Unionists were, to a large degree, astounded by the scale and
precision of the new IRA onslaught. The 'co-ordinated nature of the raids came
as a great shock to the Craig government', but the main effect of this intensive
campaign was 'to unleash a terrible sectarian backlash on the Catholic population in Belfast'.[55] More often or not, their continued attacks on police officers
and increased targeting of Protestants resulted in even bloodier revenge attacks
being committed both in rural areas such as Desertmartin and at Kinnaird
Terrace and Arnon Street in Belfast.[56] Increasingly desperate pressure from
fellow Catholics in their neighbourhoods resulted in a considerable number of
cases of indiscriminate sniping, tit-for-tat killings of Protestant workers and
bomb attacks on trams which produced many casualties.

The IRA mounted two spectacular attacks within a week in May, both in the
city centre. The onslaught on Musgrave Street police barracks on 18 May, whilst
proving to be a fiasco, was highly ambitious and revealed the 3rd Northern's aim
to utilise the anticipated haul of rifles, assorted ammunition and armoured
vehicles in a more intensive campaign against Crown forces both in the city and
across Ulster.[57] A few days later, the IRA shot William Twaddell, a Unionist MP
and fierce critic of republicanism, near his draper's shop in North Street. This
was a rare instance of the Northern Division successfully targeting a leading
member of the local unionist establishment and, of course, mirrored the
strategy adopted by their colleagues elsewhere in Ireland.[58] Both attacks illustrate that, although very much on the back foot, the 3rd Northern Division was
keen to be as innovative in the nature of its operations as the restricted security
atmosphere allowed. Another favoured strategy at this time was that of arson.

Apart from attacking railway stations and police barracks across Ulster, the IRA switched emphasis from sniping at Protestants in May and June, to a co-ordinated campaign designed directly at the commercial heart of Belfast's industry and commerce, as well as damaging the interests of 'Big House' unionists in the countryside.[59] Compensation claims for damage and injury caused by incendiary attacks during May and June exceeded £1,500,000.[60] Southern republicans were united in their support for this tactic. Sinn Féin's official organ, *Plain People*, urged northern activists to 'go on with the burnings', claiming that 'the Orangeman will not be won until he is beaten to earth.'[61] Other republicans, more circumspect over less violent tactics such as the boycott, appeared wholeheartedly in favour of direct strikes on the homes and business premises of Ulster's landed and commercial aristocracy. Collins was to later wryly remark of the IRA's arson campaign in the north:

> For a good many months we did as much as we could to get property destroyed ... I know they [unionists] think a great deal more of property than of human life.[62]

Northern nationalist feelings of besiegement and harassment were now joined by ones of isolation and abandonment as the Civil War started in July.[63] Even before hostilities commenced, nationalists were becoming increasingly aware of a reduction in interest for their predicament and as events in the south and west of Ireland took precedence for the pro-Treaty forces, the resistance of northern Catholics virtually evaporated. This disillusionment resulted in practical on-the-ground difficulties for active republicans in the city. As conceded by their own Commanding Officer, the Crown security forces used appropriate and successful tactics during the first half of 1922, tightening the screw on the IRA both in Belfast and its surrounding areas.[64] The emerging Special Powers legislation caught most republicans unawares and even if many of its major activists were not initially apprehended, they were driven underground as the wider Catholic community grew increasingly alarmed. Woods admitted in another memo to the IRA's Dublin headquarters that 'the Enemy are continually raiding and arresting, the heavy sentences and particularly the floggings make the civilians very loathe to hide "wanted men" or arms.'[65] Flogging was, understandably, the scourge of many nationalists at the time. The contents of a letter written by Crumlin Road prisoner James McAlorum to his wife, throw light on what IRA volunteers often had to endure. Ex-soldier McAlorum, who had been expelled from his workplace and shot whilst working on a tramway reconstruction site in east Belfast, had been subsequently accused of assault and robbery in a public house. Despite rather flimsy evidence, he was given a three year custodial sentence and fifteen strokes of the 'cat'. In his letter, McAlorum also described the 'degradation' he faced on the evening of 22 June when he was taken to an underground dungeon, where prison officers had erected a flogging triangle and once he had been severely tied, suffered his 15 lashes. What was especially memorable for the victim was not so much his own beating, grotesque as it was, but the predicament of a nationalist teenager who followed him to his cell. Mr McAlorum described this 'child prisoner' who, despite 'pleading to the prison doctor to intervene and save him from the cruel and unmerciful punishment', suffered the same fate.[66]

The 3rd Northern Division also suffered other reverses in June and July, including the capture of several arms dumps, as well as the discovery of many IRA documents. Many volunteers had close shave encounters with the authorities. Sean Montgomery claimed that his home was raided several times. Frequently he stored arms stolen from other sites and described one lucky escape:

> I had a Mills hand grenade that I left on the side-board under my hat. I put the two rifles in the back room and then went to bed. About two o'clock in the morning the door was knocked. I asked who was there and was answered, 'The police!' I lifted the two rifles and climbed through the back window into the yard. I jumped on to the wall, dropped the guns between a small space of about 2 foot and then made over three yards of other people. It was raining very hard. I knocked on the window of a house which belonged to friendly people. When I told them what was happening they told me to get away from them as they had a shop. I got under a table in the yard and pulled empty potato bags over me. I just got there in time as I heard two police talking in a small entry a few yards from where I was hiding.[67]

Many volunteers had been forced to go on the run in their own areas but they experienced considerable difficulty in acquiring 'safe' houses.[68] Seamus Woods described how many of his men were in 'a state of practical starvation' and told how some of the local community were turning in their frustration against them:

> The [IRA] Officers are feeling their position keenly. Recently a number of men were rounded up and detained in custody. The mother of one of the boys, when bringing him food shouted out, in the presence of Crown forces, the name of the local officer commanding and made a tirade against him for misleading her boy into this movement.[69]

Although the split in the IRA over the Treaty had little bearing on northern republicanism, most of whose members remained loyal to the Provisional Government, the commencement of the Civil War four months later provided the final blow to the 3rd Northern Division. Disillusionment both within the ranks and wider community which could be traced back a few months, resulted in nearly 1,700 republicans leaving Belfast between April and December 1922 to join the Free State Army.[70] Local republicans stressed the fatal implications of low morale in nationalist areas and the successful forays of the 'B' Specials and how these combined to stem their northern campaign. In a letter to Dublin headquarters, a 3rd Northern Division officer claimed:

> ... the enemy were able to pour in lorries [of Specials] raiding and the enemy's display of such numerically superior forces, has been considerably weakened ... B Specials with their local knowledge of the people and made it very difficult for our men to escape.[71]

Mood in the Catholic ghettoes had clearly worsened over the second half of the conflict and made it impossible for republican activity to carry on. One IRA veteran later recalled:

> With reprisals and the like, people were cowed to some extent, afraid of the knock on the door, waiting for the 'B' men or the peelers to call ... Of course the IRA did a great deal of shooting as well but they were so outnumbered and partition had cut off the nationalists so much that the IRA spent most of its time defending areas or trying to reassure people.[72]

The 3rd Northern Division met Collins on 9 July, when it was agreed that their campaign in the north should cease. The demise of the IRA was not totally appreciated by the northern authorities who appeared to misread both the strength and intentions of a depleted and demoralised force. Craig's military advisor, Major-General Arthur Solly-Flood, warned on 16 August:

It would appear from intelligence sources that reorganisation of enemy units in Ulster is now well in progress. The quiet situation is in a great measure due to an organised scheme to get the Northern Government of Ireland to release the internees, and a great amount of success is attending their efforts in this direction. There are good reasons for stating that there is every likelihood of a resumption of activities in the course of a few weeks.[73]

In conclusion, it would be incorrect to suggest that the IRA's involvement in the Twenties' conflict was mainly restricted to its final two or three months. Whilst the IRA's most frenetic response to the activity of loyalists belongs to a three month campaign in the middle of 1922, militant republicans were far from inactive during the second part of 1921 and they even had a role to play during the conflict's earliest phase. It would also be misleading to define the 3rd Northern's role as a merely defensive and reactive one. Undoubtedly at several times during the conflict self-protection was the Division's priority, as loyalist gunmen and mobs continued to snipe and attack nationalist districts, with an alarming regularity and apparent freedom. The unhealthy state of the northern IRA and the growing strength and confidence of their enemy, the Crown forces, also suggest they were not in the prime condition normally required for mounting a proactive campaign.[74] However, this argument that the Third Northern's purpose was simply to defend Catholic areas and to hold back rather than defeat Crown forces is simplistic and ignores what was happening elsewhere in Ireland. Although in the end it was internal division within the republican movement which dealt the northern IRA its death blow, republicans had used the lull provided by the Truce to reorganise in Ulster, and might have enjoyed misguided hopes for the success of their late spring onslaught, which was still two months before the beginning of the Civil War. Nor could they be totally exempted from the criticism that they became embroiled in a 'dirty war'. Whilst loyalists, both in and out of uniform, were culpable of a disproportionate number of blatantly sectarian attacks, republican forces were also guilty of indulging in tit-for-tat killings. Despite claiming the moral high ground, the 3rd Northern Division succumbed to pressure from within their own community for revenge killings and there were several instances of police and Protestant civilians being targeted in the streets, in tram-cars and at their places of work.

Assessing the IRA's culpability for events in Belfast between 1920 and 1922 is far from straightforward. In comparison with the IRA 50 years later, republicans were, to a greater degree, outnumbered and marginalized during most of this period. Although it is impossible to give a precise statistical breakdown as to the culpability for specific attacks, my estimation of IRA responsibility for fatal attacks in the city is in the region of 30%. This might suggest their role in events in the city to be peripheral. However, although they were not the sole cause of the trouble, they were arguably the most important single factor, on account of their considerable impact upon the reactions of others. It was the perceived and quite credible belief that IRA gunmen in the Short Strand, North Queen Street and Falls represented only but a small percentage of volunteers liable to be involved in greater carnage within Ulster's boundaries, that fuelled loyalist fears and resulted in further deaths. It was, in fact, the potential of IRA violence and its overthrow of the state, rather than republican sorties or attacks on trams, unionist leaders or on the 'Big Houses', which had the most important impact on the loyalist psyche.

MUTUAL RECRIMINATION AND FURTHER SLAUGHTER

Although the level of violence was not to approach that of Monday 13th February, the following day saw several further bloody incidents, some of which had fatal consequences. An early morning attack occurred at Clifton Street, off Carlisle Circus. William Waring (50), who had been the caretaker of Clifton Street Orange Hall for a decade, was opening the rear entrance of the hall at 10 a.m. when a nationalist sniper ran up from Stanhope Street and shot him at close range. The fatally wounded man, shot in the throat, initially received assistance from a passing milkman who desisted when the fleeing gunman threatened to open fire on him. Also that morning, a barman from County Armagh and an IRA officer, Frank McCoy (26), who worked in McKenna's pub on the Falls Road, was found dying in Springfield Avenue and George Harper (16), a Protestant from Earl Street, who had been standing at the corner of Little George Street, was fatally wounded during the disturbances in York Street.[75] Two Protestant labourers laying new tramlines on the Falls Road close to the War Hospital (now the Maternity Hospital) were approached by nationalist gunmen who, after enquiring their religion, gunned them down. Thomas Samuel Blair (40), of Burnaby Street, died instantly and another worker James Lindsay was wounded. Police coincidentally passed the scene of the attack and gave pursuit. As the IRA gang made their way through Dunville Park, one of them, James Morrison, received fatal wounds after the police opened fire. Another carter was targeted north of the city centre in the late morning. Henry Gallagher (40), of Little Patrick Street, was driving his horse and cart down Great George's Street when he was shot dead and another Catholic, James Rice (19), of Avondale Street, died from multiple gunshot wounds after being brutally beaten by a loyalist mob in Ravenscroft Street. Two Protestant workers loading vans at the Hughes and Dickson Flour Mill in Divis Street were challenged by a 12–strong IRA team and, separated from Catholic colleagues. One of them, John McClelland, of Christopher Street, died in the Royal Victoria Hospital, as did another Protestant, John Wales, of Enfield Street, who succumbed to injuries sustained in a previous incident.

Wednesday 15 February brought no respite, with 7 people losing their lives in the city. In another attack aimed at Protestants working in Catholic areas in west Belfast, William Duffin (24), a trainee manager in the New Northern Spinning Company in Northumberland Street, was shot dead at work in the middle of the afternoon by an IRA gang. Later that evening two Catholics, Peter McCall (22), of Tyrone Street and Owen Bond, of Stanhope Street, were shot dead by a military patrol at Carrick Hill. Three died in incidents in the north of the city. During the middle of the evening, an off-duty 'B' Special and plater, Hector Stewart (21), of Ship Street, was fatally wounded by an IRA sniper as he passed New Lodge Road on his way to meet his girlfriend. Following a flare-up of trouble on the Old Lodge Road, a fruiterer, Hugh French (39), was hit by a police bullet, following attacks on business premises in the area. Mr French, who had been reading the evening paper in his shop, subsequently died in hospital. Another Protestant, Thomas Neil, of Peveril Street, was shot dead by police, allegedly sniping from a rooftop in York Street. In the east of the city, Charles John McMullan (29), was shot in his Woodstock home and died in hospital a fortnight later. Another Catholic, John Devlin, a 5-year-old child who had been playing close to his Seaforde Street Home, died after being hit by a sniper's bullet around tea-time that day.[76]

Post-violence recrimination pursued familiar patterns. Bishop MacRory clearly attributed the latest bout of violence to the Clones incident and events elsewhere in Ireland, condemning it as an expression of 'the doctrine of vicarious punishment, according to which the Catholics of Belfast are made to suffer for the sins of their brethren elsewhere.'[77] Inevitably the press divided on who was culpable. The *Irish Independent* suggested it was not Belfast Catholics who had started 'the original pogrom', maintaining they 'would be less than human if they did not seek to defend themselves.'[78] This call for resistance was developed by the *Irish News* which suggested that if an 'organised and united' Catholic response to loyalist pressure had been adopted, 'the idea of exterminating them would not have been seriously entertained.'[79] The *Belfast Telegraph*, on the other hand, indulged itself again in assessing statistical responsibility. Denying MacRory's claim that the suffering had been exclusively Catholic, the *Telegraph* pointed out that most of the previous day's fatalities had been Protestant and said, 'This abominable shooting in the city is not so one-sided as the Bishop suggests.'[80]

Although violence subsided in its intensity on 16 February, there was still a fatal wounding and reports of further shooting, especially in the Short Strand area. James McCormick (45), a Protestant, from Roseberry Gardens, was shot in the head on his way to work in a chemical factory close to Short Strand. Despite the momentary respite on the streets, the political temperature was raised at Westminster where Joe Devlin bemoaned the plight of his constituents in west Belfast, describing them as 'the victims of a system of terrorism without parallel in any country in Europe.'[81] Meanwhile in Belfast, its elected government representatives were also expressing their concern at the 'still very unsatisfactory situation' in the city, but their proposed remedies would hardly have won the support of the nationalist leader. Spurning the possibility of introducing martial law, the Northern Ireland Cabinet appeared keener to solve the worsening security problem by deploying a greater number of soldiers on the streets. The liberal Minister for Education, Lord Londonderry, was 'of the opinion that troops should be used more liberally and also that certain fixed points should be manned by the military.'[82] There was a consensus of trust and 'great faith' in maximising military forces, but Home Affairs Minister R. Dawson Bates pointed out the 'difficulty [in] getting a sufficient number of troops.'[83]

The conflict spread to a normally quiet, trouble free area on the evening of 17th February. John Duffin (28), a Catholic from Walmer Street off the Ormeau Road area of south Belfast, had been walking along Sunnyside Street when he was approached by gunmen as he got near the King's Bridge. Severely wounded, Mr Duffin died the following day. Violence returned to an area more associated with conflict two nights later. On 19 February a bomb was thrown into Flynn's public house at the corner of Corporation Street and Great George's Street, but there were miraculously only reports of minor injuries. Publicans were, of course, a favourite target for the gunmen, especially those on the loyalist side.[84] Nearly a week later, James Reilly, of Cliftonpark Avenue, whose Old Lodge

Road pub had been rebuilt after being damaged by fire in 1920, was walking home with a barman when gunmen shot him dead as they were walking past the grounds of the Mater Hospital. Two Protestants were to lose their lives on 24 February. One of these, Edward Hardy, of Brookhill Avenue, died of injuries sustained in a previous incident, whilst James Hutton (45), a shoemaker from Central Street off the Newtownards Road, was shot dead by gunmen who burst into his home. It was alleged that, as nationalist gunmen were unlikely to execute such an attack in the middle of a loyalist area, Mr Hutton's shooting was probably a case of mistaken identity. Three people died in renewed violence within 48 hours. Isaac McMillan (22), a Protestant, of Donegone Street, was shot in the head by a Short Strand sniper, as he returned from a football match at the Oval. Also in the east of the city, David Fryer (27), an ex-serviceman and off-duty 'B' Special, was shot by a sniper operating in the Thompson Street area, dying in the Royal Victoria Hospital the following day. Mr Fryer, who was unemployed, had been looking for work and constantly assured his mother who was concerned about his safety.[85] The grief of a mother losing her son was shared that day with another woman, of a different religion and living in another part of town. James Hughes (20), of Butler Street, had been walking along the Crumlin Road with his mother when they were fired at by two gunmen. Mr Hughes died shortly afterwards from a head injury but his distraught mother escaped unhurt. Although serious disturbances were avoided for over a week, shooting and bombing incidents continued spasmodically, the most significant being a bomb attack on patrolling Specials in York Street on 28 February.

The early months of 1922 again showed that prolonged periods of calm could be abruptly ended following incidents elsewhere. The specific targeting of children at Weaver Street illustrated there were no depths to which terror gangs would not go to exhibit their hatred for the other side. This was especially true of loyalist extremists – both those in and out of uniform – who grew increasingly desperate in their actions. Meanwhile the IRA, despite being put on the back foot by a combination of loyalist terror gangs and police interventions, grew increasingly active during this period, ensuring that violence would be by no means one-sided. The resulting mutual recrimination, the tension produced by the political vacuum and the lack of certainty over security policy meant that the conflict would inevitably enter an even bloodier phase.

Chapter 15

Murder and mayhem in north Belfast

'YOU BOYS SAY YOUR PRAYERS'

The escalation of violence, especially since the start of the year, including the growing number of Protestant casualties and horrific attacks on tramcars, particularly aggrieved those loyalists who sought revenge for such outrages. Again it was the launch of an attack on members of the security forces which pre-empted the incident which most epitomises the bloody nature of this conflict. Two 'B' Specials had been killed in County Tyrone on 21 March and a similar loss of life was to occur in Belfast city centre two days later. Around lunch-time two young Specials, Thomas Cunningham (22) and William Cairnside (21) were patrolling in the busy area between Great Victoria Street and May Street when they were approached by a group of men.[1] Several shots rang out and both Specials fell to the ground mortally wounded. Retribution for the assassination of police officers was frequently sought and in the increasingly volatile political and security situation prevailing in the city, the likelihood of it occurring was high. Later that evening, two Short Strand Catholics appeared to be reprisal victims. Peter Murphy (61) and Sarah McShane (15) were shot dead in Altcar Street. However, those lusting for revenge were far from finished, even if the location for such retaliation was a little surprising.

Kinnaird Terrace, near Thorndale Avenue off the Antrim Road, consists of two rows of substantial properties and was in an affluent area cocooned from the cacophony of gunfire which blighted the nearby ghettoes.[2] Yet the occupants of number 3 Kinnaird Terrace were singularly conspicuous in that, apart from being a prosperous Catholic, the head of the family also enjoyed a high public profile. Thus, whilst such an attack was not, given the increasing tension in the city at the time, a total surprise, its nature and degree of ferocity was unparalleled and succeeded in stunning the whole community. Owen McMahon was one of five brothers, all of whom were involved in the city's licensing business.[3] McMahon (50), originally from County Down, owned the Capstan Bar in Ann Street, and, as an ex-chairman of the Northern Vintners'

Association, was one of the city's most prosperous businessmen. Although a friend of Joe Devlin, he was more involved in the city's sporting life than its political one.[4] Here, his interests were wide, ranging from horse racing and cycling to boxing and football.[5] McMahon lived with his wife Eliza, six sons, who ranged in age from 12 to 30, a daughter, niece, his pub manager, Edward McKinney and a couple of domestics in his sprawling Victorian mansion.[6]

At around one o'clock on a cold, wet spring morning a City Council workman guarding a work-site at Carlisle Circus, was approached by two men in police uniform. They persuaded him to hand over a sledge-hammer and made their way up the Crumlin Road, proceeding to Clifton Park Avenue, where they entered the grounds of a large residence, known locally as Bruce's Demesne. Here they likely met three associates and the group of five men then crossed the demesne and approached the McMahon home at 1.15 a.m.[7] Eliza McMahon recalled being in bed with her husband on the third floor when she heard a loud hammering at the front door, the smashing of glass and footsteps on the stairs. Fearing that a bomb had been through a downstairs window, she woke her husband.[8] The assailants had obviously planned the attack. Apart from the sledgehammer which was used to break down a glass panel enabling the opening of locks and for smashing down a second hallway door, they brought candles, ensuring the easy herding-together of victims in a large house. Mrs McMahon ran with her husband down a flight of stairs, almost colliding with a man in police uniform on the landing. She was ordered to return to her bed, but her anxiety was heightened by the sight of the uniformed men brandishing Webley revolvers, commanding the male McMahons to proceed swiftly downstairs.[9] Mrs McMahon failed to receive a reply from her assailants when she asked their intentions, but her husband reassured her that it was probably 'just a raid'.[10]

At this point, the male members of the family were ushered downstairs to the living-room, whilst the women (Mrs McMahon, her daughter Lily and niece, Mary Downey) remained in a first floor drawing-room. John McMahon (30), who survived serious gunshot wounds, recalled there had been five assailants, the leader of whom had been dressed in 'a dustcoat and was clean-shaven, well made and between 30 and 35 years'.[11] John recollected that a much taller, darker man did most of the shooting and that one of the attackers appeared to have an English accent.[12] Both he and the other survivor, McMahon's youngest son, Michael (12) recalled with horror how they had been escorted into the room and after a brief pause had been advised, 'You boys say your prayers.' Shortly after this chilling warning, the firing commenced. In rapid succession, each of the eight male members of the household, were targeted. Three – McKinney, Owen McMahon and one of his sons – were shot positioned by the fire, close to a window. One son was riddled with bullets as he sat on a chair. All but the youngest was hit, yet it was the decision to systematically eliminate the whole male line of the family which personified the brutality of the attack. Michael tearfully recalled his moment of horror at the inquest:

> The man in the fawn coat fired. When I saw him lift his revolver I fell under the table and began to moan and pretend to be shot. There was a number of other shots but I don't know who fired them; the result was that all the others were killed or wounded. I saw John lying near me.[13]

Fortunately the bullets ricocheted off the polished surface of the table, embedding themselves in the wall. Retaining his presence of mind, Michael hid under a sofa, pretending he had been hit. He was discovered there by his rescuers several minutes later in 'a state of abject terror'.[14]

Although the whole episode lasted barely five minutes, it was a prolonged nightmare for the distraught women. Eliza McMahon on hearing the gunfire, opened the drawing-room window and screamed, 'Murder! Murder!' As she was calling for assistance she saw a couple of the assailants retreating across Bruce's Demesne. Her cries alerted the staff of the Kinnaird Nursing Home, situated next door to the McMahon home. A nurse awakened the matron, Mrs McMurty, who phoned the police and ambulance service.[15] Other neighbours, Mrs Purdy, her daughters and the home's manager, Arthur Hamill, were awakened by the shootings and Mr Hamill met the RIC patrol which soon arrived at the murder scene from the direction of Thorndale Avenue. Even hardened police and ambulance personnel were distressed by what they found. Three of Mr McMahon's sons, Frank (24), Patrick (25) and Thomas (15), as well as his bar manager, Edward McKinney (25) were confirmed dead on arrival at the Mater Hospital, where Owen McMahon succumbed to serious stomach wounds a few hours later. Another of his sons, Bernard (26) died in the same hospital on 2 April, with only the eldest son, John (30) and the youngest, Michael (12), surviving the attack. Mrs McMahon's niece told police she heard 12 shots and confidently assured police she 'would know the face of the man in plain clothes again' as she 'clearly saw his face by the light on the landing.'[16]

The press responded in unison, condemning the attack, although unionist organs declined to speculate on who had been responsible for committing such an atrocity. However, even such sources did not attempt to minimise the scale or the horror of this attack. The *Belfast Telegraph* described it as 'a hellish Belfast deed' which represented 'the most terrible assassination that has yet stained the name of Belfast.'[17] Although it avoided mentioning the 'party' nature of the attack, the *Telegraph* certainly conveyed its bloody nature and the anguish of the relatives. Describing the scene at Kinnaird Terrace as resembling a 'slaughter-house', the report proceeded:

> The house smelt of fresh blood – it seemed scarcely cold as it spread in large pools and small rivers all over the room ... On either side of the fireplace lay large pools of blood – thick, heavy coagulated stuff, that turned one sick with horror. In places it was rubbed and disturbed as if someone had rolled in it; it was clotted in lumps as if someone had macerated fresh bullocks' liver and strewn it about.[18]

The Dublin-based *Irish Independent* suggested that 'the brutal slaughter' of the McMahons was 'a deed surpassing in atrocity anything that was done in Ireland during the Reign of Terror' and the attack was so grotesque it had 'shocked all Christian people.'[19] Noting that the outrage had been committed during curfew hours and that some of the assailants had been in uniform, the *Independent* acidly commented that 'the Belfast authorities should have little difficulty in tracking them down.'[20] For the southern audience this latest Ulster outrage epitomised the ongoing mayhem in that part of Ireland and many vaguely hoped that such a barbaric act could prove to be cathartic. The *Irish Independent* implored:

> All men of goodwill should join us in using every means to put an end to a condition of things which is disgracing Belfast and the North before the world.[21]

The English press also provided comprehensive coverage of the ghastly episode on Belfast's Antrim Road. The *Times*' report, 'Night Terrors in Belfast', focussed on 'a day of death' in the city, whilst the *Daily Telegraph*, describing the murders as a 'reprisal' for the killings of Specials the previous day, appraised the events to be 'the worst crime that has yet occurred in Belfast.'[22] Other, more critical journals queried the priorities of the Unionist administration, with the

Nation suggesting that the events at Kinnaird Terrance represented 'the worst of all those [crimes] that have made Belfast so notorious'. They claimed that Craig 'still talks as if his only business as Prime Minister of the Six Counties was to put down the IRA.'[23] The eyes of the world also converged on Belfast's horror. Irish-American journalist James Lynch's wired message outlined the last fateful moments of 'these victims of hate', dismissing the chances of a fair or successful police investigation. Lynch maintained that it was 'as certain as the Judgement Day' that the attackers of the McMahons would not be apprehended, as that was 'the way with the Belfast Police when Catholics are murdered.'[24]

The bodies of the four McMahons killed in the attack were transferred from the Mater Hospital to St Patrick's Church the following evening. Hundreds paid their last respects over the next 24 hours and at Mass on Sunday 26th March, the Reverend Bernard Laverty stressed both the enormity of the crime and its raw sectarian nature. He told his congregations that day that even the Black and Tans had 'not been guilty of anything approaching this [crime]' in its 'unspeakable barbarity', intimating that 'inoffensive citizens' such as the McMahons had been 'done to death merely because they were Catholics.'[25] However, Father Laverty asserted it was the Catholic populace which was 'on trial', imploring them 'to pray for peace' and to 'practise patience and forbearance', rather than seek revenge.[26]

The McMahon family home proved to be a Mecca for Belfast's Catholics over the next few days. A young Paddy O'Donnell recalled the scene at Kinnaird Terrace the day after the shooting and also at the funeral a few days later:

> There were enormous crowds gathered outside the McMahons' house and everyone was chattering excitedly about what had happened the previous night. There was a constant stream of people entering and leaving the house. Most of them probably didn't know the family that well, but I suppose we all had a morbid curiosity about what was going on ... A few days later I saw the four coffins as the cortege set off from St Patrick's. The whole Catholic community was united in its grief.[27]

The funeral cortege left St Patrick's church around 2 pm on Monday 27 March and made its way up Royal Avenue and Castle Street before proceeding along the Falls Road to the Milltown Cemetery. Four hearses formed the centre of the procession as it left St Patrick's on a glorious spring afternoon, Mr

McMahon's hearse in front, followed by those of his sons.[28] An enormous crowd, estimated at over 10,000, thronged the route, enveloping the graveyard. The scale of the funerals was 'unprecedented', claimed the nationalist press, and was so impressive a correspondent claimed that 'never before has such a public tribute to the dead been witnessed in Belfast.'[29] Undoubtedly most of the mourners were ordinary Catholics paying their final respects to a popular and successful Catholic family. However, there were also hundreds of representatives from the city's business community, many of them Protestant. The Bishop of Down, Dr MacRory, conducted the graveside service, assisted by the Reverend Laverty and the mourners joined in with a moving rendition of 'Faith of our Father'. A distraught Eliza McMahon, still anxious about the fate of her hospitalised sons, Bernard and John, led a legion of mourners including a host of clerics, nationalist politicians led by Joe Devlin, and C.J. Frame, the director of the American White Cross Relief in Ireland.[30] In stark contrast to the lack of security at Kinnaird Terrace the previous week, there was a heavy police and army presence around Milltown Cemetery. James Lynch described the security presence on the Falls Road:

> The commanding officer of the British forces in Belfast, fearful of an attack upon the cortege, lined the streets with a cordon of British soldiers. Leading the first hearse was a large armoured British tank car with loaded guns protruding from front and sides. Following an open carriage loaded with flowers was a smaller armoured car, while at the gate of the cemetery, two large cars were stationed. Along the line of procession at points 'believed to be dangerous' armoured cars were drawn up, manned by soldiers in trench helmets.[31]

THE POLITICAL REPERCUSSIONS

The political repercussions of the McMahon killings were profound. Michael Collins, who was anxious to restart negotiations with Belfast Unionists and was constantly wary of anti-Treaty elements within his own organisation, utilised the propaganda value of the incident to lobby Lloyd George and Churchill whom he felt might be able to pressurise a beleaguered Craig into providing improved protection for northern Catholics. For his part, Churchill had never been a proponent of Ulster Unionism.[32] He, and other colleagues in the British establishment, were becoming increasingly exasperated by the regional administration's failure to stem the tide of violence, especially as the hand-over of security from London to Belfast drew closer.[33] Nor did these security changes and other legislation introduced within a fortnight of the horrific events at Kinnaird Terrace – the establishment of the RUC and the handing-over of control of the Special Constabulary to the Belfast administration on 5 April and the passing of the Civil Authorities (Special Powers) Bill two days later – inspire confidence in those British critics already sceptical of what they perceived to be a partisan approach on the part of Unionist leaders in Belfast.[34] Therefore, some questioned the appropriateness of such punitive measures, especially in the wake of the McMahon murders. One editorial suggested that unless emergency measures were 'impartially applied' they would 'only render the plight of the Catholic minority so much more horrible' and proceeded to express a lack of confidence in the impartiality of Craig's regime.[35]

Lloyd George and Churchill, ever concerned that the spiralling violence was edging away from Craig's control at a time when he was being allocated additional powers, hastily arranged a meeting in London with Collins and Craig within four days of the Antrim Road attack. It is likely that the shift in the political pendulum, exacerbated by the McMahon murders, and evident in unionists' increasing marginalisation, precipitated his signing another pact with Collins which was more conciliatory in its tone than anticipated.[36] In his last speech before he left for these talks, Craig, who had earlier announced a £1,000 reward for information leading to the conviction of those responsible for the McMahon murders was in more bullish mood addressing his unionist colleagues in the Belfast Parliament.[37] Anxious to condemn Collins' claim that what was occurring in Belfast constituted an anti-Catholic pogrom, the N Ireland premier insisted that 'no such thing has ever been the policy of Protestants here' and reminded his audience if this had been the case, the minority Catholic populations of small towns close to Belfast 'would have been swept out of Ireland.'[38] Reminding his southern counterparts of the many 'direct instances of attack upon us here in Ulster', he hoped that outsiders would realise 'the Ulster men are up against, not Catholics, but that they are up against rebels, that they are up against murder, Bolshevism, and up against those enemies not only of Ulster but of the Empire'.[39]

The McMahon killings intensified Catholic fears that they were the helpless victims of an increasingly vicious and desperate band of pogromists. The Kinnaird Terrace attack was the latest illustration, if it was needed, that they were no longer safe in their own homes, even during the hours of curfew and from men dressed as law officers. Even those living in prosperous areas were no longer safe in their own beds at night. What depressed them even more was their failure to see where assistance was forthcoming. With their lack of confidence in the northern security forces and feeling deserted by their co-religionists in the south, it was undoubtedly tempting for many Catholics to be ambivalent in their responses to republican activity in the city. The key dilemma for many concentrated around the issue of personal protection. Joe Devlin attempted to give expression to these fears and sense of confusion shortly after the killing of his friend Owen McMahon. Speaking in parliament, Devlin identified the conundrum faced by Belfast nationalists:

> If Catholics have no revolvers to protect themselves they are murdered. If they have revolvers, they are flogged and sentenced to death.[40]

WHO WAS TO BLAME?

Attention soon turned to who was responsible for this outrage. As with other killings involving men in uniform, the loyalist press and political spokesmen expressed their disbelief at such assassinations, suggesting that the perpetrators were not necessarily bona fide police officers simply because they were wearing uniform. Proponents of such an explanation pointed out that surplus police uniforms were on sale in several Belfast shops and could, therefore, easily be purchased by terror groups.[41] Other explanations of who had been responsible for the attacks were equally flawed. Details about the calibre of weapons used on the Antrim Road were patchy and, in any event, would have failed to shed much light on culpability for the attack, as loyalist groups frequently had access to weapons used by the security forces.[42] Also, evidence supplied by witnesses was, not surprisingly given the horrific nature of the incident, contradictory in part and consequently far from reliable. Nor is the allegation that this had been a mission sanctioned by the police authorities convincing. The RIC did not have a history of sectarianism and, indeed, if this organisation had been inherently sectarian, such killings would have been considerably more numerous and widespread.

However, certain features of the Kinnaird Terrace outrage do shed light on who was responsible. What was striking about this incident and similar attacks on Catholics was the amazing degree of freedom of movement and accessibility to motor transport enjoyed by those involved in such outrages.[43] Ordinary civilians in the early 1920s would have had restricted access to motor vehicles, especially the larger cars or lorries described by witnesses as being employed in such attacks and there were few reports of active loyalist gangs being apprehended by police during curfew restrictions. It was this ease of movement, the apparent protection against detection which provides the most meaningful clue to the identity of the gunmen involved. Consequently it is hard to refute the theory that either 'rogue' policemen were directly involved in offensives such as that on the Antrim Road, or that loyalist gangs executed them with the connivance of certain police officers. The timing of the McMahon murders and their occurrence in the wake of recent killings of police personnel, prompted many to believe that a small band of hot-tempered policemen were committing retaliatory violent acts which were, at the very least, ignored by senior officers. Nearly two years after the violence in Belfast had subsided, the Defence Ministry in Dublin took the unprecedented step of publishing 'affidavits' signed by Catholic members of the northern police and collected by clergy at the time, before being handed over to Michael Collins.[44] When these documents surfaced into the public domain in February 1924, 12 officers of varying rank were specifically named as being involved in the murder of the McMahons and several other Catholics.[45]

A number of senior police officers were identified by the Defence Ministry in Dublin and these included District Inspector Nixon and County Inspector Harrison, who were allegedly the orchestrators of violence and the leaders of a gang which operated mainly out of Brown Square Barracks in the Shankill area. John Nixon, who swiftly became a pariah for the city's nationalist population, was ideally placed to lead a campaign of persecution against Catholics in the west and north of the city. Nixon, described as 'an arrant coward' in the Dublin report, was accused of being involved in the Kinnaird Terrace attack and several other killings, including the Arnon Street and Halfpenny murders, whilst his superior officer, Richard Harrison, who was in charge of the city's detective unit, had obviously easy access to information relating to individual Catholics. There can be little doubt that police chiefs and leading ministers, including Craig and Bates, were highly concerned about the activities of Nixon in particular, even if they were guarded about the true nature of these concerns, which were usually described as 'political'. Tentative approaches were made to both men to dissuade them from joining the new police force, but these were spurned by the officers who were soon, ironically, to receive official recognition for their 'services' during the conflict.[46] Despite the allegations and rumours which circulated about his activities, Nixon stubbornly refused to adopt a low profile. He had been active in campaigning against Catholics being offered jobs in the new police force and was enraged when he failed to gain promotion during the summer of 1922. In a letter to the Minister for Home Affairs, Nixon fumed:

> I tried to do my best to defeat the conspiracy against Ulster. Whether I was successful or not I cannot say, but I was vain enough to hope that I had gained the confidence of a good many loyal people in Belfast, Fermanagh, etc. ... I attach little importance to the promotion itself except that I feel as if the Sinn Féiners and their friends were laughing at me for getting left after all my exertions against them.[47]

It was the volume of grassroots support for Nixon, especially from the Orange Order and Special Constabulary which intimidated Bates. In a letter to his leader in August 1922, the Home Affairs Minister intimated the 'probable dismissal' of Nixon, confessing his concern over the inevitable 'outcry among certain of the extreme Protestant element' which would accompany such a decision.[48] The following day, Bates was under renewed pressure from the UULA who expressed their disquiet over the decision not to promote Nixon and also at the decision to recruit Catholics into the RUC.[49] Unionist embarrassment over Nixon's political posturings intensified during the next year and resulted in his downfall early in 1924. Following Craig's call for his 'immediate removal or transfer' Bates conceded that Nixon had shown 'a strong party feeling ... unbecoming in a police officer' and that the consequences of his influence in his district had been 'the Protestant hooligan is allowed to interpret in his own fashion the laws of the country'.[50] The crunch came after a speech Nixon delivered to a newly-established Orange lodge for RUC officers, when he urged his colleagues to ensure that 'not an inch of Ulster soil should be yielded.'[51] Significantly it was Nixon's 'clear breach' of updated police regulations, forbidding overt 'political' speeches by officers and not his alleged involvement in the murders of the McMahons or other Catholics, which led to his downfall.[52] Nixon, on hearing about his suspension on 6 February 1924, again exhibited supreme confidence in the impregnability of his own position. He reminded his accusers that he had 'never known an officer or man of the RIC to be suspended except when charged with a criminal offence or gross insubordination.'[53] Bolstered by a massive expression of solidarity by Shankill loyalists on 13 February, Nixon was taken aback by the decision to dismiss him, albeit on a full pension, a fortnight later.[54] A natural move was into politics, although his extreme views resulted in him being isolated on the unionist fringe.[55]

Although sections of the Nixon file are now open to the public, their contents do not categorically prove his direct involvement (or, indeed, that of his colleagues) in the McMahon case and other murders of Catholics between 1920 and 1922. What they do indicate is Nixon's supreme confidence in his position, as well as the longstanding unease and lack of confidence in his suitability as a senior officer, by those in government. However, whilst the nature and range of evidence is far from complete, one can conclude that that the McMahon outrage formed part of a campaign of targeting Catholics orchestrated by a group of 'rogue' policemen.[56] Otherwise, it is impossible to explain the easy access of gunmen to certain renowned trouble areas, both on foot and by motor vehicle during a period of curfew restrictions. Whilst the highest echelons of the police may not have had intimate knowledge of Nixon's activities, it is evident, judging from their personal correspondence, that they were cognisant of irregularities in police conduct in a restricted number of districts in the city. It was the fear of directly challenging the seemingly impregnable position of Nixon, with his massive grassroots support, that prevented his superiors taking more stringent action earlier in the Troubles, and it is revealing that disciplinary action was only taken against Nixon after the violence in the city had died down and only on account of his 'political' rather than alleged criminal activities.[57] This reluctance to directly confront a persistently blatant source of the city's communal violence personifies the lethargic response of Craig's administration and resulted in Belfast's Catholic community resigning themselves to further unnecessary slaughter in the months ahead.

Whilst interpretations of who was responsible for the murder and mayhem committed in Kinnaird Terrace that damp spring morning divided the city's populace in the weeks, months and even years ahead, there could be no denying its impact on Belfast's stunned citizens. In a devout, home-loving society, the sanctity of the family home had been breached and a deliberate attempt to eliminate the male line of an innocent family had been executed. If anyone had doubted the depth of menace stalking the city in those dark 1922 days, the events on the Antrim Road on 22 March soon reminded them of their vulnerability.

Chapter 16

'An odious persecution'

IN THE WRONG PLACE AT THE WRONG TIME

The early spring of 1922 proved to be the bloodiest period in the conflict to date, with over sixty deaths and scores of serious injuries being recorded in March alone. March was also to provide the Troubles with its most infamous and defining incident which was the subject of the previous chapter. Tension in the city was more pronounced, largely the consequence of ongoing political dialogue between the prospective leaders in Belfast and Dublin. The increasing involvement of the IRA in Belfast, often in desperate, retaliatory and sectarian attacks and the apparent invincibility of the increasingly brazen loyalist assassination gangs, became depressingly familiar features of the situation.

There was a stark tragedy about the manner in which many ordinary Belfast citizens were cruelly singled out for assassination. Like other, more fortunate people in the city at that time, they bravely endeavoured to carry on with their everyday lives during this sustained period of communal tension. Some, like Joseph Duffy, a 50-year-old labourer from Dock Lane and another Catholic, Patrick Rooney, a 24-year-old barber, were returning from work when they were shot dead in the York Street area (on the 8 and 15 March respectively). Others were carrying out their duties in the city's streets when they met a dire fate. Hugh McAnaney (34) was passing through Whitehouse on his horse and cart during the afternoon of 11 March when he was attacked by members of Robert Hazzard's funeral procession which was passing in the opposite direction. Mr McAnaney was shot dead and another Catholic, Thomas McBride, was seriously wounded in the prolonged disturbances which followed.

The dangers involved in moving around unfriendly streets could be potentially fatal. William Kane, a 50-year-old Catholic milkman from Dunmurry, was shot dead as he delivered milk to a shop on the Newtownards Road early on the morning of 16 March and John Murdock, a young Protestant mill worker was singled out for attack amongst the predominantly Catholic workforce at the Greaves Mill on the Falls Road on 23 March. Workers were not even safe on holy days. Three men were shot dead proceeding to, or returning from, their work in north Belfast bakeries on Good Friday. At around six in the morning, Matthew Carmichael (40), a foreman baker and father of five from Moyola Street, was shot in Bedeque Street off the Crumlin Road on his way home from a night shift.[1] Another Protestant bakery shift worker suffered a similar fate less than an hour later. John Sloan, of Harrison Street, unsuccessfully attempted to evade his four attackers in Geoffrey Street and around the same time, a Catholic corporation carter, Daniel Beattie (22), of Herbert Street, was shot dead off the Crumlin Road.[2] A few days later another shift worker, James Green (67), of Seaforde Street, was shot dead returning from work in the east of the city. Another Catholic, James Corr (70), was fatally wounded as he delivered coal in Dalton Street, off the Newtownards Road, on 24 March.[3] Others could not even find sanctuary indoors at their workplace. On the same day as the Protestant bakers were killed, Thomas Gillan (51), of Mountcollyer Street, a Catholic train-driver who had just completed a journey from Magherafelt to the Midland Railway Station, was shot dead by a number of assailants who had ascertained his religion, and robbed station cleaners of their wages before making their getaway. Towards the end of April, another man lost his life at his place of work. William Sibbotson, a 31-year-old Protestant time-keeper at Richardsons' Chemical Company near Short Strand, was hit by a nationalist sniper whilst working at his desk near the end of his working day on 24 April.

People were involved in humdrum activities when they were gunned down. Teenager John Roddy was shot delivering newspapers in the Peters Hill area early on 7 March and another Protestant, James Harkness (32) was out buying his evening newspaper on the Newtownards Road on 18 March when he was singled out by a Short Strand sniper. Henry Garvey (25), a Protestant accounts clerk, who had been earning extra money delivering newspapers, was shot dead riding his bicycle in North Howard Street early the following morning. Other unfortunate citizens cruelly fell to snipers active in the area through which they were walking. James Magee, a Catholic docker from Hardinge Street, was killed by a loyalist gunman in the Earl Street area during the evening of 20 March, and Sarah Keyes (27), a Protestant from Hillman Street, died from gunshot injuries received when she crossed Annadale Street in the New Lodge Road area on 10 March. Another north Belfast sniper's victim was Agnes McLarnon (30), a Catholic from Arnon Street, who was shot as she walked along the Crumlin Road on Easter Tuesday. Even those who believed they were safe in their beds during the early morning following a disturbed night's sleep, were in for a rude awakening. An especially tragic case was Mary Mullan (40), a Catholic who lived in Thompson Street. Early in the morning of 18 March, loyalist assassins crossed the Newtownards Road and, entering the slumbering Short Strand, threw a bomb through her bedroom window. Miss Mullan, asleep at the time, received horrific leg injuries and died shortly afterwards. Her aunt Rose McGreevy, who had been staying with her, also suffered serious wounds and died in hospital over a week later.

Mistaken identity cases inevitably occurred, although sometimes they may have been used as a smokescreen to discredit the 'other' side. People walking through 'strange' areas, frequently out of pure necessity, were inevitable targets for gunmen seeking easy sectarian targets. As most of the victims were not known personally to their assassins, the element of chance in such attacks was obviously high. Whilst rival papers used such uncertainty to shift the blame from their own community, such as the *Irish News* over the murders of the Protestant bakers, there were many instances where the 'wrong' victim was clearly targeted. Indeed, this was sometimes acknowledged in obituary notices placed in the press by victims' families. One such case was John McGarry, a Protestant, who was shot in Earl Street on 26 March. Mr McGarry's family recorded his death as an 'accidental' shooting in the local papers. Occasionally shootings were unintentionally provoked by the well-meaning advice of community leaders. The Catholic clergy had, in the wake of the McMahon killings, advised their flock, if threatened by those claiming to be security force members, to scream 'Murder!' and immediately run on to the street, where the alarm could be spread by whistle-blowing neighbours. When a neighbour of Maggie Savage was arrested on a 'non-party' charge at Burke Street in the Lepper Street area on 26 March, crowds quickly gathered and there was an exchange of gunfire between the security forces and the IRA. A stray bullet killed Miss Savage (21) as she sat in her parlour.

There was little consideration for the most vulnerable members of society and a number of the city's more unfortunate citizens were insufficiently sheltered from the ire of gunmen and bombers. Patrick Morgan, a blind man in his 50s, was caught out when shooting erupted at the junction of Wall and Upton Streets in the Carrick Hill district on 9 March. As he was groping to find his way to the sanctuary of a doorway, he was fatally wounded. A similar target the following month, though on the other side of the sectarian divide, was Protestant Robert Miller. Mr Miller (68) had been sitting with a friend in the parlour of his house in Beechfield Street on 23 April, when they were disturbed by armed men who had entered Mr Miller's home from the rear. The latter was shot dead and his companion was wounded. Francis Flynn (81) died a few days after a bomb was thrown through the front window of his Unity Street home towards the end of March. No dispensation was given to pregnant women. Catherine (Cassie) Neeson (27), a Catholic mother of three living in Great George's Street, had ignored threats to leave her home, including a bomb attack early in March. Mrs Neeson was expecting the arrival of her child at any time and was standing by her front door after breakfast on 11th March when she was shot by loyalist gunmen. She gave birth within an hour of the shooting but died without seeing her newly-born child.

Young children were, once again, all too predictable victims of the violence. They included Mary Wilson (4), who had been playing with her doll outside her Norfolk Street home in the Falls when she fell victim to a sniper's bullet during the early evening of 14 March. The young girl passed away the following day. Other Catholic children playing in the streets were targets for loyalist gunmen looking for easy prey. On 19 April Mary Keenan (13) and a younger friend were playing swinging games with a rope tied round a lamp-post. The girls had just returned from school and were playing at Marine Street in the north of the city, when a lone gunman approached them from Little Ship Street. His shots wounded both children, Mary fatally. Around teatime on 6 April Joseph Hannigan (9), of Maralin Street, in the New Lodge area, was shot in the head whilst he was playing in the street. There was a suspicion that the child had been killed following an accidental discharge of a military weapon and the army were obliged to support the police in quelling an angry crowd in the district. Terence Murphy (2), of Hartley Street, suffered a serious leg injury after sniping broke out in the North Thomas Street area on 9 March and he died in hospital two days later. Catholic children were also targeted in the Arnon Street shootings, but Protestant families living on the periphery of nationalist areas were also vulnerable, as illustrated by the bomb attack on the Donnelly home in the Millfield area on 31 March.[4]

Ex-soldiers who had experienced a safe passage during turbulent years in Flanders trenches were to prove less lucky in readjusting to life in their native city. At least three ex-soldiers lost their lives in March. On the 9th day of the month, Benedict Leith, a Catholic from Regent Street, who had reportedly rescued a wandering child when sniping erupted on Carrick Hill, was hit in the head by a sniper's bullet and died in the Mater two days later. Within days, another 'Tommy', William Allen, of Sackville Place, was shot, succumbing in hospital nearly a fortnight later and another Protestant ex-soldier, William Hunter, was shot dead on 22 March. Mr Hunter, who had gained the Military medal and still suffered the effects of shell-shock, was attacked by gunmen as he attended a government-funded training course for ex-soldiers in Fountain Street North.

TIT FOR TAT ATTACKS

Even normally vigilant members of the security forces were liable to momentarily drop their guard, becoming more susceptible to terror attacks. Several police and army were shot during this period, with nine members of the security forces succumbing to their wounds. A young officer in the Seaforth Highlanders, Lieutenant E. Bruce, was shot late on the evening of 10 March, following a night out in the city centre. Lieutenant Bruce, whose quarters were at the War Hospital on the Grosvenor Road, was, on account of his accent and attire, an easy target for IRA gunmen who confronted him in Alfred Street (it was rumoured he was accompanying a Catholic woman home at the time of the shooting). Two RIC constables from the Springfield Road barracks were shot in the back by IRA gunmen whilst patrolling the Falls Road around lunchtime on 10 March and both officers, James Cullen (23) and Patrick O'Connor (35) died of their injuries.[5] An alleged member of the Nixon gang, Sergeant Christopher (Christy) Clarke (41), was returning from the funerals of these officers with another policeman, Constable Caldwell three days later, when they too were attacked by a large group of men near the 'Beehive' bar at Mulholland Terrace on the Falls Road. Although wounded, Constable Caldwell returned fire at their assailants who escaped towards Broadway.[6] Clarke was the principal target of the gunmen and died instantly, despite reportedly wearing a bullet-proof vest. In the crossfire, a passer-by Daniel Rogan, a Celtic Park dog-racing official who lived on the Grosvenor Road, received fatal injuries.[7] Just over a week later two Specials, Thomas Cunningham and William Cairnside, were shot dead in the crowded Great Victoria Street area during lunchtime.[8] Two police officers lost their lives in the middle of April. Following an outbreak of IRA gunfire in the Markets area a Portadown-born Special Constable Nathaniel (Nat) McCoo was shot in the head as the Lancia vehicle in which he was travelling sped down Joy Street towards the scene of the trouble. A RIC

Sergeant, Leitrim-born John Bruin (37), who was based at Henry Street Barracks, was shot in the chest as he made enquiries at a pub in York Street. He died a week later of his wounds in the Mater Hospital.

Clearly the killing of policemen by the IRA provided the impetus for loyalist reprisals on Catholics.[9] Thus, the shooting of a Brown Square Barracks-based RIC officer, George Turner, during the evening of Saturday 1 April, sparked the grisly events which were to occur in north Belfast early the next morning. Constable Turner (41), originally from County Donegal, was shot dead whilst on foot patrol in the Old Lodge Road area. Considerable controversy surrounded this killing. It has been suggested that Constable Turner was actually shot from the roof of his own police station and not by a republican sniper operating from an empty house in Stanhope Street, which was the official version of events.[10] Alleged leaking of 'confidential' documents and 'intelligence' reports to Michael Collins in Dublin inferred that this killing was planned and executed by the Nixon gang to facilitate the condoning of a loyalist backlash, (such as in Arnon Street), which would in turn kill off any hopes for the Craig-Collins March Pact.[11] The evidence for these allegations is flimsy. The suggestion that 'rogue' officers involved in such a murder campaign were so desperate to find an 'excuse' to re-ignite further sectarian attack that they targeted a Protestant colleague, killing him from the roof of their own headquarters as he proceeded on foot patrol with a number of Specials, is far-fetched and also ignores the attack on the Donnelly family on Nixon's 'patch' the previous evening.

No matter who was behind the initial killing, the results of the violence which followed and their degree of ferocity, rarely paralleled in the conflict, are beyond doubt. Uniformed men, probably mustered spontaneously by a ringleader at the barracks, jumped in to a Lancia vehicle and, touring the surrounding nationalist side streets, took immediate revenge. Eye witnesses claimed that a large number of police charged up Stanhope Street, shouting 'Cut the guts out of them for the murder of Turner!'[12] The first victim in what became known as the Arnon Street Massacre was John McRory (40), who pleaded unsuccessfully for his life to be spared in the kitchen of his Stanhope Street home, directly opposite the scene of the Turner attack. The next casualty was Bernard McKenna (42), of Park Street, reportedly reading in bed about the progress of political negotiations in London. The last port of call for the bloodthirsty gang was Arnon Street. William Spallen (70), who lived in number 16, had just buried his wife that day and was living with his 12-year-old grandson,

Gerald Tumelty. The latter's account of his experiences that fateful night indicate that the perpetrators were local men. Young Gerald recalled:

> At 11 o'clock two men came into the room, one was in the uniform of a policeman. They asked my grandfather his name and he said William Spallen. The man in plain clothes fired three shots at my grandfather. When I cried out he said, 'lie down or I will put a bullet in you.' This man snatched the money that my grandfather had to settle up the expenses of my grandmother's funeral, it was £20 ... I could recognise the man in plain clothes. I had seen him before on the Old Lodge Road.[13]

Witnesses claimed to have heard a voice in the street exclaiming, 'Remember, everybody over 10!' and an army officer reassuring alarmed neighbours shortly after the shootings, 'Don't be alarmed – we know who did it!'[14] Using a sledgehammer, the murder gang broke down the door of the house next to Mr Spallen's and rushed upstairs where they found ex-soldier Joseph Walsh in bed with his seven year old son Michael and two year old daughter Brigid. In a frenzied attack, the gang repeatedly used a sledgehammer to kill the father, whilst Michael died from three bullet wounds the following day. Another son Frank (14), who had been sleeping downstairs, was wounded in the thigh as the gang fled. A priest discovered Joseph Walsh half an hour later 'with his skull open and empty while the whole mass of his brains lay on the bed about a foot away.'[15] Later that evening another Catholic, John Mallon (60) was shot dead further to the north of the city. Mr Mallon, a fire officer who lived in Skegoniel Avenue, was shot by three gunmen who turned their weapons on him when they discovered their intended target, Mr Mallon's son, was not at home.

The press unanimously condemned the horror and viciousness of attacks such as those in Arnon Street. Commenting on the horrors of the first weekend in April, the *Belfast Telegraph* condemned the '7 Peace Murders', maintaining that 'seldom in the history of distraught Belfast has the city passed through a more horrible weekend of bloodshed.'[16] Another unionist organ also focussed on the horrific nature of the acts of violence rather than attempt to ascertain the assailants' allegiances or motivation. The *Belfast Newsletter* therefore asked 'when is Belfast to be ridden of the murderous violence that has afflicted the city for too long, and taken toll of so many lives?'[17] The *Irish Independent*, however, went beyond merely condemning the 'barbarism' which had occurred in the northern capital over the weekend. The paper's editorial claimed that 'never, even in the worst state of the Terror in the South and West has anything like the condition of affairs which now prevail in the Northern capital been experienced.'[18] In a telegram to Craig Michael Collins demanded the establishment of an 'immediate joint enquiry' to investigate the Arnon Street outrage in order to 'prevent a disastrous situation from developing'.[19]

The raw sectarianism of many violent acts during this period were not confined to large-scale incidents such as Arnon Street or the McMahon murders, nor indeed to any one religion or political group. Such cases illustrate both the tension engendered by political negotiations elsewhere and the 'tit for tat' nature of the violence within the city itself. Other killings of Catholics at this time included those of Owen Hughes on 3 March and John Kearney on 16 March. Mr Hughes, who lived in Skegoniel Avenue, had been aboard a late evening tram passing the junction of Henry and York Streets. Asked his religion by a lone gunman, Mr. Hughes was shot dead. Mr Kearney, of Youngs Row, had been on his way to find a job at the Labour Exchange when a bomb was lobbed from Newtownards Road into Seaforde Street. Five people were injured and Mr Kearney died in hospital less than a week later. Further carnage was only narrowly avoided, as a diary insertion of a St Matthew's Priest illustrates:

> At midday today a bomb exploded in Seaforde Street. It had been thrown over the hoarding, 5 people were badly injured. The children in our school, who's duty it was to ring the bell at five minutes before twelve forgot to ring the bell. God had his divine hand in this, otherwise 200 children would have been crossing Seaforde Street just where the bomb exploded.[20]

Sacrilegious acts of violence were also committed during the early spring of 1922. No doubt using the spurious excuse that republicans periodically used the grounds of Catholic properties to direct fire into Protestant areas, some loyalists felt justified in targeting Catholics arriving for Mass. Such an attack occurred on Sunday 23 April. Just before evening mass at the much-targeted St Matthew's Church in Ballymacarrett, a hand grenade was thrown into the grounds of the church as the congregation was arriving for the service. It exploded near the door of the chapel, killing Mrs Lizzie McCabe (35) and seriously wounding a Catholic police officer, John Moriarty. A government report of the incident stated that Constable Moriarty 'saw the bomb coming through the air from the direction of Bryson Street' (a Protestant area) and suggested

that the policeman was 'not popular in the District owing to prosecutions initiated by him and it is likely that the bomb was intended for him.'[21] As the dying
woman and the severely wounded policeman were being helped into the
church, they were fired upon and the scheduled communion service had to be
abandoned. The sense of outrage inevitably felt in a religious community like
Belfast, at people being attacked as they entered a church was accompanied by
scenes of 'the utmost excitement and panic.'[22] Frightened women 'rushed
towards the altar rails but in the stampede a number stumbled and collapsed
and those who reached the altar tried to pray but the panic was too great and
they broke down and wept bitterly.'[23]

Blatant sectarianism was not solely the prerogative of loyalists. Protestant
suffering similar to the plight of some Catholic families was experienced during
the late evening of 31st March. A bomb was thrown through the front window
of a Brown Street house belonging to Francis Donnelly, who had already been
threatened by nationalists.[24] Mr Donnelly was wounded in the blast, but his
two year old son, Francis, described by a neighbour as 'the flower of the flock',
died instantly and two other children were injured. One of these, Joseph (12),
who had been preparing a meal, died a few days later in hospital. The *Belfast
Telegraph*'s report poignantly stated:

> Upstairs lies the father weeping like a child at the thought of the terrible
> destruction of his home and habitation, of the awful slaughter of his
> children.[25]

Again, the west of the city was to bear the brunt of much of the violence.
Though many of these killings had clear sectarian motives, it is difficult to
conclude that they were highly organised and premeditated. They covered a
range of people in terms of age and religion and the culpability for such offences
covered loyalist groups, IRA and the security forces. A Protestant railway clerk,
James Martin (37), was shot dead during the morning of 5 March in the
staunchly nationalist Albert Street area and during the following afternoon,
Andrew Leonard (21), an IRA volunteer from Raglan Street, was shot in the
neck near Townsend Street and died in hospital a week later. Later that day
another Catholic, Catherine Lynch (51) was shot at her home in Letitia Street
in the Falls. Increased military patrols inevitably resulted in several civilian
deaths. Thomas Heathwood, a teenager from Upton Street, was shot dead by a
military patrol in the Wall Street area on 6 March and a few hours later another

young Catholic, William Warden, was fatally wounded in the Hanover Street area. Another Catholic teenager, John Mullan, of Wall Street , who was in the Upper Library Street area during curfew hours on 7 March, was shot dead by a Specials patrol who believed he was about to fire at them.

Towards the end of the month two further Catholics, James Magee of McDonnell Street and James Neeson, of Roumania Street, were both shot dead by the army during disturbances in Raglan Street on 26 March.[26] Three Protestants were also believed to have been fatally wounded following security force fire, including one in 'mysterious' circumstances. A 38-year-old 'A' Special, Charles Vokes, of Upper Meadow Street, was shot as he tried to escape from a military patrol which had arrested him on 12 March, whilst four days later, John Taylor (52) was shot dead at the gate lodge of the New Northern Spinning Company, also in the west of the city. William Johnson (27), of Louisa Street, was fatally wounded by a soldier in the 1st Norfolk Regiment as he was allegedly sniping from an upstairs window of his home. Other Protestant fatalities in west Belfast were John Morrison (23), of Gardiner Street, who was shot in Stephen Street on 7 March and William Johnston (40), of Cavour Street, who died the following day, Herbert Woods (21), of California Street, shot dead on 10th March, Joseph Thompson (17), of Tyne Street, shot during disturbances in Hanover Street the same day and Donegall Road man Harry Brennan (19), who succumbed to head injuries sustained during gunfire on the Grosvenor Road on 26 March.[27] Further Catholic fatalities in the west of the city during March were Samuel Mullan (20), of Havana Street, assassinated by the IRA for alleged informing and teenager John Sweeney (18), of Stanhope Street, shot by a sniper in Carrick Hill at the end of March.[28]

The killing of young Mullan on 29 March was an indication of the IRA's increased 'hold' on their community. Republican punishment of suspected 'criminals' in nationalist areas also occurred. On 20 April three men who had been tarred and feathered were paraded on the Falls Road and, despite breaking free from their captors near the Falls Baths, they were given no help from an 'amused and gratified' crowd who only dispersed with the arrival of the military.[29] Police raids a few weeks earlier at St Mary's Hall and street arrests at the start of March also shows the increasing degree of IRA activity during this period. As a result of the St Mary's raids, 20 bombs, considerable ammunition and a pistol were found on 18–19 March, whilst a man arrested in North Street at the beginning of the month was caught in possession of a bomb and IRA documents.[30]

North Belfast witnessed some of the most heinous crimes of the conflict during these months, especially the McMahon and Arnon Street killings, described above. Apart from these horrific outrages, a constant stream of murderous attacks took place in the north of the city during this period. These included Robert Hazzard (24), a member of the Orange Order and the Imperial Guards, shot by the military after allegedly sniping from a roof in York Street on 8 March. The IRA planted a bomb on an Antrim Road tram on 19 March, injuring many passengers and killing Protestant Alexander Devaney (35), of Church Street East. Later that day Margaret Murphy, a Protestant married to a Catholic, living in Campbell Street in the city's Old Lodge Road area, answered a knock at her door. Mrs Murphy was fatally wounded by gunmen who decided that she should take the place of her husband, who had been their intended victim. Five days later, a Protestant car inspector, William Campbell, of Oldpark Avenue, was shot by a sniper in Ludlow Street off the New Lodge Road. A 20-year-old Catholic carter, Patrick Fitzsimons, of Frederick Street, also died of his wounds in the Mater Hospital on 24 March. Mr Fitzsimons had been shot the previous day at the corner of Fountain Street North and New Lodge Road. Incidentally, just two days before the city had been disrupted by a strike of carters who believed that they had been unfairly singled out by the gunmen and demanded more protection from the security forces.[31] Other north Belfast victims of violence at this time were John Dempster (20), from Mountcollier Avenue, who died on 30 March from gunshot wounds suffered five days previously, Andrew McCartney, also a Catholic, of Dagmar Street, who died on 21 April from an injury sustained the previous day in Henry Street, and a Protestant teenager, Thomas Best, of Louisa Street, shot dead in the mainly loyalist Oldpark area, probably the victim of mistaken identity. Particularly savage killings involved those where mob beatings preceded shooting of the victims. Such a fate befell William Kerr (27), a Catholic labourer from Mountpleasant, who was dragged on to rough ground by a loyalist gang and badly beaten before being shot.

Mob killings such as these were not restricted to the north of the city. On 20th March a Catholic Corporation worker, James Hillis (23), from Nail Street, who had allegedly been threatened by fellow workers, was attacked by a mob on the Beersbridge Road and ferociously beaten, before being shot. Nationalist mobs were also guilty of such outrages. During the evening of 30 March, a 'B' Special from Mountpottinger Barracks, Thomas Hall, had, along with a colleague, dismounted from a Short Strand tram when they were viciously beaten by a crowd and shot.[32] Although the east of the city did not experience the scale of violence as elsewhere during this period, several people lost their lives. Augustus Orange (24), a Catholic who lived on the Ravenhill Road, was shot in the Woodstock area during the morning of 18 March and died the following day, whilst Protestant John Bell (36), of My Lady's Road, was shot on the Ravenhill Road during the evening of 24 March and was found by Specials lying across tram-lines (he died two days later). Towards the end of April, however, east Belfast was to experience a more intensive, if short-lived period of violence, with at least 9 people losing their lives and about 30 receiving serious injuries. On the 19 April alone, six people perished, with about 10 suffering serious wounds and several homes in the Short Strand were destroyed. The *Irish Independent* declared that the Catholic community on the city side of the Newtownards Road were living in 'a state of siege'.³³ The violence endured from three in the afternoon until midnight, peaking at tea-time as workers were returning home. The *Belfast Telegraph* described scenes of 'great excitement' which were witnessed as crowds 'dashed for safety amidst the unceasing rattle of rifle and machine gun fire, and many were placed in imminent danger by [their] unwitting presence in the fire zone.'³⁴ Two neighbours, Mary Berry (29), a mother of five, and Rosie Dougan, both from Arran Street, were taking refuge in a relative's house in Thompson Street during a spell of heavy gunfire and disturbances when they were hit by bullets which penetrated a front window. Shortly after their deaths another Catholic, Patrick McGoldrick (27), a grocer from Madrid Street, was shot by hatchet-wielding assailants whilst serving in his shop. A Catholic 'exile', Francis Hobbs (36), over on holiday in the city from his new home in England, died from a stomach wound, believed to be the result of the army responding to gunfire in Thompson Street. Two Protestant teenagers also succumbed to the day's violence in east Belfast. John Scott (16), of Well Street, proceeding to work early that morning, was shot by a sniper operating from Thompson Street, whilst James Greer (14), of Lower Frank Street, was shot during the riots in the Short Strand, dying two days later in hospital.

The following day, 20 April, also proved to be costly in terms of human life, with 5 dying from the violence. Gunfire erupted in the east of the city as curfew ended at six. Two Catholics died in the Short Strand area which local residents felt to be the main target of attack. John Walker, a teenager shot in the Quinn Street district, was believed to have been a victim of military gunfire and Dennis Diamond (25), of Vulcan Street, who was shot by a sniper at the corner of Albertbridge Road and Short Strand. However, the casualty list also included workers proceeding to the shipyards. A foreman at Andersons and Sons, James Johnston (50), of My Lady's Road, was one such worker targeted by nationalists in the Short Strand and he died of his injuries. A 'B' Special protecting workers on the Albert Bridge was wounded, also in the early morning, and there were reports that marksmen at Short Strand were lying on the tramlines firing up the Newtownards Road.

CATHOLIC TREPIDATION

Feelings of fear and trepidation increased in many Catholic areas, especially those on the fringe of larger loyalist ones. This was especially evident after the Arnon Street killings. Only hours after those grisly events had occurred, Services of Humiliation were held throughout the Down diocese and the following day Catholic representatives voiced their 'horror and indignation' at the 'appalling crimes' committed in the city the previous weekend.[35] Catholic spokesmen endeavoured to persuade government officials to give their urgent attention to law and order issues and to admit their own culpability in failing to prevent murders from being executed by men in uniform during the curfew in areas occupied by the army and police, only two days after a peace agreement. Even though there were several days lull after the events in Arnon Street, an overnight exodus of residents from Stanhope Street and its neighbouring sidestreets continued for a number of weeks. These residents, mainly women and children, 'fearing further night attacks, and not being satisfied with the semblance of protection afforded them', left their homes in the early evening and sought refuge with relatives and friends in safer Catholic areas.[36] The *Irish News* report caught the mood of increased tension in such areas:

> No one in the Catholic district can venture into the streets or even stand at a doorway and feel certain that his or her life is safe, while children are compulsorily confined in the houses. It is under these conditions that the unhappy women and children and younger members of the families migrate cautiously before nightfall for security in other places. In most cases the men remain in charge of the threatened houses.[37]

Others were not so fortunate with temporary flits nor were they likely to have taken such a decision voluntarily. Intimidation intensified particularly when there was only a small number of Catholic families left in a loyalist area. Explicit instructions to leave such areas were not always disseminated by crude actions such as a verbal warning or a brick through the window but were something delivered in a more sophisticated, yet equally chilling manner. Such a case was the typewritten warning given to a Catholic resident of Portallo Street which, apart from four families, was exclusively Protestant. The chilling warning from the '13th gang' went on:

> We have come to learn that you are a rebel so take notice this house is required for a loyalist and his family. We give you 7 days to pack up and leave. To ignore this warning means you will be made to leave for we will bomb you out. You carry your life in your hands. In future your days are numbered, so prepare. The dreaded 13th gang is upon you![38]

More large-scale evictions of Catholics occurred in the Marrowbone district over the Easter period. These arose from violence which, not for the first time, happened as crowds were leaving a football ground. The trouble followed a football match at Cliftonville on Easter Monday. Gunfire raked the Marrowbone for an entire evening and much of the following day (18 April). Several people were wounded, including a Catholic, James Fearon (56), of Glenpark Street, who died the following day. There followed several reported cases of looting and at least 15 houses in Antigua Street were burned.[39] This street, along with neighbouring Rothesay and Saunderson Streets, suffered 'complete destruction', with the American White Cross relief agency taking the initiative in building properties in a new street, Gracehill Street, after hostilities had ceased.[40] The same area bore the brunt of disturbances the following day, with several more evictions and shootings.[41] The *Irish News* condemned the 'extraordinary inertia' of the security forces in dealing with the evictions in particular.[42] Commenting on the prevailing mood in those nationalist areas under siege, the *Irish News* proceeded:

> The people complain bitterly of the failure of the Crown forces to stop the operations, it being alleged that gunmen and looters were busily engaged at their nefarious work within range of both soldiers and police. It does seem strange that a whole street should have been practically wiped out while the city is thronged with both police and military, and the matter certainly requires further investigation.[43]

The local press carried copious reports of the major incidents during this period, though not surprisingly, they differed both in their interpretation of specific events and in their selection of news stories.[44] The range of issues debated in their editorial columns was quite wide, though inevitably many of these topics were perennials. The unionist press chose to focus on events in the south and on the attitudes of Irish leaders, rather than explain who had been responsible for much of the blood-letting in Belfast. Thus, the *Belfast Telegraph* agreed with the stance of the new Belfast Parliament, which had questioned whether Collins had 'the will, or the power, to secure ... observance of the peace which he has negotiated' and a couple of days later suggested the south was 'drifting to anarchy'.[45] The *Belfast Newsletter* also chose to focus on broader issues and 'external' factors rather than the immediate causes and responsibility for the violence on their own doorstep. Therefore, the paper noted Sinn Féin's increasing border activity which they warned would lead to Fermanagh and Tyrone, 'for the sake of peace, agree[ing] to inclusion in southern Ireland', which in turn would 'render the position of the other four counties perilous, if not untenable and would be a long step in the direction of a united Ireland.'[46] The same paper, drawing on a statement by Lord Justice Moore the previous day – in which he claimed that a comparatively small number of 'murderous ruffians' were 'holding the city up' – declared that such a small group of activists would not be able to function 'unless they were shielded and sheltered.'[47] Inferring that the wider Catholic community was culpable, the *Newsletter* concluded that 'if the shelter was denied, the police and military would soon suppress the evil.'[48]

Pressurised by their political opponents north and south of the border and by an increasingly embarrassed and impatient British administration, Craig's government also had to contend with increasing frustration about poor security among their own traditional support. Belfast businessmen, the backbone of the Unionist Party, were concerned about the damage being done to their commercial interests, both by the boycott and the enduring civil unrest in the city. A resolution adopted by the General Purposes Committee of the Belfast Chamber of Commerce was forwarded to Craig's government expressing the desire of the mainly loyalist business community that 'prompt' action should be taken by the government to overturn its 'failure' in the area of law and order. The Committee demanded that, 'without further delay one central authority shall be vested adequate powers to secure the prevention, detection and punishment of breaches of the law.'[49]

The nationalist press, on the other hand, castigated both the perpetrators of and apologists for the city's violence. In an editorial, the *Irish News* compared the lot of Belfast's Catholics with the 'odious persecution' of Bulgarians by Turks and challenging Craig and his Home Affairs Minister Bates to deny the allegation, claimed that 'not a single honest official effort had been made to get at the truth about these ghastly occurrences.'[50] The *Irish News* also made it clear that they had little confidence in the workings of Craig's administration. Reminding its readers that 'full responsibility for all these hideous deeds of terrorism and blood rests on the shoulders of the established Government of this city', it suggested that 'their failure to preserve a semblance of law and order is apparently complete.'[51]

Some London journalists on the other hand, distinguished between loyalist culpability in Belfast and the more serious transgressions of republicans elsewhere in Ulster. Informing their readers of the discovery of 'a concerted plan to precipitate a conflict between the Northern and Southern governments', the *Times* argued that the 'Sinn Féiners' appear in all cases to have been the aggressors on the border, but the situation in Belfast with the attacks on Roman Catholics and the counter-campaign of reprisals on unionists has aggravated the position.'[52] Although many of the legion of foreign journalists in the city at this time found it convenient to focus on the spectacular, others endeavoured to unravel reasons for sectarian actions and were even-handed in their analysis. Charles A. Merrill, correspondent of the *Boston Globe*, was one such pressman. Writing about 'depressing' aspects of the city's life, Merrill proceeded:

> You come in contact with the depressing side of the picture when you go through the poorer quarters of the city, particularly at a time like this, when thousands are without employment. You see mothers with shawls over their heads and babies in their arms, wandering disconsolately along miserable streets lined with two storey shops. You see pinched faces throughout the murky atmosphere, faces as expressionless as so many sphinxes. It is in such unwholesome soil that religious bigotry thrives and inflames men's minds and sets one man's hand against his neighbour. It is futile to charge any one sect or any one group in Belfast for the reign of terror.[53]

The months of March and April, with their combined tally of over 100 lives, represented by far the most concentrated violence in the conflict to date.

Political tension increased as a result of the signing and subsequent failure of the March Pact. Further crippled by delays in the handing-over of security powers to the northern authorities and the passage of time required for the passing of their own emergency legislation, those with responsibility for security appeared to accept the premise that an 'acceptable' level of violence was inevitable, at least in the short term. It seemed to many in the spring of 1922 that, despite the prevailing Truce elsewhere in Ireland, the men of violence were in the ascendancy in the North. Belfast citizens were increasingly resigned to a bloody crescendo.

Chapter 17

'A state of chassis'

LIVING HELL

Had Belfast rather than Dublin been his home town, Sean O'Casey would surely have applied his famous description of Dublin during this period to depict the electrically-charged atmosphere of Ireland's northern metropolis. The horrors and depravity witnessed during the spring of 1922 barely prepared Belfast's citizens for a month-long orgy of bloodshed which was to reach its climax in early June. This violent crescendo was, however, inevitable given the merging together of several crucial influences upon the state of security within the city. These included the perilous predicament of the Catholic minority, the increasing desperation of armed republicans, the unhindered progress of loyalist terror gangs and the repercussions of Craig's emergency legislation. All these influences combined to precipitate some of the most barbaric incidents of the conflict, including the setting on fire of a doctor's house-keeper, the deliberate drowning of a helpless man on the Queen's Bridge and a gunfire attack on a city hospital. The intensity of violence over a prolonged period of several weeks was unparalleled, as new dimensions of horror, including assassination of politicians and arson attacks on central commercial properties, were experienced.[1]

Trams continued to be popular targets for assassination gangs on both sides. Although loyalists generally refrained from hurling bombs at tramcars, a number of Catholics were either shot or hauled off trams and beaten. Spontaneous reactions on passing churches presented watching enemies with proof an individual's religious identity and sparked shooting incidents. Such an attack occurred during the morning rush-hour of 18 May. Flax-dressers Samuel McPeake (50) and James Donaghy (46), both of Ligoniel Place, had been going to work along the Crumlin Road on a packed city-bound tram. It was believed the men had been spotted crossing themselves as the vehicle passed the Holy Cross chapel and they were shot by two gunmen who escaped amongst the confusion. Another Catholic, Thomas McCaffrey, of Shore Street, was shot dead at Mountcollyer Avenue that day on a Falls-bound tram. Sectarian gangs struck again on a tram three days later.

In a particularly ferocious attack, Hugh McDonald (20), from Saul Street, was dragged off an early morning tram-car at Bridge End and savagely beaten before being shot dead in Memel Street. When unsure of the religious affiliation of potential victims, gangs asked the hapless individuals to reveal this information. This cost many people their lives during the conflict, including two Catholics in this period. During the evening of 12 May, Michael Cullen (44), of Havana Street, was shot dead in the Marrowbone district by a four-strong gang who had enquired his religion, and three weeks later another Catholic was caught in the wrong place by an armed gang. On 3 June Thomas Gough, of Mineral Street, had been leaving the Brickfields when he was stopped by loyalists who asked him his religion in Skegoniel Avenue. Mr Gough was dragged into a side street where he was shot, passing away in hospital two days later. Even passing through what was deemed 'friendly' territory posed danger for relative strangers as Protestant fruiterer Alexander Morrison, from Ballyclare, found to his cost on 26 May. Visiting a market on the Albertbridge Road, the former soldier was attacked by a loyalist gang and fatally wounded.

Those Catholics still in a job were under special pressure as sectarian attacks were concentrated on people travelling to work and also in the workplace itself. Although many Catholics avoided this danger on account of the industrial intimidation prevailing in the city, some did fall victim to preying loyalist assassins. Apprentice saw-maker Robert Monaghan (20), of Arizona Street, was shot dead as he left work on 31 May. During the mid-evening of 6 June, Patrick O'Malley (45), was shot returning from work as he approached his home in Stratheden Street and within hours John McMenermy, of Conway Street, was shot as he walked along Cupar Street. Towards the end of June Leo Rea, a teenager from Leeson Street, was fatally wounded during the early morning of 23 June as he made his way to work. Many other Catholics were attacked either on their business premises or carrying out their work duties, often in hostile areas. Disturbances occurred during the funeral procession of Robert Beattie on 16 May. Accounts of what exactly happened differed considerably, but it appears likely that harassment of passers-by and residents of homes passed on the route by some mourners prompted nationalist gunmen to open fire at the procession in Donegall Street and later in Kent Street.[2] Following this outbreak of gunfire, the crowd of mourners panicked and a number of people received minor injuries as they were trampled in the stampede. Shortly after the second outbreak of gunfire, a Catholic unloading fruit from a van outside a shop in North Street, William Madden (21), Sackville Street, was approached by a large group of men who allegedly had been part of the funeral procession and was shot dead.[3] In a separate incident two teenage cattle-drovers, Patrick McAuley, of Ton Street, and Thomas McGuigan, of Stanfield Street, were shot dead as they led cattle into the pens at the market in Duncrue Street on 20 May. Also that morning, another Catholic worker, this time an employee of J.P. Corry's timber works in Henry Street, was singled out by loyalist gunmen. John Connolly (35), of New Lodge Road, was fatally wounded. Two more Catholics were shot at work a couple of days later. Around lunchtime on 22 May, John McLarnon, of Moyola Street, a foreman ganger, was shot dead as he worked at the Midland Railway Station and Charles McMurty, of Frederick Street, suffered a similar fate as he worked at a rubbish tip. Even office workers working in less exposed environments, were far from safe. A Catholic clerk working at the Shankill Labour Exchange, Francis McHugh (27), of the New Lodge Road, was an all too easy target for loyalist gunmen on 1 June.

Catholic shopkeepers who carried out their business in a loyalist area were particularly at risk, as were their staff. Three female shop workers lost their lives in two separate attacks in May. Cecilia Kearns was shot by a loyalist gunman as she served a customer in her York Street corner shop on 20 May, whilst ten days later, Mary McElroy (52) and her daughter Rose (29) were both shot dead during the late evening in a butcher's shop on the Old Lodge Road owned by her husband, who was not in at the time. The assailants looted a Catholic-owned pub next door, though fortunately its owner escaped. During the mid morning of 12 June, a leading Belfast businessman, Edward Devine, from the Springfield Road, who was managing director of the Hughes bakery in west Belfast, was preparing a considerable sum of money (estimated at around £1,600) for banking when a seven-strong gang invaded his premises and endeavoured to snatch the moneybags. Mr Devine disarmed a gunman before being fatally wounded in front of his horrified son, John and members of his staff. The gang escaped but the money was, surprisingly, not taken. The size of the gang and the location of the attack (off the Falls Road) suggests IRA involvement, with their failure to lift the money being interpreted as a sign of panic induced by the fatal shooting of Mr Devine. Another spin on this was that it was nothing more than a botched robbery executed by 'a gang of common thieves.'[4] The *Belfast Telegraph*, with considerable justification, castigated the southern press for 'cloaking the IRA and suppressing the facts' about responsibility for the arson attacks and several of the murders being committed in the city, including the Devine killing in a nationalist part of west Belfast which had

been blamed on loyalists. It concluded that 'the likelihood [was] that the criminals were either out to replenish the coffers of the IRA or for private plunder.'[5]

Loyalist sniping attacks intensified during this period. In the main they operated from the sanctuary of their own areas, picking off people walking or
standing in Catholic streets. Many such fatal attacks occurred in the north of
the city. During the evening of 16 May, John Gribbon (21), of Gordon Street,
was shot in the chest in Great Patrick Street and died in the Mater Hospital the
following morning. That evening Nellie McMullan, of Keegan Street, was shot
at the corner of Great George's Street, whilst three days later several Catholics
were gunned down both in the north and the west of the city. These included
Francis McDermott, of Lady Street and Arthur McMurrough, from Grosvenor
Place, who were shot by loyalists as they worked in the Pumping Station.[6]
Agnes Coudet (22), of Fleet Street, and John Hickey (50), of Nelson Street, were
victims of loyalist snipers in York Street. That evening Thomas McShane (35),
of Jennymount Street was shot in the neck and Peter Prunty (35) was shot
during disturbances in Albert Street. Inside a week loyalist snipers in different
parts of the city claimed another two lives. William Toal (17), of Mayfair Street,
was shot in the chest in the Marrowbone district and died in hospital on 26
May, whilst William Smyth (21), of Moira Street, was shot at Thompson Street
in the Short Strand the next day.[7] Other Catholics to die in May shootings were
John Murphy (40), who was shot in the chest in Northumberland Street on 19
May; Joseph Murtagh, of Palmer Street, who was shot the following day;
Patrick Hughes, of Carntaul Street, killed on 21 May; and Lizzie Donnelly, of
West Street, who was a victim of sniping in the Millfield area towards the end
of the month.

Also at risk were those conducting messages at what they thought were safe
times. Two north Belfast teenagers were such victims on 14 May. Kathleen
Douglas (13), of Marine Street, was hit in the stomach by a sniper and although
managing to struggle back to her home, she died of her injuries a short time later,
whilst Ellen Dargan (19), from Emily Place, was shot as she returned from
purchasing bread and milk in Great George's Street. Another 'messenger' victim
was teenager Esther McDougall, the daughter of an ex-soldier, on 25 May. Miss
McDougall, however, was not murdered by accident. She was due to be a witness
in a forthcoming court case involving a loyalist throwing a bomb into Stanhope
Street and had been shot at the previous evening. Nipping out to fetch a jug of
milk, Miss McDougall was shot close to her house. People standing at their front
doors continued to be easy prey for snipers. John Black (50), of New Dock Street,

was another such victim, as he was shot by a sniper operating from Little Ship Street on 3 June. Less than a fortnight later another Catholic, William Smyth (54), of Hardinge Street, was shot by a Vere Street sniper as he left a shop at the corner of North Queen Street in the middle of the afternoon. More Catholics fell victim to loyalist snipers in the north of the city during June. They included Bella McKeown (22), of Arran Street, who died in the Mater Hospital three weeks after being shot on the opening day of that month, teenager Bernard McCaffrey, from the New Lodge Road, who died in the same hospital shortly after being shot on 3 June, and Thomas Johnston (26), of Frederick Street, whose body was found in Nelson Street two days previously.

Other vulnerable groups included the young, elderly, handicapped and those who had already been threatened. Toddler Brigid Skillen (3), of Herbert Street, was singled out in York Street on 20 May. Given a penny to treat herself to a bun, the poor child was struck down by a sniper as she made the short journey to a corner shop. Her distraught mother was informed within a minute by a boy who had narrowly escaped the attention of the gunman. An elderly man, Patrick Ward, was shot by a loyalist sniper in Great Patrick Street on 12 June and died nearly a fortnight later. Another old man, William Millar, of Willowfield Street in the east of the city, was the victim of an especially vicious attack just over a week later. During the middle of the evening of 21 June, Mr Millar (70) had been breaking up wood for his fire when he was confronted by three youths who had climbed over his yard wall, shooting him three times. Although a neighbour rushed to his help, Mr Millar died shortly afterwards, the likely victim of a sectarian attack against one of the few Catholics likely to have been living in that street.[8] Sheer hatred and mob fury, fuelled by the killing of Special Constable Roulston on 30 May, prompted an angry loyalist crowd to torch many homes in the mainly Catholic Peter's Place and Boyd Street in western Belfast. Two of these belonged to Jane Doran and John Jennings who were shot by the mob. Mr Jennings, who was blind and paralysed, was the only Protestant living in the street, a fact probably unknown by the vengeful crowd. A Catholic invalid, Francis James Hughes (45) was shot in his bed in Lesson Street following the death of a policeman on 29 May. Sometimes people ignored threats at their peril. Mary Grant (60), of Fleet Street, had been intimidated and asked to leave her home, and was probably an intended victim of a sniper operating from York Street. Although Mrs Grant staggered home, she died in hospital on 23 May. Others were clearly unintended victims, sometimes paying a terrible price for their spur of the moment heroism. Robert Rainey

(50), of Cyprus Street, was shot on 27 May after he went to the aid of a man injured during disturbances in the Cullingtree Road area.[9]

Seven police officers, including three members of the RIC, lost their lives during May and June. This illustrates an escalation of republican activity, especially in their strongholds, coinciding with their arson campaign. It involved ambushing policemen in broad daylight as well as during curfew hours, attacking police stations, as well as some attacks which might have been improvised.[10] Surprisingly, the majority of these attacks did not appear to precipitate a renewal of activities by 'rogue cops', although the last police fatality in May did pre-empt a ferocious response, especially by Specials in west Belfast. Apart from the audacious onslaught on the Musgrave Street barracks on 18 May in which RIC officer John Collins was killed, the other murders of police personnel occurred in nationalist areas. Also on 18 May, Cavan-born RIC officer, William Heaslip was shot by armed men in Millfield, following a botched robbery in Berry Street. A week later, on 25 May, two members of the Special Constabulary were killed in separate attacks. Special Constable James Murphy (27), who was based at Shankill Road Barracks, responded with a colleague to the request of local police for assistance during a gun battle with IRA volunteers on the Springfield Road just before six in the morning. As they approached the Falls Road end of Conway Street, Constable Murphy, a Protestant originally from Ballymena, was hit by gunfire and fatally wounded. Later that evening, just after the start of curfew, another Special Constable was killed, this time probably a result of being lured into an IRA ambush. A police patrol had entered the Cromac Street area following reports that a group of men were attempting to set fire to a building. As he endeavoured to evacuate adjoining buildings in McAuley Street, Special Constable George Connor, an ex-member of the Royal Irish Rangers and a native of Whitehead, was fatally wounded by an IRA sniper.

Another three officers lost their lives within the next week. On 29 May, Leitrim-born RIC officer, Henry O'Brien (23) who, along with a colleague had been talking to a civilian outside their barracks in Cullingtree Road, was approached by a number of gunmen who opened fire from about ten yards. Both Constable O'Brien and the pedestrian, Patrick Loughran were hit, but the other officer managed to return fire on the IRA team, which also fired into the police station before fleeing down Lady Street. Security force follow-up searches for arms in the area prompted the IRA to carry out further attacks on security forces from carefully concealed vantage points in Albert Street and the Grosvenor Road. During this four hour gun battle, a police mobile vehicle containing about ten officers, was ambushed during the early afternoon in McDonnell Street, and Special Constable John Megarritty (20), originally from County Armagh and stationed at Court Street Barracks, died instantly from a sniper's bullet. An interesting account of this operation and a subsequent stand-off between the army and the IRA is given by Sean Montgomery:

> An armoured car going through McDonnell Street was firing at anyone who moved. One of our company fired and hit the special on the head. Word was received that the Specials then went into the house of a sick man off Leeson Street and shot him dead in bed so we formed a party to go after the car ... 15 men moved in a single line on each side of the street ... I was on the corner of the road with a Thompson machine gun as we left McDonnell Street to go into Servia Street I came face to face with a British patrol. They were shocked – we stood facing each other for a short time when the Company OC gave the command to walk back-wards down McDonnell Street where we got into a house ... I think the officer who was in charge of the British patrol saw the machine gun but did not try to engage us. They moved into Albert Street.[11]

The next day, 30 May, another Special Constable lost his life in the west of the city. On this occasion, the response of loyalists and the Special Constabulary was virulent and several people subsequently lost their lives. At around 4.30 p.m., Special Constable Andrew Roulston (23) and Special Constable William Campbell were patrolling the Millfield district when they were fired upon. Both officers fell to the ground, where their assailants shot them again. Constable Roulston, originally from Strabane and stationed at Smithfield Barracks, died in the attack.[12]

As well as those who perished in crossfire between rival factions and the army, at least 10 people were killed directly by the security forces. Sometimes this occurred when a person was away from his or her own district, as was the case with Thomas Drumgoole. Mr Drumgoole, from Seaforde Street in Ballymacarrett, was shot by a police patrol in Cullingtree Road on 29 May. Four men were shot by the Specials on 30/1 May in particularly bloody arracks in the west of the city. In the aftermath of the attack on Special Constable Roulston, Patrick McGurk (34), of Ardmoulin Avenue and Arthur George Megahey (17), of Irwin Street, were hit in an exchange of gunfire between the police and the IRA. Later that evening William O'Hara (25), of McDonnell Street, was shot as he walked home from work and Hugh Kennedy (26), of Servia Street, was also shot by Specials operating in the Falls area. A few days later, a Protestant teenager, John Kane, was shot by the army during riots and alleged looting in the Peters Hill district. During the early hours of 4 June, a Catholic paid a heavy penalty for breaking the curfew regulations. Robert Hunt (50), of Millford Street, was shot by police in Ross Street during disturbances. It was reported that Mr Hunt had been on his way to feed a horse and had ignored police instructions to stop. He subsequently died in the Mater Hospital. Also that evening William Rice (25), of Fairview Street, was shot by the army in Lime Street. Inside a fortnight Thomas Mullaney (38), of East Street, who had been visiting his brother in Grove Street, was shot by a military patrol in the North Queen Street area. Mr Mullaney's visit coincided with a spell of attacks on properties in the area and apparently he had refused an army request to move away from the street and was shot as he appeared to put his hand inside his pocket. On 21 June, John Ireland (37), a Protestant from Elms Court, was shot dead by the army during disturbances in the York Street area.

Although on not nearly the same scale, Protestant suffering was also widespread and equally heart-wrenching in its nature. Protestants were particularly prone to attack, as we have seen, either proceeding to and from work or in factories and offices adjacent to nationalist districts. Robert Beattie, a postman from Palmer Street off the Crumlin Road, was shot dead by a man wielding a rifle as he delivered letters in Butler Street on Saturday 13 May.[13] On 22 May ex-soldier George Lawson (30), of Marymount Street, was returning to work in the shipyard when he was struck by a sniper operating from Seaforde Street in the nationalist Short Strand.[14] Another ex-soldier, Victor Kidd, of Brookvale Avenue was making his way to his business premises (he was a building contractor) on 26 May when he was singled out by a New Lodge sniper. Towards teatime on that day another shipyard worker was hit by a sniper as he made his journey home from work. William Shields (21), a clerk and promising Queens Island footballer, was shot as he walked with a friend down the Newtownards Road, close to Anderson Street. Those workers with early starts coinciding with the end of curfew were particularly liable for targeting. Another Protestant baker, William Collum (45), of Portallo Street in the Woodstock area, was shot dead near East Bridge Street by a Short Strand sniper in the early morning of 1 June, whilst a Protestant lorry driver, James Kane, from Limestone Road, was fatally wounded whilst sitting in his lorry on the Falls Road later that morning. On 23 June, the Protestant manager of the Hughes mill in the nation-

alist Divis Street, William Kirkwood (27), of Marlborough Place, was shot dead
by a gang as he went on his lunchbreak. Even travelling in the city centre was
not always safe. William McKnight, a carter from McTier Street, was shot
during the early morning of 18 May in Academy Street.

Placing bombs on workers' trams continued to be used by nationalists during
this period. Tram crew were, like taxi drivers more recently, a favourite quarry
of the terrorists and a tram conductor was fatally wounded during the late
evening of 11 May. Recently widowed Protestant John Mansfield (42), who had
just started duty on the Oldpark-Castlereagh tram route, had deposited an
abandoned attaché case in the cashier's officer at the Ardoyne depot, where it
exploded, killing him and wounding three colleagues. One of them, James
Kennedy, from Butler Street, recalled how other motormen had bantered
Mansfield, who had been counting his fares when there was 'a loud report and
we were all knocked helter-skelter ... My clothes went on fire and I rolled about
the floor in an endeavour to beat out the flames.'[15] Tram passengers continued to
be considered legitimate targets for the bombers. On 24 May three bombs went
off on trams and although they only caused one fatality and a handful of minor
injuries, there was considerable confusion as rush hour commuters stampeded
in their attempt to escape the blasts in North Street, Upper Donegall Street and
to the north of the city centre in Clifton Street. Grace Todd, a 30-year-old
Protestant of Bedaque Street, died from chest and leg injuries sustained in the
North Street blast. Further tragedies were only avoided because of the vigilance
of tram staff and passers-by. A conductor on a Mountpottinger tram discovered
a device on his tram as it approached Castle Junction on 15 May and an alert
flower-seller extinguished the device by dousing it with water from his vase.

As with Catholic victims, many of the Protestants who died in nationalist-
orientated violence, were easy targets. The young were particularly vulnerable
and there were three such fatalities during May and June. On 27 May, Georgina
Campbell (5), of Roxburgh Street, was hit during the mid evening by a sniper
allegedly operating from the grounds of St Matthew's Church. On the 1st June,
a 11 year old newspaper seller, Albert McMordie, from Lower Urney Street, was
hit by a sniper as he sold papers and towards the end of June, Isabella Foster, an
infant, died just before curfew after being struck by a bullet which had entered
the front window of her parents' house at Ballycarry Street in the Oldpark
district. Stationary targets like the poor newsboy and people who used to stand
chatting outside their front doors, were particularly popular targets for snipers.
Teenager John Moore, already vulnerable living in predominantly nationalist

Hooker Street, was shot outside his front door on 25 May. Another person who was in the wrong place at the wrong time was James Telford. Mr Telford (63), a grave-digger at the City Cemetery, died after being beaten and shot by a group of men outside a church in the Broadway part of the Falls, as he returned from his work on 24 May. His anguished grand-daughter, standing barely 50 yards from the attack, helplessly witnessed the unfolding events. People endeavouring to carry on with the routine of their everyday lives were also vulnerable. During the mid morning of 22 May, Thomas Boyd (25), a pub manager from the Donegall Road, was shot by a Short Strand sniper on the Albertbridge Road as he collected his bicycle from a repair shop.[16]

A number of Protestants were also killed in more dubious circumstances, most likely caught in crossfire between security forces and nationalists. Downpatrick-born Lizzie McAloney (47), of Brown Street, was shot on 14 May and three days later ex-soldier Robert Dudgeon, of Westland Street, who worked as a cleaner in the City Hall, was shot near Cupar Street at teatime, following similar exchanges. On 19th May, this time in the north of the city, Mary Donaldson (50) was caught in crossfire between the army and nationalist snipers in North Queen Street and she died of her injuries outside her the front door of her home in Spamount Street. IRA discipline was sometimes sorely tested and occasionally snapped in cases of extreme provocation. One such case occurred in Memel Street in the Newtownards Road area shortly after the horrific killing of Hugh McDonald on 21 May. Moments after this attack a Short Strand sniper struck down Robert Newell (26), of Clonallen Street. Other Protestants to lose their lives during this period were Robert Powell (35), a sailor, who was shot in Edward Street on 21st May after being asked his religion; Minnie Boyd (38) of Wilson Street, who died from a back wound sustained in the volatile Millfield area on 28 May; and Mary Semple (25), of Ardgowan Street who died from injuries at the end of June.[17] Miss Semple, a clerk, had been sitting in the kitchen of her home when a bullet fire through the window struck her in the chest. The victim, who was probably mistaken for a Catholic, died in hospital.

THE LOWEST OF THE LOW

It must have seemed to many during the early summer of 1922 that the latest evil atrocity was competing with innumerable others for the dubious accolade of ultimate barbaric act. Sometimes it was the nature of the violent attack rather than its scale or whether it resulted in a fatality, which distinguished it as a new land-mark in depravity and inhumanity. One of the most gruesome of all murders committed during the conflict was executed on 24 May. Jack O'Hare (30), a Newry-born Catholic who lived at Thompson Street in the Short Strand, had been a store-room porter at the Imperial Hotel in Donegall Street for 11 years. Following increased street tension in the east of the city, his family had phoned a message through to the hotel, advising Mr O'Hare to proceed to his mother's home on the Falls Road. Unfortunately he had left the Imperial ten minutes previously and had caught a tram to the Albert Bridge, where he dismounted to walk down to the Short Strand. A gang which had been loitering on the bridge noted where he was heading and circling him, proceeded to hand out a severe beating. Apparently his assailants had started to move on, but returned when they heard the hapless O'Hare pleading for water. This was the cue for several of them to throw their semi-conscious victim over the bridge and into the Lagan below. They moved away on account of the presence of a police patrol on the bridge, sending a few young girls to confirm that their victim had gone under. Apparently when confirmation of this was relayed to them, a cheer went up. The failure of the security forces to intervene was noted by many in the minority community. The suffering of Mr O'Hare's family did not end there. Over the next five days relatives and friends of the missing man, as well as police, had to face sniping attacks as they endeavoured to locate Mr O'Hare's body.[18]

Just over a week later, another incident occurred involving unprecedented barbarity both in terms of its nature and the subject of attack, although this did not have fatal consequences. A gang called at the house of a doctor in the mainly loyalist Donegall Pass, just south of the city centre at around nine o'clock during the evening of 1 June. His housekeeper, Susan McCormick, a Catholic, was attacked by the gang after she had advised them he was not on the premises. They burst in to the house kicking the hapless housekeeper to the ground. One of the gang proceeded to empty a tin of petrol over her, as another lit a match which ignited the housekeeper's clothing. As the gang made a hasty retreat, their distraught and badly injured victim ran screaming into the street, where she received assistance from horrified neighbours, before being rushed to hospital. This abominable attack on an innocent woman horrified a society which was more accustomed to hearing accounts of such barbarity emanating from reputedly 'uncivilised' societies thousands of miles away from Belfast. Press condemnation was universal, although unionist organs refrained from speculating on the motives behind such an attack, or indeed who the perpetrators might have been. The *Telegraph* described it as 'a deed of unqualified shame', maintaining that those who 'descended to an act so contemptible and cruel should be hunted out of society.'[19]

Another type of attack which horrified the Belfast public was that which singled out groups of workers on account of their religion. Apart from the tram attacks on loyalist workers, specific groups of workers who were targeted at this time included carters and coopers. As in the modern conflict, the direct motivation for such attacks was revenge for an assault on one's own community. Hence on 19 May, in response to killings on a tram the previous day, a nine strong IRA team entered Garrett's cooperage in Little Patrick Street during the mid afternoon, ordering Protestant workers to one side. Four of them were wounded, three fatally. They were William Patterson (35), an ex-soldier from Frazer Street who was shot in the head, Thomas Maxwell (25), of Durham Street, who was shot in the chest and Thomas Boyd (20), of Louisa Street. This blatantly sectarian act indicates the extent of republican desperation in the city. As noted elsewhere, carters were especially vulnerable as they moved across dangerous trouble areas close to the city centre. Three Catholic carters were shot dead whilst they were at work on 20 June, at least two of them by the same attackers. Around lunchtime David French (30), of Pinkerton Street, was riding a horse and cart along a deserted Duncrue Street when he became unaware of two men jumping on the back of his cart. During a struggle Mr French was shot in the back and died in hospital later that evening. In a sad sequel to the attack, a group of Specials saw the petrified horse careering across Duncrue Street. This street was the scene of another murder of a carter, James Tutton (50), later that afternoon. Mr Tutton, from Brookfield Street in the Crumlin Road area, had been driving a cart of rubbish to the dump in that area when he too was shot dead from close range. Just over an hour previously another carter, ex-soldier Charles O'Neill (46), from Plevna Street in the Falls, had been levelling the pitch at Brantwood Football Club in Skegoniel Avenue, when he and a colleague were approached by a large gang who asked his religion. Mr O'Neill was shot dead, though his friend managed to escape.

Certain buildings were – given the context of a strictly religious society in a different era – perceived as being exempt from terror attacks. Whenever such onslaughts did occur, that society expressed its collective horror. As already noticed, this especially applied to churches and schools, but also included those institutions caring for the sick, including victims of the city's street violence. The attack on the Mater Hospital during the late evening of 5 June produced such horror, as well as controversy over culpability for the attack. Following what the authorities maintained was an orchestrated sniping attack from the grounds of the hospital aimed at police across the Crumlin Road, security forces returned fire directly into the Mater Hospital. This sustained attack fortunately resulted in no casualties, but several windows at the hospital were broken, furniture was smashed and both patients and staff were 'nerve-racked by a terrible 40 minute fusillade.'[20] Medical staff instructed their patients to lie on floors during the onslaught. The following morning many of them were still distraught and several patients who did not suffer from serious illnesses decided to discharge themselves.[21]

Not for the first time, differing accounts of the origins of the gunfire and responsibility for the incident were propagated by the various sides. In a report written by the prison governor, S.C. Willis, the following day, the slant was that it was an attack directed at officers in the prison, coming from the hospital grounds. Referring to a statement by one prisoner that he had seen two men hiding in a tree in the hospital grounds at eleven o'clock shortly before the gunfire had erupted, and that another had seen men firing from inside a hospital window, Mr Willis's claim was in stark contrast with that of hospital staff.[22] Deliberately by-passing Craig's administration, the Sister Superior at the Mater wrote to the International Red Cross Society in Geneva, outlining their version of events in what she described as a 'veritable siege', describing the local police as 'easily excited and [they] shoot indiscriminately'.[23] In a statement which clearly illustrates that, even late in the conflict, Catholic community leaders retained a degree of confidence in the even-handedness of the military, if not the police, the Sister Superior suggested that the Catholic population 'desired to be protected by them.'[24] Papers gave considerable coverage to the incident, with the *Irish Independent* suggesting it was 'the lowest infamy yet' and aligning it with the recent arson attack directed towards the Donegall Pass house-keeper, claimed that these attacks illustrated 'savage instincts' which were shared by 'a large number of these uncivilised beings.'[25] The incident was raised in Parliament the following week by Joe Devlin, who complained that Crown forces had fired into the hospital, 'insulting' its patients and staff. He asked if there would be any 'redress for criminal conduct of that character carried out by officers of the Crown?'[26] In his reply, the Colonial Secretary, Winston Churchill insisted that the claims surrounding the incident had been 'very much exaggerated', suggesting it had been an attack on the prison from the Mater which had pre-empted the response of the Specials at the prison.[27]

Police stations in Belfast had proved to be difficult to target, given the heavy security base there. An exception was the attack on Musgrave Street Barracks during the evening of 17/18 May.[28] Although it was recognised as being an audacious, if not foolhardy, attempt to raid the police fortress in central Belfast just after the start of curfew, the northern IRA believed it was necessary if they were to be able to mount an effective campaign in the next few days. Up to 20 volunteers, many of them dressed in police uniform and aided by a 'mole' working at Musgrave Street gained access to the barracks where they held captive a small number of officers for several hours. In the meantime the volunteers, led by Roger McCorley and Seamus Woods, attempted to load rifles and revolvers into sacks and to prepare police vehicles for hijacking. At one point in the evening two officers, Special Constable McKeown and RIC Constable John Collins went for their weapons and both were wounded, Constable Collins fatally.[29] Other police officers on duty elsewhere in the barracks were alerted by the commotion and one of them directed machine-gun fire at the IRA team. The order was given to evacuate the building, leaving behind an arsenal of police weaponry as well as Lancia vehicles. Some of the attackers were seriously injured, and narrowly avoided arrest in their own districts.[30] The loyalist response was a mixture of bemusement and grudging admiration for republican audacity. The *Belfast Telegraph* commented; 'It would appear all the brains, all the audacity, all the enterprise and all the resources are on the side of the rebels.'[31]

'THE FALLS FIREBUGS'

The motives behind the republican movement's decision to diversify their military campaign in the north arguably varied from the stance of the nationalist leadership in Dublin to that of the on-the-ground volunteers on the streets of Belfast.[32] Southern republicans had, of course, utilised the arson tactic in their economic boycott of northern goods, destroying many of those captured products by fire. Therefore, any extension of the technique, such as targeting commercial buildings and industries which symbolised Belfast's 'difference' from the rest of the island, blended well with republican rhetoric. As the Sinn Féin newspaper urged its readers on 17 June:

> The Orangeman will not be won until he is beaten to earth. Every factory destroyed is a blow at the enemy ... [so] we say, go on with the burnings![33]

Whilst those uninvolved in the day-to-day running of the conflict could afford
to look at wider political objectives, those responsible for waging war in the north
had a much shorter term focus. For Belfast republicans, the tactic of arson offered
another way of directly attacking what they saw as the 'godfathers' of loyalist
terror, without running such high risks of inviting a backlash against already
harassed Catholics in the city. Although republicans had periodically torched
buildings since early in the conflict, their targeting of commercial properties
increased in its intensity from the end of March and especially during May and
early June. In a two month period the *Belfast Telegraph* estimated there had been
a 'carefully planned' IRA campaign of arson on between 80 and 90 commercial
properties.[34] The most vicious assault took place in 15 days in May and early June,
when there were at least 41 big fires and half a million pounds of damage to property in the city.[35] These attacks on commercial properties coincided with arson
attacks on Anglo-Irish families across Ulster. The 'Big House' blazes damaged or
destroyed irreplaceable properties including Shane's Castle, near Antrim,
Crebilly Castle near Ballymena, Glenmona House at Cushendun, Kilclief House
at Strangford and Hawethorne Hill near Armagh. Additionally, there were arson
attacks on a number of rail stations and flax mills across rural Ulster.

There was a marked increase in the number of arson attacks during the
weekend of 19 and 21 May.[36] Following at least seven fires the previous day,
including a particularly vicious one on Doran and Company premises at
Donegall Quay, another eleven businesses in the city centre were attacked on 20
May, including a furniture store in Academy Street and a seed merchants in Great
George's Street. Not for the first time would the city's fire department be
stretched, especially as many of their calls proved to be hoaxes. Buildings which
were targeted in the next few days included Ferguson's motor engineering works
in May Street (they conducted business with the security forces), a cleansing
depot in Short Strand and the Carnegie Library on the Falls Road. The most star-
tling outburst of attacks took place on 26 May when there were 13 fires between
eight and eleven o'clock that evening, most of which occurred in the Falls and
Divis Street areas. Castigating the 'Falls firebugs' they considered responsible for
these attacks, the *Belfast Telegraph* suggested that such attacks constituted 'part of
the criminal conspiracy which is going to make the Government of Northern
Ireland impossible and to make life in Belfast intolerable.'[37] Further attacks were
made on commercial property in the city over the next few days. These included
the damaging of a timber-yard in Smithfield, a pawn shop in Cromac Street, and
the destruction of a pub in King Street on 30 May.[38]

During a period when there was a distinct reduction in the number of shoot-ings and street disturbances, arson attacks continued on a regular basis, escalating towards the middle of June. These included fires on business sites in Corporation Street, Alfred Street, Academy Street, May Street and Queen Street, as well as damage done to a hotel in Donegall Square East. At least 8 serious fires were reported in the city during the weekend of 17/18 June, including an incident which shocked Belfast's animal-loving community. This involved the burning to death of twelve horses stabled in premises attached to a coal merchant's targeted by the arsonists near the city centre.[39]

Arson attacks at this time were not restricted to central Belfast. On 13 June a brewery was damaged by fire and a handkerchief factory at Mountpottinger was damaged the following evening when there was also a fire in a Cromac Street draper's shop. A couple of days later a soapworks was damaged in the Newtownards Road and other buildings were severely damaged in York Street and Kent Street. Such attacks requiring the transportation of inflammable materials, firearms and gangs of men on foot, and involving the targeting of buildings within reasonable distance of Catholic districts often in broad daylight, were both ambitious and well organised. Members of the IRA teams would have had specific roles on such missions. Some armed members were responsible for holding up staff on the business premises, whilst other either carried inflammatory materials or actually started the conflagration, (this was often the leader). Another vital group member was the 'lookout', responsible for detecting approaching members of the security forces. Whilst it was apparent to most local observers that such operations constituted a new, distinctive phase in IRA operations, others from outside the city appeared perplexed about the true origins of such attacks. The *Irish Independent* incredulously attached the blame for the arson attacks on loyalist gangs.

> Although the weekend fusillading has not been as bad as usual in Belfast, there is no abatement in the reign of terror carried out by the armed forces of the Belfast Government. Several buildings were set on fire and a considerable amount of property was damaged or destroyed.[40]

The dangers of those involved in countering the potential effects of such attacks were indicated by the injury of a fire officer, after a roof collapsed during a fire which he was attempting to extinguish in Howard Street and by sniper attack on officers attempting to extinguish a fire in a business property in Great Patrick Street on 13 June. The following evening four officers were injured trying to extinguish a fire on business property in Great Victoria Street. What with the combination of coping with a multitude of serious arson attacks and the possibility of being shot at, it was hardly surprising that these were difficult times for fire officers. Sam Jamison, who grew up in a fire station where his father worked, recalled:

> I remember the bad days in 1922. Although for us children there were perks living in the station like feeding the horses in the two stables and having the luxury of electric lighting in the station, my father and his colleagues had a rough time. They were intimidated in the streets, men threatened to burn down the station and when they were out on jobs, their hoses were often cut. Nelson Street, which was close to the station, was a lively area and we sometimes had gunfire directed at the station. I remember bullets bouncing off the steel framework in Corry's timber yard in Garmoyle Street. It got so bad that my father and his men refused to go out on a call one night until the gunfire had subsided.

Although the chief focus of the IRA arson campaign was clearly business premises in the city centre, non-commercial buildings were also targeted. One of the most controversial attacks was on the Model School in Divis Street on 26 May. This school, the majority of whose pupils were Protestant, had been attacked on two previous occasions and the arsonists were clearly bent on its destruction. At around 8 p.m. the first incendiary device exploded. Over the next three hours seven bombs with time fuses set off four explosions at 15-minute intervals, which resulted in the school being burned to the ground.[41] John Parkinson, 15 at the time, recalls the night his school burned down:

> I was at home in Distillery Street when I heard somebody outside shouting, 'Parkie, I think your school's on fire!' I rushed outside and saw smoke billowing from a building beside the great spires of St Peter's Catholic Cathedral. It had to be my school but my parents wouldn't let me explore. However, the next morning I ventured towards the school and saw its charred remains. Police were guarding the building but there was some jeering when the Divis Street boys saw us. I wasn't that surprised because there had been two previous fires at the school and we had been stoned on our way to school a few times. As this happened a few weeks before the end of the school year and the school was due to reopen on the Cliftonville Road, quite a bit away from where we lived, my father agreed to me starting work.

Places of sorely-needed need entertainment were also subject to republican arson attacks. Several picture-houses were damaged or destroyed during this period. Some of these, including the Imperial Picture-house, the Gaiety Picture Theatre in North Street and a cinema in Smithfield, were situated in the city centre, but others, including the West Belfast Picture House, the Tivoli, and Clonard cinemas, were west of the city centre. The perpetrators of such attacks were not deterred by initially unsuccessful attacks. Thus, they returned to the Tivoli picture-house in Christian Place on 21 May, the day after a botched operation and ensured that this time it was 'completely gutted'.[42] Attacks such as these indicate the sheer desperation of republicans who were prepared to countenance the wrath of many in their own community. This was partly on account of the difficulties they were experiencing in sustaining their commercial arson campaign in the city centre. Popular as this was, especially in terms of its propaganda value for external audiences, attacking commercial properties in busy city streets during daylight was fraught with danger. Indeed, at least one attack was botched, resulting in the loss of a volunteer. Republicans in the Markets area had been particularly active during the arson campaign and despite the arrest of three of its members a couple of days previously, a gang entered the premises of an oil merchants in Gloucester Street in the Cromac area on 20th June. The team intended to set fire to the premises, but as they were holding the staff at gunpoint a female employee threw a weight through a window, alerting a passing RUC patrol. Most of the would-be incendiaries fled, but section leader William Thornton (22), a former British soldier, persisted in his quest to set fire to the premises. Mr Thornton, of Catherine Street, was shot dead, as he drew his gun on the patrol.[43]

POLITICAL ASSASSINATION

With the odd celebrated exception, political assassination had not been a common characteristic of Irish conflict.[44] Northern republicans at this time were less motivated by class dogma or sectarian hatred and their chief targets were men in uniform blocking their political cause or harassing their beleaguered people. Thus casualties tended to be mainly working class people and police personnel. As the situation in the north worsened and the plight of Catholics became perilous, increasingly desperate republicans commenced targeting leading unionist politicians. Both victims of assassination were undoubtedly selected because of their high profile opposition to a united Ireland and also on account of the virulence of their speeches. This transition from targeting industrial workers on city trams and policemen patrolling Belfast's streets is indicative of the sheer desperation of on-the-ground volunteers rather than constituting evidence of either a stepping up of their military campaign or a fundamental shift in republican policy. In an atmosphere of extreme political tension and corresponding security caution, leading political figures in the city were less likely to be realistic targets for assassination, but constituency representatives such as William Twaddell and Westminster-based Unionists such as Henry Wilson, were less likely to have enjoyed round-the-clock protection and were consequently highly vulnerable to such attacks.

William Twaddell, MP for Woodvale in the northern Parliament and a Shankill councillor had been, for a considerable period, a vociferous opponent of Sinn Féin.[45] In what appears to have been a carefully planned attack, the unaccompanied Twaddell was walking through city centre streets at the start of a new working week on 22 May. He had gone down Royal Avenue and was proceeding along Garfield Street to his shop in North Street when he was attacked by IRA gunmen. The exact circumstances of this shooting were far from clear and reports of the unionist politician's last moments at his inquest on 30 June shrouded his death in even greater mystery. At this it was contended that Twaddell had only been shot after he had gone to the aid of a woman passer-by who had been shot in the arm. This would suggest that his assassins (estimates of the size of the gang varied from two to eight) had fired prematurely, but the Unionist M.P. was struck by up to six bullets and was fatally wounded, falling outside a café by the Artisans' Hall in Garfield Street, before being despatched to hospital with the injured woman. Their assailants ran down Royal Avenue and North Street, with one report suggesting that the murder weapon had been passed on to a female sympathiser. The security forces were quick to arrive at the scene and passers-by were rigorously searched. Indeed, for a considerable part of the day large parts of central Belfast were cordoned off and a landmine was discovered in a cable manhole in Arthur Square.

The unionist press that evening and for days afterwards barely concealed its anger. The *Telegraph* described the attack as 'murder most foul', claiming that the crime marked 'a new stage in the criminal campaign which Sinn Féin had been conducting.'[46] Certainly the killing of a well-known Belfast politician shocked a community unfamiliar with political assassination. The *Daily Chronicle* aptly described such an attack as constituting 'a fresh shock to a city cruelly accustomed to outrage'.[47] The *Irish News*, whilst denouncing such an outrage, condemned the premier's call for 'swift retribution', maintaining that if such 'just retribution [had] been legally exacted when the first victim fell' it would have been 'all but certain' that 'a welter of crime and bloodshed would have been averted.'[48] Sir James Craig's immediate response was a call for 'restraint' from the loyalist community, whilst at the same time reassuring them that his administration would now implement security measures which would be 'sufficiently comprehensive to meet any event that may arise.'[49] The Prime Minister paid fulsome tribute to his colleague the following day in Parliament, saying he was 'true to the honourable traditions of an Ulsterman, true to the Empire'.[50]

Grieving fellow-parliamentarians passed a resolution expressing their 'detestation of the cowardly assassination of our esteemed colleague Mr Twaddell and tenders deepest sympathy to his widow in the sorrow that has befallen her'.[51] Twaddell's funeral procession a few days later brought the city's central streets to a standstill. Craig showed considerable personal courage in walking along the whole funeral route. The *Belfast Telegraph's* emotive report summed up the feeling of many in the Protestant community:

> Few events have so stirred to the depths of an outraged community as the appalling horror which encompassed the end of this active and popular public leader, who, without a single personal enemy, suffered the venom of the assassin simply because of what he represents.[52]

The second attack is more likely to have been commissioned by republican leaders in Dublin, though there was a perception at the time that, far from being given orders to execute this attack, the assassins operated as a 'freelance' team. The target for this attack was encountered far away from Belfast's turbulent streets. Sir Henry Wilson, a distinguished military figure and recently-elected Unionist MP, had been appointed as a military advisor to the northern administration and was instrumental in recommending strong measures to be taken against the IRA. Returning from unveiling a war memorial at Liverpool Street Station, Wilson was approached by two Irish republicans near his home at Eaton Place, in London's fashionable Belgravia, and despite his attempts to ward off his assailants with a walking-stick, was shot dead. The gunmen, Reginald Dunne and Joseph O'Sullivan, had both served during the war, with O'Sullivan losing a leg at Ypres. Indeed, it was his disability which had resulted in their eventual capture following a bizarre chase during which they commandeered an open-topped Brougham carriage and wounded two policemen. Both men were tried at the Old Bailey where they received the death penalty on 18 July.[53]

Although their public fury was directed at the IRA, the unionist regime was far from happy about the London administration's failure to act on intelligence which their representatives had passed on to the Home Office authorities in Whitehall. Clearly such bad liaison was a factor in explaining the success of this republican assassination. Writing to Dawson Bates, General Solly-Flood complained:

> Over a fortnight ago, one of our Agents in London reported certain information in regard to certain addresses in London from which the activities of the IRB and other organisations emanated ... The Home Office authorities in London apparently failed to appreciate the danger of the movement [of republican personnel] and refused to accede to our request. Until the Imperial Government are brought to realise that the IRB is the driving power behind the whole of the Sinn Féin machinery ... there appears to be no real hope of a satisfactory ending to the terrible happenings which are now taking place.[54]

It was likely that the assassination of Wilson had been ordered by Collins who was conscious of the latter's virulently anti Sinn Féin and Treaty stance, but it certainly backfired on him. British spokesmen unwittingly assumed that it was the action of the anti-Treaty faction of the IRA and especially the Four Courts garrison led by Rory O'Connor, with Churchill threatening to intervene unless Collins and the Free State administration took action against the garrison. Within a week, Free State forces using heavy artillery borrowed from the British army, opened fire on the Four Courts, precipitating the Civil War. The impact of this assassination on Ulster loyalists, in the light of the Twaddell murder a few weeks previously, cannot be understated. The *Belfast Telegraph* described Sir Henry as 'Ulster's Greatest Martyr' who had been 'designated for assassination' by sections of the nationalist press and Sinn Féin on account of his opposition to the British Government's Irish policy.[55] A few days later, the *Newsletter* stressed the personal loss as Sir Henry had been 'ours by sympathy and ours by service' and that his killing was 'an epochal crime' which stood out 'stark in its fiendishness, marking for all time the criminality of the Sinn Féin movement.'[56]

Journalists and politicians outside also acknowledged the significance of the loss of Sir Henry. The *Daily Mail* wrote that 'not only Ulster [but] Great Britain and the Empire lament the death of this great and noble man' and even the *Irish Independent* described his shooting as 'a horrifying tragedy.'[57] However, Eamon de Valera's press statement which followed the assassination of Sir Henry, reminded its audience both of the suffering of the nationalist minority in Northern Ireland and Sir Henry's influential role in events there:

> The killing of any human being is an awful act, but as awful when the victim is the humble worker or peasant, unknown outside his own immediate neighbourhood, as when the victim is placed in the seats of the mighty and is known in every corner of the earth ... I know that life has been made a hell for the nationalist minority in Belfast ... I do not approve [the murder] but I must not pretend to misunderstand.[58]

'CORNER BOYS WITH GUNS'

As with later loyalist paramilitary activity the exact composition of such groups and the overall responsibility for the co-ordination of their campaign was far from clear. This was largely due to the fragmented nature of loyalist pressure groups and the tendency for overlapping between the groups and even the police. There were at this time several groups ranging from the UVF, which was more interested in its members being formally recognised, preferably within the framework of a special constabulary force and a plethora of smaller, quasi-secretive groups such as the Imperial Guards, the Cromwell Clubs and the Ulster Ex-Servicemen's Association, which were liable to adopt covert and illegal action against their opponents.[59] Unlike nationalist paramilitaries, loyalists mainly operated along freelance lines and although there was clearly some co-ordination of targets and attacks, several killings and incidents owe more to spur-of-the-moment sectarian hatred and spontaneity, aided by the wealth of weaponry, than it did to a centrally orchestrated campaign.[60]

Perhaps the group most synonymous with loyalist violence during this period was the Ulster Protestant Association (UPA), which first gained the attention of the security forces during the autumn of 1920, having grown out of the BPA which had been active during the shipyard expulsions. A police report written by a senior officer in east Belfast to Dawson Bates, Minister of

Home Affairs, in February 1923, throws some light on the structure of this organisation and the fanaticism of its members. During the conflict the UPA was believed to have operated four branches in Ballymacarrett, York Street, Shankill and the Ormeau area. According to Detective Inspector R.R. Spears, the organisation was composed of 'well-disposed citizens for the protection of Protestants and Loyalists against Sinn Féin aggression'.[61] Rather more ominous was the type of recruit attracted to the UPA. Spears noted:

> Before it had been long in existence this organisation appears to have attracted to itself a large number of the lowest and least desirable of the Protestant hooligan element … The whole aim and object of the club [is] simply the extermination of Catholics by any and every means.[62]

The east Belfast branch of the club met every Thursday evening, from 7:30 p.m. to just before the start of curfew, in the top room of Hastings' public house at Scotch Row on the Newtownards Road. It had a membership of around 150, about a third of who were considered to be active. Details about the execution of UPA operations are patchy, but internal discipline was exceptionally tight, as was the organisation's grip over the local community. Clearly some system of tracking local nationalists was in operation, with police discovering names and addresses in books and cryptic language was used in internal memos depicting weaponry. Although guns were readily available and did not need to be purchased or stolen, the UPA actively collected contributions in many areas of east Belfast.[63] As in the 1970s, loyalist paramilitaries used their powers of persuasion to extract money. Spears wrote:

> Funds for the club [UPA] were obtained at the point of a gun … Failure to subscribe entailed receipt of a threatening letter and a subsequent visit and intimidation by armed men.[64]

Similar tactics were utilised to ensure that internal discipline was maintained. Punishment was meted out to miscreants or suspected informers on a 'flogging horse', using a 'cat of nine tails.' Such 'kangaroo' courts meted out punishment to suggested informers or miscreants within their own ranks.

The exact scale of UPA operations is difficult to assess. Whilst it would be disingenuous to suggest they were behind most of the attacks attributed to loyalists during the conflict, it can be surmised that they were involved in a

considerable number.[65] As nationalist critics of Craig's administration repeatedly pointed out, the government was slow to react to such a threat, despite
their subsequent admission that they had been aware of UPA activity from an
early phase of the conflict. Why was this so? It would be wrong to conclude that
senior police chiefs approved of such activities or actively colluded with loyalist
gunmen. Indeed, Spears pointed out that the police had been 'greatly hampered
by the fact that the rough element on the Protestant side entered thoroughly
into the disturbances, met murder with murder and adopted in many respects
the tactics of the rebel gunmen.'[66] Yet the authorities' response to the threat of
these loyalist terror gangs seemed to many to be half-hearted and belated in its
nature. Those with responsibility for maintaining order pointed out that their
chief priority had to be countering the external threat posed by 'rebel' gunmen.
Once this was removed, the authorities could turn their attention to loyalist
terror. Whilst this does not justify Craig's initial lethargy to the perpetrators of
the majority of sectarian attacks in Belfast, there is evidence to suggest that both
the attitude of the northern administration and public opinion in the Province
stiffened towards loyalist activists once the republican threat had been snuffed
out. Thus, although the initial swoop on terror suspects had harvested a nearly
exclusive Catholic net, several leaders of the UPA were interned or imprisoned
as the IRA's campaign petered out.

One of the early arrests involved Robert Simpson, chairman of the UPA, on
27 March 1922. Following a tip-off, Spears led a police raid on Simpson's home
in the Beersbridge area. As the police forced entry, Simpson, described by
Spears as 'a corner-boy who never did any work', passed a packet containing 23
rounds of ammunition to his mother who promptly tossed it into the fire.[67]
Although the UPA leader was to receive a custodial sentence (11 months 'hard
labour'), his removal from the streets did not provoke an immediate onslaught
directed against loyalist terrorists. Indeed, persuaded by General Solly-Flood
that some of the more reliable elements of the UPA might be suitable recruits
for the Special Constabulary, Craig entrusted his Chief Whip, Captain Herbert
Dixon, to liaise with the group early in June 1922 so that some of their ranks
might join the Specials and consequently the behaviour of the wider group
might be regulated in a more effective manner. Predictably these negotiations
broke down and a further spate of loyalist killings broke out in September,
prompting Bates to be more proactive in his treatment of suspected UPA
members. The first of a series of internment orders for four loyalists who 'had
regarded themselves as immune to further interference' was executed on 5

November.[68] Inside six weeks, another dozen men had been interned and several others jailed for firearm offences. The organisation broke up in February 1923. Patrick Buckland's assertion that there can be 'no denying that this [removal of the UPA threat] could have been achieved earlier and lives saved had the government been willing to use its powers as fully against loyalists as it [did] against nationalists' is hard to refute.[69] However, given Craig's insistence that the central problem facing the Belfast community was the threat posed by Sinn Féin, it was perhaps inevitable that he would turn his attention to dealing with counter-terrorism once the problems posed by the IRA had eroded.

Inevitably, the activists in both communities became known both to police and many within the locality, who knew of them either on account of a reputation based on rumour or because they had seen them in action firing around street corners. Some of the loyalist marksmen warranted a fearsome reputation, not only in bordering Catholic areas, but also with their co-religionists. Eddie Steele and John Parkinson remember seeing loyalist gunmen in action on the unionist side of the Grosvenor Road. They recalled:

> We used to stand at a distance and see these fellows, usually with revolvers, firing across into Cullingtree Road. Sometimes, when they had the bravado, they would cross the road and fire straight into the Catholic streets. They made no attempt to cover their faces and the smoke was still coming from their weapons as they ran past us and into safe houses. We knew some of them by reputation, including the Guiney brothers, but we didn't pay a lot of attention to them. They were corner boys with guns . . .

Many members of the UPA and similar groups had criminal records and a raw hatred of Catholics. Perhaps the most infamous loyalist gunman was Alexander Robinson from York Street. 'Buck Alec' as he was known, barely 20 at the time, was acknowledged by police as 'a dangerous gunman and leader of a murderous gang'. Though based in the area around Andrew Street and described in the press as 'the Dockland bomber and gunman', Robinson was engaged in 'freelance' terror, involving himself in shootings and bombings across the city. A colourful character, Robinson's infamy as a killer of Catholics was unsurpassed and despite a criminal record, managed to serve as a 'C' Special, before being interned in November 1922.[70] Another leading north Belfast UPA man was 'Big Davy' Duncan, an ex-Guardsman, who was also highly active on his York Street patch.[71] Other UPA men well known to the authorities included 'Snatch'

McCracken, George Scott, the UPA leader on the Shankill, Robert Moore and east Belfast gunmen Joseph Arthurs, Frederick Pollock, Thomas Pentland and Robert Simpson.[72]

'A FATALISTIC COMPLACENCY'

Dispute over the relative degree of culpability peaked along with the scale of violence during this time. Rival organs condemned the actions of violent men in a ritualistic manner but illustrated selective amnesia over who was responsible and which acts should be featured in depth. The unionist press criticised both southern and English papers for failing to detect nationalist involvement in several attacks, castigating the pro-unity *Daily News* for its suggestion that Protestants were responsible for 90% of the deaths in Ulster.[73] Some unionist papers even suggested that the blame for the 'deplorable' state of Belfast rested 'exclusively' on Sinn Féin which was responsible for attempting to overthrow the northern administration by 'murder and fire-raising'. The conclusion was that they were 'responsible for all the violent deaths, whether … perpetrated by themselves or provoked by them.'[74] A constant theme of unionist leading articles was the 'war' against Protestants all over the Irish island and to inform the British public about 'the systematic persecution' of Protestants in the south and west of Ireland, claiming that 'not since the Rebellion of 1641 have the minority been in greater danger.' In the same article, the *Belfast Telegraph* claimed that the northern 'war' was pointless, as the Belfast administration would 'never be cowed by the incendiary and the murderer' as they were 'made of sterner stuff' and realised there was 'a widespread conspiracy to make life and government impossible and that it has to be crushed.'[75] However, loyalist observers also turned their critical eye, if not their scorn, on their own political leadership. Noting that the previous week had been 'the worst the citizens of Belfast have experienced', the *Belfast Newsletter* called out for 'more drastic measures of suppression' to be taken against 'the assassin, the incendiary and the armed bandit' who had been allowed to 'prey on the city' with relative 'impunity'.[76]

The nationalist press, both north and south of the new border, was also inclined to be self-righteous and sweeping in their condemnation of opponents. In one unqualified statement they maintained that 'authentic records extending over 100 years prove that on no occasion whatever did the Catholic minority begin, or provoke, the "riots" and scenes of bloodshed and destruction that have made the city's name a byword throughout the world.'[77] Ignoring the bloody scenes which had occurred in their own capital, the *Irish Independent* asked of the Belfast administration:

> The streets of their capital have become a shambles; the homes of their citizens are the mark for the sniper. Is the bullet to become the normal arbiter in Belfast? Are death and tragedy to become the daily lot of its people?[78]

Nationalist indignation at the lack of governmental intervention to calm the situation in Belfast, intensified during this period. The *Irish Independent*, under the headline, 'New Armenia-Belfast Pogrom goes on', informed its readers early in June that ongoing events in the city were part of 'a plan for the extermination' of Catholics there and lamented that 'not the slightest effort' had been made to trace the culprits.[79] Much of the coverage of such papers concentrated on describing the unique plight of people in Catholic communities. Gunfire, bombing and arson attacks could trap people within their own immediate areas for several hours. Such was the case on the Falls Road during the evening of 24 May when three people were killed and over twenty injured on the Falls Road. The *Irish News* reported:

> At times the firing, especially in the upper portion of the Falls Road, was of unprecedented intensity, and the residents were in a state of nerve-wrecking terror. Hundreds of people were unable to reach home, while others who were on the Falls Road, and who had to make their way city-wards, were unable to do so. The residents of the Falls Road were the greatest sufferers from the activities of the gunmen, and for upwards of three hours a terrible bombardment of houses was maintained. A couple of large concerns were set on fire on the road, while a tram car was also set alight, and was practically gutted.[80]

Within a week, west Belfast was to experience another 'tornado'. On this occasion machine-guns, rifles and revolvers were used and 'entire blocks of dwelling-houses were burned to the ground.' The *Irish News* report proceeded:

> On the Peters Hill side of Millfield mobs assembled from the Shankill and Old Lodge Roads, and, seizing opportunities, bore down with

savage ferocity upon streets occupied solely by Catholics. Supported on each flank by bodies of men well equipped with arms and ammunition, they experienced little difficulty in reaching their objectives. Many members of the mobs carried biscuit tins containing petrol, which was used upon the exterior and the interior of each house.[81]

Even when the violence was at its peak, the local press endeavoured to cheer up their readers by making light of serious situations. The *Belfast Telegraph* informed its readers that a southern English firm expressed interest in placing an appeal in its advertising section about selling 'a number of steel body shield bullet proof vests [which] might sell in your city'.[82] The following day a report in the same paper told of how a medical student had managed to evade attackers near Dunville Park, sprinting into the nearby Royal Victoria Hospital, observing that his assailants 'couldn't run for nuts!'[83]

Several British papers, especially the *Manchester Guardian*, *Daily News* and the *Daily Herald* were strongly critical of the northern administration's handling of events. The *Daily Herald* had an intriguing slant on the inter-relationship between border violence and disturbances in Belfast, suggesting that the former was the 'direct sequel' of the latter, maintaining there could be 'no settlement and no peace until there [is] in Belfast a Government which will stand up to the Orange lodges.'[84] Guarded support for the Unionist position came from familiar sources. The *Times*, in two leading articles, reiterated its belief that the Treaty was 'the inviolable charter of Ulster's right', reminding nationalists that a republic was 'impossible' and that Britain would 'tolerate no aggression upon the established liberties of N. Ireland.'[85] Also, Stephen Gwynn, writing in the *Observer*, warned northern Catholics about the threat from the south of 'subsidised acts of brigandage' and on the subject of the new Belfast Parliament asked 'are they more likely to change it to their liking by a refusal to touch it, recognise or obey it, or by co-operating in its work?'[86]

The fury of the nationalist press and the despair of English and indeed, many unionist observers, was perfectly understandable. At a time when violent incidents were comparatively rare elsewhere in Ireland, disturbances proceeded unabated in Belfast, escalating on an almost daily basis, despite the increased security presence and emergency powers.[87] However, they largely represented the death-throws of militant republicanism in the city – precipitated by both the gradual impact of the emergency legislation and the declining morale of IRA volunteers, and accelerated by the onset, within weeks, of civil war – which also reduced the need for loyalist retribution. Yet the horrors of the early summer of 1922 should not be deprecated. At no other time during the conflict had such a wide range of terrorist activity – the tracking, beating and shooting of victims, arson attacks on commercial buildings, the assassination of political leaders, tram bombings, attacks on hospitals and police stations – coincided, producing a singularly high death toll. Indeed, the situation in the city had deteriorated so greatly that its citizens were fast becoming oblivious to the brutality occurring all around them. Matthew Anderson noted in the *Manchester Guardian*:

> The familiar clang of fire engines accompanied city people to their offices this morning, but only the stranger's head turned round to watch the furious progress of the engines. A fire engine in a Belfast main road is as common a sight as a milk cart in a Manchester suburb. Its presence is accepted with a fatalistic complacency which is not a little bewildering in a western business city.[88]

Chapter 18

Return to normality

HONEST BROKERS?

Several factors were to result in the general subsidence in the levels of violence during the summer of 1922. These included the start of the civil war in the rest of Ireland which divided the republican movement and left northern nationalists increasingly isolated, as well as the increasing success of the security forces in dealing with civil unrest (largely a consequence of the Specials Power legislation). A number of questions will be asked in this section. How did the political and security problems encountered by both London and Belfast administrations determine their responses to the ongoing violence on Belfast's streets, especially during the summer of 1922? What differences were there in attitudes and proposed measures to stem such violence, by both of these administrations? What behind the scene initiatives involving community leaders, senior British politicians and civil servants were conducted by Westminster in order to defuse tension on the streets of Belfast? What challenges did the Unionist government face during this difficult time and what range of measures did they consider using to deal with the unprecedented problems they were encountering on Belfast's streets? How did these come to a head in the summer of 1922?

The ultimate responsibility for the governance and maintenance of order in the north of Ireland for most of this period, lay in the hands of the Westminster administration. British attitudes to Ireland had, of course, shifted substantially since the Home Rule agitation before the start of the Great War. As a result of the 1916 Rising and the changing political landscape in most of Ireland, the British government clearly recognised that different political provision would be necessary for the two distinctive parts of Ireland in the post-war world. An altered political climate in Britain – where a coalition government was less susceptible to the temptations engendered by a culture of political expediency in pre-war Britain, the impact of the self-determination principle at Versailles and a growing conviction amongst British politicians and public that the time had come for political leaders to finally address the long term nature of relationships between the two islands – all mitigated against the unionist position, undoubtedly making them less likely to compromise. Lloyd George believed he had devised a compromise settlement of the Irish question. Political compromise was the essence of the Government of Ireland Act, the Treaty and pact negotiations. However, the furious and bloody nature of the Anglo-Irish war and its demands on British military resources had resulted in the shelving of the northern question. Thus, until at least two months after the Treaty, British politicians were content to delegate security responsibility to locals, content in the knowledge that these 'loyal citizens' would be only too willing to deal with the common enemy, namely the IRA.

Having theoretically at least, delegated substantial security and political responsibility to the local administration, Britain thought it prudent to assume an honest broker's role in the north, especially from 1922. As the number of attacks on Catholics increased, Liberal members of the British Cabinet became increasingly concerned about the about the Belfast administration's handling of the security situation.[1] In a letter to Churchill in June 1922, Lloyd George underlined the dichotomy between the high number of Catholic fatalities in Belfast and their significantly lower population concentration, concluding that 'our Ulster case is not a very good one'.[2] Early in June Churchill and Lloyd George tried to persuade Craig to hold a judicial enquiry into the Belfast disturbances, but Craig only agreed to the principle of a private one on the grounds that a public enquiry would only exacerbate the situation. These and other statements, especially in the wake of the Weaver Street and Kinnaird Terrace atrocities, illustrate the 'guilt' experienced by many British politicians as the killing ratio became more one-sided during 1922. Arguably, London might have put more pressure on the Belfast regime to produce more arrests and to react in a more obviously proactive way to the increase in violence. Also, they might have paid more attention to the pleas from the Catholic community for military reinforcements to be used instead of the Special Constabulary on Belfast's streets. Expensive as it might have been, a higher profile military presence, sharper liaison between the local police and the army, and a smoother transition of responsibility from London to Belfast would have alleviated the situation in the north and possibly led to a marked reduction in the level of violence.[3] Politically, more effective channels of communication might have been developed between the government and the representatives of constitutional nationalism and more heed might have been taken of the concerns of the northern Catholic clergy.[4]

British politicians believed that sending senior civil servants to act in an advisory role to the northern administration would constitute evidence of them taking a responsible 'broker's' role in the north. Two such advisory or inspectorial appointments were made during the conflict, one towards its beginning and the other near its conclusion. Sir Ernest Clark had been appointed as Assistant Under-Secretary to Irish Chief Secretary Sir Hamar Greenwood in mid-September 1920.[5] Clark's main brief was to address the issue of the recently expelled Catholic workers. In this task, Clark attempted a prognosis of the origins of the conflict, concluding that such expulsions constituted an emotional reaction to the spread of the IRA terror campaign into Ulster and that there was no evidence of a Craig-led conspiracy to create a systematic pogrom of Catholics. Like other intermediaries and, indeed, political leaders, Clark was overwhelmed by the effects of spiralling violence and gradually assumed the unionist position that a 'security' initiative should be at the centre of a solution to the Province's problems. Therefore, he believed that the establishment of a Special Constabulary would not only reassure loyalists but would also remove the likelihood of further industrial expulsions. Although Clark's main brief was the issue of industrial expulsions, his appointment was important in that it helped pave the way for a smooth administrative transition from Dublin Castle to Belfast.

Another official who would broadly concur with the unionist interpretation of events visited Belfast for a ten day period towards the end of June 1922 to report on the collapse of the March Pact and to assess whether a full public enquiry should be conducted to ascertain the reasons behind the collapse of political initiatives and the eruption of communal violence. Sir Stephen Tallents' recommendations were staunchly unionist and anti-republican in their nature. Referring to the failure of the March Pact, Tallents suggested that it was unsuccessful 'chiefly because it dealt with minor issues before the major issues which really govern them were decided'. 'Currents', such as the unpredictable future of the provisional Government in the south; the Boundary Commission clause in the Treaty; the 'organised conspiracy of violence' in the north – which was, in Tallents' view, 'in substantial measure an undercover operation planned with the knowledge and support of Collins himself'; and the failure of the northern minority to acknowledge Craig's administration', resulted in the 'the light anchors of the March agreement (being) soon swept away'.[6] Although critical of the Special Constabulary and certain members of the unionist administration, (notably Bates), Tallents' interpretation of the causes of violence and his apparent dismissal of anti-Catholic outrages were generally shared by unionists. Consequently his conclusion that there was no need to hold a judicial enquiry into northern violence surprised few. He justified this decision by claiming it would 'lead to a revival of propaganda about matters that are best forgotten. Inadvertently it would encourage the Northern Catholics in their refusal to recognise the Northern Government.'[7]

Clearly Lloyd George's appointment of two senior and respected government observers did not produce the fresh insight into the problems of the north which he and his colleagues had anticipated. However, it did not stop the British Government exploring other diplomatic channels with representatives of the northern Catholic minority. Therefore, meetings involving senior Cabinet members, including Sir James Craig and leading members of Belfast's business community, including Raymond Burke and Hugh Dougal, were indicative of creative but ultimately doomed attempts to maximise Catholic support for the new administration. Burke and Dougal were involved in discussions during April 1922 with Craig and his officials over the possibility of recruiting Catholic Specials, who would have initially operated in the city's Markets area. Early in June they met with Churchill to discuss ways in which Craig's regime might entice sections of Belfast's minority community into acknowledging the legitimacy of the new administration. Whilst the motives of businessmen like Burke and Dougal might have been genuine, their readiness to recognise and do business with Craig's government was far from typical of the response of the wider Catholic community in the city, which was more concerned about evictions from workplace and home.[8]

Unionists were not, of course, totally in control of their own destiny. As noted earlier, they had been persuaded into compromising on at least the nature of their political governance into accepting the Government of Ireland legislation. The amount of political pressure placed on the Unionist leadership would have added considerably to loyalist unease in Belfast. Craig was under pressure not only from his political opponents, Sinn Féin and Devlin's nationalist group, but also from the IRA's 3rd Northern Division increasingly encroaching on his administration's territory; the British Cabinet in London; from a foreign audience ranging from governments and heads of state to concerned pressure groups, and even from within his own political party.[9] Whilst Craig deftly handled criticism from fellow Unionists, ensuring it did not lead to a leadership challenge like some of his successors were obliged to encounter, the pressure he had to endure from several of his parliamentary colleagues and from a range of loyalist groups, was considerable. One instance of grassroots opinion losing patience with a previously unassailable leader was the Ulster Protestant Voters Defence Association's complaint to Craig on 22 June 1922, notifying him of a resolution passed by their group following the killing of four Protestants at Altnaveigh in County Armagh. In it they called upon 'the men who were elected on 24 May 1921, to throw aside the lackadaisical mantle that seems at present to enshroud them, otherwise we will have no alternative but to take immediate steps to protect our own great protestant community – steps that IRA assassins shall not dare to despise, and politicians shall not presume to ignore.'[10]

Within the Belfast Parliament Craig had to encounter 'the usual little gang of Coote, Lynn and McGuffin'.[11] William Coote's criticisms of Craig's administration were numerous, ranging from his concern over government expenditure and its relationships with London to its handling of Sinn Féin. A parliamentary speech in September 1921 was especially critical of the government's security policy. Referring to recent deaths in Belfast, Coote argued:

> We had peace until this truce began, and until gunmen came down in pairs and dozens – they are in the city today. We know they are there. There is a camp at Ballykinlar, about four hundred strong, with the Sinn Féin flag flying there. Is the Prime Minister aware of this? Has he made any protest to the Dublin authorities? I charge the Government with weakness. I charge the Government with over-confidence in the British Government. I believe we are being made the catspaw of the British Government.[12]

Although Craig's critics only constituted a small proportion of his parliamentary party and didn't pose a serious challenge to his leadership, their presence was of considerable nuisance value and probably explains his occasional bellicose statements in the northern Parliament and in correspondence with British politicians. Writing to Austen Chamberlain about this time, Craig reminded his external audience how unionists might be tempted into adopting the strongarm tactics of their opponents:

> Loyalists may declare independence on their own behalf, seize the Customs and other Government Departments and set up an authority of their own. Many already believe that violence is the only language understood by Mr Lloyd George and his Ministers.[13]

As the conflict deepened, Unionists gained a growing degree of day-to-day control over security in the province, and were therefore, increasingly liable to charges of culpability, on account of excessive police reaction and a low number of terrorist prosecutions. As they assumed more responsibility for policing, so did voices of opposition increase in their volume at the one-dimensional nature and low success rate of their response. Despite the validity of such claims they ignored Sir James Craig's fear that internal pressure would result in his Cabinet having to introduce even more draconian measures. These included martial law, the proclamation of organisations like Sinn Féin and the IRA, and the death penalty for terror crimes. Many advisors, including local magistrates, encouraged Craig and his Cabinet to introduce martial law for a trial period, but the latter were reluctant to do so, largely because it was felt it might have reflected badly on their capacity to manage their own security operations.[14] A committee of magistrates informed Craig on 16 June 1922 that 'a considerable majority' of their group supported martial law as 'the only method of bringing about peace and the abolition of terrorism' and complained that their feelings had been ignored by Bates and the security forces.[15] Also around this time, Solly-Flood's proposal regarding the proscription of certain societies did not warrant much backing amongst the Cabinet and it was decided not to proceed with this suggestion 'unless the Minister for Home Affairs found there was special reason to do so.'[16] The Cabinet also deferred on Solly-Flood's recommendation for investigating the death penalty 'in all cases of persons found carrying firearms' and his request the establishment of a special court to deal with such cases.[17]

Despite the rejection of these proposed measures, a number of other extreme proposals, including curfew and Special Powers legislation (specifically that relating to internment) were introduced. Curfew restrictions had been introduced early in the conflict and there were variations both in terms of the restricted hours and the specified locations for curfew, depending on the scale of violence in a particular area at a particular time.[18] Many groups, particularly business institutions and places of entertainment, had concerns over the length of curfew restrictions. Groups as disparate as the Belfast Philharmonic Society and the city's branch of the British Empire Union joined in requesting the delaying of curfew by an hour (for it to start at 11:30, rather than 10:30 p.m.).[19] Another casualty of the curfew was the tram service which tended to stop running from the city centre shortly after 9 p.m. This resulted in huge financial losses for the Corporation (an estimated £1,200 a week) and a subsequent decision to allow trams to run until ten in the evenings.[20]

How culpable was Craig's administration for the security disaster which unfolded, particularly during the first half of 1922? On the surface, their response was, to a greater or lesser degree, partisan, reactive and piecemeal, without there being evidence of a wider plan. Although loyalists would eventually be interned, the vast majority of internees rounded up in May 1922 were nationalists and though some loyalist terrorists were later apprehended, Catholics were clearly prioritised as the chief targets for such draconian action. Many critics argued that the paucity of arrests and prosecutions illustrated the unionist government's lethargic approach and even when Craig offered financial rewards for information leading to the conviction of those responsible, many felt it was a case of too little, too late.[21] It was the failure to make inroads in the war against terrorism and a tendency to focus on the threat from outside rather than the more stark one at the epicentre of their new state, which many could not comprehend. However, this reluctance or inability to deal with those individuals or organisations responsible for many of the attacks did not mean that unionism's leaders were necessarily in collusion with the godfathers of terror. Nor did the draconian nature of the Special Powers legislation equate with the more drastic emergency measures instigated in the south by a government acting against its erstwhile colleagues. Also, the lack of progress on the security front was not aided by the hostility of the Catholic Church to the new administration and the active role taken by Sinn Féin and the IRA both inside and outside the N Ireland boundaries. Much of the official condemnation of violence and requests for it to cease tended to be cloaked in partisan language or hyperbole. Exceptions to this rule came in the form of appeals for peace made by the Lord Mayor of the city in June and early July 1922. Appealing to 'all creeds and classes', Sir William Coates asked all to 'refrain for the next 10 days from all acts of violence and disorder and from all burning and looting.'[22] These appeals would have been heard by the vast majority of Belfast's citizens. Apart from their inclusion in newspapers, 'peace' posters were displayed on advertising hoardings all over the city. In his second appeal, the Lord Mayor welcomed 'a substantial degree of success' of the first plea for peace ten days previously, urging that 'all sections of the community will continue to do their utmost to give to our city the blessings of a permanent peace.'[23]

WINNING THE WAR

Responding to a complex and developing political situation at a time of considerable political change would have been difficult enough for Craig's administration. Dealing simultaneously and imaginatively with a worsening security situation in the north would have proved a most onerous task for an administration more gifted than Craig's. However, as already noted, the undoubted problem posed by the crisis facing both British and unionist admin-istrations in the early 1920s does not excuse the limitations of their response. What is of key significance is the perception which the Belfast administration had of security in the north and how this actually impacted upon their approach. Convinced that the kernel of the security situation was the threat posed by Sinn Féin both inside and outside Ulster, Craig and his colleagues regarded loyalist violence as basically reactive and merely of nuisance value, believing it would dissipate once the nationalist threat was removed.[24] This understanding of the security situation was reflected in the administration's approach which involved, at least in its initial stages, the prioritisation of the threat posed by republicans and the adoption of a range of draconian measures to deal with such a menace.

The spiralling nature of violence in the first part of 1922 had prompted the northern government, which had taken over responsibility for security on 21 November, to consider a range of special powers at a Cabinet meeting on 13 March.[25] Although IRA personnel were the intended targets of Bates, the archi-tect of the legislation hastily drafted around this time, the measure also reflects loyalists' frustration over the low number of culprits brought to justice for the escalating attacks in their city.[26] The Civil Authorities (Special Powers) Act (N Ireland) became law on 7 April. The Act permitted internment without trial, exclusion of suspects from all or part of N Ireland and flogging for possession of firearms on top of the custodial sentence.[27] Regulations 23 (concerned with arrest and indefinite detention) and 23B (internment) permitted the May sweep, which had obviously been planned, rather than simply constituting a knee-jerk response to the murder of William Twaddell. Thus, minutes of a Cabinet meeting held at Craig's Cabin Hill home late in May indicate his concern that people might regard these measures to be a sudden response to the North Street murder and arson attacks on Anglo-Irish properties. Rather they 'should know the steps which had, and were being taken, had been in contem-plation for some time and were now put into force on account of the second organised attack against Ulster'.[28]

The legislation provoked a wrath of fury from nationalists north and south of the border. The *Irish News* claimed that Craig's internment initiative consti-tuted 'martial law' and suggested that the Government's methods equated to 'coercion, naked and unashamed, drastic beyond comparison.'[29] They claimed such extreme powers were unparalleled in international history:

> It is doubtful if any Government-in the Russia of the Czars or Napoleonic France or Rome of the Caesars, or Egypt of the Pharaohs – ever made more elaborate arrangements for the establishment of a system of rule by armed force than those outlined by Sir James Craig yesterday.[30]

The *Manchester Guardian* also found the new legislation more draconian than the Restoration of Order Act which it replaced. It also alleged:

> Whilst envenomed politicians in the Ulster Parliament are voting themselves power to use torture and capital punishment against citizens whom they forbid to defend themselves whilst they scarcely attempt to protect them from massacre, some of their own partisans in Belfast carry wholesale murder to refinements of barbarity hardly surpassed in Armenia and Constantinople.[31]

In Dublin, Michael Collins despatched a letter to Churchill condemning the British government for handing over 'virtually unlimited' powers to Bates who was 'notorious for his antipathy to our people.'[32] Collins concluded that if 'these offensive, not protective, measures were enacted against Catholics', he could not be held accountable for 'the awful consequences which must ensue.'[33] The *Irish Independent* also condemned the 'furiously partisan' security initiative of Craig's administration, accusing it of double standards regarding the pursuit of those responsible for murder in the city. It fumed:

> When the McMahon family was butchered under circumstances of barbarity of which cannibals would be ashamed, where was the vigorous pursuit of evil-doers, whose identity, to say the least, was not shrouded in mystery? ... But now when persecution and injustice have brought their terrible aftermath of reprisal and counter-reprisal Sir James Craig launches his thunderbolts.[34]

Even the minister most associated with the emergency legislation, Dawson Bates, described it as a 'most drastic' provision declaring 'we are at war with the

IRA.'[35] Unionists, whilst not denying the scale of the measure, claimed it was both justifiable and in response to nationalists' requests for stronger action against the forces of terror. The *Belfast Telegraph* accused nationalist critics of the measure of employing double standards, arguing that Craig's administration had been 'called on by the Nationalist press to govern and now when it seeks to root out a formidable conspiracy of murder, arson and outrage, it is accused of persecution.'[36] Some Unionists thought the government was not going far enough. Robert Lynn, MP for Belfast Central and editor of the *Northern Whig*, suggested it was 'no time for indulging in legal hair-splitting' and pointedly asked,' is civilisation going to be allowed to exist, or is there going to be anarchy?'[37]

However radical and significant the measures were in terms of their long-term effects, the legislation was mild compared to actions taken against political opponents during the Irish Civil War. It has been estimated that during the last six months of the civil war that almost twice as many republican prisoners were executed by the Free State authorities as had been executed by the British during the whole struggle between 1916 and 1921. Referring to the execution of at least 67 anti-Treaty prisoners in reprisal for assassination of government supporters, Tom Wilson surmised: 'One can readily envisage the horrified reaction there would have been, not only in Ireland but in England and abroad, if the British authorities had behaved in this way, and the outrage that would have been provoked if the hard-pressed Ulster government had done so.'[38] Regulations 23 and 23B of the emergency legislation resulted in the Belfast administration gaining considerable powers of arrest and indefinite detention. These were utilised during the late evening of 22 May and the early morning of 23 May.[39] Controversially, the task of arresting suspects was delegated to 'A' and 'B' Specials. Unlike internment arrangements in 1971, the Unionist Government acted swiftly and, in most cases, those arrested were caught unawares. Both in Belfast and in the Ulster countryside that evening, over 200 suspects, exclusively nationalist, were lifted.[40] Denise Kleinrichert gives an evocative account of 'Internment Night':

> Wooden doors crashed in splintered shards under the weight of rifle butts breaking the quiet in the early hours of a May morning, sending chairs and tables clattering across the cool, damp floors. Dogs growled at the heels of uniformed military-style figures in the doorways of rural and city homes, startling the residents from deep slumber. Shouts of racial,

sectarian epithets spewed along with the seizure of men from their homes. The wail of children, as if from nightmares, as fathers, uncles and youthful brothers were dragged from the warmth of their beds to the stark realities of arrest, search and seizure of the local police.[41]

Although the operation was swiftly implemented and was on a province-wide scale, it appears that the authorities were not always clear who they were looking for. Thus, where the named suspect was unavailable, another male member of the family was whisked away in his place.[42] Although there were no serious injuries reported during the round-up of nationalists in Belfast, those suspects resisting arrest were often beaten and a few received minor gunshot injuries. Many were subsequently released due to cases of mistaken identity, or, where evidence remained flimsy, others were given their freedom if they agreed to keep the peace or by promising to leave northern territory.[43]

Figures on the number of people detained in the north vary from the government's early estimation of less than 350 to press estimates of just over 200. Inside four months the government admitted that 446 had been interned, whilst an estimated 728 men were detained between May 1922 and the end of 1924.[44] Internees were temporarily held in Belfast Prison, Newtownards military camp and in Larne, before being moved a few weeks later to the *Argenta* prison ship. The comparatively small number of republicans detained in Belfast (29) is highly significant given that the bulk of serious violence in the northern area for a two year period had been confined to its capital. Whilst a number of IRA personnel were arrested in the city, several key figures were ignored, which is surprising, given that there had been major intelligence gains following the raid on St Mary's Hall in March.[45]

Holding internees in prisons and army barracks was, of course, a temporary measure. Craig's government had commissioned an American cargo ship, SS *Argenta*, on 17 May for such a purpose and following outfitting at Harland and Wolff's, the ship was brought into service as a prison.[46] On 19–20 June in a high risk security operation over 300 detainees were moved from the various holding centres to the *Argenta*, which was berthed in Belfast Lough.[47] There were 8 cages on the vessel, each containing up to 56 beds (each cage was 40 feet long by 20 feet wide and 8 feet high). Conditions were obviously cramped, with open latrines less than a yard from prisoners' beds and complaints of roaming rodents and lack of opportunities for fresh air and exercise abounding. Discipline was tight on board the boat, and with little realistic opportunity of escape, morale among detainees was low.[48] Despite being described as 'Craig's torture chamber', the Minister for Home Affairs tried to persuade his supporters that the vessel had the facilities of a third class steamer. Many prisoners expressed their feeling of resentment at conditions on board the *Argenta* in the form of verse. One prisoner wrote:

> Where Belfast spews its poison filth to mingle with the sea,
> The convict ship is anchored, bound by cruel men's decree.
> She rides within the mire and filth, to leeward in the pool,
> A prison made by savage hate and shaped by savage rule.[49]

It was necessary to transport prisoners, both those appearing in court in the city and especially moving detainees from other holding-centres to Crumlin Road Prison, and later the *Argenta*. The proximity of a loyalist hotbed, Sandy Row, to the city's main rail terminus in Great Victoria Street, resulted in blatant intimidation of republican prisoners.[50] Rumours concerning the movement of internees meant that many angry Protestants awaited the arrival of trains from the farthermost edges of the province. When these pulled into Great Victoria Street station, hostile crowds, mainly consisting of women, abused and attacked the handcuffed prisoners. Sometimes the assaults were verbal in their nature and were confined to swearing and spitting. However, occasionally when prisoners had to await motor transportation to Crumlin Road, the angry mobs kicked and assaulted them.[51]

The tight security in the city's prisons and the obviously restricted opportunities offered to those planning escape from prison ships, meant that serious escape bids from penal institutions were few and far between. Although dissent amongst prisoners was not as great as during the H Blocks dispute in the early 1980s, there were instances of disorder, involving both nationalists and unionists in the prisons, especially at Crumlin Road. These were generally anticipated by the prison authorities who accordingly took preventative measures. The Deputy Governor of Belfast Prison expressed such fears on 4 September 1922, claiming that 'the sole aim of the above [viz. detention and internee] prisoners is to destroy prison discipline among the other prisoners.'[52] Captain F.M. Stuart's subsequent report described the 'outbreak of disorder' the previous evening:

> Immediately after the 8pm bell for bed rang, 8 prisoners located in 'C' wing, 2 prisoners in 'D' wing, began to break up their cell furniture and

to throw some through cell windows ... In all ten prisoners had to be held in restraint. Owing to the promptness with which the situation was met the damage to furniture is not extensive; in all, to the value of £1 18s. Among the prisoners who resisted, prisoner R Simpson attempted to strike warder Newell with the leg of a cell table. In being restrained he received a scalp wound.[53]

The lot of prisoners, especially republican, was therefore, far from being a happy one. This distress often started over annoyance caused by an apparent lack of equity in court sentencing. Captain Stuart, in an earlier letter to Dawson Bates, discussed how two court cases involving prisoners in his care, had been brought to his attention. In one, a loyalist prisoner had been sentenced to a mere three years in prison after being caught with 'a smoking revolver' following the shooting of two children, whilst two Catholic brothers were given slightly longer custodial sentences for having guns in their possession (one of them also received 25 strokes of the birch).[54]

Apart from the problems they had to encounter either in Crumlin Prison or on the *Argenta*, republican prisoners in particular had to cope with worries relating to their families and homes. These concerns were mainly financial but also involved the well-being of wives and families. The government did not provide any financial assistance for prisoners' families and the latter were dependent on help from charity groups. As noted elsewhere, the American White Cross agency, which was established at the beginning of 1921 to help families afflicted by the conflict, provided generous financial and housing support to many Catholics evicted from jobs and homes, and another group, the Irish Republican Prisoners' Dependent Fund gave £2 a week subsidies to supplement the family income of imprisoned volunteers. Other psychological concerns superceded financial fears, especially for those Catholic internees whose homes were located in mainly loyalist areas. The sister of Michael Waters, of Lady Street, a shipyard worker and father of two, recalled that after he had been interned, his home was ransacked by his neighbours, and his family, along with his parents and her, were forced to flee to Dublin, where they had to endure a 'Poor House tenement lifestyle'.[55]

THE BEGINNING OF THE END

Although the emergency legislation, increased security measures and the effects of the Civil War clearly started to bite during the summer of 1922, resulting in a highly significant decrease in the levels of violence, disturbances did not completely disappear from Belfast's streets overnight.[56] Indeed, some especially horrific and vicious onslaughts occurred during July, August and September, with the last recorded sectarian killing in the city happening early in October.

The arrival of another marching season prompted an increase in the levels of tension, especially in the interface areas. A Catholic was wounded in Foundry Street as an Orange parade was passing along the Newtownards Road during the evening of 1st July and there were reports of Catholics being forced out of their homes in Conway Street the following morning. Daniel Duffy, of Moyola Street, was seriously wounded on his way to work on Monday 3 July and later that day Lizzie McKeown, from Foundry Street, was also wounded. In addition, an explosion was reported in Frederick Street that evening. The next day produced two fatalities and a number of other incidents. During the early hours police raided St Peter's Club in Sultan Street off the Falls. These premises had previously been used as a social and welfare club, but in the raid the police seized IRA documents and detained 11 men. Also, in the west of the city that morning, Joseph Hurson (15), a Catholic apprentice cabinet-maker, who had been standing at the front door of his Unity Street home, was shot in the head by a sniper operating from the Hanover Street area. The teenager died in the Mater Hospital later that day. That evening there was firing from Millfield directed into Upper North Street, which resulted in the killing of an elderly Protestant, James Mooney (70), of Third Street. Mr Mooney suffered serious wounds to his side and died in hospital a couple of days later. The random nature of many of these attacks and the narrow distinction between misfortune and good luck was illustrated by the narrow escape of James Mullaney when a bullet cut the sleeve of his coat but left him unharmed.

Although there was to be no loss of life for another few days, a spate of shootings continued in different parts of the city over the next 48 hours. These included the beating and shooting of a sailor in Edward Street, the shooting of a man fixing a window in New Dock Street, the wounding of a young woman outside her home in the York Street area and a couple of shootings in the Shankill area. Just before curfew on 8 July an attack by a 30-strong mob on the Catholic residents of Conway Street resulted in several leaving their properties, reportedly under threat of an armed attack. Another attempt to intimidate Catholics from their properties was foiled the following evening after an intervention by Specials based in the Falls Road Library. The mob was driven back, in some cases by officers using their rifle butts, and the evicted residents of Norfolk and Conway Streets were escorted back to their properties. The *Irish News* reported that the Catholic residents concerned spoke 'very highly of the prompt action' of the police in 'putting an end to a very serious situation.'[57] Also that evening in the west of the city, a Protestant teenager Frank McAleer, on arriving close to his front door just a few minutes after curfew, refused the call to halt by the police and was shot dead. Young McAleer, who had just left a fish and chip café, was carried into his house, where the police were forbidden entry by a hostile crowd until an ambulance arrived to take away his body.[58]

Off-duty police officers had mixed fortunes endeavouring to intervene in city centre robberies. A detective foiled an attempted robbery in a Victoria Square pub, wounding one assailant and arresting two others, whilst a policeman attempting to intervene in a robbery in a restaurant in Commercial Court, was wounded. Early the following morning there was an arms find in Marrowbone and 11 Catholics were arrested in Ballymacarrett and Cromac Square. Barely 24 hours before the Twelfth, heavy firing was reported in Peters Hill, with at least two injuries being recorded. Across the city a recently married Protestant tram conductor, Harry Little, of Bramcote Street, was shot dead trying to intervene on behalf of Catholic neighbours who were being evicted.[59] Tensions again erupted in the Conway and Argyll Street area of the Shankill during the early hours of the Twelfth. Three explosions were heard in these and surrounding streets but although no injuries were reported, several houses were damaged.

The big parades in the city, shepherded by a large security presence, passed off peacefully. Craig, who had travelled to the city after addressing Orangemen in Glasgow, adopted a conciliatory approach, with the emphasis in his speech on the imminent return of peace to Belfast. The *Belfast Telegraph* proudly proclaimed that, 'if nowhere else in Ireland, the Union Jack at least flies in Ulster' and, detailing Sinn Féin's 'war' upon Ulster, promised the spirit of its people would 'never be broken.'[60] The *Northern Whig* also condemned republicans, describing them as 'experts in mendacity' who excelled at 'wholesale mud-slinging' at their political opponents in the hope that 'a large proportion of the mud will stick, and that the Orange Order will fall into bad repute throughout the civilised world.'[61] Although expressing its 'greatest admiration for the Orange Institution – as a machine', the *Irish News* were far from impressed by the Unionist leader's speech which they said was 'an illustration of how easy' it was to 'humbug an intelligent community once it has been machined into the proper state of discipline.'[62]

The number of violent incidents in the second half of July declined markedly, but the city was by no means quiet or back to normal. The day after the parades a Protestant, Robert Boyd, of Convention Street, was crushed by a Crossley tender during minor disturbances on the Newtownards Road and died shortly afterwards. Shooting was reported that evening in Ardilea Street and there was a fire in Academy Street. A group of children were fired upon as they played in Glenview Street during the morning of 14 July and an eight year old girl, Maggie Hunter, was seriously wounded. In a follow-up arms search, weapons and IRA documents were found in the Marrowbone. In another unfortunate case where people returning home were caught out by the curfew restrictions, Francis Crilly, a Protestant, was shot on 15 July. A few days later, two members of the security forces, a Special and a Norfolk Regiment soldier, were wounded in the Marrowbone and a pedestrian was shot in Church Lane. At teatime on 20 July, in one of several cases where cyclists were seriously assaulted for refusing to hand over their bicycles, an apprentice electrician, William McClelland, of Duncairn Gardens, was shot in the chest as he cycled down May Street. In a 'neutral' city centre area, it is likely that this shooting was neither premeditated nor sectarian, but rather was symptomatic of the state of lawlessness existing in the city at the time. Towards the end of July there was rioting in the Springfield area, a bomb caused damage at the Ministry of Labour in Upper Library Street, three youths were arrested carrying a gun and ammunition near Falls Park, a young boy, John Walsh, was injured by a bomb flung into Youngs Row in the east of the city and two men were charged with the possession of guns in the Marrowbone.[63] On 29 July Patrick McGivern, of Tyrone Street, who had been delivering fruit to a shop on the Old Lodge Road with a friend, was fatally wounded by a gunman and his friend had to make a hasty retreat on his cart. The following day a patrol of 'B' Specials were passing Carlisle Circus when they were fired at from Stanhope Street. In the crossfire which ensued, a young woman, Elizabeth Savage, who had been walking along Trinity Street, was shot in the leg.[64]

Although the Specials escaped serious injury at Carlisle Circus, one of their off-duty colleagues was to be less fortunate in what was regarded 'safe' territory barely a week later. During the early evening of Saturday 5 August, 'C' Special Samuel Hayes was having a drink with a friend in the Britannic public-house on the Newtownards Road, when he was fatally wounded by a gunman. Several shooting incidents were to occur within the next few days. The following evening William Mathers was shot in the chest in the Old Lodge Road area and on Tuesday 8 August a Catholic labourer, Patrick McGuigan, of Seymour Street, was shot by two men as he worked near the County Down railway. Mr McGuigan died in the Mater Hospital a few days later. Other shooting casualties included George Doherty who received a leg wound at Millfield on 11 August and a young mechanic, Joseph Bradley, who suffered similar injuries in Kashmir Road two days later.

More frequent and impromptu searching, both of householders and pedestrians, was carried out at this time. The *Belfast Telegraph* reported how 'surprise' searches had been conducted in the city earlier in the day when 'many pedestrians were held up and subjected to a close examination.'[65] Police transport in the form of Lancia and Crossley vehicles, were busy operating in several parts of the city and raids on suspected premises continued to be carried out under heavy guard. Just before lunchtime on Sunday 13 August, constabulary surrounded a hall in Currie Street, off Cullingtree Road, and found 30 men assembled there. These men were detained, but although republican literature was found, no weaponry was discovered.[66]

A month-long printers' strike in the north during the mid-summer stirred the rumour cauldron in Belfast. Rumours circulated in the city that there had been another IRA assassination attempt on a leading unionist, as well as an IRA attack on the shipyards and speculation that a settlement of the Boundary Commission was imminent. Shortly after the strike ended on 21 August, a major news story emerged from elsewhere in Ireland, which was to have a significant psychological impact upon Belfast's nationalist community. The news that Michael Collins had been killed by anti-Treaty forces in County Cork dominated press coverage throughout Ireland, and indeed Britain, for several days. Nationalist opinion in the north lamented the passing of the man most closely associated with the Treaty. Reflecting the admittedly qualified support of many northern Catholics for the London agreement, the *Irish News* despaired at the passing of 'a wonderful Irishman', declaring that he 'gave his life in defence of the Treaty that must be maintained if Ireland is to be saved at all.'[67] A few days earlier the same paper had reminded its readers that 'good comes out of evil on occasions', trusting that 'the fate of General Collins may awaken the dumb and dominant populace to a sense of their peril and of their responsibility to Ireland.'[68] The unionist press exhibited no such mourning for a man who they believed had met his just reward. Relishing the divisions within the republican movement which had resulted in this assassination, the *Northern Whig* commented that Collins' death 'brings home to us with renewed force the truth of the Scripture saying that he who taketh the sword shall perish by the sword.'[69] Although many northern nationalists had reservations about a Treaty which had politically marginalized them, they were, in the main, supportive of Collins who had consistently represented their case in his dealings both within the new administration in the south and in negotiations with Britain. Now he was gone, a civil war was raging, and their position was inevitably going to be downplayed.

Sniping, bomb-throwing and occasional close-range shootings continued, albeit intermittently, throughout the rest of the summer. Thus, a bomb was thrown from Cupar Street into Kashmir Road late on 16 August, fortunately causing no injuries and a policeman was equally lucky to escape injury when a bomb thrown into Corporation Street exploded outside Sinclair Seamen's Schoolhouse (temporarily used as a Special Constabulary barracks) just over a week later. Shooting was reported in the Marrowbone and Cromac Street on 20 August and James McKeating was seriously injured off the Old Lodge Road as he hurried home before curfew on 25 August. During the following few days there were reports of sniping in Bryson Street, Boundary Street (where a soldier was wounded), the Marrowbone and in Millfield. Three armed men burst into a spirit grocery in the Oldpark area on 28 August and shot Luke McGrane who had tried to intervene and his colleague Anthony Brady. The following evening another worker was shot as he went about his duty. Peter Mullan (65), who had moved to Joy Street in the Markets area after being forced out of his Ormeau Road home a few weeks previously, was an attendant in the Crumlin Road Picture House. A press report gave a vivid account of the panic caused when Mr Mullan was shot in the head at close range by a gunman at around nine o'clock:

> There was a rush for the exit doors on the part of a number of the spectators, and within the building all was at once a scene of confusion, those who heard the shots not knowing that others would follow, while some of the younger people who were present on the occasion fainted.[70]

At a similar time elsewhere in the north of the city, a bomb was thrown at a group of children playing in Earl Street, near North Queen Street, causing eight injuries, three of them serious. Another Catholic worker was targeted in unfa-

miliar territory at the start of September. George Higgins (30), a postman originally from Sligo, had been on the Shankill 'run' for most of his year working
in Belfast, but was attacked as he worked on a new stretch in the isolated
Musgrave Channel Road, where his body was found near the Electric Power
Station.[71] The first weekend in the new month saw four bomb attacks, two
shootings and at least two serious injuries. The bombs were thrown at Catholic-
owned houses in Glenview Street and Louisa Street in the Oldpark area, where
the injuries were sustained. A bomb exploded in Upton Street, injuring Maggie
Ward (12) and another young Catholic, Mary McCann was hit in the back by
a sniper's bullet in Broadbent Street, as she visited her aunt. That weekend two
men were stabbed returning from the cinema and there were reports of gunfire
in Short Strand, the Ravenhill Road and Woodstock areas. Monday, 4
September saw a renewal of gunfire into Old Lodge Road and, more sensation-
ally, 'an organised attack of cell wrecking and destruction of prison property', in
the early evening, an event which had been pre-warned. Consequently the
'damage to furniture [was] not extensive' and ten prisoners had to be held in
restraint.[72] After a few days of comparative quiet trouble was renewed on 8
September when there were a couple of bank robberies in High Street and on
the Falls and a Special Constable, Edward Brown (31), from Mountpottinger
Barracks, was shot near the Ravenhill Road. That morning the Special had
caught a man with a rifle and a jeering mob surrounded the officer, leading to
the escape of his prisoner and his own wounding.

A week's comparative absence of trouble ended on 13 September when a
number of violent incidents were experienced in north Belfast. A teenage
Protestant message-boy, John Walker, from Molyneaux Street, was standing at
the corner of Little George Street during the early evening with a group of
friends, when a man emerged from a side street and shot him dead. Two others
were wounded in the York Street area, including a farmer who had been delivering potatoes at a North Queen Street shop. Police raided a house in Grove
Street, off North Queen Street, and there was a rumour of an explosion on the
Argenta prison ship.[73] The following evening, in an attack reminiscent of that
over six months previously in Weaver Street, nine children were hurt, three seriously, in a bomb attack near Cullingtree Road in the west of the city. Children
were taking full advantage of a more relaxed atmosphere and were playing in
the street, when a man emerged from Devonshire Street, allegedly pretending
to light a pipe. Instead however, he lobbed a bomb into the middle of the
playing children in Ton Street, who were caught unawares by the blast.

Teenagers Alexander McKenna and Edward Fitzpatrick suffered serious arm and shoulder injuries, but Louisa Cannon (30), of Frederick Lane, died from her wounds the following day. Also that evening, Arthur Heaney (21), of Havana Street, was shot in the stomach in Oldpark, rushing home just before curfew. Over the next few days it appeared to many in the city that the hopes for peace and stability engendered by a marked reduction in violence, were being over-turned. The previous evening the *Belfast Telegraph* had asked:

> The peace of Belfast does not apparently meet with favour in some quarters, as, after a good period off welcome orderliness, some persons of the hooligan type have been doing their best to revive the awful deeds which disgraced the city several months ago.[74]

On Saturday 16 September there were isolated incidents of unrest in the York Street area in particular. Catholic homes were damaged in Grove Street and buildings were burned in York Street and towards the city centre. Elsewhere in the city there had been an explosion at a soap-works on the Newtownards Road earlier that day. Worse was to follow on Sunday 17 September, when three people lost their lives and others were seriously injured. Most of the trouble was in the York Street area which had been in 'a disturbed state' from the morning.[75] Two Catholic men were killed by sniper fire during the afternoon. At around two o'clock Thomas McCullagh (40), a carter, of Hardinge Street, had been going towards North Queen Street and was shot when he stopped at the corner of Great George's Street. Mr McCullagh died before he reached the Mater Hospital and in a follow-up police search, a sniper's post was found in a loft in Great George's Street, with a rifle and ammunition. Within an hour a seaman, James McCluskey (41), of Marine Street, who had just returned to Belfast to visit his wife and family, was shot on his own doorstep. Later that evening, Jane Rafferty (40) answered a knock at her New Andrew Street home in the Garmoyle Street area and four men rushed in, shooting her in the head. This was a particularly cowardly attack on a defenceless woman whose Protestant husband was at sea, and who was known to be the only Catholic living in the street. During heavy police presence in the district, a Special was fired at in Little George Street.

The next few days saw a reduction in the number of shootings, although gunfire raked the Millfield area on 18 September and Margaret Kelly was wounded on the Woodstock Road the following day. However, despite the reduction in the number of sniping incidents, there were eight serious fires in the city on the 17th and 18th, including the attack on a picture-house in Smithfield and a blaze gutted a commercial property in Mill Street. In an especially callous arson attack, 12 horses were burned to death in a Ballymacarrett stables. Love of animals cost James Spratt (50), of Wigton Street, his life on 22 September, in what proved to be another curfew tragedy. Mr Spratt, a Protestant, was shot dead in Westmoreland Street near his home, ignoring a police challenge to stop. He had been going to feed a donkey in stables, but did not possess a curfew permit and had been trying to dodge detection by police. That evening there was also a bomb attack on a house in Bryson Street and reports of gunfire in nearby Foundry Street, but the improved security situation had prompted the authorities to delay curfew until 11.30 p.m. The last series of concentrated incidents occurred during the weekend of 30 September and 1st October, and was described as 'a renewal of disorder.'[76] Only one person was seriously injured in these attacks. Henry McAuley (42), of Chatham Street, had been buying a newspaper on the evening of 30 September and had been chatting to a friend in Herbert Street when he was struck in the chest by gunfire directed from the Shankill.

The last victim of the conflict turned out to be Mary Sherlock (34), a Catholic from Vulcan Street off the Newtownards Road. On 5 October, Mrs Sherlock, who had only resumed shopping on the busy Newtownards Road after the reduction in violence, left home just before 11 o'clock , proceeding on to the main road via a wooden barrier at Seaforde Street, where it was believed she was spotted and followed by the gang who subsequently killed her. She had just entered a butcher's shop when she was shot in the head by one of the gang. Unusually, the police mounted a search of houses in the loyalist area and the government again offered a reward for information leading to a prosecution (this time £2,000). At Mary Sherlock's inquest, her brother described how he had been worried when he saw a group (three men and a woman) following his sister as she turned into the Newtownards Road and became alarmed when he heard a shot ten minutes later. The Coroner expressed his dismay at the renewed violence, expressing the feelings of many that they had entered 'a new era of peace' in the city and hoped that 'the whole people of the city would set their faces determinedly and these murderers and have them put down.'[77] Later that day another Catholic, Samuel Dines (38), from Anderson Street, was seriously wounded following sniper attack. Having started in the east of the city, the last fatality and bombing incidents also occurred there. At least two bombs were thrown into Short Strand on 18 and 22 October, with four suffering injuries in the first attack in Stanhope Street.

As 1922 drew to its conclusion, the chances of renewed sectarian violence had all but evaporated. A combination of the effects of the Special Powers legislation and the increasing security grip enjoyed by the new police force and the USC, the onset of civil war in the rest of Ireland, the dip in the morale of northern republicans and their migration south to participate in the Civil War, and the northern administration's generally tougher stance against loyalist terror gangs meant that the initiative swung back into the hands of Craig's security forces. Although political tension, especially over the deliberations of the Boundary Commission, remained for some time, the enduring influence of the emergency legislation throughout the formative years of the new state and the narrow self-preservation focus of the new southern administration meant that northern Catholics were unlikely to receive meaningful assistance from their co-religionists in the south. The result of all this was the return of a peaceful, if somewhat strained, atmosphere to the city. Indeed, as early as mid September, the *Belfast Telegraph* had, rather mischievously, referred to Belfast as a 'bright spot' in 'the midst of the darkness and gloom that hang over southern Ireland', claiming that 'the conditions in the Six Counties are as free from bloodshed and crime as are Kent and Lancashire.'[78]

Conclusions

The conflict which erupted during the mid summer of 1920 occurred more as the result of a fusion of factors and events rather than being the outcome of a planned campaign of violence by one group upon another. This is not to deny that sinister elements on the loyalist side had been preparing for such an opportunity since the commencement of the IRA's war against the British. The UVF had been organising the stockpiling of a considerable arsenal and the timing of the shipyard evictions – as workers returned from their summer holiday – was certainly opportune. Both within the ranks of the security forces and the various sections of the Belfast community, there were growing tensions and expectations that spectacular events were imminent. This was largely attributed to a lengthening in the list of loyalist grievances. Often unable to return to their employment in the shipyards, Protestants were also aggrieved by uncertainty over Ireland's political future and by the worsening plight of southern Protestants. As the IRA encroached into Ulster territory, these fears appeared to be justified. The commencement of an organised boycott campaign within weeks of the industrial expulsions also accounts for unionists' reluctance to distinguish between the threat posed by the IRA nationally and that presented by its weakened northern division.

Suggestions that Belfast's violence was the result of an orchestrated campaign of sectarian killing are flawed in that they fail to provide a complete explanation for the bloodshed. Industrial expulsion was not confined to Catholics, with many 'rotten Prods', or socialists, also being evicted from the workplace. This would suggest that political affiliation was even more important than church membership. Nor did the BPA distinguish between different groups of Catholics, such as ex-servicemen or suspected members of Sinn Féin. Many loyalist attacks were led by alcohol-fuelled mobs, often executed as spontaneous reactions to nationalist violence, and there were relatively few sophisticated operations against high-ranking republicans. Despite the virulence of political speeches, there was no 'grand plan' involving senior politicians in the orchestration of such violence. Although links between the political leadership and the UVF were close before the war, there is a dearth of evidence to suggest that this alliance was systematically co-ordinating such a campaign. However, members of the BPA and other loyalist splinter groups undoubtedly benefited from easy access to their considerable arsenal and were certainly responsible for the initial industrial expulsions and several sectarian murders.

Although the unionist establishment may not have co-ordinated the campaign of violence, it is undeniable that the Belfast authorities had been bracing themselves for an outbreak of communal disturbances during the summer of 1920. In the light of these fears, the failure of the city's political and civic leadership to avert, or at least curtail, such disturbances was palpable. Few precautionary measures were adopted in the first half of 1920 and, despite the justified excuse of significant shortfalls in available security personnel, more incisive deployment of troops in strategic Belfast locations would undoubtedly have reduced the likelihood of skirmishes breaking out in the city's industrial heartland. Yet efficient security force intervention was hardly helped by the uncertainty over specific responsibility for security arrangements in the north. The provisions of the Government of Ireland Act meant that responsibility for policing would be ultimately passed on to the local administration in Belfast, but this did not actually happen until November 1921, and it would be another six months before a new police force, the RUC, would be up and running. Consequently, much of the responsibility for coping with the disturbances fell upon the shoulders of the RIC and especially the USC. In spite of the latter force being involved in a disproportionately high number of killings of Catholics, this was partly explained by their heavy deployment in troubled nationalist areas. Though the majority of Specials were not involved in controversial incidents, it is likely that some police officers were guilty either of direct involvement in the murder of Catholics, or else of collusion with loyalist terrorists. Certainly the Specials became pariah figures for many Catholics, who preferred military patrols in their streets, as they believed these would be less likely to turn a blind eye to loyalist snipers.

The main charge against the authorities was that failure to adopt firm action against loyalist troublemakers, especially during the early stages of the conflict, set the pattern for future security incidents. The administration of Sir James Craig prioritised the republican threat, dealing with it comprehensively before turning its belated attention to agitators from within their own section of the community. This pragmatic, as distinct from impartial, focus epitomises the approach of Craig's administration to the violence. Such a focus was reflected in the emergency legislation implemented in the early summer of 1922. The effects of these measures and the start of the Civil War elsewhere in Ireland led to a decline in morale and the speedy defeat of the IRA in Belfast. The emphatic nature of this victory and the dissipation of loyalist terrorism in its wake, illustrates the success of this policy, at least in the short term. However, the ill feeling engendered by such a policy resulted in festering Catholic dissatisfaction and resentment.

POLITICS OF THE STREET

Undoubtedly the strain and stress produced by prolonged political negotiations was to frequently result in an intensification of street violence. This was evident during the Treaty negotiations, and over 30 died in Belfast disturbances in November 1921. Yet intense spells of political activity did not always lead to a significant increase in the level of violence. Despite strong nationalist feelings of abandonment and initial unionist reticence over the impending legislation, the last quarter of 1920 was a comparatively quiet period. On occasion, a bout of excessive blood-letting in the city could produce an, albeit short-lived, atmosphere dominated by hopes of political compromise and optimism, rather than one of fear and distrust. Such events could lead directly to positive political action and an apparent desire for compromise. This seemed to be the case with the orgy of violence in Belfast during March 1922, culminating in the horrific attack on the McMahon family and the signing of the second Craig-Collins agreement within days of the Kinnaird Terrace incident. Often more elaborate security arrangements resulted in an uneasy calm in the city for a short period, though this did not necessarily result in a corresponding decline in communal tension. Thus, by temporarily deploying an increased number of military and constabulary in the city during the run-up to the elections for the new Northern Ireland Parliament in May 1921 and for the royal visit to formally open this institution the following month, Craig's administration was successful in preventing potentially embarrassing outbreaks of disturbances.

What impact did local press coverage have on determining the levels of tension on Belfast's streets? Certainly journalists on both sides of the political divide might have done more to defuse edginess from within their own section of the community. Systematic selection and manipulation of news stories likely to be sympathetically received by their readers – often at the expense of more newsworthy but less favourable stories – resulted in these readers developing a one-dimensional interpretation of events. Therefore, the loyalist press would focus on issues involving republican transgressions both in the city and elsewhere in Ireland, often at the expense of loyalist attacks, which , if they were reported, were normally dismissed as being the work of 'hooligans'. On the other hand, nationalist organs would constantly turn their spotlight on the failure of the local authorities to take firm action against loyalist terror gangs, rather than attempting to ascertain responsibility for the arson attacks in Belfast during May and June 1922, or to assess the moral case for continuing the boycott of northern goods. Despite these failings, few mainstream papers advocated that their readers should resort to violence and they also acted as a public information service, educating their readership on a variety of safety issues, including the dangers of loitering on street corners and entering sealed-off buildings, as well as informing them on updated curfew regulations.

It is important to gauge the extent to which the political aspirations and fears of one section of the community clashed with those from the other side. Attempts to assess culpability for violence divided Belfast society at the time and have continued to spark different responses during the intervening years. Nationalists had ambivalent feelings towards the political gains enjoyed by their co-religionists elsewhere in Ireland. Any feelings of joy they would have shared with Dublin and its winning of self-government, or for British military withdrawal from the south, would have been tempered by their fears of the repercussions of such gains on their own delicate position in Ulster. Increasingly besieged and isolated, Northern Catholics rarely felt in a position to collectively express their discontent. Months before the Civil War started in August 1922, republican activists in Belfast were privately expressing their feelings of isolation and desperation. The results of this desperation were several inflammatory attacks on Protestants and their commercial properties. To a large extent, these actions, designed as warnings to loyalists, reflected the mood of the people the IRA claimed to represent.

Catholic vulnerability in Belfast was not just psychological in its nature. From the Catholic viewpoint, a far from favourable demographic composition meant that they were especially conspicuous and prone to attack. Their perilous predicament was exacerbated by the IRA's mass kidnapping of elderly Orangemen, their assassination of Ulster-born policemen and politicians, as well as the bombing of workers' trams. Yet the northern IRA remained relatively weak throughout the conflict and, with the exception of the post-Truce period, political and military developments tended to work against the interests of Belfast republicans. Not the least of these problems was the introduction of effective counter-terror measures by a Unionist administration which was resolute in its determination to protect its territory. Sacrificed by their colleagues in the south and suffering a dip in volunteer morale, the IRA, reduced to sectarian outrages, finally ceased its Northern operations.

Although the nature of their concern was different, unionist anxiety persisted throughout the entire conflict. Despite their clear numerical superiority in Belfast, loyalists were vexed about increasing IRA encroachment in Ulster and also by ongoing political negotiations in London. Worried by a fundamental shift in British policy and opinion, which was now more concerned about easing in a settlement of the broader Irish problem than empathising with the interests of any political group, unionists were even more disturbed by the apparent strengthening of Sinn Féin's bargaining position. In their eyes, such trends helped justify the bloody events on Belfast's streets. Therefore, to many Protestants, attacks on Belfast Catholics, in both their homes and workplaces, had an air of regrettable inevitability, as they assumed the role of scapegoats. Increasing political tension, the easy availability of weapons and the presence of many vulnerable Catholic victims provided loyalist marksmen with unlimited opportunity to satisfy their sectarian bloodlust. By striking at Catholics in Belfast, loyalist paramilitaries saw themselves as reaffirming their political opposition to a united Ireland and to the IRA's campaign elsewhere. Splinter groups and gangs of individual, maverick gunmen were responsible for many of the attacks attributed to loyalists. Though the character of such violence was normally random and opportunistic, this should not conceal its large scale – loyalists of one ilk or another were responsible for well over half of the deaths in Belfast during the conflict – or its widespread nature, with assassins proving to be active in several areas. The victims of these terrorists tended to be individual Catholics, targeted either in their streets or homes, or sometimes at work. Most of them fell to snipers operating from the sanctuary of their own districts, though others were killed during mob invasions or bombing of Catholic areas. The presence of security forces unquestionably kept the lid on much potential loyalist violence, until it evaporated after the end of the IRA campaign and the internment of their own leaders and activists. However, the ambivalent approach of the Unionist Government to loyalist violence and the paucity of prosecutions resulted in the prolonging of the terror campaign and also moulded the long-lasting impression that these gangs were able to do what they wanted.

AN 'UNHOLY' WAR

Whilst sharing some of the characteristics of previous disturbances, the 1920s' Troubles also had their own distinctive features. These included an extension in the range and type of terrorist activity (including long and short range gunfire attacks and the use of machine-gun, as well as rifle and revolver), the stark repercussions of governmental indecision and inappropriate troop deployment, retaliatory killings on both sides, violence set in a clear political context, the indiscriminate nature of many attacks and the sectarian persecution of political opponents. The scale of the violence was also striking. Fatality rates far exceeded those of the nineteenth century and although constituting only a fraction of the slaughter of the modern conflict, the total number of fatal incidents was higher than in most two-year periods of the late twentieth-century Troubles.

Given its significance, what type of conflict was it? Though sharing such features with the wider Irish conflict, especially the Civil War, the Northern Troubles were unique on account of their sectarian nature and urban focus. Did they constitute a 'pogrom' as some commentators have claimed? The term implies the elimination or large scale massacre of a minority religious group in a particular area, orchestrated by its central authority. Though not restricted in its historical application to any one particular religious or ethnic group, it is most often associated with attacks on Jews, either in Tsarist Russia during the early 1880s, or in eastern Europe over the next year 20 years, and, of course, those outrages committed by Nazis during the 1930s. Some of the more obvious features of a 'pogrom' did occur in Belfast during the early 1920s. These included the disproportionately high number of Catholic victims of violence, the blatantly sectarian nature of the majority of killings and the stock-piling of weaponry for a considerable period before the commencement of hostilities. Yet this term is imperfect and unhelpful in explaining the events of this period. Central to such an interpretation of a 'pogrom' is the persecution of one group, with large scale suffering and loss of life normally restricted to the members of that persecuted group. Despite disproportionate loss of life and serious injury amongst the Catholic community, there were also hundreds of Protestant dead and injured, not to mention those experiencing financial or commercial losses.

A 'pogrom' also implies that the violence affected the whole of the persecuted community. Whilst not intending to minimise the significant degree of genuine suffering endured by its community, the Catholic fatality count of less than 300 constituted considerably less than 1% of the city's Catholic population at that time. Also, though those intimidated from job and home represent much higher percentages, most of the suffering was temporary in its nature and even then, figures constituted a minority of that community. Co-ordination of the murder campaign was not executed by the official administration for the area and many killings appeared to have been done in a random and reactive fashion. Thus, notwithstanding the essentially sectarian nature of the 1920s' conflict in Belfast, it can not be considered as a fully-fledged 'pogrom', mainly because suffering was neither one-sided nor the result of a campaign by the region's governing administration. No one term adequately catches the multifarious nature of this conflict, though the 'unholy' character of disturbances between two communities, each justifiably claiming their sense of isolation and besiegement, perhaps comes closest to describing it.

What was the legacy of this conflict? It is probably more helpful to separately assess its short and longer term repercussions. In the short term, the trauma experienced by many citizens and the restrictions on their personal liberty prevented an imminent, fresh outbreak of trouble and provided the new Unionist administration with vital breathing space. The longer term legacy, however, was far from productive. The bitterness and suspicion provoked by the events of these two years created an atmosphere of mistrust and non co-operation which resulted in the pent-up frustration and resentment prevalent in the North on the eve of the modern conflict. The Twenties' Troubles were different from those of the nineteenth century on account of their sheer scale and, due to the more sophisticated weaponry and range of terrorist tactics, was the first 'modern' conflict in the city. Apart from its enduring legacy, the conflict also illustrated the underlying vulnerability of both sections of the community, as well as the inter-relationship between imminent political change and communal disturbances.

LIVING WITH THE TROUBLES

Life in Belfast during these two turbulent years at the start of the twentieth century's second decade was very difficult and in some ways the anxieties experienced by its people were comparable to those encountered by another generation 50 years later. Therefore, although the 1920s' conflict differed from the modern one in that the security forces were clearly victorious, there were striking similarities in other spheres. One was in the sheer intensity of violence over prolonged periods of time, with a wide range in the types of security incidents occurring over several areas of the city. Many attacks were retaliatory in their nature with the most vulnerable, especially those living on the periphery of loyalist areas, being the subject of frequent attack. The excitement, stress and anguish caused by proximity to such events undoubtedly affected the majority of Belfast's citizens. However, this paled into insignificance when compared with the suffering of those forced out of job and home and, most of all, the heartache for those thousands of family circle members who had lost loved ones on account of the violence. There were also similarities in that both conflicts experienced lulls in the fighting which provided welcome, if short-lived, relief from the strain of communal warfare.

Whilst those suffering most from the Troubles were mainly working class and constituted a minority of the city's population, all of Belfast's citizens were affected by the strife to one extent or another. Everyone was liable to experience curfew restrictions, street-searching, the all-pervading presence of police or army and the outburst of gunfire or explosions on busy central streets. Although most had to carry on with their everyday lives, many were forced to vary their routine. Therefore, workers fearing attack would take longer, but safer, routes to their place of work, whilst those intimidated from their homes sought temporary refuge in homes in 'friendly' districts. Many aspects of ordinary life suddenly became fraught with danger. Travelling to work on a tram-car, fetching milk or bread from a corner shop, attending a church service or football match, or having a drink in a city bar before rushing home, all had to be reconsidered in the light of the terror. For many, the excitement caused by increased levels of danger and one's natural curiosity to move closer to the source of the danger, would end in tragedy. This apparently magnetic attraction to danger was commonly found in children. Many of those whom I interviewed vividly recalled their excitement at finding bullets lodged in walls, seeing gunmen fire around street corners, witnessing the aftermath of terror attacks, seeking shelter following the outbreak of gunfire and their interrupted games due to the imminence of curfew hour. However, despite these interruptions to their normal routine, most of them continued to attend school and to play with their friends.

The effect of the 1920s' Troubles on the lives of ordinary people was undoubtedly profound. Obliged to carry on with the rigours of everyday life, working class people in the city's ghettoes had to cope with a mixture of sectarian street fighting, evictions from work and home, bombs on trams, arson attacks upon homes and business premises and sniping attacks in their own areas. They tended to adopt a pragmatic response to the ongoing terror, combining an approach which minimised the risk of injury with one of not interrupting the routine of their personal lives. Clearly there is a deep resonance between such experiences and feelings with those experienced by subsequent Belfast generations. One experiences an eerie *déjà-vu* on taking a stroll down similar Belfast streets today. Although the city has undergone considerable demographic change as well as witnessing improvements in the quality of housing, one can still obtain a feel of what it must have been like to have lived there over 80 years ago. Neat two-up, two-down Housing Executive properties with charming patio gardens have taken the place of the kitchen-houses of that period. However, women still chat over garden walls and treat strangers with caution in Little George Street, a long narrow street linking North Queen Street and York Street. One can imagine the trepidation of policemen patrolling the street, ever-wary of preying nationalist snipers, and of anxious mothers, concerned that the play of their blissfully unaware children would be cruelly broken by spying loyalist snipers in York Street. Perhaps the last word on the similarities between past and more recent conflict in Belfast should belong to a 'veteran' of both. John Parkinson recalls:

> A lot of things then were the same as during the recent Troubles. You know, people standing around in groups on their street, discussing what had happened, who had been shot the previous evening. As youngsters we generally obeyed our parents but sometimes we couldn't help sneaking out to see what all the fuss was about. The big difference about the Twenties' Troubles was that they were over much sooner; we knew they were hard times but we didn't expect them to last for ever. But we also used to wish all the trouble would be over so we could get on with our normal lives. That hasn't really changed, has it?

Appendices

1920

25 February	Better Government of Ireland Bill introduced at Westminster by Lloyd George.
June–July	Nearly 40 killed in communal disturbances in Derry.
12 July	Carson's platform rhetoric arouses Orangemen at Finaghy demonstration.
18 July	Cork killing of Ulster-born senior police officer, Col. Gerald Smyth.
21 July	Around 7,000 Catholics and socialists forced from the Belfast shipyards.
22 July	Evictions of 'non-loyal' workers commence in other industries. Start of sectarian disturbances in several parts of the city, resulting in 20 deaths inside three days. Catholic-owned business premises destroyed, especially in east of city. Start of intimidation of several hundred Catholics from their homes.
6 August	Establishment of Belfast Boycott Committee.
22 August	Lisburn assassination of Detective Inspector Oswald Swanzy sparks second spate of sectarian disturbances in Belfast. 33 die inside 10 days.
31 August	Start of curfew restrictions in several parts of the city.
1 November	Recruitment starts for Special Constabulary.
23 December	Passing of Government of Ireland Act proposing devolved parliaments in Belfast and Dublin.

1921

26 January	2 RIC officers shot by IRA in city hotel.
4 February	Sir James Craig appointed Unionist Party leader.
12 March	3 'Black and Tans' killed in city centre attack.
23 April	Killing of 2 further 'Black and Tans' in central Belfast sparks reprisal attack on Duffin brothers.
24 May	Unionists win landslide victory in elections for new Belfast Parliament.
7 June	Craig elected Prime Minister.
10–12 June	14 killed in city, including 'uniform' attack.
22 June	George V formally opens the new Parliament in the city. An IRA bomb attack on military train near border kills 6 the following day.
9 July	Truce announced between military forces and the IRA. Bloody response in Belfast, sparked off by Raglan Street attack on police. At least 16 die the following day, known as Belfast's 'Bloody Sunday'.

29 August– 1 September	Up to 20 die in street disturbances in north and west Belfast.
21–25 November	Over 30 die in Belfast violence, including 7 in tram attacks.
6 December	Anglo-Irish Treaty signed in London.

1922

8 January	Treaty narrowly approved in Dáil. This was followed by the establishment of a Provisional Government and the withdrawal of British forces from the south.
21 January	Signing of first Craig-Collins Pact.
9–11 February	IRA border kidnappings of Protestants and attack on Special Constabulary at Clones provoked bloodshed in city.
12–16 February	Over 30 die in Belfast, including 6 in a loyalist bomb outrage involving children in Weaver Street.
March	60 die in shooting and bombing attacks all over city.
24 March	Uniformed men attack the McMahon home off the Antrim Road, killing 6.
30 March	Signing of second Craig–Collins Pact.
April	Over 30 die in continued disturbances including 5 Catholics in a 'uniform' attack in the Arnon Street area.
7 April	Passing of Special Powers Act by Craig's administration.
May	At least 75 deaths reported in Belfast in the most bloody month of the conflict.
18 May	Daring IRA attack on Musgrave Street police barracks.
20 May	Start of sustained IRA arson campaign.
22 May	William Twaddell, Unionist MP, shot by the IRA in city centre.
23 May	Implementation of Special Powers Act, with over 200 interned in initial sweep and soon interned on 'Argenta' prison ship.
June	Continued outbursts of violence, claiming over 30 lives, but not on the scale of the previous month. Large numbers of Catholics seek temporary accommodation in and Glasgow and Dublin. Recruitment starts for the RUC.
22 June	Assassination of Field Marshal Sir Henry Wilson by the IRA in London.
August	Virtual halt to IRA activities in city and overall a significantly reduced level of violence (6 deaths reported in July and August).
22 August	Killing of Michael Collins in County Cork.
13–17 September	5 killed in final flurry of trouble.
5 October	Last reported conflict killing in Ballymacarrett.

APPENDIX 2: DRAMATIS PERSONAE

Sir Edward Carson (1854–1935). Born in Dublin and educated at Portorlington School and Trinity College, Dublin. He was called to the Irish Bar in 1889 and appointed Solicitor-General in 1892. He served as Unionist MP for Dublin University between 1892 and 1918. Carson earned a reputation as one of Britain's leading lawyers, especially for his advocacy in controversial cases, including the Oscar Wilde trial (1895) and the 'Winslow Boy' case (1909). Knighted in 1900 and appointed Solicitor-General in the same year. Succeeded Walter Long as leader of the Irish Unionist Party in 1910 and orchestrated Ulster resistance to the 3rd Home Rule Bill (1912–14). Carson served as Attorney General (1915) and First Lord of the Admiralty (1916). He represented Belfast Duncairn at Westminster (1918–21). Carson resigned as Unionist leader early in 1921, declining the opportunity of becoming Northern Ireland premier. Created Baron Carson of Duncairn the same year and served as Lord of Appeal (1921–9).

Sir Winston Churchill (1874–1965). Grandson of the Duke of Marlborough and son of Randolph – 'Ulster will fight and Ulster will be right!' – Churchill. Educated at Harrow and Sandhurst. He sprung to national prominence following his journalistic exploits during the Boer War. Returned as Conservative MP for Oldham in 1900, but switched to the Liberals in 1904, becoming MP for Manchester North West (1906–08) and for Dundee (1908–22). Gained experience of Government as President of the Board of Trade (1908–10), Home Secretary (1910–11) and First Lord of the Admiralty (1911–15). A supporter of Irish home rule, he narrowly escaped physical injury during a visit to Belfast in 1912. Served as Minister of Munitions (1917–19), Secretary for War (1919–21) and Colonial Secretary during the partition period (1921–22). Conservative MP for Woodford (1924–64). He was Chancellor of the Exchequer for five years in the Twenties (1924–29) before leaving the Tory shadow cabinet and entering political obscurity in 1931. Political career revived in 1939, when he returned to the War Cabinet as First Lord of the Admiralty (1939). Succeeded Chamberlain as Prime Minister in 1940. Churchill appreciated Northern Ireland's war contribution. Defeated by Clement Atlee's Labour Party in 1945 election, leading the Conservatives in opposition. He again became Prime Minister (1951–55) and was knighted in 1953.

Sir Ernest Clark (1864–1951). English-born, Clark entered the Civil Service in 1884 and was awarded a CBE in 1918. Appointed Assistant Secretary of Inland Revenue in 1919 and knighted the following year. Served as Irish Assistant Under-Secretary (1920–21) and was responsible for drafting Northern Ireland's constitution. He was made Permanent Secretary of Northern Ireland's Ministry of Finance, as well as the overall head of the region's Civil Service (1921–5). Clark served as a director of Harland and Wolff (1925–33) before being appointed as Governor of Tasmania (1933–45).

Michael Collins (1890–1922). Born in County Cork but moved to London in 1906 where he worked as a Post Office clerk. He returned to Ireland in 1915 and joined the Irish Volunteers. Collins participated in the 1916 Rising but later rose to prominence as the Director of the IRA's Intelligence section. He was a member of Dáil Éireann (1918–22) and was appointed Minister of Finance, masterminding the economic boycott of northern goods (1920–22). Collins was believed to have been responsible for the reorganisation of the northern IRA during the Truce period. He led the Irish delegation at the Treaty negotiations (1921). After the split in Sinn Féin, Collins led the pro-Treaty faction and was Chair of the Provisional Government of the Irish Free State (1922). Co-signatory of the ill-fated 'peace' pacts with James Craig (January and March 1922). Commander-in-chief of government forces during the Civil War, he was killed during an ambush in his native county (August 1922).

Sir James Craig (1871–1940). Born in Belfast, Craig was both a landowner and businessman, primarily as a director of Dunville's distillery. He served as a Captain in the Royal Irish Rifles during the Boer War (1900–01). Represented County Down as a Unionist M.P (1906–18) and also Mid Down (1918–21).Quarter Master General of the 36th Ulster Division 1914–16, Craig was knighted in 1918. Gained experience in government as Parliamentary Secretary at the Ministry of Pensions (1919–20) and Finance Secretary to Admiralty (1920–1). Succeeded Carson as leader of the Ulster Unionist Party in February 1921. Represented County Down in the northern Parliament (1921–40). Served as Northern Ireland's first Prime Minister between 1921 and 1940. Head of administration which introduced draconian anti-terror legislation in May 1922. Created Viscount Craigavon in 1927.

Frederick Crawford (1861–1952). Served in Boer War, rising to rank of Lieutenant-Colonel in the British army. He was also to become a senior officer in the UVF and was responsible for organising the Larne gun-running in 1914. Behind secret reorganisation of UVF in 1920. Crawford joined the Special Constabulary in 1920, becoming a District Commander in the 'B' Specials. A small businessman, Crawford also worked for the Northern Ireland Ministry of Home Affairs (1925–36).

Eamon de Valera (1882–1975). Born in New York of mixed Spanish and Irish blood, and brought up in County Limerick. Educated at Christian Brothers school, Blackrock College and University College, Dublin. He joined the Gaelic League in 1908 and the Irish Volunteers in 1913. De Valera was one of the leaders of the 1916 Rising, being spared the death penalty due to his American parentage. Sinn Féin MP for East Clare (1917), President of Sinn Féin (1918) and President of first Dáil Éireann (1919). Elected to northern Parliament in May 1921 but refused to take up seat. President of Irish Free State in August 1921 but resigned four months later when Dáil ratified Treaty. He formed the anti-Treaty party and later helped to establish Fianna Fail (1926). Responsible for drafting of Irish constitution (1937). Irish Prime Minister 1937–48, 1951–4 and 1957–9. President of the Irish Republic 1959–73.

Joseph Devlin (1871–1934). Popularly known as 'Wee Joe', he was born in west Belfast, although his family originally came from County Tyrone. Educated at Divis Street Christian Brothers School, he started his working life as a barman, before taking up positions as a clerk in a jam factory and a reporter for the *Irish News*. He became Secretary of the United Irish League (1901) and represented Kilkenny as a Home Rule MP (1902–6). Appointed General Secretary Home Rule Party (1904–20) and served as President of the Ancient Order of Hibernians (1905–34). Represented West Belfast at Westminster between 1906 and 1918. He was regarded as the political voice of northern nationalism throughout the Twenties' conflict. Elected MP in northern Parliament (1921–34), where he became leader of the Nationalist Opposition (1925–34). Represented Fermanagh and South Tyrone (1929–34).

David Lloyd George (1863–1945). Born in Manchester but educated at a Welsh Church school before training as a solicitor. Served as a Liberal MP at Westminster between 1890 and 1945. Supporter of Irish home rule (1912–14). Cabinet experience as Chancellor of the Exchequer

(1908–15), Minister of Munitions (1915–16) and Secretary for War (1916). Succeeded Asquith as Prime Minister in 1916. Architect of the Government of Ireland Act (1920) and mastermind of the Treaty negotiations (1921). His attitudes and policies towards Ulster fluctuated between political and financial endorsement of unionist policy and a growing scepticism over Craig's failure to stem the tide of loyalist violence in particular. Prime Minister 1916–1922. Leader of the Liberal Party (1926–31). Created Earl Lloyd George in 1945.

Richard D.W. Harrison (1883–1982). Born in Kilkenny and educated at Trinity College, Dublin, Harrison joined the RIC in 1906. His appointments included a spell in charge of the Belfast Detective Division, RIC County Inspector and RUC City Commissioner (appointed in 1922). He was awarded the OBE in 1923. Harrison was strongly suspected of being involved with John Nixon in orchestrating a 'rogue cop' campaign against individual Catholics.

Joseph MacRory (1861–1945). Born at Ballygawley, County Tyrone and educated at Maynooth. He entered the priesthood in 1885 and became a professor at Oscott College in Birmingham and later at Maynooth (1899–1915). Appointed Bishop of Down and Connor (1915–28), he was to be regarded as the 'protector' of Belfast's Catholic community during the conflict. MacRory adopted a quasi-political role, helping to establish the Belfast Boycott Committee and aligning himself closely with Collins and the pro-Treaty section of Sinn Féin. MacRory's 17-year period as Archbishop of Armagh started in 1928 and he became a Cardinal the following year. He refused to recognise the 'British' institutions of the northern state and later suggested that the Irish Protestant Church was 'not even a part of the Church of Christ'. MacRory was also accused by his opponents of having sympathies with the Nazis.

John W. Nixon (1879–1949). Born in County Cavan, Nixon joined the RIC in 1899 and had risen to the rank of Detective Inspector by 1917. He later served in Belfast, becoming Commander of 'C' police district, based at Brown Square in the Shankill area. He became a pariah figure for Belfast Catholics during the early Twenties when he was strongly suspected of leading several forays by 'police' murder gangs. He became Worshipful Master of Peel Memorial RUC Orange lodge and joined the RUC as Detective Inspector (1922). Awarded the MBE in 1923, he was to fall from grace and was dismissed from the RUC for 'political' activities in 1924. Elected as an Independent Unionist councillor for the Old Lodge area (1925–49) and as a MP for Woodvale in the Northern Ireland Parliament (1929–49). Founder of the Ulster Protestant League in 1931.

Eoin O'Duffy (1892–1944). Born in County Monaghan, he became a local government engineer before joining the IRA in 1917. Director of IRA Organisation in 1921 and Truce Liaison Officer in Belfast (1921–22). O'Duffy later became Chief of Free State forces and the first Commander of Garda Siochana (1922–33). First President of Fine Gael (1933–34). O'Duffy's right wing leanings were epitomised by his leadership of the paramilitary group, the Blueshirts, and his mission to Spain in 1936 where he led a pro-Franco Irish Brigade.

Alexander Robinson (b.1902). Born and reared in north Belfast, 'Buck Alec' Robinson was known as a petty criminal to local police from his early teens. He was strongly suspected of the murders of several Catholics during the Twenties conflict and was interned on the *Argenta*. Following a short period of enforced exile in England, he moved to America where it was rumoured he found employment as a wrestler and later as a bodyguard to the infamous gangster Al Capone. Returning to Belfast he became a greyhound trainer – one of his dogs was called after his favourite catch-phrase, 'It's a geg!' (*sic*) – and also won the Irish middleweight boxing championship. Robinson reportedly took great pride in walking his 'pet' lions along York Street. 'Buck Alec' lived well into his 90s.

Lieutenant-Colonel Sir Wilfred B. Spender (1876–1960). English-born, he was educated at Winchester and Camberley Staff College. Joining the army in 1897, he served in India and in 1911 became the youngest officer on the General Staff. He signed the British Covenant for Ulster and helped to finance the anti Home Rule petition (1912). He resigned from General Staff to join UVF headquarters in 1913, returning to General Staff on the outbreak of war. Serving with the 36th Ulster Division, he was promoted to the rank of Lieutenant-Colonel in 1916 and awarded the DSO and MC in 1918. Spender was made Commanding Officer of the UVF in 1919 and worked with Craig at the Ministry of Pensions (1919–20). He helped in the establishment of the USC in 1920 and was awarded the CBE in 1921. First Secretary to the Northern Ireland Cabinet (1921–5) and Permanent Secretary to the Ministry of Finance and the Head of the Civil Service (1925–44).

Sir Stephen W. Tallents (1884–1958). English-born civil servant who was involved in the organisation of food rationing during the Great War. British Commissioner in the Baltic States 1919–20. Moving to Ireland, he became Private Secretary to the Lord Lieutenant in 1921 and was Imperial Secretary in Belfast (1922–6). Later Tallents worked with the Empire Marketing Board, the GPO and the BBC (1926–41) . His last major post was as Principal Assistant Secretary at the Ministry of Town and Country Planning (1943–6).

William Twaddell (1877–1922). Belfast-born, Twaddell owned an outfitter's shop in the city. A city councillor and Unionist MP in the new Parliament, Twaddell was a fierce critic of the IRA and had been threatened by them a few months before his assassination in May 1922. A leading thoroughfare in the Woodvale area is named after him.

Lieutenant-Colonel Sir Charles Wickham (1879–1971). Born into a well-to-do Yorkshire family, he was educated at Harrow. Joining the Norfolk Regiment in 1899, he served in the Boer War and also saw service in the Great War. Involved in British military mission to Russia (1918–20). RIC Divisional Commissioner for Northern Ireland (1920–2). Served as Inspector-General in the RUC (1922–45). Head of British police and prisons mission to Greece (1945–52).

Field Marshal Sir Henry H. Wilson (1864–1922). Born in County Longford and educated at Marlborough College. He served in the Boer War and in Burma. Appointed Director of Military Operations at the War Office (1910) and made a Major-General in 1913. Wilson backed the Curragh Mutiny in 1914. On outbreak of war he was appointed Deputy Chief of General Staff and was promoted to Lieutenant-General in 1915. Wilson was Chief of Imperial Staff (1918–22). Made a Field Marshal and offered a knighthood in July 1919. Wilson was elected Unionist MP for North Down in February 1922 and was also security adviser to the Craig administration. A fierce critic of the IRA, he was assassinated by them in London during June 1922.

Seamus Woods (1898–1976). Born near Ardglass in County Down, Woods trained as an accountant. He was appointed a Colonel in the Free State army early in 1922. Woods was the Officer Commanding the 3rd Northern Division from April 1922. As a pro-Treaty leader he was critical of the lack of southern support for northern Catholics. Woods was active in many attacks in Belfast between April and June 1922, including the Musgrave Street attack. Appointed Dublin GHQ Assistant Chief of Staff in 1923, he was also charged that year for the Twaddell murder. Interned in Belfast Prison and on the *Argenta*, Woods was eventually freed in April 1924. Later appointed a Captain in the Free State Army.

APPENDIX 3: REPORT FOR COMMISSIONER RIC, 1 JUNE 1922
(based on incidents for 31 May and taken from HA5/151 PRONI)

At 11.15 a.m. 3 men armed with revolvers entered the timber yard of Messrs McKelvey in Smithfield. They held up Mr McKelvey and 4 of his employees and set fire to the premises on the first floor. After seeing the fire was making progress they made off. The Fire Brigade got the fire under control but not before considerable damage was done. Protestant firm in RC area.

At about 4.30 p.m. 2 Special Constables named Campbell and Roulston who were on duty in Millfield, were fired upon by a party of armed men and seriously wounded. They were conveyed to hospital where Constable Roulston died shortly after admission. Crown forces replied to the fire and two unknown civilians were shot dead and at least 2 wounded. RC area.

At 5.20 p.m. the pawn office of J. McBride [P], 81–3 Cromac Street, was maliciously set on fire and almost completely destroyed. RC area.

At 5 p.m. a number of artisan houses in Boyd Street, 13 in all, were set on fire and destroyed. RC area in the neighbourhood of a Protestant area. There was heavy firing going on at the time between the rioters and Crown forces. The fire brigade could not operate in this area.

At about the same hour a number of artisans' houses were set on fire in Peters Place. RC area in neighbourhood of a Protestant area. Heavy firing was going on at the time and an old man and woman were shot dead. The fire brigade could not operate. 14 houses were burned out.

At 8.30 p.m. James McEntee's public house, 57 King Street, was wrecked during rioting. RC area, RC firm.

From 8.30 to 9.30 heavy fighting took place around Cullingtree Road and College Square, RC area, consisting mainly of sniping at Crown forces, and at College Square RIC barracks. Military and police replied to the fire. Number of casualties at present is unknown.

During the firing in the area around Peters Hill, Millfield and King Street there were a large number of casualties. The following being reported from the Hospitals, viz. RV Hospital: S/Const Andrew Roulston [P] Dead; wounded S/Const Wm Campbell [P], Smithfields Barracks. Edward Robinson [P], 25 years, Hamill St, George Martin, RC, 26 years, Bond St, John Doran, RC, 27 years, McMillan's Place. Mater Hospital: Dead: 3 unknown men, one unknown woman;

Robert Monaghan, RC, Arizona St, Mary McCrory, RC, 28 Old Lodge Road, Rose McIlroy, RC, 29 years, 28 Old Lodge Road, William O'Hare, RC, 40 years, McDonnell Street, Henry Kennedy, RC, Service Street. Wounded: Roger McKay, RC, North Queen Street, James Campbell, RC, Millfield, Edward Rogan, RC, Cullingtree Road, James Toner, RC, Peters Place.

About 8 p.m. the confectionery shop of H. McGee, RC, 3 Ormeau Road, Protestant area, was attacked by a mob. Windows were broken and some goods looted. The mob was dispersed by police.

At 8.20 p.m. the vacant public house, 28 Bankmore Street, Protestant area, the property of John McGurk, RC, was set on fire and completely destroyed.

At 8.30 p.m. the spirit grocery of John Morgan, RC, 13 Elm Street, Protestant area, was attacked. Windows were broken and some goods looted. At the same time the spirit grocery of Patrick Griffiths, 2 Taggart St, Protestant area, was attack and partially looted. Mobs dispersed by police.

At 9 p.m. the dwelling house of William Benson [atheist], 1 Belmore St, was attacked and chairs and windows broken and partially looted. The mob was dispersed by police.

About 9 p.m. the dwelling house of Joseph McGuiness, RC, 3 Belmore St, was attacked and some property looted. Protestant area.

At 9.40 p.m. a man named Lutane, RC, living at 66 Cook St, Protestant area, private house, was wounded in the hand by a man who fired at him through the back door while he was in the back yard.

APPENDIX 5: BOYCOTT POSTER

The
BOYCOTT
BARRIER

Men and Women of Ulster!

Are you aware that a powerful barrier of lawlessness, which hitherto the Provisional Government of Southern Ireland has failed to deal with, has been raised around the Six Counties of Northern Ireland, whereby the manufactures of this area are prevented from being transported to any other portion of Ireland?

Are you aware that the barrier is more completely under the control of this unchristian organisation of men who are pledged to the economic ruin of our manufacturers and traders—and of you—than the traffic in a city is controlled by the pointsmen?

Do you know, further, that the products and merchandise of the people who are manipulating the unholy exclusion of Belfast and Ulster in the hope of throttling your industries still come into the Six Counties area freely, and are being purchased by Ulster men and women—perhaps by yourself?

Are you going to allow this to continue?

Don't buy a single article from anybody until you are perfectly certain that its purchase by you will not bring a penny of profit to the men who are endeavouring to crush you.

Some of the merchandise the Boycotter is sending you. Look out for it ➡

STOUT,	CIGARETTES,	WRAPPING PAPER,	PIPES,	BRUSHES,
WHISKEY,	SOAP,	PRINTING,	CLOTHING,	POPLINS,
BUTTER,	SWEETS,	PAPER BAGS,	TWEEDS,	SLATES,
MARGARINE,	HOSIERY,	ENGRAVING,	AGRICULTURAL	CONDENSED MILK,
EGGS,	SHIRTS,	BEEF,	IMPLEMENTS,	LEATHER,
BACON,	CARPETS,	MUTTON,	CHEMICAL	CONFECTIONERY,
HAMS,	MINERALS,	PORK,	MANURES,	CHOCOLATES,
BISCUITS,	INK,	SAUSAGES,	CATTLE FOODS,	FURNITURE,
TOBACCO,	NEWSPAPERS,	BOOTS,	SEEDS,	POLISHES,

NOT A PENNY TO THE BOYCOTTER.

ULSTER TRADES' DEFENCE ASSOCIATION.

Notes

INTRODUCTION

1. Therefore, there are countless studies of the *Titanic*, the battle of the Somme, Belfast's Blitz and, of course, the modern conflict. 2. Ballymacarrett Research Group, *Lagan Enclave* and M. Farrell's *Orange State* discussed which of these terms was more appropriate without reaching a firm conclusion. 3. G.B. Kenna, *Facts and Figures*, J. Redmond, *Church, State and Industry in Belfast*, A. Boyd, *Holy War;* J. Bardon, *A History of Ulster*, M. Elliott, *The Catholics of Ulster*, G. MacTeer, *Down the Falls* and K. McPhillips, *The Falls – a history.* 4. M. Farrell, *Arming the Protestants,* J. McDermott, *Northern Divisions*, D. Kleinrichert, *Republican Internment.* 5. B.A. Follis, *A State under Siege.* 6. Boyd, *Holy War*, p. 183. 7. I. Budge and C. O'Leary, *Belfast: approach to crisis*, p. 143. 8. Kenna, *Facts and Figures*; A. Morgan, *Labour and Partition*; J. Graham, *In the Name of Carsonia*; P. Buckland, *A Factory of Grievances*; B.A. Follis, A *State under Siege*. 9. E. Phoenix, *Northern Nationalism;* Kenna, op. cit., Farrell, *Arming the Protestants;* Buckland, *A Factory of Grievances;* Redmond, op. cit. 10. Phoenix, *Northern Nationalism*, and Farrell, *Arming the Protestants.* 11. J. Beckett, in *The Making of Modern Ireland*, p. 449, wrote about the limitations of Unionist response to the violence. 12. A.T.Q. Stewart, *The Narrow Ground*, argues that the raw sectarianism of the 1920s' riots ushered in the terminal decay of non-sectarian ideals in the city. 13. Whenever certain 'closed' or 'restricted access' papers did become available, their guardedness and comparative dearth of revelatory material disappointed the reader (a good example of this is the Nixon file). 14. Yet the reminiscences of both the 'great and the good' also paint a vital and vivid picture of the period. Contemporary accounts of life during this time form an essential part of this book. 15. Morgan, *Labour and Partition*, p. 302. 16. Ibid. 17. This, of course, excludes the modern Ulster conflict. Andrew Boyd suggested that the 1920s violence proved to be 'far more terrifying than all the disturbances of the nineteenth century'; in *Holy War*, p. 176. 18. According to T. Hennessy, *A History of Northern Ireland*, 557 were killed in the northern area during the period of conflict, 416 of these being killed in Belfast. Apart from major attacks outside the city, I will not address the IRA's border campaign in depth. 19. Boyd's figure of 452 casualties, including 267 Catholics and 185 Protestants, falls into this category. The Catholic casualty rates – over 60% of the total number of conflict fatalities – was significant in a city where Protestants outnumbered Catholics by nearly three to one. 20. Figures are from Hennessy and Boyd, *Holy War*. I consulted available police records and press reports, recording every single Troubles-related incident between July 1920 and October 1922. They are, I believe, accurate in their nature and detail. 21. Boyd, *Holy War*, p. 205. 22. This was due to a number of reasons. Some, especially those involving the small number of Protestants evicted, did not always receive aid or even report their situation to interested authorities or charity groups. Others were forced out of their jobs or homes on more than one occasion, hence complicating the statistics. 23. Boyd, op. cit., p. 205. 24. See Stewart, *The Narrow Ground*, p. 148. Certainly goading of opponents frequently led to stone-throwing and eventual use of firearms, with the need for police or military intervention. However, the early phases or 'defined stages of violence' were frequently bypassed in the 1920s' conflict. 25. Although many familiar battlegrounds, especially in the west of the city, were to feature in the 1920s' riots, there was a sharp increase in the number of locations which were to be involved: see below. 26. 1972 was by far the bloodiest year of the conflict. In a year when political power shifted from Stormont to Westminster, 496 people lost their lives. 27. This was reflected in a comparatively weak IRA, especially in 1920, and also by the fact that political realities at that time did not augur well for Ulster nationalists. 28. This apparent contradiction was the theme of my paper, 'Belfast 1845–1914: Economic Prosperity and Political Entrenchment', delivered at the European Social History Conference, Amsterdam, 1998. 29. This proved to be a central cause of the riots in August 1864, though loyalists were enraged by local nationalist support for the erection of a statue to Daniel O'Connell in Dublin. Another feature of these riots, when at least 12 people lost their lives, was the allegation of collusion between loyalist rioters and members of the police force. An informative account of these riots is given in J. Magee, *Barney – Bernard Hughes of Belfast.* 30. See Stewart, *The Narrow Ground*. 31. C. Hirst, *Religion,*

Politics and Violence, p. 81, points out that such rioting in the first half of the nineteenth century was ritual-istic in its nature, contrasting sharply with the politically-motivated disturbances of the 1870s and 1880s. **32.** These disturbances started after an Orange parade and involved the burning of Catholic property and the fatal shooting of a Catholic child. **33.** *Illustrated London News*, 15 August 1872. **34.** The official fatality count was conservatively estimated at 31. **35.** See Bardon, *A History of Ulster, pp* 380–2. Despite its political context, the actual 'spark' for the violence was believed to have been the intimidation of a Protestant in the mainly Catholic docks workforce. A distinctive feature of these disturbances was 'the degree of legitimacy enjoyed by the rioters in the wider Protestant community', which accounts for 'the severity and longevity' of these riots in 1886; in Hirst, *Religion, Politics and Violence*, p. 180. **36.** When John Redmond's National Volunteers attempted a similar gun-running exercise at Howth a few months later, the response of the author-ities was considerably more assertive. A vivid account of UVF activities at this time can be found in Stewart's *Ulster Crisis*. **37.** The degree of support for Unionists in Great Britain was phenomenal, illustrated by the collection of over two million signatures for the British Covenant and the revelation that cavalry officers based at the Curragh near Dublin had intended to refuse orders to enforce the requirements of the Home Rule Bill when it became law. See my MA dissertation, 'Ulster will fight and Ulster will be right!', which looked at unionists' propaganda success during this period. **38.** Minor disturbances were reported in the shipyard at the start of 1912 and during a football match at Celtic Park shortly before the signing of the Ulster Covenant in September. **39.** See P. Orr's book, *The Road to the Somme*. Many Ulster Catholics also served in other Irish regiments, including several future victims of the 1920s' disturbances. **40.** The Government of Ireland legislation is considered in detail in Chapter 6.

CHAPTER 1

1. This theme is discussed in greater detail in Chapter 7. **2.** Reported in *Belfast Newsletter*, 9 June 1920. **3.** Redmond, *Church, State and Industry*, p. 12. **4.** See R. Gallagher, *Violence ... Derry City*. Belfast experi-enced its own disquiet around the time of the Derry riots. There were skirmishes in Sandy Row following a mob attack on a spirit grocery and Cavan born Head Constable Perrott died in hospital, after being struck on the head by a stone. **5.** *The Times*, 7 July 1920. **6.** *Northern Whig*, 13 July 1920. **7.** *Times* 13 July 1920. **8.** Carson, quoted in Farrell, *Orange State*, p. 27. **9.** Carson quoted in *Northern Whig*, 13 July 1920. **10.** *Manchester Guardian*, 13 July 1920. **11.** See Boyce, *Englishmen and Irish Troubles* for an analysis of British press coverage of the Irish crisis. **12.** *The Times*, 13 July 1920. **13.** Ibid. **14.** *Northern Whig*, 13 July 1920. **15.** Ibid. **16.** J. Kelly, *Bonfires on the Hillside* p. 12. **17.** Ibid. **18.** *Irish News*, 10 July 1920. **19.** Ibid., 12 July 1920. **20.** Ibid., 13 July 1920. **21.** Ibid., 14 July 1920. **22.** Ibid. The Catholic hierarchy also lambasted Carson, suggesting that he, rather than the threat of IRA activity in the north, was the main reason for this build up of tension. Dr Joseph MacRory, Bishop of Down and Connor, later informed Colonial Secretary Winston Churchill that it had been 'well know for a considerable period before [the outbreak of violence] by our people that Carson and his henchmen were working up this business': in p. 53/153, UCD Archives. **23.** Smyth, quoted in D. McArdle, *The Irish Republic*, p. 332. **24.** *Northern Whig*, 19 July 1920. **25.** Ibid. It wasn't just loyalists who called for a more urgent governmental response. Referring to the assignation of Smyth, *The Times*, 19 July 1920, suggested the government should regard the Irish problem as 'the greatest and most insistent issue in the whole field of British statesmanship'. **26.** Many of the weapons smuggled into the north before 1914 were still in circulation. **27.** The City's 'Island Men' were perceived to embody both the Protestant work ethic and political loyalty to Britain. **28.** Redmond, *Church, State, and Industry*, p. 12. This category of 'decent' Catholic tended to be confined to ex-servicemen working in the shipyards. **29.** Conor Kostick believes this economic explanation of the shipyard disturbances has been understated. Noting Belfast's disproportionately high unemployment rate in the early 1920s (over 26% compared to 17% in Great Britain), Kostick argues that the expulsions had 'very specific causes in the imme-diate defeat of a great strike and the onset of recession' and can be considered part of a pattern of post-war 'reactionary mobilisations of workers', including similar attacks on black dockers in Cardiff, the 1919 Chicago race riots and disturbances in Germany. Kostick concludes that the Belfast expulsions did 'not result from the same inherent prejudice amongst Protestant workers': in C. Kostick, *Revolution in Ireland*, p. 157. **30.** Ironically the expulsions of thousands of Catholics from the shipyards and factories and their temporary replacement by loyalists did not result in enjoying the wage levels of their predecessors, as the violence got progressively worse and the unions' economic bargaining position weakened, resulting in many workers' wages actually being reduced – joiners were reportedly earning 12s. a week less in 1921 than they had been the previous year – and an increase in the number of unemployed. **31.** Although unusual, such solidarity across the divided community was not unprecedented, as was experienced during the dock strike in the city in 1907. In the 1919 stoppage, some workers were demanding a 10-hour reduction in their working week (from 54 to

44 hours) and the creation of more jobs.   **32.** Three UULA members were successfully returned to Westminster at the end of 1918. Fears of the Bolshevik menace were evident in many European countries.   **33.** *Westminster Gazette*, quoted in *Irish News*, 26 July 1920.   **34.** *Irish News*, 22 July 1920.   **35.** McArdle, *The Irish Republic*, p. 329.   **36.** *Belfast Newsletter*, 15 July 1920.   **37.** Carson; in Hansard 22 July 1920, 5th series vol. 132 col. 617.   **38.** I return to this subject later.   **39.** Joe Graham, *In the Name of Carsonia*, claims that weapons had been bought by industrialists and businessmen and distributed amongst their workforce. **40.** Crawford Papers, D640, PRONI.   **41.** As in more recent times, there was a plethora of loyalist groups in the 1920s. With membership frequently overlapping, other groups believed to have been involved in staging the shipyard meeting including the UULA.   **42.** The meeting coincided with the Smyth funeral in Banbridge. Shipyard managers, who had experience of small-scale yard evictions in 1912 and should have been bracing themselves for trouble, were fiercely criticised for waiving their ban on political meetings taking place on yard property.   **43.** This term was used to embrace both Catholic workers and trade unionists, or 'rotten Prods'.   **44.** Estimates of the size of the mobs ranged from 300 to over 1,000. They were mainly young apprentices, especially platers' helpers.   **45.** Quoted in Farrell, *Orange State*, p. 28. Another worker reportedly had to swim to Sydenham where, dripping wet but having evaded his pursuers, he boarded a tram back to the city.   **46.** *Irish News*, 31 July 1920.   **47.** J. Kelly *Bonfires on the Hillside*, p. 12.   **48.** *Irish News*, 23 July 1920.   **49.** Even in larger factories, especially where the majority of the workforce was female, many Catholic workers returned to their jobs, sometimes within a matter of days (an example was linen workers). Others were also able to eventually find work elsewhere, especially in workplaces where intimidation was less prominent. Robert Preston recalls how an acquaintance, a Catholic foreman joiner who had been forced out of the shipyards soon found temporary work with a city building firm.   **50.** This happened where Protestants constituted a minority of the workforce, such as in the docks or the catering industry.   **51.** Also, some workers were intimidated more than once and others were even forced to leave a replacement position. Additionally some eventually returned to their jobs.   **52.** Although this still constituted a minority of the city's estimated 93,000 Catholics, the number of dependents affected by such intimidation would have been in the region of 40,000. Many female Gallahers' employees and textile workers receiving police protection had returned to work by the end of July.   **53.** Later waves of expulsions included Catholic employees in the rail industry and bakery trade, who also became popular targets for sectarian attacks.   **54.** It was alleged that this meeting had been arranged to coincide with the Catholic workers' attendance at a funeral of a colleague killed in an accident at the mill; reported in *Irish News*, 11 August 1920.   **55.** Reported in D. Curran, *St Paul's*, p. 53.   **56.** In *Irish News*, 29 July. This threat by predominantly Protestant workforces to 'down tools' if Catholics were allowed to return to work without signing the 'loyalty' pledge was repeated elsewhere and condemned by leading Catholic spokesmen such as Bishop MacRory.   **57.** Ibid. Such was the advice given to a young Catholic worker assaulted with an iron bar by a gang which entered a factory.   **58.** Davy Matthews' uncle, a Belfast Corporation painter who was relocated to a council depot in Ardoyne, was one such case.   **59.** Estimates of their numbers are put at around 1,800, nearly a quarter of all those evicted from the shipyards; in Morgan, *Labour and Partition*, p. 269. The prolonged absence of these officials from the yards and factory floors resulted in workers' economic rights receiving less profiled coverage, leading in turn to a drop in wages over the next couple of years and the temporary replacement of many union shop stewards by members of loyalist vigilante committees.   **60.** The Independent Labour Party hall at Langley Street in the north of the city was burned to the ground that summer. Victimisation of Belfast socialists carried on throughout the Troubles, especially surfacing during the election campaign for the new northern parliament in May 1921 when labour meetings were interrupted or even abandoned.   **61.** *TUC Report* 1921, p. 268; quoted in Morgan, *Labour and Partition*, p. 270.   **62.** In K. Middlemas, *Thomas Jones – Whitehall Diary*, p. 38.   **63.** *TUC Report* 1920, quoted in Morgan, *Labour and Partition*, p. 269.   **64.** These included the Belfast Branch of the INVA which met at the Tivoli picture-house on 7 August to register expelled Catholic ex-servicemen.   **65.** *Irish News*, 29 July 1920.   **66.** Engineering workers registered in Clonard Street Hall, joiners in the Garfield Street Rooms, with the other workers meeting at St Mary's Hall in Bank Street. **67.** *Irish News*, 13 August 1920.   **68.** St Mary's Hall staged concerts on at least three occasions in October 1920 with each concert receiving capacity audiences.   **69.** Bishop MacRory contributed £100 to the fund and Joe Devlin gave £50.   **70.** Expatriate group were especially generous. The Liverpool Irish Society contributed £150 to the fund in August 1920.   **71.** In MacRory files.   **72.** Ibid.   **73.** In *Irish News*, 13 August 1920.   **74.** Ibid., 20 August 1920.   **75.** Ibid., 6 October 1920.   **76.** Ibid.   **77.** Ibid., 7 September 1920.   **78.** Ibid., 9 August 1920.   **79.** MacRory files, 12 August 1920.   **80.** Ibid.   **81.** MacRory in a letter to Mr H Devine, 6 August 1920: quoted in Phoenix, *Northern Nationalism*, p. 91.   **82.** Hansard HOC vol. 134 cols 1452–5. Devlin absented himself from Westminster in protest over the Government's inaction in this area.   **83.** Hansard vol. 132 cols 194–197, 2 August 1920.   **84.** According to J McColgan, *British policy and*

the Irish administration 1920–1922, p. 132, the opening of this Belfast office 'not only presaged partition four months before the 1920 Act became law but initiated it in a practical way by the establishment of a central administration apparently working in the interests of the prospective Northern Ireland Government'. **85.** Sir Hamar Greenwood; quoted in Follis, *A State under Siege*, p. 12. **86.** Clark's observations of events in Belfast were rather typical of an upper class English observer. Having dinner with senior police chiefs Galston and Harrison during his first night in the city, Clark was struck by their lack of concern over the sound of sniper fire from the York Street area: see D1022/2/2 PRONI. **87.** Ex-soldiers were paid £1 9s. a week and all insured workers received £1 per week. **88.** *Irish News*, 18 September 1920.

CHAPTER 2

1. At her inquest the following week, it was claimed that a police sergeant had stumbled and, as a result, his pistol discharged, fatally wounding Mrs Noade. **2.** St Matthew's was one of the oldest Catholic churches in the city, having first opened its doors in 1833. **3.** This description by monk P.J. Gannon is found in Boyd, *Holy War*, p. 187. Both the first and last fatalities of the conflict were members of the parish and apart from those killed, over 150 were seriously injured. A more recent description of the church has stressed its strategic role as 'a rallying point of defence that has contributed to its present day survival'; in *Lagan Enclave*, p. 15. **4.** Inside a couple of days, sisters at the 20-year-old convent, acting on security advice, temporarily vacated their premises which were subsequently fire-bombed. A further assault on the Cross and Passion the following month was 'repulsed by parishioners' and the sisters' decision to return to Ballymacarrett proved to be 'a consolation and comfort' for their parishioners who were pleased that 'the sisters were still amongst them'; in Cross and Passion records, *Belfast Centenary Celebrations*. **5.** Inquest, reported in *Northern Whig*, 11 August, 1920. Samuel Faulkner was more fortunate that evening on the Newtownards Road. Two bullets passed through his coat but he was unharmed. **6.** Two youths were wounded going to Mr McAuley's assistance. **7.** Estimates of the size of the mob varied from the army's figure of a few hundred to the *Irish News* view (26 July) that it was 'several thousand strong'. Incredulously, the *Northern Whig* (24 July) informed its readers that the convent attack was 'the work of 1 or 2 lads with whom the crowd had no connection or sympathy.' **8.** Although the most serious damage to spirit groceries was experienced in the east of the city over a three day period at the end of July 1920, they proved to be a target for arsonists and gunmen periodically during the conflict. **9.** Whilst Ballymacarrett proved to be by far the biggest problem, there were reported cases of looting and excessive drunken behaviour in Sandy Row and west Belfast. **10.** In Redmond, *Church, State and Industry*, p. 21. This correlation between involvement both in attacks on the liquor stores and the wider disturbances on the streets, is significant. Drunken assailants making impromptu attacks on spirit groceries challenges those interpretations centred on the premise that the violence was premeditated and executed by people fully cognisant of the repercussions of their actions. **11.** *Irish News*, 23 July 1920. **12.** Ibid. **13.** *Northern Whig*, 24 July 1920. **14.** Ibid. **15.** In some cases, Catholics evicted from their spirit groceries were replaced, at least in the short term, by Protestants. This was more likely to have occurred in rented property. Robert Preston remembers Paddy Nugent, a spirit grocer on the Donegall Road, being forced out of his premises and a local Protestant taking over his trade. **16.** In *Lagan Enclave*, p. 16. Another vivid account of the plight of Catholic families evicted from their businesses and homes was given in Radio Ulster's *The State We're in*, 11 January 1992. A particularly poignant case of an elderly Belfast widow, whose son had been killed during the Great War, being forced out of her east Belfast home and suffering the ignominy of her possessions being tossed on to the street, was given in the *Irish News*, 26 July. A more detailed account of Catholic refugees is provided in Chapter 3. **17.** Mr Gray's learned colleague informed him that when a crowd of several hundred was attacking a property the owner was 'wise to clear out'; reported in *Irish News*, 29 July 1920. **18.** Quoted in the *Irish News*, 5 May 1921. It is likely that many spirit grocers, in dreaded anticipation of a similar outcome, copied Mr Hoey's example and itemised their existing stock. However, some were even less fortunate in their claims requests. Another east Belfast spirit grocer, William Bergin, of Ashmore Street, near Dee Street, received a mere £1,350 of his £5,500 claim for damage to his business; in *Irish News*, 16 April 1921. **19.** In Redmond, *Church, State and Industry*, p. 12. **20.** Ibid., p. 20. This curiosity theme is developed later. **21.** Although pubs and spirit groceries were the first port of call for looters and rioters, they also turned their attention to other shops in Ballymacarrett owned by Protestants. Walking down the Newtownards Road, Redmond was horrified to 'find Mr Dick's boot shop in the last stages of being looted' and saw men coming out with 'arms full of boots and shoes and women with aprons full'; Redmond, quoted in Boyd, *Holy War*, p. 188. **22.** Redmond, *Church, State and Industry*, p. 13. **23.** In *Irish News*, 31 August 1920; on 20 August, the *Irish News* also noted that Redmond did 'very good work controlling mobs'. **24.** *Belfast Newsletter*, 26 August 1920. **25.** *Northern Whig*, 26 July 1920. **26.** Ibid. **27.** Redmond's tactic of organising volunteers to patrol local districts was copied in areas like Willowfield and even spread outside the city to towns like Lisburn and Lurgan.   **28.** Although there may not have been a substantial difference in the personnel involved, the fundamental role of Redmond's unarmed vigilantes was, of course, vastly different to that assumed by the USC in November 1920.   **29.** In *Northern Whig*, 3 August 1920. **30.** Ibid.   **31.** The assassination of DI Swanzy is covered in greater detail in the next section.   **32.** *Irish News*, 26 August 1920.   **33.** The inquest verdict exonerated them from involvement in the disturbances but conceded they had been killed by blasts of military fire which had been used to disperse unruly crowds in that area.   **34.** *Belfast Telegraph*, 26 August 1920.   **35.** *Irish News*, 26 August 1920. As noted earlier, the convent's own account of the incident was quite different.   **36.** *Irish News*, 26 August 1920.   **37.** *Northern Whig*, 26 August 1920.   **38.** Charles Murray, 12 at the time, recalled yard workers 'going over the bridge at Frazer Street, going to their work in Harland and Wolff's engine-works and being targeted as they went up the steps of the bridge by snipers that were in the tower of the Roman Catholic Church'. Mr Murray also remembered the infamous Malcolmson brothers who crossed the city in 'a car fitted with machineguns' and the utter fear of people on the Newtownards Road as they drove along 'firing in every direction, particularly through the Catholic quarters'; in *The Century Speaks: Ulster Voices*, p. 88.   **39.** *Irish News*, 27 August 1920. **40.** The *Irish News*, 28 August, whimsically noted that an American journalist was threatened on the Newtownards Road by a number of men who demanded to know his religion. Even young children were threatened on the streets. Ten-year-old Jack Reid was walking with an older friend in this area when passers-by suddenly pulled a gun on his friend. Serious injury was only avoided because one of the assailants realised they had failed to pick their intended target; in Boyd, *Holy War*, p. 196.   **41.** There were a number of clashes over the next two years between loyalist shipyard workers and the city's mainly nationalist dock workers. Although most incidents occurred during the journeys to and from work, this attack was one of many which occurred during the period when most men would be at work.

CHAPTER 3

1. *Irish News*, 23 July 1920.   **2.** J. McDonnell estimates IRA strength in the city in July 1920 at around 1,000 and despite internal organisational problems, the Third Northern Division had in its possession, 600 rifles and 5 Thompson machine-guns; in McDonnell, *Northern Divisions*, pp 36–7.   **3.** In Boyd, *Holy War*, p. 190. This is also corroborated by an old republican who claimed 'we used to lie all night around Clonard Chapel on standby against the Orangemen': in G. Adams, *Falls Memories*, p. 67.   **4.** At the following month's inquest the jury, in discussing the deaths which occurred during the Kashmir Road disturbances, ruled that 'in the sniping no revolver shots were heard coming from the unionist side' (in Cupar Street); in *Northern Whig*, 11 August.   **5.** As he lay dying in the street, Mr. Robinson received the last rites.   **6.** Rev. J Kelly, writing to Rev. Burke, 26 July;in Clonard Monastery records, T1. Incidentally, Brother Morgan was buried in a vault at the monastery.   **7.** In *Irish News*, 26 July 1920.   **8.** In *Northern Whig*, 12 August 1920.   **9.** *Irish News*, 26 July 1920.   **10.** Mr Conn had been going to the assistance of Mr Dunning.   **11.** HOC 2 641 vol. 132, Hansard July/August 1920. Devlin also disputed the claim that it was an attack on republicans, suggesting it was an onslaught on Catholics in general.   **12.** Ibid.   **13.** Ibid.   **14.** Ibid.   **15.** Sir Ernest Clark was eventually appointed as the Under Secretary directly accountable to the Irish Secretary: see Chapter 18. **16.** *Belfast Newsletter*, 24 July 1920.   **17.** Hansard vol. 132 cols 1974–7, 2 August 1920.   **18.** *The Times*, 23 July 1920.   **19.** *Nation*, 31 July 1920. Hundreds of Indians had been massacred by British forces the previous year.   **20.** *Irish News*, 23 July 1920.   **21.** Ibid. Incidentally, another report in the same edition of the paper counteracts the suggestion that Belfast citizens had been anticipating the outbreak of violence. The *Irish News* noted that on the day violence broke out in the city, there had not been 'a whisper or hint of disturbances' and rather people 'in all parts were going about their business without thinking of impending disaster.' **22.** Devlin, in *Irish News*, 23 July 1920.   **23.** In *Irish News*, 26 July, 1920.   **24.** *Irish News*, 27 July, 1920. **25.** A more detailed account of Catholic migration is provided later in this chapter.   **26.** *Northern Whig*, 27 July 1920.   **27.** *Northern Whig*, 24 July 1920.   **28.** Coates, in *Irish News*, 24 July 1920.   **29.** Ibid. Loitering in public thoroughfares was a constant concern for the authorities and despite an information campaign, curiosity was to cost several people their lives.   **30.** Crawford diary, D640/11/1, 6 August 1920, PRONI. **31.** 'Daily News', 31 August 1920, quoted in *Irish News*, 2 September 1920. Martin's estimate of the arson damage was 180 fires in six days. One of unionism's most outspoken critics, Hugh Martin described the attacks on Catholics as being 'probably unmatched outside the area of Russian or Polish pogroms.' **32.** *Daily Herald*, 31 August 1920.   **33.** *Nation*, 4 September 1920.   **34.** Ibid., 8 September.   **35.** *Daily Mail*, 1 September 1920.   **36.** *Times*, 1 September 1920. Other sympathetic journals gave warnings to Ulster Unionists. The *Birmingham Post* warned Ulster that continued ill-treatment of Catholics would 'alienate the sympathies of people who desire to help her'; quoted in Bardon *A History of Ulster*, pp 473–4. The economic damage which was being caused by 'the anti-Catholic campaign' had brought the city to 'the verge of bankruptcy'; in *Daily News,* 31 August.   **37.** *Daily Express,* 1 September 1920.   **38.** *Daily Chronicle,* 1 September 1920.   **39.** Ibid., 15 September, 1920. However, as George Boyce, *Englishmen and Irish Troubles,* p. 108, points out, the change in post-war attitudes to the Irish crisis and the unfavourable manner in which the Belfast disturbances were reported in the British press, 'seemed to make nonsense of the Ulster Unionist claim that they represented the most progressive and civilised element in Irish life'. Even southern Anglican clergy were critical of northern protestants, with the Bishop of Meath confirming the 'happy relationship in both commercial and social life' existing between all religion groups in southern Ireland; in *Irish News,* 23 August 1920.   **40.** *Irish News,* 29 July 1920.   **41.** Ibid., 27 July 1920.   **42.** Ibid.   **43.** *Irish News,* 29 July 1920.   **44.** Ibid., 13 August 1920.   **45.** Ibid., 29 July 1920.   **46.** Also, it did not, as subsequent events in the Short Strand area were to illustrate, necessarily guarantee safety and it was likely that several families moved to safer areas in the west and north of the city.   **47.** J Boyd, *Out of My Class,* p. 40. Although the vast majority of families intimidated from their homes were Catholic, some Protestants who lived in Catholic areas, were to suffer the same fate. A respondent, who wishes to remain anonymous, remembered how her parents and older siblings were forced out their Percy Street home. Their furniture was removed and placed in the road, but fortunately her father contacted a local priest and they were able to transport their undamaged furniture and possessions to a house vacated by a Catholic family on the Crumlin Road. Later her father told her how the Catholic carter who had been hastily hired to transport their possessions, briskly covered the name on his vehicle as they approached the loyalist Crumlin Road!   **48.** *Irish News,* 28 August 1920.   **49.** Ibid.   **50.** Ibid., 26 August & 28 August 1920.   **51.** In contrast, unionist papers like the *Belfast Telegraph, Northern Whig* and the *Belfast Newsletter* rarely reported such evictions in depth.   **52.** Quoted in *Irish News,* 18 August 1920.   **53.** One estimate of the Free State administration was that 303 houses belonging to Catholics were burned beyond repair between July 1920 and April 1922; in p. 53/176, UCD Archives.   **54.** Paddy O'Donnell's frequent moves during these turbulent times would not have been uncommon for many Catholics. Paddy's family moved across the city from the loyalist Donegall Road to the Antrim Road around the start of the Troubles and, after short periods in Dublin and Castlederg (his mother's home town), they eventually returned to Belfast (unlike some of his cousins who continued to live in the south).   **55.** In *Irish News,* 21 June 1921.   **56.** In *Irish News,* 28 July 1920.   **57.** In *Irish News,* 29 July 1920.   **58.** P53/178, UCD Archives.   **59.** MacRory's telegram to Churchill 21 April 1922: quoted in *Irish Independent,* 22 April 1922.   **60.** In July 1922 Churchill suggested that Craig's administration should consider reimbursing the Free State for housing its northern refugees.   **61.** For instance, many homes in the parish of St Paul's in west Belfast were constructed using such funds: see Curran, *St Paul's,* p. 56. Indeed, one street, Amcomri Street was an acronym of the American Committee for Relief of Ireland.   **62.** *Irish Independent,* 6 June 1922.   **63.** Quoted in *Irish Independent,* 15 June 1922.   **64.** *Irish Independent,* 1 June 1922.   **65.** Ibid.   **66.** Quoted in *Irish Independent,* 12 June 1922.   **67.** Quoted in *Belfast Newsletter,* 21 June 1922.   **68.** The streets involved included Lower California Street, Peter's Place, Maryville Street, and the Grosvenor Road.   **69.** *Freeman's Journal,* 7 June 1922; in MacRory files (Armagh). Another nationalist claim regarding the damage caused to the property of Catholics over a period covering the duration of most of the conflict (July 1920–April 1922) was that over 300 Catholic houses were destroyed: in p. 53/176 UCD Archives.   **70.** CAB 9 B 41/1, PRONI.   **71.** *Irish Independent,* 3 June 1922.   **72.** *Belfast Newsletter,* 18 July 1922.   **73.** An abortive attempt to kill Swanzy had been made shortly before, when he had been stationed in Downpatrick. The assassination squad was believed to have been mostly from Cork, though Joe McKelvey was believed to have done reconnaissance for the attack. Indeed, it was claimed he had a conversation with Swanzy in a park close to Lisburn Cathedral.   **74.** The taxi had been hired from a firm in Belfast's Upper Library Street and was driven by Sligo-born IRA volunteer, Sean Leonard.   **75.** Leonard's death sentence was commuted to 12 years' imprisonment.   **76.** *Northern Whig,* 23 August 1920.   **77.** *Irish News,* 24 August, 1920.   **78.** Fred Crawford's diary, D640/11/1 PRONI.   **79.** In *Irish News,* 9 September, 1920.   **80.** Curfew restrictions started at 10.30 p.m. and ended at 5 a.m. No civilians were allowed on the streets during these hours, unless they had special permits.   **81.** Another soldier, Charles Harold, died of his injuries on 4 September.   **82.** It was reported in the nationalist press that Mr. Saye, an ex-soldier, was suspected of being involved in the 'torching' of a pub in Apsley Street. The sixth death, incidentally, was that of James Cromie, described in the previous chapter.   **83.** *Irish News,* 1 September 1920.   **84.** Ibid.   **85.** It was estimated that there were 122 fires, mainly on Catholic homes and business premises in a nine day period (from 25 August until 2 September), causing over £1 million damage: see p. 53/155 UCD Archives.   **86.** Constable Leonard's family were awarded £3,500 compensation in September 1921.   **87.** See account in Curran, *St Paul's,* p. 59 and the account of an old IRA volunteer in Adams, *Falls Memories,* p. 66.   **88.** Hansard 5th series, vol. 143, cols 335–42.   **89.** It was claimed that Harrison and Head Constable Giff had been responsible for the actual shootings, although other gang members, including Clarke, Glover and Hicks were also likely to have been involved: in Nixon file, Blythe papers p. 24/176, UCD Archives. **90.** There was paramilitary involvement at both the funerals of Edward Trodden and Sean Gaynor. Thousands attended the Gaynor funeral, with an estimated 500 volunteers led by Sean O'Neill and Joe McKelvey following the cortege. Armoured cars kept a discreet distance from the cortege and legend has it that when the British officer in charge of the leading car turned his machine gun on Mr Gaynor senior and other family members, threatening to open fire unless the tricolour was removed from the coffin, Liam Gaynor refused and the flag remained on his son's coffin; in McDonnell, *Northern Divisions*, p. 62. **91.** Hansard 5th series, vol. 143, cols 335–42. **92.** *Daily Express*, 27 September 1920. **93.** In *Irish News*, 29 September 1920. **94.** Reported in *Belfast Newsletter*, 6 October, 1920. During the Sinn Féin funerals, Protestant-owned shops were ordered to close by the IRA: in *Belfast Telegraph*, 29 September.

CHAPTER 4

1. M. Hopkinson, in *The Irish War of Independence*, p. 160, claimed that Galway traders had staged a boycott of northern businesses as far back as December 1919 and there were instances of widespread activity during the following six months. **2.** Rev. J. Hassan, a priest at St Mary's, using the pseudonym G.B. Kenna, wrote *Facts and Figures – The Belfast Progroms 1920–22*. MacRory's initiative in this area is indicative of the unparalleled involvement of a senior member of the Catholic hierarchy in quasi-political affairs. However, not all Catholic clergy favoured the boycott strategy. A County Louth priest, Rev. N. Lawless, suggested that such a measure was unnecessary because the upheaval in Belfast had been largely due to IRA violence. He claimed: 'it is those [IRA] crimes that enraged – and no wonder – the workers of Belfast who have said they will let Catholic workers back when the shooting of RIC men and others stops': in A. Mitchell, *Revolutionary Government in Ireland*, p. 170. **3.** Quoted in Hennessy, *A History of Northern Ireland*, p. 14. **4.** Undated circular, headed 'Belfast Trade Boycott', SPO DE 2/110. **5.** Ibid. **6.** Ibid. It was claimed that depots for such goods had been established in Liverpool, Glasgow and Manchester, with 'goods being redirected to Ireland under bogus names.' **7.** See D.S. Johnson, 'The Belfast Boycott 1920–22', in *Irish Population, Economy and Society*, p. 292. Northern government records illustrate the extent of boycotting in the border areas over the next year. In February 1922 there were at least 8 prosecutions in the Fintona district of County Tyrone, including 2 grocers, for alleged misdemeanours including the posting of boycott notices, the delivery of threatening letters to shopkeepers still selling Belfast goods and open attempts to dissuade potential customers from entering such premises; in HA 5/111, PRONI. **8.** In *Northern Whig*, 18 August 1921. Nationalist sources maintained that there was a reduction of nearly 50% on northern trade with the south. **9.** *Irish News*, 10 May 1921. **10.** In *Belfast Telegraph*, 6 April 1921. **11.** Quoted in D Kennedy, *The Widening Gulf*, p. 88. Incidentally, Sir James Craig owned the northern-based distillery. **12.** Quoted in L. Curtis, *The Causes of Ireland*, p. 335. **13.** Johnson, 'The Belfast Boycott 1920–22', p. 299, estimates that deposits in northern banks fell by 6.1% in the late 1920 to 1922 period with a corresponding 9.3% rise in business in the south. **14.** An Ulster Bank circular, 12 October 1920 FIN 18/1/185, PRONI. **15.** CAB 6/23, PRONI. **16.** CAB/4/23/6, 22 September 1921, PRONI. **17.** Ibid. **18.** CAB 4/23/5, PRONI. **19.** CAB 4/23/9, PRONI. **20.** Michael Collins annoyed Bishop MacRory by his opinion that the boycott was 'comparatively ineffective'; quoted in Kennedy, *The Widening Gulf*, p. 87. **21.** Dáil Éireann, Treaty Debate, p. 225: quoted in Kennedy, *The Widening Gulf*, p. 86. **22.** A more detailed analysis of this is provided in chapter 13. **23.** Quoted in *Irish Times*, 23 January 1922. **24.** The most active support for the boycott tactic in 1922 came from the anti Treaty section of Sinn Féin. **25.** Even Collins, who was far from convinced about the tactic, seriously considered the possibility of reintroducing an official boycott. This was largely due to pressure from the Belfast Boycott committee and Collins' compromise was to establish a North Eastern Advisory committee to monitor the situation in the north. **26.** In one bizarre case a Dublin art gallery was threatened and advised to withdraw paintings exhibited by northern artists! **27.** In *Times*, 27 April, 1922. **28.** In *Northern Whig*, 5 April, 1921. **29.** In *Northern Whig*, 28 October 1921. **30.** Ibid. **31.** *Northern Whig*, 15 April, 1921. **32.** As early as 20 January 1922, the UTDA had placed an advertisement in the *Belfast Telegraph*, asking if Belfast people were 'going to purchase his [the southern boycotter's] goods whilst he refuses to buy theirs, and chases their salesmen and tips into the river or burns the products of the mills and factories that give our sons and daughters employment?' **33.** *Belfast Telegraph*, 17 May 1922. **34.** Ulster Trades' Defence Association advert, CAB 6/23,PRONI. **35.** Ibid. **36.** *Belfast Newsletter*, 7 April 1922. Loyalists claimed the moral high ground over the issue. In a report the following month, the *Belfast Telegraph*, 1 May 1922, reminded its readers that 'Jameson's whiskey, Guinness's porter, Jacob's biscuits and Limerick bacon are retailed as freely in Belfast as in Dublin' and pointed out that 'no armed gunmen go about here collecting debts due to these firms in the way that gunmen go around in Dublin and elsewhere in the south openly and illegally collecting and appropriating the debts due to Northern traders.' **37.** *Belfast Newsletter*,

10 May 1921. **38.** Ibid. **39.** *Belfast Newsletter*, 2 February 1921 and *Northern Whig*, 2 May 1921. **40.** *Belfast Telegraph*, 6 April 1921. **41.** *Belfast Newsletter*, 10 May 1921. The *Newsletter* claimed that less than 20% of the city's trade was with the rest of Ireland. This economic self-sufficiency theme was also reflected in sympathetic British press treatment of the boycott. **42.** D Kennedy in *The Widening Gulf*, p. 89, reckoned that even a couple of years after the termination of the boycott, exports from Northern Ireland to the Irish Free State were only half those of 1920 levels. **43.** See Phoenix, *Northern Nationalism*, p. 92. **44.** P.S. O'Hegarty, 'The Victory of Sinn Féin', quoted in Kostick, *Revolution in Ireland*, p. 159. **45.** Ibid. Winston Churchill was also to write about the psychological damage inflicted upon the notion of Irish unity by the use of a tactic which proved to be 'merely a blind suicidal contribution to the general hate.' Indeed, Churchill maintained that the boycott of northern goods 'recognised and established real partition, spirited and voluntary partition, before physical partition had been established'; in W Churchill, *The World Crisis and the Aftermath*, p. 318. **46.** See Kennedy, *The Widening Gulf*, pp 88–9. **47.** Ibid. **48.** However, cross-border trade continued to be adversely affected for a number of years. **49.** D.S. Johnson, 'The Belfast Boycott', p. 306. **50.** Dennis Kennedy in *The Widening Gulf*, p. 89, notes that the boycott was still being enforced in the second half of 1921 by the same Sinn Féin leaders who were being welcomed in London as negotiators, and how this did 'nothing to encourage Unionist confidence in the British Government.' M. Hopkinson, *The Irish War of Independence*, p. 161, also argues that the boycott policy 'amounted to little more than gesture politics'.

CHAPTER 5

1. This is arguably the case with Michael Farrell's *Arming the Protestants*. **2.** CAB 23/37, 356–62, 2 September, PRONI. **3.** Ibid. An earlier Craig memo to the British government warned of 'rebel plans' to establish by 'working in conjunction with Bolshevik Forces elsewhere … a Republic hostile to the British Empire' and, in demanding 'immediate action' from those in power, warned that in order to prevent 'civil war on a very large scale', it might be 'advisable' for them to see what steps could be taken towards 'a system of *organised* reprisals'; quoted in K. Middlemas, *Thomas Jones – Whitehall Diary*, p. 38. **4.** However, not everyone was happy about the creation of such a force, especially General Macready, the military officer commanding British forces in Ireland. **5.** Additionally, as R. Abbott, *Police Casualties in Ireland 1919–22*, p. 145, points out, IRA intimidation of Catholics elsewhere in Ireland deterred recruitment to the RIC, which compounded its existing shortfall in personnel. **6.** The organisation of Specials within the Belfast area was to be administered differently, relating closely to the organisation of existing police divisions in Belfast: in A. Hezlet, *The B Specials: a history of the Ulster Special Constabulary*, pp 29–30. Basing Special Constables in regular police stations would have significant bearing on subsequent incidents in the city. **7.** Regulations clearly stated the subordinate role of the Special Constabulary. One such rule stated, 'Special Constables will not under any circumstances act on their own initiative. In particular, an 'order to fire' must come from the senior member of the RIC present': quoted in Hezlet, *The B Specials*, p. 31. Raids or searches involving Special Constables were subject to the permission of the RIC County Inspector (in the case of the Belfast area, this was DI Harrison, regarded by many as leader of the murder gang) and, if this was granted, RIC personnel had to be present. **8.** Modifications of the 'C' branch of the force took place in April 1921 when a C1 group was established. Organised on a territorial basis for emergency use only, it was officially separated from the rest of the Special Constabulary, following the creation of the RUC in May 1922. **9.** Advertisements for recruitment to the Special Constabulary subdivided into county lists, were printed in the press throughout November. This one refers to Belfast; quoted in *Belfast Telegraph*, 1 November 1920. **10.** In Hezlet, *The B Specials*, p. 23. **11.** Quoted in Hezlet, *The B Specials*, p. 27. **12.** Spender, quoted in C. Ryder, *The R.U.C. – A Force under Fire*, pp 37–40. **13.** Recruitment for the comparatively well-paid 'A' Constabulary was brisker, with 1700 applications province-wide inside six weeks. **14.** D 1700/5/16B, 16 December,1920, PRONI. **15.** *Northern Whig*, 18 April 1921. **16.** Quoted in M Hopkinson, *The Irish War of Independence*, pp 52–3. **17.** C. Wickham, 9 November 1921: quoted in Kenna, *Facts and Figures*, pp 57–8. **18.** Wickham circular: quoted in Kenna, *Facts and Figures*, pp 57–62. **19.** The outcome of the so-called 'Wickham Circular' scandal was the shelving of such recruitment into the plain clothes 'C' category, but also an increase in the numbers of both the 'B' section (by nearly 5,000) and the full-time 'A' section (by about 700). Although the Special Constabulary was enlarged to contain escalating violence in 1922 – A Hezlet, *The B Specials*, p. 88, estimates its membership peaked at around 5,500 'A' Specials, 19,000 'B's and 7,500 'C's, resulting in an astronomical security bill of one and a half million pounds for 1921 and £2.7 million for 1922 – it never reached its required quota and, especially in those areas where it was most needed, under-recruited. **20.** Joe Devlin, UK Parliamentary Debates, 25 October 1920, HOC 5th series, vol. 133. **21.** *Irish News*, 1 November 1920. **22.** Ibid. **23.** Ibid. **24.** *Times;* quoted in Phoenix, *Northern Nationalism*, p. 93. **25.** *Daily Mail*, 15

September 1920, quoted in Kenna *Facts and Figures,* p. 37. **26.** Ibid. **27.** *Westminster Gazette,* 16 September 1920. **28.** *Nation,* 18   September, 1920. **29.** *Fermanagh Herald,* 27 November 1920. **30.** *Belfast Telegraph,* 29 November 1920. **31.** This apparent standing-down of the Specials particularly galled Craig who was aware of IRA training around the border area during the Truce period. **32.** Of the 49 Special Constables killed during the conflict, only 11 lost their lives whilst serving in the city. This may well have been due to republicans' stronger position in these areas. **33.** Hezlet, *The B Specials,* p. 46. **34.** MIC 127/27, 6 April 1921, PRONI. **35.** However, some Catholics, including Sarah O'Hare, did not have direct experience of hostile treatment from the Specials. **36.** Attacks which were allegedly carried out by Specials or by 'rogue' policemen are described later. **37.** Indeed, many of those accused of vicious attacks on Catholics were members of the RIC rather than the Special Constabulary. Also, weaponry regulations meant it was more difficult for Specials to have easy access to 'official' weapons, so it was likely that the fire-arms used in many of these controversial cases were either privately owned or were weapons belonging to the regular police, which implies the collusion of some police officers. **38.** Although tragic shootings of Catholics grabbed the headlines, the most common complaints against them involved over-aggressive personal searching, minor assault, sectarian name-calling and especially provocative searching and damaging of personal possessions during security force raids. **39.** Kelly, *Bonfires on the Hillside,* pp 16–17. **40.** The USC was not to celebrate its half century. Following the damning indictment of the Hunt Report which investigated policing issues at the start of the modern conflict, the Special Constabulary was disbanded in 1969. **41.** Follis, *A State under Siege,* p. 16. **42.** Hezlet, *The B Specials,* p. 47. **43.** Fitzpatrick, *The Two Irelands – 1912–39,* p. 119. **44.** Ibid. Ironically, despite the bigoted motives of some members, the force precipitated the conclusion of a sectarian conflict. **45.** B Griffin, 'A Force Divided: Policing Ireland 1900–60', in *History Today,* October 1999, p. 28. **46.** Ibid., p. 27. **47.** See Farrell, *Arming the Protestants,* p. 166. Craig's administration was reassured by the news on 9 February 1921 that Westminster would fund approximately half of USC costs, approximately £850,000. **48.** Ibid., p. 166. **49.** The RIC was disbanded in the north on 31 May 1922 and it was some time before the RUC took the field against the IRA (it only had 1,000 recruits by July 1922). In practice at least, the USC constituted the main counter-insurgency force in the pivotal period between November 1921 and the end of the conflict: see Follis, *State under Siege,* p. 86. **50.** One should note that the problems which the army had in coping with loyalist mobs were accentuated by the locals' close relationship with the USC. Thus, a senior army officer was to complain of the Specials' failure to support the military on 3 June 1922 when they were being attacked by a mob on the Newtownards Road; 6 June 1922, CAB 6/43, PRONI.

CHAPTER 6

1. However, during this period there were at least 7 additional deaths of people injured in earlier disturbances. Protestants who succumbed to their wounds were John Lawther, of Everton Street, John McClean, of Glenallen Street, and Joseph Morrison, of Boyne Street, whilst Catholics William Bell, of Brown Street and William Mullen, of Urney Street also died of their injuries. Two members of the security forces also died in the city during November. RIC officer Samuel Lucas, shot by the IRA in County Fermanagh, passed away in the Royal Victoria Hospital, and soldier Arthur Bundy died on 21 November. **2.** Reported in *Belfast Telegraph,* 8 October 1920. **3.** There were at least another four cases of civilians being struck and fatally wounded by police or military vehicles during the conflict. **4.** A Catholic, Henry Megaw, described by witnesses as having cheered and waved his cap in the air as Mr McLeod fell, was later acquitted of his murder. **5.** MacRory, quoted in Curran, *St Paul's – the Pivotal Point,* p. 56. **6.** MacRory, in a letter to the Belfast Expelled Workers Fund, 20 November; in Bishop MacRory files, folder 11. **7.** Ibid. **8.** Ibid., folder 11, dated 24 December. Similar letters were sent to French bishops. The Irish Catholic hierarchy also professed their support for northern Catholics, claiming in October that 'in no other part of Ireland' was 'a minority persecuted;' quoted in M. Harris, *The Catholic Church and the foundation of the Northern Irish State,* p. 86. **9.** Ibid. **10.** *Belfast Telegraph,* 22 November and 15 December respectively. **11.** *Belfast Newsletter,* 13 November 1920. **12.** *Belfast Telegraph,* 29 November 1920. **13.** D 640/11/1, 6 September 1920, PRONI. **14.** The Act came into force on 1 May 1921. Although described by Brian Follis, *A State under Siege,* p. 185, as an attempt to find 'a broadly acceptable compromise between the conflicting aspirations of loyalism and nationalism', the legislation failed to directly address the needs of nationalists within Ulster. **15.** The crucial difference between the two pieces of legislation was, of course, that only one, Dublin-based administration was proposed in the 1912 bill. **16.** A more detailed account of the provisions of the Government of Ireland Act can be found in D. Fitzpatrick, *The Two Irelands, 1912–1939,* p. 100. **17.** Carson was to express such long-term optimism during the Westminster debate on the Bill, hoping that it would result in an Ireland 'one and individual, loyal to this country and loyal to the Empire'; in HOC Debates, vol. 134, col. 1422, 11

November 1920. Sinn Féin , on the other hand, were horrified that, under section 75 of the bill, 'the supreme authority of the Parliament of the United Kingdom shall remain unaffected and undiminished over all serious matters and things in N Ireland'; quoted in Buckland, *Factory of Grievances*, p. 3. **18.** This was reflected in the second clause of the Bill. Indeed, the Act actually specified that the Council of Ireland should be constituted 'with a view to the essential establishment of a Parliament for the whole of Ireland': the Government of Ireland Act: quoted in Hopkinson, *The Irish War of Independence*, pp 212–13. **19.** HOC Debates 5th series, vol. 127 col. 98, 29 March 1920. **20.** HOC Debates 5th series, vol. 134, col. 1447, 11 November 1920. **21.** Ibid., col. 1455. Devlin dismissed the parliament, alleging it would be 'merely a familiar party of profiteers, puppets and placemen'. **22.** HOC Debates 5th series, vol. 127, cols 1139–49, 30 March 1920. **23.** *Irish News*, 24 December 1920. **24.** Ibid. **25.** *Nation*, 24 December 1920. **26.** *Times*, 24 December 1920. Apart from towards the end of its parliamentary passage, the Bill tended to receive relatively low-key coverage. **27.** Ibid. **28.** *Daily Chronicle*, 26 November, 1920. **29.** *Belfast Telegraph*, 22 December 1920. **30.** Ibid. **31.** *Irish News*, 1 January 1921. **32.** This discount was announced in Warnock's Royal Avenue sale; quoted in *Belfast Telegraph*, 13 December 1920. **33.** In *Belfast Telegraph*, 10 November, 1920. **34.** In *Belfast Telegraph*, 13 December, 1920. **35.** However, tram billboards would have reminded them of the imminent arrival of new rolling-stock for the City's Tram Department.

CHAPTER 7
1. *Northern Whig*, 2 January 1921. **2.** *Belfast Telegraph*, 1 January 1921. **3.** Ibid. **4.** *Northern Whig*, 1 January 1921. **5.** *Irish News*, 1 January, 1921. The year they were referring to was 1801, when the Act of Union was implemented. **6.** Reported in *Northern Whig*, 2 & 3 January, 1921. **7.** *Northern Whig*, 4 & 5 January, 1921. **8.** It was suggested that a hotel barman, who was an IRA member, had become suspicious of the armed guard sometimes placed outside rooms at the top of the hotel, and had noted how meals were brought to the occupants of these rooms. The IRA were alerted and the shooting sanctioned, probably by Collins. Experienced IRA personnel, including Roger McCorley, were believed to have been involved in this ruthless operation. **9.** *Northern Whig*, 27 January 1921. The paper, which had led with the headline, 'Two Police Murdered in Belfast – Shot Dead in Bed', used the outrage to express their concern at worrying recruitment levels for the Specials in Belfast. **10.** *Belfast Telegraph*, 27 January 1921. **11.** In *Irish News*, 28 January 1921. **12.** *Northern Whig*, 28 January 1921. **13.** Mr McGarvey was believed to have been a victim of mistaken identity. It has been suggested that the Nixon gang, in their urgency to eke out revenge, incorrectly fingered Mr McGarvey whose name and background were similar to that of the barman suspected of setting up the attack. **14.** The killing of Special Constable John Cummings in an IRA attack at Warrenpoint in Co. Down on 6 February and the jeering of the Oldpark-born officer's coffin by republican prisoners as it passed the Crumlin Road Goal did little to ease such tension. **15.** *Northern Whig*, 15 February 1921. **16.** Ibid., 18 February 1921. **17.** See *Northern Whig*, 11, 14, 17, 21, 24 and 25 January 1921. **18.** *Belfast Telegraph*, 27 January 1921. **19.** Ibid., 28 April7 1921. The *Belfast Newsletter*, 9 May 1921, also condemned the 'systematic persecution of Protestants' claiming that, 'not since 1641 have the [Protestant] minority been in greater danger'. **20.** D 989 C/1/51 PRONI. Statistical information was more in evidence the following year when the plight of southern Protestants worsened. Presbyterian Home Mission reports claimed that the Protestant population in several counties was seriously shrinking with an estimated 45% decline between 1915 and 1922. Dennis Kennedy, *The Widening Gulf*, p. 127, suggests that the 32% decline in the overall southern Protestant population between 1911–1926 reflected the scale of the problem, as well as the genuine fear of northern loyalists. **21.** Quoted in *Northern Whig*, 21 January 1921. **22.** *Belfast Telegraph*, 10 January 1921. **23.** *Northern Whig*, 8 February 1921. **24.** Ibid., 14 February, 1921. The *Belfast Telegraph* also denounced Devlin's abstentionist policy in its 5 April edition. **25.** *Northern Whig*, 24 January 1921. The *Observer*, 6 February, approved of Craig's appointment, describing his acceptance speech as 'forward-looking, constructive and conciliatory.' **26.** *Northern Whig*, 4 February 1921. **27.** Carson in the *Northern Whig*, 4 February 1921. **28.** Carson, speaking on 4 February 1921; quoted in H. Montgomery Hyde, *Carson*, p. 449. **29.** Craig, quoted in *Belfast Newsletter*, 8 February 1921. **30.** In *Irish News*, 14 February 1921. **31.** In *Northern Whig*, 14 February 1921. **32.** In *Irish News*, 15 April 1921. Devlin was the most popular speaker to appear at St Mary's Hall at this time. Sarah O'Hare recalls going to St Mary's a few times with her parents and being impressed both by his eloquence and sartorial elegance! **33.** De Valera, in 'Weekly Freeman', 5 February; quoted in J Bowman, *De Valera and the Ulster Question*, p. 44. **34.** *Irish News*, 26 January 1921. **35.** Ibid., 21 February 1921. **36.** Ibid., 29 March 1921. **37.** All three officers were 26 years of age and had military service to their credit. **38.** Mr Allen, a widower and father of eight children, was a joiner in the shipyards, who had experienced a fortunate escape nearly a decade previously. He had sailed to Southampton on the *Titanic*, as it prepared to embark on its maiden voyage to America. **39.** Events in the city at this time neatly fit into the pattern of

'Belfast violence' described by A.T.Q. Stewart in *The Narrow Ground*. Stone-throwing between small groups from either side of the sectarian divide had led to a significant increase in the number of those involved and the subsequent difficulty experienced by police in dispersing large crowds. Revolver fire broke out and brought an immediate police response and a call for reinforcements as gunfire continued to rage.   40. They were acquitted of this charge on 9 June.   41. Easter was not trouble-free elsewhere in the north. Over a ten day period, a policeman was killed in Derry, three were shot dead at Dromore in County Tyrone and a Special Constable was shot dead near Crossmaglen.   42. In *Northern Whig*, 6 April 1921.   43. Ibid.   44. The attack shows the IRA's often impromptu response to changing security force deployment in the city. Reportedly tipped off by a boy who had seen Tans enter a city hotel, an IRA team was 'scrambled' later in the day. One of the gang had a fortunate escape after the attack. Finding the gates at one end of the Queen's Arcade locked, the republican activist handed his gun to a passing girl who happened to be a friend of his mother; Montgomery, quoted in McDermott, *Northern Divisions*, p. 75–76.   45. *Irish News*, 25 April, 1921. 46. Joe Graham, *In the Name of Carsonia*, suggests that the gang comprised Sergeant Christy Clarke, Sergeant Hicks, Constable Golding and Constable Caldwell.   47. Kenna, *The Belfast Pogroms 1920–22*, p. 40, described them as 'two of the most respectable and well-conducted young Catholic men in the city.' 48. Jimmy Kelly remembers being told by the headmaster of St Paul's that his teacher had been 'shot by bad men' the previous night. Jimmy also recalls Christy Clarke's children attending St Paul's School at this time and how they used to be collected from school in a police vehicle.   49. It was believed that a silencer was used to nullify the sound of firing and therefore the rest of the family did not hear the shooting. John Duffin caught a brief glimpse of his brother's assassins leaving their home and noted an apparent lack of haste, a distinctive characteristic of the murder gang.   50. *Irish News*, 26 April 1921.   51. See Graham, *In the Name of Carsonia*. Shooting occurred in the Old Lodge Road area after the funeral, when 5 people suffered gunshot wounds.

CHAPTER 8
1. Craig, quoted in the *Irish News*, 11 May 1921.   2. Craig, quoted in Hennessy, *A History of Northern Ireland*, p. 15.   3. The Unionist leader boasted to Irish Secretary Greenwood that loyalist candidates had been selected without dissension and that 'unanimity prevails'; in PM 1/20, 7 April 1921, PRONI. Consequently, the Unionist Party managed to avoid a situation where independent unionists competed with 'official' candidates for the loyalist vote.   4. *Northern Whig*, 4 May 1921.   5. Ibid. A couple of days earlier the *Whig* had castigated the 'murderous ruffians of the so-called Irish Republican Army' which they suggested, were 'not leading the population of Ireland' but rather were 'driving' them; in *Northern Whig*, 2 May 1921.   6. J.V. Bates, in *Northern Whig*, 2 May 1921.   7. *Belfast Newsletter*, 14 May 1921. Sections of the loyalist press refused to allow Labour candidates to advertise their meetings and labour meetings scheduled for the Ulster Hall to be abandoned on account of loyalist intimidation.   8. *Belfast Newsletter*, 23 May 1921. 9. *Irish Independent*, quoted in *Belfast Telegraph*, 3 May 1921.   10. *Belfast Telegraph*, 13 May 1921.   11. Taken from W Ewart, 'A Journey in Ireland 1921'; in Craig, *Belfast Anthology*, p. 198.   12. Ibid.   13. Ibid. 14. *Belfast Telegraph*, 21 and 24 May 1921.   15. Carson, in *Belfast Telegraph*, 23 May, 1921. Craig was also active during the campaign. Robert Preston recalled seeing him, surrounded by 'A' Specials, travelling from one meeting to another in a yellow touring car.   16. MacRory, quoted in *Irish News*, 23 May 1921.   17. The arrangement had been agreed by Sean MacEntee and Joe Devlin towards the end of March.   18. The northern perspectives of de Valera and Collins could not have been any more stark, both in terms of style and substance. De Valera was an ideologue who quickly grew more obsessed with the issues of a 'republic' and sovereignty than with closely associating himself with the plight of Catholics in the Six Counties. Collins, on the other hand, was more of a pragmatist than a political thinker and empathised more closely with the beleaguered Catholic northern minority.   19. The Sinn Féin candidates in Belfast were John Dolan, Sean MacEntee, Denis McCullough, Denis Barnes and Michael Carolan.   20. *Irish News*, 10 and 24 May 1921. Incidentally, de Valera made a fleeting high security visit to Belfast during the election campaign. John Parkinson remembers hearing an impassioned de Valera addressing a large crowd on spare ground near Christ Church in Hamill Street and recalls grim-faced RIC officers 'watching his every move like hawks at the back of the crowd'.   21. *Irish News*, 23 May, 1921.   22. In *Weekly Northern Whig*, 7 May 1921.   23. *Belfast Telegraph*, 6 May 1921. Other loyalists were far less relaxed about such a meeting. Speaking to a group of North Belfast Unionists, loyalist firebrand Sam McGuffin said he had been 'astonished' by the Dublin Castle meeting and suggested their leader had been 'inveigled' into such an interview: reported in *Irish News*, 6 May 1921.   24. *Morning Post*, 9 May 1921.   25. The meeting is memorable only for de Valera's lengthy diatribe on Irish history which Craig stoically ignored. This abortive meeting was another blow to northern nationalists, who felt that Dublin republicans were unresponsive to their plight. Jimmy Kelly's father was one Belfast

Catholic disillusioned by Dublin's lukewarm response to the position of northern Catholics.   **26.** In *Irish News*, 7 May, 1921.   **27.** Ibid.   **28.** Ibid., 13 and 17 May. Christy Robinson remembers how 'curiosity' led him to Dunville Park on the Falls Road where Devlin, accompanied by a band and flag-waving supporters, was speaking.   **29.** Devlin; quoted in *Irish News*, 7 May 1921.   **30.** Campbell; quoted in *Irish News*, 2 May 1921.   **31.** Ibid.   **32.** *Irish News*, 4 and 2 May 1921.   **33.** Ibid., 23 May 1921.   **34.** *Belfast Newsletter*, 24 May 1921.   **35.** *Daily Telegraph*, 25 May, 1921.   **36.** Ibid.   **37.** Quoted in Buckland, *Craig*, p. 59.   **38.** *Irish News*, 27 May, 1921. British papers on the left, including the 'Daily News' and 'Manchester Guardian' were also critical of the manner in which the election was conducted. On 25 May the *Manchester Guardian* suggested; 'It would be hard to find even in the rather corrupt history of Irish politics an election fought with such ruthlessness, such corruption and such unfairness as the election for the Northern Parliament, which ended today.'   **39.** Also, in Lisburn a train transporting expelled workers from Belfast, who were attempting to cast their votes in the areas where they were registered, was attacked in the station.   **40.** In his autobiography, *Fifty Years of Ulster 1890–1940*, p. 108, T.J. Campbell recalled escorting an elderly Catholic voter, 'with blood streaming from a wound on his face' to an empty police barracks at Mountpottinger. A British soldier approached the pair of them and pointing to the injured man said, 'We think, sir, that you people over here are all mad.'   **41.** Clark, in a letter to Greenwood, 28 May 1921, FIN 18/1/86 PRONI.   **42.** Entry in diary of F. Crawford, 28 May 1921; D 640/11 PRONI.   **43.** *Belfast Newsletter*, 25 May 1921.   **44.** *Belfast Newsletter*, 27 May 1921.   **45.** Sinn Féin failed to return a candidate in Belfast. The *Belfast Telegraph*, 27 May 1921, duly celebrated the 'rout of Sinn Féin'.   **46.** *Irish News*, 28 May 1921. In the previous day's edition, the *Irish News* had sniped at the 'docile stupidity' of the loyalist electorate.   **47.** Reported in *Belfast Newsletter*, 20 May 1921. Three serious injuries were reported.   **48.** Devlin, quoted in Follis, *A State under Siege*, p. 57.   **49.** From an internal IRA memo, 'Belfast Brigade Operation for the Month of May', dated 27 May 1921: P/23, UCD Archives.   **50.** Ibid.   **51.** Sean Montgomery later recalled that 'when the news arrived that he [Ferris] would live our Battalion Officer Commanding almost cried': quoted in McDonnell, *Northern Divisions*, p. 80.   **52.** Internal IRA report, P/23, UCD Archives.   **53.** Ibid.   **54.** The Coroner, Dr J. Graham, criticised unionists' 'foolish' decision to take the city-bound route via the Newtownards Road, suggesting that in future they 'should obey the police instructions and go by settled routes'; in *Irish News*, 1 June 1921.   **55.** Levels of tension were also high in other areas. That morning (19th) an estimated 300 Catholic workers, mainly women, were escorted from its York Road site following alleged intimidation and there were also disturbances that evening in York Street and Townsend Street.

CHAPTER 9

1. After the oaths of allegiance to the Crown ceremony, the Parliament adjourned until its official opening by King George V on 22 June.   **2.** *Irish News*, 8 June 1921.   **3.** Not surprisingly, the *Irish News* report (8 June) described FitzAlan's drive through 'silent streets' to the City Hall.   **4.** FitzAlan, in *Belfast Newsletter*, 8 June 1921.   **5.** *Times*, 8 June 1921.   **6.** *Daily News*, 8 June 1921.   **7.** Parliamentary proceedings were soon to transfer from the City Hall to the Presbyterian Assembly Theological College, near Queen's University, where they remained until the opening of Stormont in 1932.   **8.** *Belfast Newsletter*, 22 June 1921.   **9.** Ibid.   **10.** *Irish News*, 21 June 1921.   **11.** Ibid.   **12.** In *Irish News*, 20 June 1921.   **13.** Norman Douglas, a year younger at the time, recalls how difficult it was to get a glimpse of the royals as they proceeded along Ann Street on account of the police who 'all seemed to be six-footers'.   **14.** D 1415/B/38, 22 June 1921, PRONI.   **15.** Harry recalled that George and he had exchanged salutes – 'His was brisker than mine.'   **16.** *Belfast Newsletter*, 23 June 1921.   **17.** Lady Craig's diary; op. cit.   **18.** John Boyd, who had queued up for hours before their arrival, was positioned outside the City Hall when the royal pair approached in their open carriage. He was quite surprised when the King dismounted from the landau, as he proved to be 'a small man at the centre of great fuss'.   **19.** King George V, quoted in H. Montgomery Hyde, *Carson*, p. 458.   **20.** *Belfast Newsletter*, 23 June 1921.   **21.** *Irish News*, 23 June, 1921. Indeed, the speech was believed to have been written by Lloyd George's special adviser, Edward Grigg (see his son John's article about this occasion in *The Times*, 22 June 1996).   **22.** Lady Craig's diary, op. cit.   **23.** *Daily Express*, 23 June, 1921.   **24.** Lady Craig's diary, op. cit.   **25.** *Belfast Telegraph*, 22 June 1921.   **26.** However, some critical papers such as the *Daily News* believed that the new Northern Parliament would entrench itself 'behind its orange barricades with the blessing of Imperial authority': quoted in Boyce, *Englishmen and Irish Troubles*, p. 116.   **27.** *Daily Chronicle*, 23 June 1921.   **28.** *Irish News*, 23 June 1921.   **29.** Ibid.   **30.** *Belfast Telegraph*, 24 June 1921.   **31.** NI HOC Debate cols 36/7, 23 June 1921.   **32.** Ibid.   **33.** Follis, *A State under Siege*, p. 50, has maintained that the royal visit 'accelerated negotiations between the British Government and Sinn Féin'.   **34.** Their sense of satisfied well-being was not to last long, what with the attack on the royal train and other security incidents, not to mention growing resentment amongst loyalists about the delay in handing over responsibility for security to the Belfast government.   **35.** Horse-loving Irishmen's involvement in destroying so many animals was a central theme of the reporting of this attack, just as it was in a subsequent IRA outrage, in London's Hyde Park in 1982.   **36.** In J. Brewer, *The RIC – an oral history*, p. 83.   **37.** *Belfast Telegraph*, 25 June 1921.   **38.** An illustration of how bureaucratic incompetence nearly resulted in tragedy involved an unemployed ex-soldier, Thomas Molloy, who made a speedy retreat in a trap from an angry loyalist mob following his re-direction from the Labour Exchange in Frederick Street to an employment bureau on the Shankill Road; in *Irish News*, 10 June 1921. Also, the firms of Hursts, Johnstons and Hasletts were all targeted by the 'C' Company of the IRA's 2nd Battalion, with 'a considerable amount of damage 'being meted out to Hursts Motor Garage: Belfast Brigade HQ diary of operations, 6 July 1921, P/23, UCD Archives.   **39.** Glover appears to have been specifically targeted by the 1st Battalion of the IRA which carried out the attack. In the Belfast Brigade's report of its operations for that month, Constable Glover was described as being 'long wanted for the murder of some civilians who were killed during curfew'; Diary of Operations, 6 July 1921, P/23, UCD Archives.   **40.** *Irish News*, 11 June 1921.   **41.** Mr McBride, a member of Sinn Féin, was reportedly found clasping rosaries.   **42.** It was alleged there were bayonet wounds in the soles of Mr Halfpenny's feet and around his testicles. There are grisly similarities between these killings and the horrific deeds of the Shankill Butchers half a century later.   **43.** The demand for an adjournment was defeated by 192–64. Devlin had to be physically removed from the Commons after protesting vehemently against its decision.   **44.** Devlin, in *Irish News*, 15 June 1921.   **45.** Ibid.   **46.** Constable Sturdy was the first Special to be killed in Belfast.   **47.** In a test legal case, Mr Miller's widow, Sadie, made a £1,500 claim for compensation against the Belfast Corporation under the terms of the Criminal Injuries Act. Arguing that as four men 'dressed the same as peelers' had attacked her husband, the Corporation should accept responsibility for the crime, Mrs Miller's claim was rejected by the Deputy Recorder on 27 April 1922; in HA5/251 PRONI.   **48.** *Irish News*, 14 June 1921.   **49.** Ibid., 15 June 1921.   **50.** This case was particularly tragic for his parents who had lost two other sons a few years previously. The boys had drowned going to the rescue of a friend who had fallen through broken ice on the Springfield dam; in J. Baker, *The McMahon Family Murders*.   **51.** A passing RIC patrol later found both bodies in Ashmore Street.   **52.** The IRA's claim that a ferocious gun battle in the city on 20 June had resulted in four casualties, two of them suffering fatal injuries, cannot be substantiated.

CHAPTER 10

1. It came into effect at noon on 11 July 1921.   **2.** Eamon de Valera brought a political team to Whitehall inside the next couple of days for the first phase of negotiations. Following talks on the offer in the Dáil during August and September, a disillusioned de Valera despatched Collins to London when the new phase of talks commenced in mid October.   **3.** Indeed, for some time Craig could do little more than pester the British administration to improve security. It was likely that those gangs of loyalist assassins already active in the period before the truce, felt obliged to fill the void created by these operational restrictions on the part of the Crown forces and consequently believed that they had an excuse to increase their campaign of terror.   **4.** As Helen Litton, *The Irish Civil War – an illustrated history*, p. 15, points out, more guns were imported during the six-month period of the Truce than in the previous year.   **5.** Fitzpatrick, *The Two Irelands*, p. 105.   **6.** CAB 4/7, 5 July 1921, PRONI.   **7.** *New Statesman*, 9 July 1921.   **8.** Ibid.   **9.** D 1633/2/24, PRONI.   **10.** Brian Follis estimates that there was over 1,200 men in the 3rd Northern Division around this time, half of whom were in the Belfast Battalion: in Follis, *A State under Siege*, p. 22.   **11.** See Phoenix, *Northern Nationalism*, p. 141.   **12.** D 1633/2/24, PRONI. Such uncertainty and disagreement between the military and police was apparent even towards the end of the following month when Home Affairs Minister Dawson Bates conceded that it was 'due to this difference of opinion[over troop deployment] and the lack of preventative measures, that serious loss of life occurred'; CAB 4/19, 12 September 1921, PRONI. He also admitted 'we don't appear to have made any progress for guarding against a recurrence of such outbreaks': ibid.   **13.** Mulcahy file, 10–16 August 1921, p. 7 A/26, U.C.D. Archives.   **14.** Ibid. McCorley also noted £27 expenses incurred for the funeral of a Belfast volunteer killed in action in Donegal.   **15.** Ibid.   **16.** CO 904151, 8 September 1921, PRO.   **17.** Ibid.   **18.** In *Irish News*, 3 September 1921.   **19.** *Belfast Telegraph*, 12 July 1921.   **20.** *Daily Mail*, 14 July 1921.   **21.** *Belfast Telegraph*, 15 July 1921.   **22.** Nationalists were largely indifferent to the arguments made for and against the curfew restrictions.   **23.** *Belfast Telegraph*, 6 August 1921. Naturally observers were dumfounded by this fatal shooting. Jim McDermott, in *Northern Divisions*, p. 108, suggests that the two IRA volunteers were probably reconnoitring the leafy avenue, home of a leading IRA target, R.I.C. County Inspector, Richard Harrison.   **24.** *Irish News*, 29 August 1921.   **25.** *Belfast Telegraph*, 30 August, 1921.   **26.** Ibid. The *Telegraph* also warned its readers that another favourite quarry for the gunmen were people peering round street corners.   **27.** The young girl, like several other victims of the violence, had been standing at her front door. Mr Smith, an ex-soldier who had been out looking for work, had been shielding a child when he was shot dead.   **28.** Nationalists believed that a weekend speech delivered in County Down by Unionist firebrand William Cootes had sparked off the Belfast disturbances.   **29.** As noted below, there were three additional fatal shootings in the west of the city that day. The press noted how a wide range of ordinary people were targets of the gunmen, ranging from the curious bystander who was shot on the nose peering round a corner to a Nelson Street centenarian who received a gunshot wound to her arm. **30.** *Belfast Telegraph*, 19 September 1921.   **31.** A resident of Vere Street, Francis Corr, was charged with their murders.   **32.** *Belfast Telegraph*, 24 September 1921.   **33.** *Belfast Telegraph*, 26 September 1921.   **34.** Father Fullerton's diary 23/24 September, in Down and Connor Diocesan Archives.   **35.** *Belfast Telegraph*, 26 September 1921.   **36.** Kenna, *Facts and Figures*, p. 47.   **37.** Quoted in G. Adams, *Falls Memories*, p. 67. **38.** Ibid. Incidentally, there is a stained glass window dedicated to Murtagh McAstocker in St Matthew's Church.   **39.** *Belfast Telegraph*, 27 September 1921.   **40.** Funerals provided trouble-makers with ideal opportunities for further attacks and several people were killed or seriously injured attending funerals. Also military reports indicated the degree of intimidation of both Catholic and Protestant workers on the Crumlin and Springfield Roads: quoted in Phoenix, *Northern Nationalism*, p. 442.   **41.** Whilst nineteenth century violence was witnessed both in the city centre and in districts other than the west of the city, by far the most serious and prolonged fighting had been in the Falls and Shankill areas. I estimate that over 40% of the fatalities during the 1920s' conflict perished in west Belfast.   **42.** In an unusual incident on 8 July, men assembling an Orange arch in Sandy Row intercepted a man who had just robbed a Post Office in Great Victoria Street.   **43.** Four people were shot dead in the Newry area on 5 and 6 July.   **44.** *Belfast Telegraph*, 6 July 1921.   **45.** Several Catholic dockers working on the steamship 'Baltic' were physically assaulted and chased from their work on 7 July.   **46.** Security forces claimed that IRA casualties were 'very heavy', although there were no reports of civilians receiving hospital treatment. This might indicate that republicans whisked dead and injured away from the scene for treatment by sympathetic doctors or for secret burials. **47.** See Kenna, *Facts and Figures*.   **48.** Sean Maclomaire, speaking in 1983: in Adams, *Falls Memories*. **49.** Constable Conlon, who had 13 years service in the RIC, had no relatives in Ireland as his sister had emigrated to America barely two weeks previously and he was buried at Newtownbreda.   **50.** The significance of this west Belfast incident and its indication that armed resistance was still present, was commented upon in the British press, with the *New Statesman*, 16 July, suggesting Raglan Street 'added a new complication to the crisis' in the north.   **51.** In G. McAteer's *Down the Falls*, p. 17.   **52.** *Irish News*, 12 July 1921. This report highlighted the eviction of an elderly widow whose furniture was burned in the street.   **53.** Although apparently off duty at the time, James Ledlie was an IRA squad commander and he received a republican funeral.   **54.** In *Belfast Telegraph*, 18 August 1921.   **55.** *Belfast Telegraph*, 13 July 1921.   **56.** *Irish News*, 13 October 1921.   **57.** Ibid. The coroner also called for the authorities to take more strenuous measures to protect the lives of loyalist citizens going to and from work.   **58.** In *Irish Independent*, 3 September 1921. **59.** Accounts of what happened when they failed to do so are given elsewhere.   **60.** McElborough, *The Autobiography of a Belfast Working Man*, p. 20.   **61.** Ibid.   **62.** As regular police were supposed to accompany such patrols, and were eventually forbidden to patrol 'mixed' areas, it was probably likely that the extent of their misdemeanours has been exaggerated.   **63.** Kelly, *Bonfires on the Hillside*, p. 15.   **64.** In McAteer, *Down the Falls*.   **65.** Davy Matthews' father and aunt, who had recently been evicted from east Belfast, stayed temporarily on the Falls, often told him about these 'dark' Twenties' days. One of their anecdotes illustrates that, even in such stressful times, a sense of humour prevailed. Apparently one interloper found in a house by the Specials claimed he lived there. Most of the police were about to leave when one sharp-witted officer asked him to call 'his' children into the room. When they didn't respond, he was arrested!   **66.** Curran, *St Paul's*, p. 55.   **67.** *Belfast Telegraph*, 11 July 1921.   **68.** Ibid.   **69.** Craig; in *Belfast Newletter*, 13 July 1921.   **70.** *Belfast Telegraph*, 15 July 1921.   **71.** *Belfast Newsletter*, 6 August 1921.   **72.** Ibid.   **73.** *Belfast Newsletter*, 17 August 1921.   **74.** *Belfast Telegraph*, 18 August 1921.   **75.** *Belfast Telegraph*, 1 September 1921. **76.** *Westminster Gazette*, 1 September. 1921.   **77.** Ibid.   **78.** Ibid., 2 September 1921.   **79.** *Daily Chronicle*, 1 September 1921.   **80.** *Manchester Guardian*, quoted in Kenna, *Facts and Figures*, p. 43.   **81.** *Nation*, 20 August 1921.   **82.** *Morning Post*, 31 August 1921.   **83.** Ibid.   **84.** *Irish News*, 1 August 1921.   **85.** Ibid., 3 August 1921.   **86.** Ibid., 30 September 1921.   **87.** In MacRory files, folder no. 11, 7 July, 1921.   **88.** Ibid. **89.** *Irish News*, 11 July 1921.   **90.** Ibid., 12 July 1921. It wasn't just nationalist opinion that pointed to the failure of the security forces to cope effectively with disorder. The Home Affairs Minister R. Dawson Bates, admitted to his Cabinet colleagues that 'certain differences of opinion' between police and army, as well as a general 'lack of preventative measures', had resulted in 'perilous loss of life' during the late summer of 1921. Bates also conceded that 'we don't appear to have made any real progress for guarding against a re-occurrence of these events': CAB 4/19, 12 September 1921, PRONI.   **91.** Ibid.

CHAPTER 11

1. *Northern Whig*, 3 October 1921.   2. The *Irish News*, 7 October 1921, condemned the closing of this National school due to 'Orange intimidation'. Jim McDermott suggests there might have been another motive for targeting this school. Its principal, Frank Crummey, was a leading IRA figure in the city and had, since the Truce, resumed teaching in the school, a fact which had come to the attention of loyalists in the area; in McDermott, *Northern Divisions*, pp 119–20.   3. Quoted in *Northern Whig*, 1 October 1921.   4. Crawford papers, D640/11/1, 24 November 1921, PRONI.   5. In practice, he was not a formal participant in the talks, but a most interested observer, reminding Lloyd George of the unionist position before the conference formally opened on 11th October and visiting him early in November to urgently remind him that the pressure of negotiations could not be used as an excuse to manoeuvre Ulster into an all-Ireland republic.   6. *Daily News*, 10 October 1921 and Stachey, writing in *Northern Whig*, 14 October 1921.   7. *Daily Express*, 3 October 1921.   8. *Irish News*, 18 October 1921.   9. Irish Bulletin', 17 October 1921; quoted in *Northern Whig*, 18 October.   10. Craig, quoted in *Northern Whig*, 18 October 1921.   11. *Irish News*, 28 October 1921. Practical support for northern Catholics was offered by Free State Trade Minister, Ernest Blythe, who addressed nationalists in St Mary's Hall, advising them 'to stick right here'; quoted in *Northern Whig*, 25 October 1921.   12. *Irish News*, 4 October 1921.   13. In *Northern Whig*, 7 October 1921.   14. In *Northern Whig*, 12 October 1921.   15. In *Northern Whig*, 5 October 1921.   16. In *Northern Whig*, 7 November 1921. Mr Hunt, a Protestant, claimed to have been held for 15 days, during which time he had been beaten by an IRA gang and taken to a Sinn Féin prison camp near Dublin. Jim McDermott, *Northern Divisions*, examines in detail the argument that, rather than being an ordinary Protestant picked up off the streets by the IRA, he was either a common criminal or a police spy. In either case, several republicans were arrested and IRA information was seized.   17. *Irish News*, 22 November 1921.   18. *Belfast Newsletter*, 23 November 1921.   19. Ibid.   20. The following day, the *Belfast Newsletter*, 23 November 1921, interpreted the escalation of violence as a sign that the IRA had started war on Belfast's loyalist population, claiming this constituted 'a rebel reply to the transfer of powers'.   21. In *Northern Whig*, 24 November 1921. Also see HA/32/1/7, PRONI. The new curfew restrictions were from 9 p.m. to 5 a.m.   22. Boyd, *Holy War in Belfast*, p. 185. However, paramilitaries were also ingenious and the IRA soon devised a hook-bomb which could be hung onto the wire mesh.   23. *Northern Whig*, 23 November 1921.   24. Mr Graham's widow, Isabella, later claimed £5,000 in compensation for the loss of her husband. He had earned a respectable £5 a week wage but on his death she was reduced to living off a £1 donation from the Loyalist Relief Fund and a one-off payment of £40 from a Queens Island charity raffle. Like most compensation cases, she received considerably less than her original claim, in her case £850; quoted in *Irish News*, 1 July 1922.   25. *Northern Whig*, 25 November 1921. An eyewitness, James Bell, recovering in hospital, talked of 'the awful, steamy smoky smell of the explosive, followed by darkness.'   26. *Northern Whig*, 26 November 1921.   27. Ex-soldier David Duncan was later acquitted of Mr McIvor's murder.   28. Eerily his body lay for several minutes in the deserted streets until a police officer arrived at the scene.   29. Two other men died of their injuries at this time. Protestants Joseph Blakely (23), of Campbell Street and David Cunningham (19), of Lendrick Street, who had been shot during the summer, both passed away in hospital. Even the privileged in the leafy suburbs were affected by the disturbances. A guest of Lady Spender, who had earlier enjoyed 'tea and music', gratefully accepted her offer of staying overnight, following a warning from a neighbour whose train had been fired upon: Lady Spender's diary, 4 December 1921, D 1633/2/25, PRONI.   30. Loyalist fears of a step-up in IRA activity were apparently well-founded, as the northern authorities were also bracing themselves for an attack at this time. An internal police memo detailed RIC intelligence of Sinn Féin personnel in the border counties, which suggested they were on 'standby' for action in the north. DI Gillihan warned his superior officers that, 'in the event of the truce terminating, it is the intention of the Sinn Féin authorities to send 500 men to Ulster to carry on guerrilla warfare'; HA5/1398, 2 December 1921, PRONI.   31. A few days previously an infant had been wounded in the arms of its mother on the Castlereagh and two people had been shot dead in Derry jail.   32. *Northern Whig*, 8 December 1921.   33. He died in hospital the following day. John Porter, of Ballycarry Street, was charged with Mr Crudden's murder, but was acquitted on 21 February.   34. In *Belfast Telegraph*, 6 January 1922. However, his sister admitted he was an IRA volunteer who had been carrying a revolver at the time of his death.   35. The particular vulnerability of tram workers is described elsewhere.   36. At his inquest on 26 January his lawyer claimed police had fired the fatal bullet from a mere 15 yards.   37. There was criticism in the nationalist press of the police for the manner in which the Donnelly shop and other Catholic homes in east Belfast were searched, with accusations of prayer-books being thrown in the fire and sacred objects being smashed or burned.   38. *Northern Whig*, 19 December 1921.   39. *Irish News*, 19 December 1921.   40. *Northern Whig*, 29 December 1921.

CHAPTER 12

1. Well over 30 people under the age of sixteen lost their lives in the conflict.   2. Kelly, *Bonfires on the Hillsides*, p. 13. This followed an IRA attack on a loyalist workers' tram elsewhere in the city.   3. Ibid.   4. Ibid.   5. J. Parkinson, *A Belfastman's Tale*, p. 16.   6. Others were more fortunate in using the Short Strand route as a short-cut. John Boyd's father used to regularly cut across the Short Strand to get to the railway station and experienced no problems.   7. John's father told him that John Green still kept in touch with him and returned to his job in the shipyards when the disturbances ended.   8. Harry Currie, who travelled from his home on the Ormeau Road to his work as an apprentice upholsterer in Wright and Arthurs in Arthur Street, also experienced few problems, but he was fortunate in being able to avoid 'mixed' areas on his way to work.   9. McElborough, *The Autobiography of a Belfast Working Man*, pp 19–20.   10. Paddy was later ordained as a priest!   11. A more detailed account of Catholic migration is provided in Chapter 3.   12. However, there is no doubt that such fears were held by many in Catholic areas.   13. At least 25 people lost their lives in tram shootings and bombings with many others suffering physical attack and intimidation.   14. Kelly, *Bonfires on the Hillside*, p. 15.   15. At least 30 civilians and members of the security forces lost their lives during curfew hours.   16. Ena McKenna, in A Murphy, *When Dublin was the Capital*, p. 146.   17. On a number of occasions, such 'search' parties missed the late arrival of youngsters and instead ran into trouble themselves with the authorities, sometimes with tragic consequences.   18. The lack of opportunities for outdoor play resulted in a studious John discovering his local library at an early age (he later became a celebrated local writer). This chasing of youngsters off the streets before the start of curfew, especially in loyalist areas, illustrates the authorities' recognition that children playing in the streets were easy targets for bombers and gunmen. Incidentally, John remembered the 'corner-boys who hung about outside the two pubs and spirit grocery at our end of Chatsworth Street' collecting money to buy a 'Jack' which was proudly displayed at the top of the totem pole around the Twelfth.   19. In Murphy, *When Dublin was the Capital*, p. 150. Norman Douglas remembers a trip to a picture-house in High Street and how, when walking down Ann Street, an army lorry whizzed round the corner of Church Lane and soldiers jumped out, firing wildly up Skipper Street. Hemmed in by gunfire, a young and frightened Norman was unable to escape for nearly an hour.   20. Robert Preston also remembers lying in bed, assessing how bad the shooting was both by its frequency and volume – 'if we heard machine-gun fire, we knew it must be bad.' Robert lived off the Donegall Road and could often hear gunfire coming from the Falls.   21. Ena McKenna, quoted in Murphy, *When Dublin Was the Capital*, p. 146.   22. Kelly, *Bonfire on the Hillside*, p. 16.   23. Ibid.   24. Some of the worst exchanges of feeling involving the military were displayed at sporting matches between the various regiments. Robert Preston remembers watching a challenge soccer match between a Scottish regiment and the Norfolk Regiment at Windsor Park which ended in fisticuffs both on and off the pitch!   25. Kelly, *Bonfires on the Hillside*, p. 17. Eddie Steele who attended Erskine's School, near Dunville Park, also remembered a 'real strong' romance between one of his teachers and an officer in a nearby military garrison.   26. Even today, Norman Douglas recalls the distinctive and menacing cage-cars, which were military vehicles with a V-shaped cage covering the top of the van with a 12-inch gun opening.   27. 'Inst' is the nickname of the Royal Belfast Academical Institution, a well-known 300-year-old grammar school situated close to the city centre. Christy was also fascinated by a machine-gun perched in the railings by Queen Victoria School, opposite his home in Durham Street. John Parkinson, too, recalls heavily armed soldiers positioned behind sandbags at the end of Distillery Street.   28. Robert Preston also remembers his aunt's dog taking a clear dislike to a Scottish foot soldier patrolling the streets near his Donegall Road home and how the flustered soldier resorted to pointing his rifle at the offending animal's head!   29. Apparently there was a house in Twomey Street which was especially renowned for sheltering IRA volunteers.   30. Sam also remembered seeing gunmen in action at street corners and being ordered to disappear. Both he and Jimmy recalled that, in the tightly-knit communities of north and west Belfast, residents were frequently warned in advance of imminent shooting attacks.   31. Other children had to be equally creative in their leisure pursuits. Towards the end of the conflict, the 10-year-old John Boyd along with a friend, 'mitched' off Sunday School and made his way over the Albert Bridge to the Custom House, where they listened to a variety of political and religious speakers 'serving up great craic.' The orators included his aunt who was a socialist and a couple nicknamed 'Laurel and Hardy', who entertained large crowds with their religious duologues.   32. However, frequently such innocent games of football had to be conducted along sectarian lines, and children had to move from one playing field to another to avoid marauding sectarian gangs. Paddy O'Donnell recalls being chased away from playing fields at Alexandra Park by a loyalist gang and having to move up to the Cavehill Road to finish matches off.   33. Eddie's love of sport was inspired by his brother Alex, who went on to play professional football in England and represented Ireland at senior level.   34. Ibid. John recalls that in those days a Raleigh bicycle cost £5, a fortune for working class boys.   35. Kelly, *Bonfires on the Hillside*, p. 14.   36. Whilst there was no

direct loss of life following such attacks on children attending school, or on actual school buildings, press reports indicate that such attacks happened on a regular basis.   37. However, many young people continued to enjoy city centre attractions unaffected by curfew restrictions. John Parkinson remembers enjoying the latest Charlie Chaplin film at the Coliseum Picture House in Sandy Row on a Saturday afternoon.

CHAPTER 13
1. A *Belfast Telegraph* leading article (6 January 1922) condemned British apathy towards Ireland, claiming that 'England as a whole wants rid of Ireland, loyal and disloyal, and its Government, its Press, and many of its people do not care one iota who is sacrificed so long as they get rid of this country from Westminster.'   2. Gavin Duffy and Erskine Childers were also members of the Sinn Féin group. De Valera, who had been elected President of the Dáil on 26 August, opted not to attend this conference. Citing his new position as the reason for not absenting himself from Dublin for a prolonged period, Eamon de Valera would have been aware of the likelihood of a real political dilemma facing the leader of the Irish delegation.   3. Lloyd George had narrowly survived a Commons motion of censure led by Conservatives in October 1921 and a potentially hostile Bonar Law-led Tory administration was waiting in the wings at Westminster.   4. Lloyd George, quoted in F. Owen, *Tempestuous Journey – Lloyd George his Life and Times*, p. 587.   5. Michael Collins, 6 December 1921; quoted in L. Ó Broin, *Michael Collins*, p. 113.   6. *Irish News*, 8 December 1921.   7. The British military left Ireland on 16 January 1922, just over a week after the Dáil's ratification of the Treaty.   8. See R. Foster, *Modern Ireland 1600–1972*, p. 506.   9. DE p. 24 19/12.   10. DE Treaty Debates, pp 152–8, 22 December 1921.   11. E. O'Duffy, quoted in *Irish Independent*, 5 January 1922.   12. *Irish News*, 4 January 1922.   13. In *Manchester Guardian*, 7 December 1921.   14. See McDermott, *Northern Divisions*, p. 115. McDermott points out that republicans in Belfast avoided the bad blood caused elsewhere by divisions over the Treaty.   15. HOC Debates, 5th series, vol. 147, cols 1389–93, 31 October 1921.   16. Ibid. Unionists were also perturbed by the withdrawal of Special Constabulary street patrols, a consequence of the Treaty, and more especially, by the increasing political uncertainty caused by the London negotiations and its inevitable impact unto communal tension in Belfast.   17. These included increased troop deployment, more frequent use of armoured vehicles and more vigorous arms searches.   18. Craig met Lloyd George on 7, 17 and 25 November.   19. Carson speaking in the House of Lords. See HOL, vol 48, Debates 5, cols 44–50, 14 December 1921.   20. Quoted in Middlemas, *Thomas Jones – a Whitehall Diary*, p. 190.   21. NIHOC Debates, vol. 2, col. 1149, 7 December 1921.   22. *Northern Whig*, 3 November 1921. This is not to suggest that Ulster Unionists were without friends in Great Britain at this time. A meeting organised by the National Constitutional Association at the Queen's Hall in London on 21 November pledged support for northern loyalists under the slogan, 'No Betrayal of our Friends'; in *Belfast Newsletter*, 22 November 1921.   23. *Northern Whig*, 3 November 1921. The *Whig* concluded that those who 'now revile her [Ulster] for 'blocking the way' will one day be thankful for her caution and forethought.'   24. *Northern Whig*, 7 November 1921 and *Belfast Newsletter*, 2 November.   25. *Belfast Newsletter*, 16 November 1921. Despite their anxiety, loyalist popular opinion seemed to condone Craig's meeting with Lloyd George at this time. For instance, a large loyalist rally supporting their leader was staged at Newtownards on 27 November.   26. *Northern Whig*, 15 December and 11 December 1021.   27. *Belfast Newsletter*, 17 December 1921 and *Northern Whig*, 12 December 1921.   28. *Northern Whig*, 10 December 1921.   29. *Belfast Newsletter*, 23 January 1921. English opinion was united in its support for the Treaty. Months after its signing and in the mists of sectarian turmoil and political dispute, the *Times* (25 May) described the Treaty as 'the inviolable charter of Ulster rights as well as those in the rest of Ireland' and as such it stood as 'the one clear criterion in the present obscurity'.   30. The Irish Free State and N. Ireland governments were each to appoint a representative to report to Collins and Craig who, it was hoped, would eventually reach mutual agreement over the boundaries between the two states.   31. *Belfast Telegraph*, 23 January 1922.   32. Ibid. Despite its broadly favourable reaction to the Pact, the *Telegraph* again illustrated its loyalist credentials by reminding its readers that the boycott had been 'from every point of view a failure', claiming that barely 10% of the city's trade had been affected by the boycott.   33. *Belfast Newsletter*, 23 January 1922. The *Northern Whig*, 23 January, also expressed its hope that the agreement would prove to be 'a harbinger of peace in Ireland.'   34. *Times*, 23 January, 1922.   35. *Manchester Guardian* and *Daily News*, 23 January 1922.   36. *Irish News*, 23 January and *Irish Independent*, 23 January 1922.   37. *Irish Independent*, 23 January 1922.   38. The *Belfast Telegraph* stoutly defended Craig's decision to meet de Valera in Dublin in its editions of 2 and 3 February. Yet this did not end the speculation in Dublin surrounding such a meeting. The *Irish Independent*, 1 February 1922, argued that unionists were beginning to realise that partition is as burdensome in the economy, as it is unnatural in the political sphere.'   39. Fitzpatrick, *The Two Irelands*, p. 121.   40. Pact, quoted in A.C. Hepburn, *Ireland 1905–25*, pp 214–15.   41. This particularly annoyed many loyalists, including Sir Henry Wilson.   42. This formed the fifth clause

of the pact: in Hepburn, *Ireland 1905–25*, p. 215.   43. Ibid.   44. Arguably the pact, like more recent political agreements in the north, was designed more for the benefit of the 'external' audience, rather than as a serious attempt to precipitate an internal political solution.   45. *Irish Independent*, 1 April 1922.   46. MacRory, quoted in *Irish Independent*, 1 April 1922.   47. *Irish News*, 31 March 1922.   48. *Northern Whig*, 31 March 1922.   49. *Belfast Telegraph* 31 March 1922.   50. *Belfast Newsletter*, 31 March 1922.   51. Lady Craig's diary, D1415/B/38, 31 March 1922, PRONI.   52. Ibid., 4 April 1922.   53. The Police Advisory Committee folded after three acrimonious meetings and the Conciliation Committee collapsed after six meetings.   54. HA/32/1/142, 7 June 1922, PRONI. He alleged that 26 shots had been fired in to his Presbytery and he hadn't received an apology or explanation from the security forces which had forced him to conclude 'these Forces had at least the tacit approval and protection of the Authorities in the City.'   55. Ibid. These included cases of 7 refugee families being burned out of accommodation in Divis Street provided by the American White Cross and that of a distressed Catholic mother watching her house burn to the ground with police allegedly looking on and having to flee to Dublin with her three children the following day. Fr Laverty also complained of Catholic factory girls being 'maltreated' on their way to Gallahers with Specials 'jeering and looking on.'   56. This was especially evident on the police committee and despite a valiant attempt by Burke and others to encourage Catholics in the Markets to join the Specials, there was little progress for this group. Indeed, the suspicions of the loyalist members of such a committee were hardly surprising, given Burke's confession that Collins had encouraged Sinn Féiners to participate in such bodies for intelligence-gathering purposes.   57. For instance, they couldn't call witnesses or submit reports and all they could do was proffer advice to a reluctant Minister for Home Affairs, Bates, who refused requests to formalise their powers. See Phoenix, *Northern Nationalism*, p. 215.   58. *Irish News*, 15 April 1922.   59. Burke, who along with Dougal acted as an unofficial 'link' between the Belfast and Dublin administration which were unwilling to openly communicate with each other, was an interesting character. At times sycophantic towards the Unionist regime, Burke, a wealthy shipbroker and part-time diplomat (he was Belfast's Counsel for at least six countries), was reputedly influential in gaining the release of the kidnapped border loyalists.   60. In *Northern Whig*, 6 May 1922.   61. Ibid. Craig had discussed this with the ultra group, the Belfast Loyalist Workers' Committee and had managed to extract from them an acceptance of the principle of the return of Catholic workers as suggested in the pact, but he realised that shipyard fortunes had to rise and unemployment be reduced first.

CHAPTER 14

1. *Belfast Telegraph*, 2 January 1922.   2. It was alleged that the military were returning fire following the attack on Private Barnes and that he had been a sniper: see Kenna *Facts and Figures*, p. 66.   3. The *Belfast Telegraph*, 4 January 1922, alleged that nationalists had flung a bomb at a tram in Foundry Street and that five loyalists had been wounded by the army as they chased their assailants.   4. *Belfast Telegraph*, 5 January 1922.   5. Ibid.   6. *Belfast Telegraph*, 7 January 1922.   7. Terrorist groups frequently calculated on such impromptu gatherings by organising follow-up explosions or shootings in order to maximise the number of casualties.   8. Whilst it was undoubtedly true curiosity cost several people their lives during the conflict, it was equally the case that many people, occasionally those from outside the city's boundaries, were simply in the wrong place at the wrong time. For instance, the *Belfast Telegraph*, reported on 6 January that a Mallusk farmer, Henry Caruth, was shot in the thigh as he led a horse and cart across North Queen Street.   9. The *Belfast Telegraph* report, 11 January, also assured its readers that the Loyalist Relief Fund would 'care for the orphans'.   10. *Belfast Telegraph*, 14 January 1922.   11. Mr Hogg had gained the impression that she had been targeted because they suspected her of passing on information.   12. In private they were less reluctant to verbalise their concern over increased loyalist violence and the impact this was having on their image. Cabinet records maintained this was 'very adverse to the loyalist cause' and R.D. Bates, the Minister for Home Affairs, was 'strongly advised to liase closely with the Divisional Commander of Police and Lord Mayor to see what further steps could be taken to restore order'; in CAB/4/32, 14 February 1922, PRONI.   13. Quoted in the *Belfast Telegraph*, 13 January 1922.   14. The *Belfast Telegraph*, 25 January 1922, observed how a culprit in an armed robbery in a city post office, got a 'meagre' four months custodial sentence.   15. Ibid., 13 January 1922.   16. Ibid.   17. McElborough, *The Autobiography of a Belfast Working Man*, p. 19.   18. Mr Gray, who had an address in Earl Street, was given an IRA funeral the following week.   19. These included many Special Constables, a prominent police officer and the son of William Coote, MP.   20. *Belfast Telegraph*, 10 February 1922.   21. *Belfast Newsletter*, 9 February 1922.   22. Churchill later claimed that an error had resulted in police passing through Clones rather than Omagh; in *Irish Independent*, 14 February 1922.   23. An interesting account of the IRA's frantic preparations for the attack can be found in Shea, *Voices and the Sound of Drums*.   24. *Irish Independent*, 13 February 1922.   25. The IRA squad used

a machine-gun during the 20-minute attack. In the subsequent chase, the police made five arrests. The Special who lost their lives during the Clones attack were Sergeant Dougherty and Constables Lewis, McFarland and McMahon.   **26.** *Glasgow Herald,* 13 February 1922.   **27.** *Times,* 13 February 1922.   **28.** *Irish Independent,* 14 February 1922. Some believed that the 'football team' was a gang on its way to 'spring' IRA prisoners from Derry gaol. In a controversial jury statement it was claimed at the inquest; 'We condemn the action of those responsible for sending through our area uniformed and armed men, contrary to the liaison arrangements'; in *Irish News,* 14 February 1922.   **29.** Quoted in Phoenix, *Northern Nationalism,* p. 334.   **30.** Paddy Lambe's funeral procession was attacked a few days later.   **31.** *Belfast Telegraph,* 14 February 1922.   **32.** Ibid. **33.** An allegation was made by a resident of Weaver Street to the Provisional Government in Dublin that an 'A' Special had moved the group of playing children from Milewater Street to Weaver Street barely half an hour before the blast, thus concentrating potential victims in a confined space; in 'Freeman's Journal', quoted in M. Hayes Papers, p 53/163, UCD Archives.   **34.** *Belfast Telegraph,* 14 February 1922. Interestingly, the *Telegraph* described the Weaver Street attack as 'a dreadful outrage' but omitted mentioning its sectarian dimension, devoting more space to the Waring killing the following morning.   **35.** At the inquest into the killings, a witness claimed Specials had spoken to two men in the vicinity shortly before the explosion took place; in *Northern Whig,* 4 March 1922.   **36.** *Belfast Telegraph,* 14 February 1922. The *Telegraph* claimed that the blast had shattered windows in neighbouring streets and the noise could be heard at Castle Junction, nearly two miles away.   **37.** Ibid.   **38.** M Hayes Papers p. 53/167, UCD Archives.   **39.** In *Irish News,* 15 February 1922.In a Lenten Pastoral, Bishop MacRory also condemned 'this doctrine of vicarious punishment according to which the Catholics of Belfast are made to suffer for the sins of their brethren elsewhere': in MacRory papers, 21 February 1922.   **40.** The horrors of such a blast for some endured right to the grave. Robina Ryan (née McAllister) suffered serious neck injuries and at her funeral in Philadelphia in 1973, the message on a wreath read 'Suffer little children': in Graham, *In the Name of Carsonia.*   **41.** In Phoenix, *Northern Nationalism,* p. 37.   **42.** In Morgan, *Labour and Partition,* p. 286. Even at the height of the conflict, republicans in the north-east barely constituted 5% of the estimated 72,000 strong IRA force, with the number of volunteers in the city peaking at around 1000. Seamus Woods claimed that there were up to 800 volunteers active in the city, having access to an arsenal of 181 rifles, 11,600 rounds of ammunition, 306 revolvers and 5 machine-guns.   **43.** The shooting of police auxiliaries Bolim and Bailes on 23rd April was apparently unplanned. According to Sean Montgomery who was involved in the attack, a reported sighting of the officers in a city hotel by a schoolboy resulted in a group of officers being tailed for a couple of hours by a hastily-assembled IRA team which assassinated them when a suitable opportunity arose; in J. McDermott, *Northern Divisions,* p. 75–6.   **44.** Training camps were held near Ballycastle and in the Sperrins – the camp was raided on 24 December – and there were reports of 200 west Belfast men parading in Hannastown in August.   **45.** O'Duffy had been a vociferous propagandist for Sinn Féin over the past year. Speaking at Armagh in September 1921 O'Duffy had said of Ulster Unionists; 'These people are standing on a bridgehead for the British Government in this country...If they were for Ireland then they[Sinn Féin] would extend the hand of welcome to them as they had done in the past, but if they decided they were against Ireland, and against their fellow countrymen they would have to take appropriate action' (quoted in Farrell, *The Orange State,* p. 43).   **46.** HA/32/1/130, PRONI.   **47.** Megaw speaking in the Northern Ireland Parliament, NIHC vol. 2, col. 84, March 1922, PRONI.   **48.** UCD RMP p. 7/B/77, 27 July 1922. **49.** Police reports indicate a certain degree of paranoia on the part of the authorities towards the end of 1921. In one memo DI Gillihan, referring to a 'fairly reliable source' in County Tyrone, informed a superior officer that 'in the event of the truce terminating, it is the intention of the Sinn Féin authorities to send 500 men to Ulster to carry a guerrilla warfare'; in HA 5/1398/H3020, PRONI.   **50.** Jim McDermott restricts their campaign to being a 'defensive' one, with occasional attacks on the security forces.   **51.** Sean Montgomery; quoted in McDermott, *Northern Divisions,* p. 130.   **52.** E. Staunton, *The Nationalists of N Ireland 1918–73,* p. 50.   **53.** Tim Pat Coogan writes of Collins' deception in the Irish Parliament: 'Janus-faced he stood in Dáil Éireann, arguing fiercely for the Treaty and the establishment of law and order in a democratic independent Irish State, while at the same time he acted with the vigour, intent and methodology of any chief of staff of the Provisional IRA to wreak the other State enshrined in that Treaty, 'Ulster'.' In Coogan, *Michael Collins – a biography,* p. 333.   **54.** Dennis McCullough, 21 February 1922; quoted in Phoenix, *Northern Nationalism,* p. 188.   **55.** Phoenix, *Northern Nationalism,* p. 219.   **56.** Although it is difficult to be precise about the exact number of IRA casualties during the conflict, it is fair to conclude that compared to their military colleagues elsewhere in Ireland, the number of Sinn Féin/IRA losses was relatively low (my estimated figure is around 10). As observed earlier, the OC Northern Division, Seamus Woods was to admit to Richard Mulcahy that prior to the signing of the Truce the IRA 'could only command the sympathy of 25% Catholics of the area'; in Phoenix, *Northern Nationalism,* p. 141.   **57.** A team of 21 IRA men led by Seamus Woods shot two policemen, one fatally, and assumed control of the situation for several hours, before abandoning the building. A more detailed account is given in Chapter 17. **58.** Impossibly tight protection of unionist figures, strengthened even more in the wake of Twaddell's assassination, and the introduction of internment resulted in the abandonment of likely attacks on other prestigious establishment figures. **59.** A detailed account of this arson campaign and how it prompted a further sectarian backlash on Belfast's streets, is given elsewhere. At least five stately homes were severely damaged or destroyed, including the homes of Sir Hugh O'Neill, Speaker of the N. Ireland House of Commons, and Roland MacNeill, MP. **60.** Compensation claims relating to these incendiary attacks in Belfast amounted to £794,678 in May 1922 and £760,018 for June; quoted in Follis, *A State under Siege*, p. 98. **61.** 'Plain People', 17 June 1922; quoted in Farrell, *The Orange State*, p. 57. **62.** In T.R. Dwyer, *Big Fellow, Long Fellow*, p. 293. **63.** Hopkinson, *The Irish War of Independence*, p. 164. Hopkinson queries southern commitment to the plight of northern Catholics. He writes: 'Southern nationalists had failed to make a priority of the Northern Question and for all their protestations on the subject, to defend minority interests in the north effectively.' **64.** S. Woods, in p. 713/97, UCD Archives. **65.** P7/B/11/77, 27 July 1922, UCD Archives. **66.** Quoted in Kenna, *Facts and Figures*, pp 97–9. **67.** Sean Montgomery, quoted in McDermott, *Northern Divisions*, p. 73. **68.** In one internal report, 17 men were captured in a refugee's house; in Phoenix, *Northern Nationalism*, p. 381. **69.** P7/B/11/77, 27 July 1922, UCD Archives. **70.** Quoted in Staunton, *The Nationalists of Northern Ireland 1918–73*, p. 71. Staunton also notes the 'friendly' relations which developed between people in the Falls area and Special Constables during that summer (p.68). **71.** S McGouran, 3rd Northern Division, writing to IRA Chief of Staff, 7 July 1922, Mulcahy papers p. 7B/77, UCD Archives. **72.** In Adams, *Falls Memories*, p. 67. **73.** Solly-Flood, 8 September 1922, HA/32/1/257, PRONI. **74.** However, certain aspects of IRA activity had an air of slickness about them. One of these was in the area of intelligence gathering where IRA 'moles' operated from the very centre of British security operations. Perhaps the most successful intelligence-gatherers were Sergeant Matt McCarthy of the RIC and Pat Stapleton who worked in General Solly-Flood's office in Waring Street. Stapleton, who also became an 'A' Special, confiscated security files at the end of a working day for IRA intelligence officers to digest, before replacing them the following morning; in HA/32/1/271, PRONI. **75.** It was rumoured that the Nixon gang had been involved in the killing of Frank McCoy. **76.** Another Catholic died in the east of the city that day. Mrs Brennan, who had just given birth, died of shock following a RIC raid at her home on My Lady's Road. **77.** Quoted in Phoenix, *Northern Nationalism*, p. 34. **78.** *Irish Independent*, 15 February 1922. **79.** *Irish News*, 15 February 1922. **80.** *Belfast Telegraph*, 15 February 1922. **81.** Hansard HOC Debates 5 series col. 1363–4, 16 February 1922. **82.** CAB 4/33, 16 February 1922, PRONI. **83.** Ibid. **84.** The majority of publicans were Catholics and many were comparatively well off, in contrast with their loyalist assailants. **85.** The *Belfast Telegraph's* 28th February report followed such a reassurance – 'Mother you know I will not get into trouble' – with a dramatic end to its report, 'but in a short time his body reposed in the morgue.'

CHAPTER 15

1. Constable Cunningham, an 'A' Special, was originally from County Cavan, and residing on the Ormeau Road, whilst Constable Cairnside, a native of Portaferry in County Down, had a mere three months' service in the 'B' Specials. **2.** Although many of the buildings in Kinnaird Terrace today are sub-divided into flats, they remain impressive properties. **3.** One of them, Bernard, had been burned out of his 'Great Eastern' pub in Ballymacarrett during the violence in the summer of 1920. **4.** Despite his apparent lack of interest in politics, there were suggestions that McMahon had contributed to republican funds and that this may have motivated his assassins; in McDonnell, *Northern Divisions*, p. 94. **5.** Owen McMahon was benefactor and former President of the Old Ivy Cycling Club and a director of Glentoran Football Club. **6.** However, neither of his domestic servants were at home that fateful March evening. **7.** There was some confusion over the size of the gang. Although only five were believed to have been involved in the attack, rumours suggested there were further accomplices. **8.** Mrs McMahon, speaking at the City Hall inquest on 11 August 1922; in H 828/508, PRONI. **9.** The next day police found evidence in the bedroom suggesting that some of the McMahons had initially resisted these demands. **10.** John, on telling an assailant that one of his brothers was receiving hospital treatment, was told not to worry! **11.** In H 828/508, PRONI. Mrs McMahon also testified that there had been five assailants, including one in a trench-coat. Incidentally her son's description corresponds with that of Nixon, though the latter was in his forties at the time. **12.** Ibid. **13.** Ibid. **14.** In *The Times*, 25 March 1922. His badly injured brother, John, was lying close to him. **15.** The matron had been unaware of the attack, since her bedroom was at the back of the property. **16.** Mary Catherine Downey, speaking on 24 March 1922; in HA 32/1/257 PRONI. **17.** *Belfast Telegraph*, 24 March 1922. **18.** Ibid. **19.** *Irish Independent*, 25 March 1922. TJ Campbell, *Fifty Years of Ulster 1890–1940*, p. 28, also stressed the unchristian nature of the attack, claiming that 'in the annals of Oriental devilry this crime could not be matched.'   20. Ibid.   21. Ibid.   22. *The Times*, 25 March 1922 and the *Daily Telegraph*, 26 March 1922. The *Observer*, 27 March, suggested that 'with the appalling slaughter of the McMahon family, mob law has reached the last point of infamy.'   23. *Nation*, 1 April 1922.   24. Lynch, writing for 'America'; in State Paper Office S1801/A.   25. In *Irish News*, 27 March 1922.   26. Ibid.   27. O'Donnell interview, op. cit.   28. Edward McKinney was buried in his home town of Buncrana in County Donegal.   29. *Irish News*, 28 March 1922.   30. Mrs McMahon's youngest son, Michael, who had survived the ordeal a few days previously, courageously attended the funeral.   31. Lynch; in S/1801/A.   32. Churchill suggested that one would have to 'search all over Europe to find instances of equal atrocity, cold-bloodedness and inhuman cannibal vengeance'; quoted in D. Smyth, *Sailortown – a Reign of Terror*, p. 28.   33. Indeed, Churchill was 'quiet prepared to consider the possibility of placing a portion of the City definitely under martial law' as that was 'greatly desired' by Catholics who would be re-assured that control over law and order would be in 'the hands of more or less impartial Imperial troops': Churchill, speaking in the House of Commons 27 March 1922, quoted in Campbell, *Fifty Years of Ulster*, p. 117–8.   34. Under this Civil Authorities legislation, draconian powers were invested in the Minister of Home Affairs who had the right to detain suspects for an unspecified period and courts of summary jurisdiction, which could detain suspects without trial, issue severe sentences (including whippings) were established. This is covered in greater detail in Chapter 18.   35. *Westminster Gazette*, 27 March 1922.   36. A detailed account of this meeting and the terms of the second Pact was given in Chapter 13.   37. Incidentally, apart from the ritualistic condemnation of ongoing violence, there were few references in parliamentary debates to the McMahon murders, regarded by many outside the city to be a watershed in the conflict.   38. N Ireland House of Commons Debates, 28 March 1922, vol. 2, cols 223–9.   39. Ibid.   40. Joe Devlin, 25 March 1922; quoted in Macardle, *The Irish Republic*, p. 683. A few days later Devlin alleged at Westminster that what was happening was 'a deliberate plot to exterminate the Catholics of Belfast', and condemning additional expenditure on the Special Constabulary, suggested that 'surely some more useful purpose could be served by the expenditure of this money'; M. Hayes Papers, p. 53/165 UCD Archives.   41. This assertion was made during a parliamentary debate by William Grant, a N Ireland MP; N Ireland House of Commons Debates, 18 May 1922, vol. 2, col. 557.   42. This access could have been gained through both legal gun clubs and arms illegally smuggled into the Belfast area over a ten year period.   43. Although their immediate access to Kinnard Terrance had been by foot, it is believed that some of the assailants used a getaway vehicle.   44. In the wake of the McMahon murders, Collins' request of an inquiry into the events in north Belfast had been rejected by Craig, so prompting Collins to initiate his own 'enquiry'.   45. Dublin Department of Defence memo, quoted in M. Farrell, *Arming the Protestants*, p. 298. A number of these alleged police 'miscreants', including Sergeant Christopher Clarke, Constable James Glover and Constable Sterritt were targets for subsequent IRA assassination squads. The Dublin Defence Ministry suggested that the Nixon gang had, apart from the McMahon murders, been involved in the killings of Trodden, Gaynor and McFadden, the shooting of Michael McGarvey, the Duffin brothers, the Halfpenny, Kerr and MacBride murders, as well as the Arnon Street and Stanhope attacks.   46. It was even rumoured that Nixon had been offered a job in the Canadian Mounted Police. He was awarded a MBE for 'valued services' in 1923.   47. HA/32/1/254, 11 July 1922, PRONI.   48. Ibid., 15 August 1922.   49. Several loyalist groups expressed their displeasure at this time to Bates and Craig. One group, the Adam and Eve Royal Black Preceptory, based at Limestone Road, also condemned Bates for his 'disloyalty' to the unionist electorate over the question of police appointments, demanding the 'instant dismissal' of the newly-appointed southern City Commissioner.   50. HA/32/1/254, 23 October 1922, PRONI. Craig was also influenced by the imminent publication of the dossier on Nixon.   51. Ibid., 30 January 1924, report of Nixon's speech to Sir Robert Peel Memorial Lodge. The 'not an inch' loyalist slogan is attributed to Nixon.   52. A detailed description of Nixon's dismissal is given in Chris Ryder's *The RUC – a Force under Fire*, pp 60–4.   53. Ibid., p. 62.   54. Accompanied by several loyalist bands, an estimated 10,000 crowd marched from the Shankill to the City Hall, where they demanded Nixon's reinstatement. On his dismissal, the discredited District Inspector threatened to 'blow the whistle' on other senior officers and politicians. This was no idle threat, as Nixon was believed to have kept a black book, listing all officers involved in terror attacks and alleged government contacts.   55. His belief in his own invincibility persisted and he was to win considerable legal damages from the 'Derry Journal' and the Methuen publishing group for alleging his involvement in the McMahon murders.   56. Another possible theory is that there was direct collusion between some police officers and loyalist terror gangs both in the planning and execution of such terror attacks.   57. The timing of his dismissal was crucial. If such a decision had been taken when the violence was at its height and if criminal charges against Nixon and his colleagues had been pursued, the new police force would have been severely discredited at a most sensitive time.

CHAPTER 16
1. Mr Carmichael, a native of Derry and a leading freemason, had only resided a few months in the city. 2. Ironically, the same ambulance ferried both the bodies of Beattie and Sloan to the mortuary. Predictably the rival newspapers interpreted these killings quite differently. The *Belfast Telegraph*, 15 April, claimed that the murders were 'indisputably the work of Sinn Féin gunmen', whilst the *Irish News* qualified their assertion that 'the question of party does not arise when wilful murder is done' by proceeding to claim 'there is not a man in Belfast who does not know in his heart ... that Carmichael and Sloan met their fate because it was believed they were Catholic working men.' 3. A distinctive feature of the violence was the number of victims who were elderly men still endeavouring to make a living. 4. Both incidents are discussed later. Also, a Protestant child William Cowan died of gunshot wounds sustained in Templemore Avenue during the middle of April. 5. Constable O'Connor was a member of a County Clare family with strong police connections, and had a distinguished war record, whilst Wexford-born Constable Cullen had barely two months experience in Belfast. 6. Interestingly, Clarke and the other two officers who had recently died were Catholics originating from outside Belfast. Many RIC officers in the city had been drafted in from stations all over Ireland. 7. Mr Rogan died of his injuries in the Royal Victoria Hospital on 19 March. A detailed account of Christy Clarke's alleged involvement is given in Graham, *In the Name of Carsonia*. 8. These killings precipitated the McMahon killings and were outlined in the previous chapter. 9. However, each incident involving a security force fatality, did not necessarily result in a 'spectacular' loyalist response, such as the McMahon or Arnon Street killings. The decision to execute such attacks owed more to logistical matters and having available personnel to carry out the attacks than they did to a plan to target specific Catholics. 10. This argument is developed in Graham, *In the Name of Carsonia*. 11. S/1801/A– 'Extracts from Statutory Declarations re Arnon Street and Stanhope Street Massacre', National Archives Dublin. 12. P53/165, UCD Archives. 13. S/1801/A, National Archives, Dublin. 14. Ibid. 15. Ibid. Another priest, Father Gannon, picked up a few fragments of bone and kept them as 'a gruesome reminder of Belfast civilisation and of an Empire's gratitude to the men who fought for it.': in Boyd, *Holy War*, p. 202. The report was also explicit in its condemnation of Nixon, Harrison and Giff who were, it claimed, 'up to their knees in crime – yet these are the men who keep the 'peace' of Belfast today.' 16. *Belfast Telegraph*, 3 April, 1922. 17. *Belfast Newsletter*, 3 April 1922. 18. *Irish Independent*, 3 April 1922. Incidentally, there were many reports in the *Independent* of southern unionist condemnation of the atrocities committed by their co-religionists in the north. One such report, dated 12th April, noted the 'unanimous passing' of a resolution by Protestants at Roundstone, Connemara, 'strongly protesting against the heartless and cold-blooded murders of Catholics in Belfast' and comparing such horrors in the north with the 'very friendly relations' in their own district, where the Protestant minority had 'never been interfered with on account of their religion.' 19. S 1801/A, 4 April 1922, National Archives Dublin. 20. Father Fullerton's St Matthew's Diary, in Down and Connor Archives. 21. HA5/209, PRONI. The report stated that a police Lancia vehicle which had been in the vicinity of the chapel had been distracted due to gunfire in the Youngs Row area, and that a military patrol on the Newtownards Road had been quickly on the scene though 'no trace of the miscreants could be found.' 22. *Irish News*, 24 April 1922. 23. Ibid. There was also strong condemnation of the attack in the British press, with the *Westminster Gazette*, 24 April, calling it 'a dastardly outrage'. 24. Due to the location of the attack and the name of the family, they were described in the southern press as 'Catholic', therefore giving the impression that northern violence was one-dimensional in its nature. 25. *Belfast Telegraph*, 1 April 1922. 26. Two other Catholics died in uncertain circumstances during this period. They were Hugh McNally, of Maple Terrace, and Thomas Mullan, who came from the Short Strand. 27. Other Protestants to die in uncertain circumstances during April were teenager William Steele, of Disraeli Street, who appeared to suffer accidental injuries after handling a revolver, and Ellen Greer of Enniskillen Street. 28. Indeed, the indiscriminate nature of much of this violence was reflected in the sniping from those areas, such as Carrick Hill and Millfield which were in close proximity to the centre. Describing such an attack on 8/9 March, the *Belfast Telegraph*, 9 March, wrote about how 'screaming women and frightened men sought the scanty protection of doorways, shops and offices' and how 'dozens of people in tramcars were compelled to throw themselves flat.' 29. Reported in *Belfast Telegraph*, 21 April – apparently one of their victims was prosecuted for theft the following week. 30. St Mary's Hall, in Bank Street, which had been used by a number of Catholic community groups for 'social' purposes, was regarded by the government as the IRA's Belfast headquarters. It was closed by the Home Affairs Ministry after this raid and requests to hand it back were ignored by Bates until the conflict was over; in HA/32/1/129, PRONI. 31. In *Belfast Telegraph*, 21 March 1922. 32. Mr Hall, originally from Lurgan, had served for 17 years in the Royal Irish Rifles and died in hospital the following day. 33. *Irish Independent*, 20 April 1922. 34. *Belfast Telegraph*, 20 April 1922. 35. In *Irish News*, 4 April 1922. 36. *Irish News*, 7 April 1922. 37. Ibid. 38. Quoted in *Irish Independent*, 7 April 1922. In an interesting

sequel to this case, a man was arrested for making a verbal threat to the family mentioned above, as he passed their home.   **39.** The number of Catholic families 'rendered homeless' on account of these Marrowbone attacks was estimated at the end of the two day onslaught at between 40 and 50; in *Irish News*, 19 April, 1922. M. Liggett, in *A District called the Bone*, estimates that over the duration of the conflict 244 families were forced to leave the area, with 57 homes being burned and 17 residents of the Marrowbone losing their lives. **40.** See Ligget, *A District called the Bone*, p. 15.   **41.** One report described, in vivid detail, the various stages of attack, in particular how both loyalist gunmen and army, employing machine-guns, were firing from within the area. The consequence of this for the residents – 'like rats in a trap' – was that their only way of escape was 'over the back yard walls and in this perilous task they were not even immune from the attentions of their assailants, who fired at them in relentless fashion'; in *Irish News*, 19 April 1922.   **42.** Ibid. The paper returned to the same theme the following day when it claimed that the unfortunate Catholic residents were the victims of 'a persecution more odious than that by the Turks in Bulgaria'.   **43.** Ibid. Although such intimidation was generally endured by Catholics living in predominantly loyalist areas, Protestants could also experience such isolation and fear. Towards the beginning of March, the *Belfast Telegraph* drew the attention of its readers to the 'persecution' of Protestant families in Cupar Street in western Belfast, where three people had been injured the previous evening in a bomb attack. There were also complaints that Protestant churches like Albert Street Presbyterian, were being desecrated by 'Raglan Street hooligans'; in *Belfast Telegraph*, 4 March, 10 April and 12 April.   **44.** Newspaper coverage of the McMahon outrage was considered in the previous chapter.   **45.** *Belfast Telegraph*, 5, 6 and 7th April respectively.   **46.** *Belfast Newsletter*, 17 April 1922.   **47.** *Belfast Newsletter*, 27 April 1922.   **48.** Ibid. This perception enjoyed generous space in press columns in subsequent conflicts.   **49.** Quoted in *Northern Whig*, 4 March 1922. The resolution also called for 'immediate' practical action to be taken 'to compel the capture of all arms and ammunition in unauthorised possession within the city.'   **50.** *Irish News*, 20 April 1922.   **51.** *Irish News*, 24 April 1922.   **52.** *The Times*, 22 March 1922.   **53.** Quoted in *Belfast Telegraph*, 15 April 1922.

CHAPTER 17

1. The authorities were fully aware of the threat and had made arrangements to cope with the anticipated upsurge in violence. Military re-enforcements had been drafted into the city (there were 8 battalions in Belfast by May), the curfew restrictions were extended to cover the period between 9 p.m. and 7 a.m., and road blocks were set up at a number of the city's approach roads. This increase in the volume of security incidents is reflected in the daily police reports on Belfast's disturbances (see a copy of one of these in the appendices). **2.** Kenna, *Fact and Figures*, p. 90, described this as a 'mauling'.   **3.** In one version of this shooting Mr Madden was asked his religion and shot before he could reply, whilst in another, he had run from the first outburst of gunfire.   **4.** Kenna, *Facts and Figures*, p. 96.   **5.** *Belfast Telegraph*, 15 June 1922.   **6.** It has been suggested that loyalists had been unable to find Mr McDermott's more active republican sons and chose their father as an easy target: see McDermott, *Northern Divisions*, pp 231–4, for a detailed account of the killing of his great-grandfather.   **7.** Loyalists were reported to have jeered the unfortunate man as he lay dying in the street.   **8.** A neighbour rushed to his aid but to no avail. When Mr Millar's sister arrived home shortly afterwards, she found the tea he had prepared for her on the kitchen table and collapsed.   **9.** There were disturbances in Albert Street during Mr Rainey's funeral.   **10.** There was a deep suspicion amongst many Protestants that members of the largely Catholic regular police force were colluding with the IRA. In his diary Fred Crawford expressed his concern over one particular police barracks (Glenravel Station) where he claimed, only 24 out of 81 officers were Protestants. Crawford suggested that the station 'demanded immediate re-construction', part of which would involve the transfer of DI McConnell, who had 'strong Sinn Féin sympathies', and the increased use of 'A' Specials: in D640/6/18, 28 June 1921, PRONI.   **11.** Taken from S. Montgomery memoir, pp 18–19, 29 May 1922; quoted in McDermott, *Northern Divisions*, pp 240–1.   **12.** Other attacks on police during this period included the wounding of Special Constable George Dobson on the Falls Road on 1 June and a republican attack on Brown Street Barracks on 2 June.   **13.** The timing of this shooting was especially tragic, as Mr Beattie, an Orangeman, had been due to transfer to London, his wife's home city. Mr Beattie's funeral a few days later was raked by nationalist gunfire.   **14.** Also around this time, James Brady, a Catholic of Kilmood Street, was shot as he turned into Seaforde Street, probably an unintended victim of the same sniper.   **15.** *Belfast Telegraph*, 12 May 1922.   **16.** A couple of other people were wounded riding their bicycles the following month in Donegall Street and Oldpark Avenue.   **17.** Although serious attacks were still confined to working class areas, the city's middle class were not totally insulated from such horrors. Laurence McIveen, described as 'a well-known Belfast violinist', was wounded as he played tennis in the exclusive Cavehill Lawn Tennis Club: reported in *Belfast Telegraph* 20 May 1922.   **18.** His body was found on 29 May. On 7 June a similar tragedy was narrowly averted at the same spot when a Specials patrol intervened after two Catholic girls had been beaten and their assailants were attempting to throw them into the Lagan. **19.** *Belfast Telegraph,* 2 June 1922. **20.** *Irish News,* 6 June 1922. **21.** Many of those distraught by the attack were children, including victims of the Weaver Street attack a few months previously, with an estimated 50 patients under the age of 16; see Macardle, *The Irish Republic,* p. 729. **22.** HA5/235, PRONI. **23.** In *Irish News,* 9 June 1922. **24.** Ibid. **25.** *Irish Independent,* 6 June 1922. **26.** Devlin, quoted in *Irish News,* 16 June 1922. **27.** Ibid. Churchill acidly pointed out that the only 'casualties' of the incident were a few broken windows. **28.** There were also attacks on Cullingtree Road and Smithfield barracks. **29.** Constable Collins (49), a native of County Cork, had been due to leave the force after 26 years service. **30.** A full account of S. Woods' account of this aborted mission – in the form of a report to Eoin O'Duffy, 19 May 1922 – is given in McDonnell, *Northern Divisions,* pp 226–7. **31.** *Belfast Telegraph,* 19 May 1922. **32.** The IRA continued to employ existing strategies and orchestrated a massive robbery in South Belfast on 12 May. Over £2,500 of Railway workers' wages was snatched from wage clerks and bosses at the Windsor sheds of the Belfast Great Northern Railway. **33.** 'Plain People', quoted in *Belfast Telegraph,* 19 June 1922. **34.** *Belfast Telegraph,* 27 May 1922. **35.** In Bardon, *A History of Ulster,* p. 491. Additionally the estimated rates loss for buildings damaged or destroyed during this period was, according to the city's Lord Mayor, an estimated £16,000: in *Irish Times,* 2 August 1922. **36.** This coincided with the arrival of the Yorkshire Regiment on a fresh tour of duty. **37.** *Belfast Telegraph,* 27 May 1922. **38.** Some loyalists eked out their revenge for such attacks by damaging or destroying the property of Catholics in their own districts. On the same day as these commercial attacks, there were assaults on a Catholic-owned pub, spirit grocery and confectionery on the Ormeau Road. **39.** Luckier animals included a cat and its three kittens rescued by the Fire Brigade during a blaze which destroyed a tobacconist's shop in North Street. **40.** *Irish Independent,* 12 June 1922. **41.** This popular school, which had been established in 1857, attracted a number of Catholics who received separate R.E. lessons from Mr O'Sullivan, one of the teachers. It was not the only school to be targeted by arsonists. St Silas' National School, on the Oldpark Road, was also 'torched' during this period. **42.** Police report, 31 May 1922, HA5/151, PRONI. **43.** As Jim McDermott has pointed out, Thornton was the first IRA volunteer to be killed by the RUC. Despite his rank and the fact he was killed on active service, there was no republican funeral, or even a press insertion, which was indicative of the growing pressure on republicans in the city: see McDermott, *Northern Divisions,* p. 254. **44.** There were a number of notable exceptions. These included the Phoenix Park murders of Cavendish and Burke in 1886 and, of course, the assassination of Michael Collins in August 1922. **45.** A notorious hard-liner Twaddell had referred to the appointment of Catholic Lord FitzAlan, to the position of Lord Lieutenant the previous year as being 'contrary to the constitution of this country': quoted in *Irish News,* 5 May 1921. Incidentally, there is a striking similarity between the fate of Twaddell and that of another Unionist critic of the IRA sixty years later, Robert Bradford. **46.** *Belfast Telegraph,* 22 May 1922. **47.** *Daily Chronicle,* 23 May 1922. **48.** *Irish News,* 23 May 1922. **49.** In *Belfast Telegraph,* 22 May 1922. The speedy setting up of stringent security in the wake of the Twaddell was in sharp contrast with a lax approach sometimes adopted by the authorities in the past. **50.** Official Report, Northern Ireland Parliamentary debates (Hansard), 1922. **51.** CAB 4/44/13, PRONI. **52.** *Belfast Telegraph,* 25 May 1922. Seamus Woods, who had allegedly been spotted in Royal Avenue by an army officer at the time of the killing, was acquitted of Twaddell's murder at a trial in 1924 and later confessed that two volunteers from Carrick Hill had been responsible: in McDonnell, *Northern Divisions,* p. 234. **53.** They were executed in Wandsworth Prison on 10 August. In an undelivered speech during his trial, he had written;' You can condemn us to death today but you cannot deprive us of the belief that what we have done was necessary to preserve the lives and happiness of our countrymen in Ireland'; quoted in *Irish Independent,* 21 July 1922. **54.** HA/32/1/183, 26 June 1922, PRONI. **55.** *Belfast Telegraph,* 23 June 1922. **56.** *Belfast Newsletter,* 27 June 1922. Though there was not a sectarian backlash in Belfast, 3 Catholics were killed by specials in Cushendall the day after the Wilson assassination. **57.** *Daily Mail* and *Irish Independent,* both 23 June 1922. **58.** Eamon de Valera quoted in M Moynihan, *Speeches and Statements by Eamon de Valera 1917–73,* pp 105–6. **59.** An IRA intelligence officer claimed at the end of 1921 that men in these groups were 'armed, paid and hand-picked' and reportedly organised from the City's Old Town Hall, with the object of establishing amongst the Catholic community 'a system of terror by shootings and ambushes'; in Phoenix, *Northern Nationalism,* p. 376. **60.** The regimented nature of the UVF's organisation and its large number of members mitigated against its involvement in a guerrilla campaign, especially when that would likely involve them in action against the security forces of the Crown. **61.** Detective Inspector R.R. Speers to the Minister of Home Affairs, T/2258, 7 February 1923, PRONI. **62.** Ibid. **63.** The money went towards paying the legal expenses for UPA suspects, as well as going into the pockets of its leaders. **64.** T/2258/2, PRONI. **65.** Speers estimated that between June and October 1922 the UPA killed at least six Catholics in east Belfast. **66.** T/2258/2 PRONI. **67.** Ibid. **68.** Quoted in Farrell,

Arming the Protestants p. 114.   **69.** Buckland, *Factory of Grievances*, p. 218.   **70.** Robinson's reputation as a character should not deflect from his record as a vicious sectarian killer. Indeed, he boasted of his involvement in several killings of Catholics, including 'hits' on trams, in cinemas, shops and pubs.   **71.** He was acquitted of murdering James McIvor.   **72.** Arthurs and Pollock (the latter an infamous Newtownards Road gunman) were, along with Robinson and other UPA men, interned in November 1922, whilst Pentland was acquitted of killing IRA volunteer Murtagh McAstocker in east Belfast (he claimed he had been merely going to the dying man's assistance).   **73.** Quoted in *Belfast Telegraph*, 25 May 1922. Following the movement of troop to the border areas in the wake of IRA attacks in the County Fermanagh village of Pettigo early in June, the *Daily News*, 6 June queried: 'murder and outrage continue much more persistently and continually in Belfast than on the border. Yet it is the smaller job that is handed over to the troops.'   **74.** *Belfast Newsletter*, 1 June 1922.   **75.** *Belfast Telegraph*, 25 May 1922.   **76.** *Belfast Newsletter*, 20 May 1922.   **77.** *Irish News*, 25 May 1922.   **78.** *Irish Independent*, 25 May 1922.   **79.** *Irish Independent*, 5 June 1922.   **80.** *Irish News*, 25 May 1922.   **81.** *Irish News*, 1 June 1922. Nationalist papers also devoted considerable coverage to blatant sectarian targeting of Catholics elsewhere in Ulster during May. These included the killing of three brothers in Magherfelt on 11 May, four Catholics in Desertmartin on 19 May and two others in the Glens of Antrim on the 24th of the month.   **82.** *Belfast Telegraph* 24 May 1922.   **83.** *Belfast Telegraph* 25 May 1922.   **84.** *Daily Herald*, 6 June 1922.   **85.** *Times* 25 May and 29 May 1922.   **86.** *Observer*, 28 May 1922.   **87.** The unprecedented fury experienced in the city during May and early June, even when considered in the context of the conflict's most bloody phase is illustrated by the number of criminal injury claims lodged for May. These came to £794,678 out of an estimated total of over £2,950,000 for the period between January and October 1922: in CAB6/11, PRONI. The total claim for the period between July 1920 and mid-May 1922 was around £4 million: in CAB6/37, PRONI.   **88.** *Manchester Guardian*, 15 June 1922.

CHAPTER 18

1. Lloyd George and Churchill saw the Boundary Commission clause as a back door route towards Irish unification, surmising that significant redefinition of the border would make the N Ireland state untenable.   **2.** Lloyd George; quoted in M. Gilbert, *Churchill*, p. 729.   **3.** A number of instances of poor liaison between the forces and a lack of respect, especially by the army for the Special Constabulary, are noted elsewhere. For instance, the leading army officer in the north, General Macready, had 'a very low regard' for the Specials; in CO 739/1/13691, PRO.   **4.** As noted earlier, Lloyd George and Churchill did maintain contact with Belfast Catholic businessmen.   **5.** Loyalists were disappointed that a unionist politician, such as Captain Charles Craig, had not been appointed to this post.   **6.** Tallents to Masterton-Smith, CO 906/25, 4 July 1922, PRO.   **7.** CO 906/30, PRO.   **8.** See Phoenix, *Northern Nationalism* p. 228.   **9.** One such North American group, the Ottawa Catholic Association, wrote to Craig on 25 May 1922, informing him of a resolution 'unanimously adopted' by the group the previous week: 'The Catholic population of the capital city of Canada behold with horror the atrocious acts of inhumanity taking place in the city of Belfast and the murder of four Catholic kinsmen and, in God's name, implore you as head of the government of N Ireland to take some measures to end the terrible slaughter and bring relief to the suffering citizens of that city': in CAB 6/37, PRONI.   **10.** HA/32/1/193, PRONI.   **11.** D1415 B/38 PRONI. William Coote represented County Tyrone, whilst Robert John Lynn and Samuel McGuffin represented west Belfast. Each of these unionist hard-liners were also sitting Westminster MPs.   **12.** Northern Ireland House of Commnons Debates, vol. 1 cols 64–8.   **13.** Craig, writing to Austen Chamberlain, in K. Middlemas [ed.] *Whitehall Diary, Vol. 3, Ireland 1918–25*, p. 190.   **14.** The Minister for Finance had proposed this in cabinet on 16 February but received a lukewarm response from his colleagues: in CAB 4/33/3, PRONI.   **15.** CAB 6/37, PRONI.   **16.** CAB 4/42, 16 May 1922, PRONI. The groups specified for proscription were the IRA, Sinn Féin clubs and the Irish Republican Brotherhood.   **17.** CAB 4/44, PRONI.   **18.** People continued to take chances, breaking curfew on a regular basis. For instance, 13 people were arrested for being on the streets during curfew hours on 13 September 1920, 15 the following evening and 22 on 2 October.   **19.** Other organisations and institutions were adversely affected by the curfew restrictions. A Presbyterian Mission Conference in the city had to be abandoned and the number of students enrolling for the new academic year at the Belfast Technical College was down 1,500 on the previous session; in *Irish News*, 11 October 1920.   **20.** Opposition to stringent curfew regulations, perhaps surprisingly, came from unionist stalwarts like Lynn who argued in parliament that many killings had taken place during curfew hours and that the restrictions were having 'a crippling effect on business in the city'; in *Irish Independent*, 18 May 1922.   **21.** The first offer of a reward occurred after the McMahon murders.   **22.** Belfast's Lord Mayor speaking on 27 June 1922; quoted in *Irish Independent*, 28 June 1922.   **23.** Quoted in *Northern Whig*, 7 July 1922.   **24.** Whilst this long-term prognosis proved to be largely accurate, it failed to suggest measures to cope with the immediate threat posed by loyalist murder gangs.   **25.** Follis, *A State under Siege*, p. 109, claims that the introduction of the Special Powers legislation had been forced upon Craig's administration on account of the army's reluctance to use its powers under the Restoration of Order (Ireland) Act.   **26.** Bates later shifted the blame for the lack of convictions on to the public. He complained: 'Not a man was brought to justice. The people knew who committed those murders, but no one had the courage to come forward and give evidence': in Buckland, *A History of N. Ireland*, p. 46.   **27.** Major-General A Solly-Flood, the military advisor in charge of the round-up of suspects had also proposed the death penalty for the carrying of firearms, as in the south, and the issuing of identification books, but these options were unpopular with Craig's cabinet.   **28.** CAB 4/44/13, 23 May 1922, PRONI.   **29.** *Irish News*, 24 May 1922.   **30.** Ibid.   **31.** 'Manchester Guardian', quoted in Bardon, *A History of Ulster*, p. 490.   **32.** CAB 24/134,CP 3884, PRO.   **33.** Ibid.   **34.** *Irish Independent*, 24 May 1922.   **35.** In *Irish Independent*, 16 March 1922.   **36.** *Belfast Telegraph*, 25 May 1922.   **37.** Parl. Debates NIHOC, vol. 2, col. 91, 21 March 1922.   **38.** T. Wilson, *Conflict and Consent*, p. 63.   **39.** Although the majority of internees were lifted that evening, some were arrested the following day and indeed, over the next few weeks.   **40.** A smaller number of loyalists were subsequently interned.   **41.** D. Kleinrichert, *Republican Internment and the Prison Ship Argenta 1922*, p. 18.   **42.** Also, in several cases more than one member of the same family was snatched.   **43.** Such a case involved Dr Charles Maguire, believed to be an active republican who had been arrested 'after seeing a patient' in Fermanagh. Dr Maguire was released from Derry Jail on 18 June, following a promise to 'solemnly undertake under no circumstances to enter the 6 Counties for such period as you may desire': in HA/5/1796, PRONI.   **44.** Up to 8 September 1922 the Belfast Government estimated that 446 men had been interned (13 were subsequently released): in HA/32/257, PRONI.   **45.** Leading republicans arrested included the 3rd Northern Division's Intelligence Officer, Francis Crumney, from Raglan Street and later, Seamus Woods, but the majority of internees were lower rank republicans or nationalists, with little apparent effort to distinguish between pro- and anti-Treaty Sinn Féin members. This might well reflect the Craig administration's rush to arrest suspects in the wake of the Twaddell killing and consequent failure to prepare quality and systematic intelligence which would have facilitated the arrest of key republican personnel. Conversely, the internment of low-level republicans might indicate an indirect admission on Craig's part that those responsible for many of the recent atrocities did not emanate from the Catholic community.   **46.** The *Argenta* was built in 1917 at a cost of £110,000 and was used as an emergency vessel during World War One. The vessel – 3,343 tons, 298 feet long and 49 feet wide – was removed from service in March 1922 and bought by the N. Ireland government for £3,000.   **47.** The maximum number of prisoners 'housed' on the vessel was around 370. The *Argenta* moved to Larne Harbour following a minor collision with another vessel.   **48.** Flogging was another penalty legalised by emergency measures and at least 21 prisoners, including 3 loyalists, were flogged between 26 April and 17 July 1922: in D Kleinrichert, *Republican Internment 1922*, p. 47.   **49.** Ibid., p. 148.   **50.** Incidents involving Sandy Row crowns and Catholic groups travelling to and from Great Victoria Street Station can be traced back to the times of Daniel O'Connell.   **51.** See descriptions of such attacks on Derry and Enniskillen prisoners in Kleinrichert, *Republican Internment*, p. 47.   **52.** CAB 6/7, 5 August 1922, PRONI.   **53.** Ibid. 'R. Simpson' probably referred to the leader of the UPA.   **54.** Ibid. Discrepancy of treatment was not just apparent in legal cases. An internal memo warned Ministers that all government officials holding republican views would be 'inappropriate office-bearers and should either be dismissed or transferred to the south'. Cabinet members and other senior officials were advised that 'the new government officials and all new appointments to the constabulary should all be those who are prepared to accept this new form of government, otherwise they will intrigue against the government they are being asked to help establish': in CAB5/1, 9 August 1922, PRONI.   **55.** Ann Dignam and her family also had limited access to her brother and when the Civil War started, they and many other refugees returned to Belfast: in Kleinrichert, *Republican Internment*, p. 196.   **56.** Consequently curfew regulations stayed in place throughout this period and indeed, on a restricted basis until towards the end of 1923.   **57.** *Irish News*, 10 July 1922. It is likely that this action was regarded by many as being a belated attempt by the authorities to appear to be even-handed.   **58.** During a meeting at the Ministry of Home Affairs on 14 October, a member of the McAleer family alleged that the police party on duty in the Cupar Street area at the time were intoxicated. At Frank McAleer's inquest in October, the Coroner concluded that 'the deceased was shot by Crown forces in the execution of their duty', adding he was satisfied the teenager was 'not associated with any disorderly mob'. As in several other such cases, the government would not accept liability for the victim's death and were therefore not liable to pay compensation to his family: in HA 5/935, PRONI.   **59.** Thomas Bowles, of East Bread Street, was arrested in connection with this killing, but the case was later dismissed.   **60.** *Belfast Telegraph*, 12 July 1922.   **61.** *Northern Whig*, 13 July 1922.   **62.** *Irish News*, 13 July 1922.   **63.** Those found guilty of possessing firearms and bombs received what were considered to be heavy sentences for such crimes. Thus, the *Belfast Telegraph*, 31 July, reporting on court cases where such sentences were handed out – 3 years and 25 strokes of the birch – led with the headline, 'Cat and Birch busy.'   **64.** Miss Savage's sister had been shot dead in a previous attack. **65.** *Belfast Telegraph*, 9 August 1922.   **66.** The Ministry of Home Affairs statement, reported in the *Belfast Telegraph*, 14 August, claimed they had 'in their possession mobilisation orders for this date for C Coy. 1st Battalion, No. 1 Brigade, N Division IRA, for the hall in which they were found.'   **67.** *Irish News*, 29 August 1922.   **68.** Ibid., 23 August 1922.   **69.** *Northern Whig*, 24 August 1922.   **70.** Ibid., 30 August 1922. **71.** The killing of Mr Higgins prompted the government to offer a reward of £1,000 for information leading to the conviction of those responsible.   **72.** CAB/6/7, PRONI.   **73.** Quoted in *Belfast Telegraph*, 14 September 1922.   **74.** *Belfast Telegraph*, 16 September 1922.   **75.** *Irish News*, 18 September 1922. The renewal of violence in north Belfast at this time precipitated an interesting exchange of opinion between Sir James Craig's military advisor, General Arthur Solly-Flood and police chiefs. On 13 September, Solly-Flood criticised the police for failing 'to take immediate and drastic steps' in districts such as Stanhope Street and Little George Street'. In his reply, W. Gelston, the Police Commissioner, whilst insisting that the police continued to surround and search districts once gunfire was reported, stressed the changed nature and scale of recent shooting attacks: in HA/32/1/278, PRONI.   **76.** *Irish News*, 2 October 1922.   **77.** Ibid., 7 October 1922.   **78.** *Belfast Telegraph*, 18 September 1922.

Bibliography

PRIMARY SOURCES

National Archives of Ireland (Dublin)
Dáil Éireann papers, including Dáil Treaty Debates & the Belfast Boycott (DE 2/110)
Provisional Government/Free State files (especially S/1801 series)

Public Record Office (London)
Papers consulted include:
   Cabinet Minutes (CAB 23 & 24, CAB 43)
   Colonial Office papers
   Parliamentary papers, especially HOC Hansard 5th series (Vol. 132)

Public Record Office of N. Ireland (Belfast)
Papers consulted include:
   Minutes of Cabinet meetings (CAB 4)
   Diaries & memoirs, including Crawford papers (D640), Lady Craig's diary (D1415 series) &
      Lady Spender's diary (D1633)
Home Affairs papers (HA series, especially HA5 & HA 32)
Police records & reports (CAB 6)
Prime Minister papers (PM 6 & PM 7)
Parliamentary papers, including Northern Ireland HOC Hansard Vols 1 &2

UCD Archive (Dublin)
Ernest Blythe papers (P24 series)
Richard Mulcahy papers (P7)
Michael Hayes collection (P53)

Various
Catholic Diocesan Records
Ara Coeli, Armagh: Logue, O'Donnell and MacRory papers
Clonard Monastery records
Cross and Passion records, including 'Belfast Centenary Celebrations'
Down and Connor records [including Father Fullerton's diary]

Newspapers and journals

Belfast Newsletter
Belfast Telegraph
Daily Chronicle
Daily Express
Daily Mail
Daily News
Daily Telegraph
Fermanagh Herald
Freeman's Journal
Illustrated London News
Irish Independent
Irish News

Irish Times
Manchester Guardian
Morning Post
Nation
Northern Whig
Observer
Pall Mall Gazette
Plain People
Spectator
Times
Westminster Gazette

Other printed sources

Boyd, J.	*Out of My Class*, Belfast 1985
Campbell, T.J.	*Fifty Years of Ulster 1890–1940*, Belfast 1940
Kelly, J.	*Bonfires on the Hillside – an eyewitness account of political upheaval in Northern Ireland*, Belfast 1995
Kenna, G.B.	*Facts and Figures of the Belfast Pogrom 1920–22*, Dublin 1922
McElborough, R.	*The Autobiography of a Belfast Working Man*, PRONI 1994
Parkinson, J.	*A Belfastman's Tale*, Belfast 1999
Redmond, J.	*Church, State and Industry in Belfast 1827–1929*, Belfast 1960
Shea, P.	*Voices and the Sound of Drums – an Irish autobiography*, Belfast 1981

Interviews

John Boyd, 11 August 2001
Harry Currie, 20 April 1998
Norman Douglas, 28 April 2000
Sam Jamison, 6 April 1999
Jimmy Kelly, 9 January 1999
John McKenna, 14 July 1999
Nora McMullan, 11 May 1999

George Morrison, 1 April 1999
Sarah O'Hare, 19 August 2000
Paddy O'Donnell, 18 December 2001
John Parkinson, 25 August 1998
Robert Preston, 31 August 1998
Christy Robinson, 25 August 1998
Eddie Steele, 31 August 1998

SECONDARY SOURCES

Abbott, R., *Police Casualties in Ireland 1919–22* (Cork, 2000)
Adams, G., *Falls Memories* (Dingle, 1982)
Baker, J., *The McMahon Family Murders and the Belfast Troubles 1920–2* (Belfast, undated)
Ballymacarrett Research Group, *Lagan Enclave – the Short Strand 1886–1997* (Belfast, 1997)
Bardon, J., *Belfast – an illustrated history* (Belfast, 1982)
—— *A History of Ulster* (Belfast, 1992)

BBC (N. Ireland), *The Century Speaks – Ulster voices* (Dublin, 1999)

Beckett, J., *The Making of Modern Ireland 1603–1923* (London, 1981)

Bell, J Bowyer, *Secret Army: History of the IRA 1916–79* (Dublin, 1983)

Berresford-Ellis, P., *A History of the Irish Working Class* (London, 1985)

Bew, P., Gibbon, P., & Patterson, H., *Northern Ireland 1921–94 – Political forces and social classes* (London, 1995)

Bowman, J., *De Valera and the Ulster Question 1917–73* (Oxford, 1989)

Boyce, D.G., *Englishmen and Irish Troubles – British public opinion and the making of Irish policy 1918–72* (London, 1972)

Boyd, A., *Holy War in Belfast* (Tralee, 1969)

Brewer, J., *The RIC – an oral history* (Belfast, 1990)

Buckland, P., *A Factory of Grievances: devolved government in Northern Ireland 1921–39* (Dublin, 1979)

—— *James Craig* (Dublin, 1979)

—— *A History of Northern Ireland* (Dublin, 1981)

Budge, I. and O'Leary, C., *Belfast, approach to crisis – a study of Belfast politics 1603–1970* (London, 1973)

Canning, P., *British Policy towards Ireland 1921–81* (Oxford, 1985)

Coogan, T.P., *Michael Collins – a biography* (London, 1990)

Craig, P. (ed.) *The Belfast Anthology* (Belfast, 1999)

Curran, D., (ed.) *St. Paul's – the Pivotal Point on the Falls 1887–1987* (Belfast, 1987)

Curtis, L., *The Causes of Ireland – from the United Irishmen to Partition* (Belfast, 1994)

Dwyer, T.R., *Big Fellow, Long Fellow – a joint biography of Collins and de Valera* (Dublin, 1999)

Elliott, M., *The Catholics of Ulster – a history* (London, 2000)

English, R., *Armed Struggle – a history of the I.R.A.* (London, 2003)

Farrell, M., *Northern Ireland – the Orange State* (London, 1976)

—— *Arming the Protestants – the formation of the USC and the RUC 1920–27* (Dingle, 1983)

Fitzpatrick, D., *The Two Irelands 1912–39* (Oxford, 1998)

Follis, B.A., *A State under siege – the establishment of Northern Ireland 1920–5* (Oxford, 1995)

Foster, R., *Modern Ireland – 1600–1972* (London, 1972)

Fraser, T.G., *Ireland in conflict 1922–98* (London, 2000)

Gallagher, R., *Violence and Nationalist Politics in Derry City 1920–3* (Dublin, 2003)

Garvin, T., *1922 – the Birth of Irish Democracy* (Dublin, 1996)

Gilbert, M., *Winston S. Churchill, vol. 4, 1916–22* (London, 1975)

Goldring,M., *Belfast – from Loyalty to Rebellion* (London, 1991)

Graham, J., *In the Name of Carsonia* (Belfast, undated)

Griffin, B., 'A Force Divided – Policing Ireland 1900–60' in *History Today* (London, October 1999)

Harkness, D., *Northern Ireland since 1920* (Dublin, 1983)

Harris, M., *The Catholic Church and the Foundation of the Northern Irish State* (Cork, 1994)

Heatley, F., *St. Joseph's Centenary 1872–1972 – story of a dockside parish* (Belfast, 1972)

Hennessey, T., *A History of Northern Ireland 1920–96* (Dublin, 1997)

Hepburn, A.C., *A Past Apart – studies in the history of Catholic Belfast 1850–1950* (Belfast, 1996)

—— *Ireland 1905–25, vol. 2, Documents and Analysis* (Newtownards, 1998)

Hezlett, A., *The B Specials – a history of the USC* (London, 1973)

Hirst, C., *Religion, Politics and Violence in late 19th century Belfast – The Pound and Sandy Row* (Dublin, 2002)

Hopkinson, M., *The Irish War of Independence* (Dublin, 2002)

Hyde, H. *Montgomery, Carson* (London, 1987 edition)

Johnson, D.S., 'The Belfast Boycott 1920–1' in J.N. Goldstrom & L.A. Clarkson (eds.) *Irish Population, Economy and Society* (Oxford, 1981)

Kennedy, D., *The Widening Gulf – northern attitudes to the independent Irish state 1919–49* (Belfast, 1988)

Kleinrichert, D., *Republican Internment and the Prison Ship 'Argenta' 1922* (Dublin, 2001)

Kostick, C., *Revolution in Ireland – Popular Militancy 1917–22* (London, 1996)

Lawlor, S., *Britain and Ireland 1914–23* (Dublin, 1983)

Liggett, M., *A District called the Bone* (Belfast, 1994)

Litton, H., *The Irish Civil War – an illustrated history* (Dublin, 1997)

Mackay, J., *Michael Collins – a life* (Edinburgh, 1996)

Magee, J., *Barney – Bernard Hughes of Belfast* (Belfast, 2001)

McArdle, D. *The Irish Republic* (London, 1951)

McAteer, G., *Down the Falls* (Belfast, 1983)

McColgan, J. *British Policy and the Irish Administration 1920–22* (London, 1983)

McDermott, J., *Northern Divisions – the old IRA and the Belfast Pogroms 1920–22* (Belfast 2001)

McPhillips, K., *The Falls –a history* (Belfast, 1992)

Middlemas, K. (ed.) *Thomas Jones – Whitehall Diary, vol. 3, Ireland 1918–25* (Oxford, 1971)

Mitchell, A., *Revolutionary Government in Ireland – Dáil Éireann 1919–22* (Dublin, 1995)

Morgan, A., *Labour and Partition: the Belfast working class 1905–23* (London, 1991)

Moynihan, M. (ed.) *Speeches and Statements by Eamon de Valera 1917–73* (Dublin, 1980)

Murphy, A., *When Dublin was the Capital – Northern life remembered* (Belfast, 2000)

O'Broin, L., *Michael Collins* (Dublin, 1980)

Orr, P., *The Road to the Somme* (Belfast, 1987)

Owen, F., *Tempestuous Journey – Lloyd George, his life and times* (London, 1954)

Parkinson, A.F., 'Ulster Will Fight and Ulster Will Be Right!' – The Presentation of the Anti-Home Rule case in Great Britain, 1912–14', M.A. dissertation, University of Westminster (1989).

—— *Ulster Loyalism and the British Media* (Dublin, 1998)

Patterson, H., *Class Conflict and Sectarianism – the Protestant working class and the Belfast labour movement 1868–1920* (Belfast, 1980)

Phoenix, E., *Northern Nationalism – nationalist politics, Partition and the Catholic minority in Northern Ireland 1890–1940* (Belfast, 1994)

Quinn, R.J. *The Troubles – a history of Northern Ireland conflict* (Belfast, 2001)

Ryder, C., *The R.U.C. – a force under fire* (London, 1990)

Stewart, A.T.Q., *The Ulster Crisis – resistance to Home Rule 1912–14*, London (1967)

Smyth, D. *Sailortown – a community in character* (Belfast, undated)

Staunton, E., *The Nationalists of N. Ireland – 1918–73* (Dublin, 2001)

Stewart, A.T.Q. *The Narrow Ground – aspects of Ulster 1609–1969* (London, 1977)

—— *Edward Carson* (Dublin, 1981)

Townsend, C., *Political Violence in Ireland* (Oxford, 1983)

—— *Ireland – the Twentieth Century* (London, 1999)

Wilson, T., *Ulster Conflict and Consent* (Oxford, 1989)

Index